Introducing PHP 7/MySQL

CADCIM Technologies
525 St. Andrews Drive
Schererville, IN 46375, USA
(www.cadcim.com)

Contributing Author
Prof. Sham Tickoo
Purdue University Northwest
Hammond, Indiana
USA

CADCIM Technologies

Introducing PHP 7/MySQL
Sham Tickoo

CADCIM Technologies
525 St Andrews Drive
Schererville, Indiana 46375, USA
www.cadcim.com

Copyright © 2018 by CADCIM Technologies, USA. All rights reserved. Printed in the United States of America except as permitted under the United States Copyright Act of 1976.

No part of this publication may be reproduced or distributed in any form or by any means, or stored in the database or retrieval system without the prior permission of CADCIM Technologies.

ISBN 978-1-942689-71-3

NOTICE TO THE READER

Publisher does not warrant or guarantee any of the products described in the text or perform any independent analysis in connection with any of the product information contained in the text. Publisher does not assume, and expressly disclaims, any obligation to obtain and include information other than that provided to it by the manufacturer.

The reader is expressly warned to consider and adopt all safety precautions that might be indicated by the activities herein and to avoid all potential hazards. By following the instructions contained herein, the reader willingly assumes all risks in connection with such instructions.

The Publisher makes no representation or warranties of any kind, including but not limited to, the warranties of fitness for particular purpose or merchantability, nor are any such representations implied with respect to the material set forth herein, and the publisher takes no responsibility with respect to such material. The publisher shall not be liable for any special, consequential, or exemplary damages resulting, in whole or part, from the reader's use of, or reliance upon, this material.

www.cadcim.com

DEDICATION

*To teachers, who make it possible to disseminate knowledge
to enlighten the young and curious minds
of our future generations*

*To students, who are dedicated to learning new technologies
and making the world a better place to live in*

THANKS

To employees of CADCIM Technologies for their valuable help

Online Training Program Offered by CADCIM Technologies

CADCIM Technologies provides effective and affordable virtual online training on various software packages including Computer Aided Design and Manufacturing and Engineering (CAD/CAM/CAE), computer programming languages, animation, architecture, and GIS. The training is delivered 'live' via Internet at any time, any place, and at any pace to individuals as well as the students of colleges, universities, and CAD/CAM training centers. The main features of this program are:

Training for Students and Companies in a Classroom Setting

Highly experienced instructors and qualified engineers at CADCIM Technologies conduct the classes under the guidance of Prof. Sham Tickoo of Purdue University Northwest, USA. This team has authored several textbooks that are rated "one of the best" in their categories and are used in various colleges, universities, and training centers in North America, Europe, and in other parts of the world.

Training for Individuals

CADCIM Technologies with its cost effective and time saving initiative strives to deliver the training in the comfort of your home or work place, thereby relieving you from the hassles of traveling to training centers.

Training Offered on Software Packages

CADCIM provides basic and advanced training on the following software packages:

CAD/CAM/CAE: CATIA, Pro/ENGINEER Wildfire, PTC Creo Parametric, Creo Direct, SOLIDWORKS, Autodesk Inventor, Solid Edge, NX, AutoCAD, AutoCAD LT, AutoCAD Plant 3D, Customizing AutoCAD, EdgeCAM, and ANSYS

Architecture and GIS: Autodesk Revit Architecture, AutoCAD Civil 3D, Autodesk Revit Structure, AutoCAD Map 3D, Revit MEP, Navisworks, Primavera, and Bentley STAAD Pro

Animation and Styling: Autodesk 3ds Max, Autodesk 3ds Max Design, Autodesk Maya, Autodesk Alias, The Foundry NukeX, MAXON CINEMA 4D, Adobe Flash, and Adobe Premiere

Web and Programming: C/C++, HTML5/CSS, VB.NET, Oracle, AJAX, and Java

For more information, please visit the following link: **http://www.cadcim.com**

Note
If you are a faculty member, you can register by clicking on the following link to access the teaching resources: *www.cadcim.com/Registration.aspx*. The student resources are available at *//www.cadcim.com*. We also provide **Live Virtual Online Training** on various software packages. For more information, write us at *sales@cadcim.com*.

Table of Contents

Dedication   iii
Preface   xiii

Chapter 1: Introduction to Dynamic Websites

Introduction	1-2
Basic Terms Used in Website Development	1-2
WWW	1-2
HTTP	1-2
HTML	1-2
URI	1-3
Request/Response Process	1-5
Basic Request/Response	1-5
Dynamic Request/Response	1-5
Static Vs Dynamic Website	1-6
Static Website	1-6
Dynamic Website	1-6
Web Server	1-7
PHP and Its Evolution	1-7
PHP/FI (Version 1.0)	1-8
PHP/FI 2 (Version 2.0)	1-8
PHP 3 (Version 3.0)	1-8
PHP 4 (Version 4.0)	1-8
PHP 5 and Later Versions	1-8
PHP 7.0	1-8
Benefits of Using PHP	1-9
Easy to Learn	1-9
Technical Support	1-9
Freedom	1-9
PHP Frameworks	1-9
Easier to Fix Errors	1-10
Object Oriented Programming	1-10
More Control	1-10
Speed	1-10
Self-Evaluation Test	1-10
Review Questions	1-11

Chapter 2: Setting Up the Development Environment

Introduction	2-2
Requirements to Work With PHP	2-2
PHP Enabled Server or Web Server	2-2
Text Editor or IDE	2-2
PHP Installed	2-2
Database Management System (MySQL)	2-2

Local Development Environment	2-3
LAMP	2-3
WAMP	2-3
MAMP	2-3
XAMPP	2-3
XAMPP on Windows	2-4
Downloading XAMPP on Windows	2-4
Installing XAMPP on Windows	2-6
Testing the Local Server	2-12
Document Root	2-13
Accessing the Document Root in XAMPP	2-13
Working Remotely	2-14
Logging into a Server	2-14
Using FTP	2-14
TEXT Editor	2-15
IDE	2-16
Self-Evaluation Test	2-17
Review Questions	2-17

Chapter 3: Fundamentals of PHP

Introduction	3-2
PHP File	3-2
Syntax of PHP	3-2
Comments in PHP	3-2
One-Line Comment	3-3
Multiple Line Comment	3-3
Echo and Print Statements	3-4
Echo Statement	3-4
Print Statement	3-7
Use of Special Symbols	3-9
Use of the ; Symbol	3-9
Use of the $ Symbol	3-10
Case Sensitivity	3-10
Data Types	3-11
Scalar Data Types	3-12
Compound Data Types	3-16
Special Data Types	3-18
Type Declaration	3-19
Scalar Type Declaration	3-19
Return Type Declaration	3-21
Self-Evaluation Test	3-22
Review Questions	3-22
Exercise 1	3-24
Exercise 2	3-24

Chapter 4: Variables, Constants, and Strings

Introduction	4-2
Variables	4-2

Table of Contents

Variable Name	4-2
Variable Scope	4-4
Local Variables	4-4
Global Variables	4-7
Static Variables	4-9
Superglobal Variables	4-12
Constants	4-13
Constant Name	4-13
Syntax of Constant	4-13
constant() Function	4-16
Magic Constants	4-16
String	4-17
Types of String	4-17
String Concatenation Operator	4-20
Escape Sequence	4-21
String Functions	4-24
strtolower()	4-24
strtoupper()	4-24
strlen()	4-25
str_word_count()	4-25
strrev()	4-26
str_replace()	4-26
substr_compare()	4-27
Self-Evaluation Test	4-27
Review Questions	4-28
Exercise 1	4-29
Exercise 2	4-29

Chapter 5: Operators

Introduction	5-2
Operators	5-2
Arithmetic Operator	5-2
Assignment Operators	5-5
Bitwise Operator	5-9
Comparison Operators	5-14
Logical Operators	5-17
The Increment(++) or Decrement(--) Operators	5-20
The String Operators	5-23
The Array Operators	5-24
Null Coalescing(??) Operator	5-25
Operator Precedence	5-26
Operator Associativity	5-27
Left to Right Associativity	5-27
Right to Left Associativity	5-27
Self-Evaluation Test	5-28
Review Questions	5-29
Exercise 1	5-30

Chapter 6: Control Structures

Introduction	6-2
Flowchart	6-2
Oval	6-2
Rectangle	6-2
Diamond	6-2
Arrow	6-2
Parallelogram	6-2
Control Structures	6-3
Conditional Control Structure	6-3
Iteration or Loop Control Structure	6-17
The Jump Statements	6-27
Alternate Syntax for Control Structures	6-36
Alternate Syntax for if Structure	6-37
Alternate Syntax for the if-else and if-elseif Structures	6-38
Alternate Syntax of the while and for Loop Control Structures	6-39
Alternate Syntax for the switch Structure	6-40
Logical Operators	6-41
Self-Evaluation Test	6-43
Review Questions	6-44
Exercise 1	6-45
Exercise 2	6-45

Chapter 7: Functions, Classes, and Objects

Introduction	7-2
Functions	7-2
User Defined Functions	7-2
Function Arguments	7-4
Function Return Value	7-6
Dynamic Function Call	7-7
In-built Functions	7-7
CSPRNG Functions	7-9
random_bytes()	7-9
random_int()	7-11
File Inclusion Statements	7-12
The include Statement	7-12
The require Statement	7-12
Classes	7-14
Declaring a Class	7-14
Property and Method Scope	7-15
Objects	7-16
Creating an Object	7-17
Accessing Members Using Objects	7-17
Object Cloning	7-20
Constructor	7-22
Destructor	7-22
Class Constant	7-24

Static Methods and Properties	7-25
Inheritance	7-30
The parent Keyword	7-33
The final Keyword	7-35
The instanceof Operator	7-37
Interface	7-38
Declaring an Interface	7-39
Implementing an Interface	7-39
Extending an Interface	7-40
Anonymous Class	7-43
Self-Evaluation Test	7-45
Review Questions	7-46
Exercise 1	7-47
Exercise 2	7-47

Chapter 8: Arrays

Introduction	8-2
Arrays	8-2
Indexed Array	8-2
Associative Array	8-7
Multidimensional Array	8-9
The foreach Loop	8-20
The print_r() Function	8-24
Array Functions	8-27
sort()	8-27
asort()	8-28
arsort()	8-28
ksort()	8-29
krsort()	8-30
count()	8-33
compact()	8-34
explode()	8-36
Conditional Testing Using Array Operators	8-37
Self-Evaluation Test	8-40
Review Questions	8-41
Exercise 1	8-42
Exercise 2	8-42

Chapter 9: Form Implementation and Validation

Introduction	9-2
HTML Form Elements	9-2
Attributes	9-2
Form Input Element	9-2
Form select Element	9-7
Form datalist Element	9-7
Form textarea Element	9-8
Form button Element	9-8
Form fieldset Element	9-8

Form Methods and Action	9-11
The get Method	9-11
The post Method	9-12
Form Action	9-12
Receiving Form Data in PHP	9-12
The $_GET Supergloblal Variable	9-12
The $_POST Supergloblal Variable	9-15
isset()	9-18
trim()	9-19
stripslashes()	9-19
htmlspecialchars()	9-20
The $_SERVER Supergloblal Variable	9-20
JavaScript(JS)	9-25
JS with HTML	9-26
JS Output	9-26
innerHTML	9-26
document.write()	9-28
window.alert()	9-28
console.log()	9-30
JavaScript Variables	9-31
Form Validation Using JS	9-33
Regular Expression	9-33
Regular Expression Modifiers	9-35
Regular Expression Functions in PHP	9-43
Self-Evaluation Test	9-45
Review Questions	9-45
Exercise 1	9-46
Exercise 2	9-46

Chapter 10: File Handling, Sessions, and Cookies

Introduction	10-2
File Handling	10-2
Opening a File	10-2
fopen() Function	10-3
Creating a File	10-3
Checking the Existence of File	10-4
exit() or die()	10-4
filesize()	10-5
Writing in the File	10-5
Reading a File	10-7
fgets()	10-8
feof()	10-9
Closing a File	10-10
Copying a File	10-12
Renaming a File	10-13
Deleting a File	10-14
Handling File Upload	10-15
enctype Attribute	10-15

Table of Contents

The $_FILES Superglobal Variable	10-15
move_uploaded_file() Function	10-16
Sessions	10-20
Starting a Session	10-20
The $_SESSION Superglobal Variable	10-21
Destroying a Session	10-24
Cookies	10-25
Creating a Cookie	10-25
Deleting a Cookie	10-28
Self-Evaluation Test	10-29
Review Questions	10-29
Exercise 1	10-30
Exercise 2	10-30
Exercise 3	10-30

Chapter 11: Introduction to MySQL

Introduction	11-2
RDBMS Terminologies	11-2
Database	11-2
Table	11-2
Record	11-2
Field	11-3
Column	11-3
Interacting with MySQL	11-3
Using Command-Line on Windows Command Prompt	11-3
Using Command-Line in phpMyAdmin	11-5
Creating Database	11-6
Creating Users for Accessing Database	11-8
Data Types in MySQL	11-10
Character Data Type	11-11
Binary Data Type	11-11
BLOB Data Type	11-12
Text Data Type	11-13
Numeric Data Type	11-14
Date and Time Data Type	11-17
ENUM Data Type	11-18
Constraints	11-18
Primary Key Constraint	11-19
Unique Constraint	11-20
Foreign Key Constraint	11-20
Creating a Table	11-21
Describing a Table	11-23
Alter Table	11-24
Renaming a Table	11-24
Renaming a Column	11-25
Modifying the Data Type	11-26
Adding a Column	11-27

Deleting a Column	11-28
Deleting a Constraint	11-29
Deleting a Table	11-30
Inserting Data in a Table	11-31
The Select Statement	11-34
Selecting Distinct Rows	11-36
Selecting Rows with the Where Clause	11-37
Count Function	11-38
Updating and Deleting Existing Table Rows	11-39
Updating Table Rows	11-39
Deleting Table Rows	11-40
Order by Clause	11-41
Group by Clause	11-42
Transaction Management	11-43
Transaction Storage Engine	11-44
The Begin Statement	11-45
The Commit Statement	11-46
The Rollback Statement	11-46
Self-Evaluation Test	11-48
Review Questions	11-49
Exercise 1	11-49

Chapter 12: PHP and MySQL Integration

Introduction	12-2
Connecting to the Database	12-2
mysqli_connect() Function	12-2
mysqli_connect_errno() Function	12-3
mysqli_select_db() Function	12-7
Building SQL Query	12-9
mysqli_query() Function	12-9
Fetching the SQL Query Result	12-11
mysqli_num_rows() Function	12-12
mysqli_fetch_assoc() Function	12-12
Closing MySQL Database Connection	12-16
Practical Implementation	12-16
Creating Table for Form Data	12-16
Creating HTML Form and Sending Data in Database	12-18
Self-Evaluation Test	12-25
Review Questions	12-25
Exercise 1	12-26
Exercise 2	12-26

Index	**I-1**

Preface

PHP 7/MySQL

PHP is a server-side scripting language used for web development and was developed by Rasmus Lerdorf in 1994. PHP, over the period, has undergone many changes and improvements. Originally PHP stood for Personal Home Page, and now it is known as Hypertext Preprocessor which is the recursive acronym of PHP. MySQL is an open source Relational Database Management System (RDBMS) which is used to interact with database along with PHP. The syntax, style, and features of these languages are very easy to understand.

Introducing PHP 7/MySQL is an example based textbook which is written to cater to the needs of the novice users who wish to learn PHP 7 and MySQL. It is quite helpful for the experienced web developers as well who want to develop efficient programs. The textbook highlights PHP and MySQL as the easiest languages for learning web development and also explains various features of the languages in a simple and easy style.

The highlight of the textbook is that each concept introduced in it has been exemplified by a program to clarify and facilitate better understanding. Also, the line-by-line explanation of each program ensures that the users with no previous programming experience are able to understand the concepts and master the programming techniques and use them with flexibility while designing programs.

The main features of the textbook are as follows:

Programming Approach: This textbook introduces the key ideas of web development in an intuitive way. The concepts are illustrated through best programming examples, covering all aspects of PHP and MySQL.

Notes and Tips: Additional information is provided to the users in the form of notes and tips.

Illustrations: There is an extensive use of examples, schematic representation, flow-charts, tables, screen capture images, and programming exercises.

Learning Objectives: The first page of every chapter summarizes the topics that are covered in it.

Self-Evaluation Test, Review Questions, and Exercises: Each chapter ends with a Self-Evaluation Test so that the users can assess their knowledge. The answers of the Self-Evaluation Test are given at the end of the chapter. Also, the Review Questions and Exercises are given at the end of each chapter that can be used by the Instructors as test questions and exercises.

Free Companion Website

It has been our constant endeavor to provide you the best textbooks and services at affordable price. In this endeavor, we have come out with a Free Companion Website that will facilitate the process of teaching and learning of PHP and MySQL. If you purchase this textbook, you will get access to the files on the Companion website. The following resources are available for faculty and students in this website:

Faculty Resources

- **Technical Support**

    You can get online technical support by contacting *techsupport@cadcim.com*.

- **Instructor Guide**

    Solutions to all review questions and exercises in the textbook are provided to help the faculty members test the skills of the students.

- **Example Files**

    The PHP program files used in examples are available for free download.

Student Resources

- **Technical Support**

    You can get online technical support by contacting *techsupport@cadcim.com*.

- **Example Files**

    The PHP program files used in examples are available for free download.

If you face any problem in accessing these files, please contact the publisher at *sales@cadcim.com* or the author at *stickoo@pnw.edu* or *tickoo525@gmail.com*.

Stay Connected

You can now stay connected with us through Facebook and Twitter to get the latest information about our textbooks, videos, and teaching/learning resources. To stay informed of such updates, follow us on Facebook *(www.facebook.com/cadcim)* and Twitter (@cadcimtech). You can also subscribe to our YouTube channel *(www.youtube.com/cadcimtech)* to get the information about our latest video tutorials.

Chapter 1

Introduction to Dynamic Websites

Learning Objectives

After completing this chapter, you will be able to:
- *Understand the basic terms used in website development*
- *Understand the request/response process*
- *Understand the meaning of static and dynamic websites*
- *Understand the use of web server*
- *Know about the evolution of PHP*
- *Understand the benefits of using PHP*

INTRODUCTION

A website is a collection of related web pages. Every web page you access through Internet is a website or a part of website. There are two types of websites, Static and Dynamic. These websites are designed and developed by using HTML, CSS, JavaScript, PHP, and MySQL languages.

BASIC TERMS USED IN WEBSITE DEVELOPMENT

In this chapter, you will learn about the basic terminology such as www, HTML, HTTP, URI used in website development; the request/response process; the static or dynamic nature of websites; web server; evolution of PHP; and benefits of using PHP.

Some basic terms that are generally used in relation to websites are explained next.

WWW

The World Wide Web or WWW in short, is the base of today's web which supports specially formatted documents also known as web pages on Internet servers. These web pages are formatted in a markup language called HTML (HyperText Markup Language). HTML is the part of basic web technologies.

In 1990, Tim-Berners-Lee invented three basic technologies, namely HyperText Transfer Protocol (HTTP), HyperText Markup Language (HTML), and Uniform Resource Identifier (URI) which together formed a global information medium called World Wide Web that operates on Internet.

HTTP

HTTP stands for Hypertext Transfer Protocol. It is an application protocol for regulating the request and response between the client (web browser running on the end user's system) and a web server. It runs on top of the TCP/IP suite of protocols and by default port 80 is used for HTTP traffic. It is designed to enable communications between clients and servers.

For example, if a user is sending a request (URL) such as *www.cadcim.com* which is actually an HTTP command, to the server through a web browser, then the browser is known as the client. Whereas the server is a system that accepts the request made by the client and returns a response message to the client in the form of HTML pages, websites, and other content. In short, client makes a request and server responds to that request.

Note
http:// and ftp:// are the protocols also known as access mechanisms.

HTML

HTML stands for Hypertext Markup Language. It defines the structure of web pages displayed on World Wide Web. Any website or web page you see on Internet consists of an HTML code. HTML is the base to form electronic documents (web pages). A website is a collection of related web pages. For a website, proper formatting of text and images can be done with the help of an HTML code. An HTML code ensures that the website is displayed on the Internet browser

Introduction to Dynamic Websites

as it is intended to look. Formatting of websites or web pages are done with the help of various HTML tags. The latest version of HTML is HTML5.

Tip
For better understanding, before learning PHP, you must go through HTML. The HTML code in this book will be explained wherever used.

Standard HTML Template
Given below is the standard HTML page template.

```
<!Doctype html>
<html>
<head>
<title>Title of web page</title>
</head>
<body>
<!--Content of the webpage......-->
</body>
</html>
```

Explanation

- **<!Doctype html>** defines the document to be HTML5 (HTML version 5).
- The text between **<html>** and **</html>** describes HTML document.
- The text between **<head>** and **</head>** provides information about the document.
- The text between **<title>** and **</title>** provides a title for the document.
- The text between **<body>** and **</body>** describes the visible page content.
- **<!--Content of the webpage......-->** is a comment which will not be displayed on the browser.

Note
HTML is case-insensitive, implying that it does not matter whether the HTML tags are written in UPPERCASE, lowercase, or camelCase.

URI

URI is an acronym of Uniform Resource Identifier. It is a string of characters used to identify names or resources on the Internet and is commonly used to specify the address of any website or related web page. Whenever users browse any website, they are actually browsing for the URI of that website which is the only medium to reach the site. URI can be further classified as Uniform Resource Locator (URL), Uniform Resource Name (URN), or both.

Note
An access mechanism is added in front of a URN to make it a URL.

For example:

http://www.cadcim.com/cadcimDesignCenter.aspx?loagPage=multimedia.htm

In this example, **http://** is the protocol (access mechanim) and **www.cadcim.com/cadcimDesignCenter.aspx?loagPage=multimedia.htm** is the URN which together forms a URI. Here, **www** is the subdomain, and **cadcim.com** is the domain name.

URL

URL stands for Uniform Resource Locator. It is part of the URI. When an access mechanism is included in front of URN, it becomes a URL. It helps in locating the resource on the World Wide Web. First part of the URL is the protocol used and second part is the IP address or domain name where the resource is located. URL is a human readable alias for an IP address.

For example:

http://www.cadcim.com/

In this example, **http://** is the protocol used, **www** is the subdomain, and **cadcim.com** is the domain name. These all together form a URL.

URN

URN stands for Uniform Resource Name. It is also a subset of URI and is completely unique. URN identifies a source by name in a given namespace. A group of names or identifiers is known as namespace. URN is different from URL as it does not include any protocol. The best example of URN is ISBN number which is used to identify a book uniquely.

For example:

www.cadcim.com/ProductDetails.htm?ISBN=978-1-942689-44-7

In this example, **www** is subdomain, **cadcim.com** is the domain name, **ProductDetails.htm** is the resource location, and **ISBN=978-1-942689-44-7** is an ISBN number which is a part of the URN. These together form a URI. URN does not include any access mechanism.

In other words, both URN and URL are part of Uniform Resource Identifier (URI), as illustrated in Figure 1-1.

Introduction to Dynamic Websites

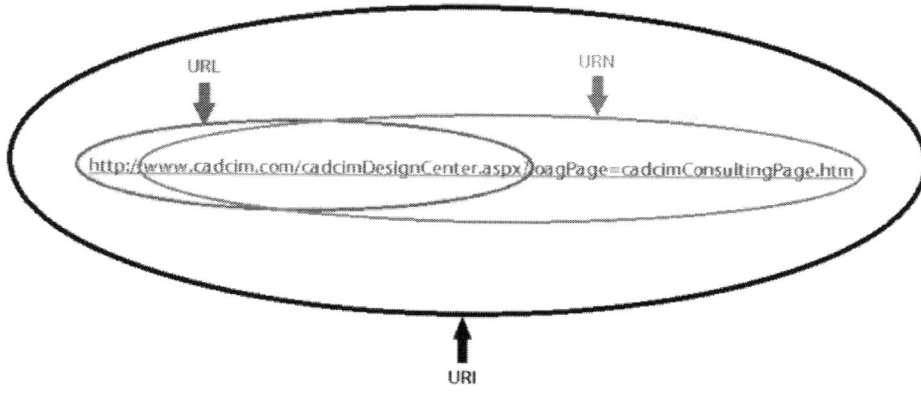

Figure 1-1 URI

From Figure 1-1, you can conclude that:

- *htttp://www.cadcim.com/cadcimDesignCenter.aspx?loagPage=cadcimConsultingPage.htm* is URI.
- *htttp://www.cadcim.com/cadcimDesignCenter.aspx* is URL.
- *www.cadcim.com/cadcimDesignCenter.aspx?loagPage=cadcimConsultingPage.htm* is URN.

REQUEST/RESPONSE PROCESS

Request / Response cycle is the process in which the user browses for the content and requests the web server for the same. The web server receives the request and sends back the requested page to the browser. There are two types of Request/Response processes. They are discussed next.

Basic Request/Response

The process of basic Request/Response is as follows:

1. User enters URL into the address bar of any web browser. For example, *http://www.cadcim.com*.
2. The browser looks up the IP address in the browser cache for the *cadcim.com* (domain name). If not found, it sends a request to DNS (Domain name system).
3. The browser makes a request for the home page at *cadcim.com*.
4. The request through Internet is relayed to the web server of *cadcim.com*.
5. The web server receives the request made by the user and looks for the web page on its disk.
6. The server retrieves the web page and return it to the web browser.
7. The web browser receives it and displays the web page to the user.

Dynamic Request/Response

The process of dynamic Request/Response is as follows:

1. User enters URL into the address bar of any web browser. For example, *http://www.cadcim.com*.

2. The browser looks up the IP address in its browser cache for the *cadcim.com* (domain name). If not found, it sends a request to DNS (Domain name system).
3. The browser makes a request for the home page at *cadcim.com*.
4. The request through Internet is relayed to the web server of *cadcim.com*.
5. The web server receives the request made by the user and looks for the web page on its hard disk.
6. The web server notices that the file in the memory is incorporating PHP scripting language and to interpret (translate) the file server sends it to the PHP interpreter.
7. The code is executed by the PHP interpreter.
8. If there are MySQL statements in the file then PHP interpreter passes the file to the MySQL database engine.
9. The MySQL database engine sends the result of the statements back to the PHP interpreter.
10. The PHP interpreter returns the results of PHP code and MySQL statements to the web server.
11. The web server receives the requested page and sends it to the web browser which displays the received page.

STATIC VS DYNAMIC WEBSITE
The differences between the static and dynamic websites are discussed next.

Static Website
Static website is the one in which the content of the site remains static, means it does not change automatically. To change the content of the site, designer needs to change it manually by making changes in the source code. It can be designed by using HTML(Hypertext Markup Language) and CSS(Cascading Style Sheets). These languages are used to design front-end part of a website and therefore are known as client-side scripting languages. For example, the date displayed on a website would remain same forever unless it is changed manually in the source code. In other words, the content of a static website is fixed.

Note
Web content is the data (text, images, videos, and so on) that you read or see on a web page.

Dynamic Website
Dynamic website is the one in which the content changes automatically at run time. It can connect the website with the database, organize data in structured way, and easily fetch information from the database to display it on the site. It can also send data from the site to the database.

Dynamic websites are interactive and user friendly and help in maintaining data. Any change or update required can be done easily on dynamic website as compared to static website. Server-side scripting languages including PHP and JavaScript are used for developing dynamic websites. These languages work with HTML, CSS, and MySQL to form a dynamic website.

All e-commerce sites and online shopping sites are dynamic websites. Dynamic websites are capable of producing different content for different visitors from the same source code file. Such

Introduction to Dynamic Websites

as, in any online shopping website, the content displayed on the home page keeps on changing according to the likes and dislikes of the visitors. For example, if a user repeatedly searches for laptops and other electronic gadgets on a website then the website will start displaying similar suggestions on its home page. The dynamic websites contain web pages that are generated in real-time. Whenever a dynamic web page is accessed, the code within the page is parsed on the web server and the resulting HTML is sent to the client's web browser.

> **Note**
> *Apart from PHP, MySQL, and JavaScript, there are various other languages such as ASP.Net, Python, and Ruby on Rails that are used to build a dynamic website.*

WEB SERVER

A web server is used to develop and test a dynamic website. It processes requests made by the client through HTTP and returns the response message to the client in form of HTML pages or web pages. There are many web servers available. In this book, you will read about the Apache web server.

Apache web server is the most commonly used web server all over the world. About 60% of the web server machines use this web server. It is developed and maintained by Apache Software Foundation, it is an open source software which is free to use and can be installed in almost every operating system such as Linux, UNIX, Windows, Mac OS X, and so on.

Apache provides a variety of multiprocessing modules instead of implementing just a single architecture. This allows Apache to run in a process-based, hybrid (thread and process), or event-hybrid mode, to match the demands of a particular infrastructure. The design of Apache ensures reliable and consistent processing of request within a given time-frame by increasing the rate of process and reducing the latency.

PHP AND ITS EVOLUTION

PHP is a server-side scripting and general-purpose programming language used for web development. It was developed by Rasmus Lerdorf in 1994. Originally PHP stood for Personal Home Page, and was initially designed for tracking visits to the personal online resume of the developer, Rasmus Lerdorf. As he needed additional functionality in the 'Personal Home Page Tools', he added more features to it and rewrote the PHP tools and now it is known as 'Hypertext Preprocessor' which is the recursive acronym of PHP.

In 1995, PHP source code was made available for general public under open source platform. Initially it was a simple set of Common Gateway Interface (CGI) binaries written in the C programming language but now it is capable of database interaction, managing dynamic content, session tracking, building entire e-commerce sites, and so on.

Over the period of time, starting from PHP/FI to PHP 7, many improved versions of PHP have been introduced. The evolution of PHP starting from 1995 is discussed next.

PHP/FI (Version 1.0)
PHP was expanded in 1995 and the name 'Personal Home Page' was dropped for a short period of time. A new name, FI which stands for 'Forms Interpreter', was given to this language. In April, 1996 a complete makeover of the code was done and by combining the past names - PHP and FI, Rasmus Lerdorf introduced a new name PHP/FI. This implementation began to evolve PHP from a suite of tools to a programing language. It included built-in support for DBM(Database Management), cookies, user defined functions, and so on.

PHP/FI 2 (Version 2.0)
PHP/FI 2 was officially released in November, 1997 after Beta testing. It evolved to the point where it could work with HTML files and instead of just making personal home page setup, it was now used for an entire website. Now it did not require small Perl CGI programs as it was able to directly work with HTML files. Due to this, the overall performance of the web pages got improved and speed got enhanced.

PHP 3 (Version 3.0)
PHP/FI 2 was rewritten in 1997 by Zeev Suraski and Andi Gutmans. They were the programmers at Technion IIT. PHP/FI 2 was an entirely new language which was released with the new name, PHP, a recursive acronym for Hypertext Preprocessor. PHP 3.0 was the first version that closely resembles existing PHP.

PHP 4 (Version 4.0)
In 1998, after the release of PHP 3.0, Andi Gutmans and Zeev Suraski started working on PHP core. Their goal was to improve the complex applications and modularity of PHP code because designing complex application and handling it efficiently with PHP 3.0 was not possible.

The Zend Engine (Zend is comprised of their first names, Zeev and Andi) successfully reached the goal by following a new paradigm of "compile first, execute later." and introduced PHP 4.0 in mid 1994. They added wide range of new features such as highly improved performance, support for many more web servers, output buffering, HTTP sessions, more secure way to handle user input, and several other new language constructs in PHP 4.0 and released it in May 2000.

PHP 5 and Later Versions
Soon after the release of PHP 4, the demand for more object-oriented features increased so Andi came up with the idea to rewrite the object-oriented part of Zend Engine. Zeev and Andi along with a team of developers created Zend Engine 2.0 which became heart of PHP 5.

Over a period of time, PHP 5.1 to PHP 5.5 were introduced. In August 2014, stable version of PHP 5.6 was released. Debugging was re-factored in PHP 5.6 with phpdbg as an interactive integrated debugger SAPI.

PHP 7.0
During 2014 and 2015, a new version of PHP was developed. This version was named as PHP7 and was released on 3 December 2015, with huge performance improvement. It is the latest PHP version which powers everything from website and mobile to enterprises and the cloud.

Introduction to Dynamic Websites

The new Zend Engine 3.0 (PHP 7) has drastically reduced the memory consumption, improved exception hierarchy and converted many fatal errors to exception. It gives up to 2x faster performance than PHP 5.6. It also removed old and unsupported SAPIs and extensions and so on. This version allows you to serve more users without adding any extra hardware.

Note
PHP 6 was abandoned due to shortage of developers and performance issues with UTF-16 conversions.

BENEFITS OF USING PHP

PHP is widely used for developing websites all over the world. The reasons behind the success of PHP are discussed next.

Easy to Learn

PHP scripting language is easy to learn and understand. The syntax of PHP is very simple and the PHP documents are clean and organized. In PHP documents or files, it is not necessary to follow an order of functionality. The developers can quickly add or remove any function in PHP file without disturbing the functionality of other functions in that file. So, developer can easily learn and work with this language to develop the website which makes PHP language easy.

Technical Support

PHP is widely used as scripting language and getting help on any technical issue is very easy. Finding online help or documentation for PHP is extremely easy. The fact that PHP is open source also contributes to the large support community of PHP as the PHP group (developers community, where they share their scripts as well as doubts.) provides the complete source code for customization and extension.

Freedom

PHP is open source meaning that everyone has free access to the source code made available by PHP group and can use it for developing websites. It is compatible with most web servers and operating systems. As compared to other languages, PHP does not need any specific text editor for writing it. Developer can use any text editor such as Brackets, Notepad++, Sublime Text, or even Notepad.

PHP Frameworks

PHP frameworks provide basic structure of PHP code where users can build web applications very easily and quickly. It helps in creating more stable web applications with less repetitive coding. There are many PHP frameworks available which work as helping hand for database access libraries, session management, or in code reuse.

Most popular PHP frameworks are:

1. Laravel
2. Symfony
3. codeigniter
4. Yii 2

5. Phalcon
6. CakePHP
7. Zend
8. Slim
9. FuelPHP
10. PHPixie

Easier to Fix Errors

It is easy to fix errors in PHP. Every request in PHP is independent. So, any change or problem in one request will not necessarily affect another request, thereby making it easier to find out the problem.

Object Oriented Programming

PHP works on Object Oriented Programing (OOP) concept. It is object based programing which involves the use of classes to organize the structure and data of web applications. PHP has the ability to call Java and Windows COM objects.

Note
You will learn about PHP objects and classes in later chapters.

More Control

PHP has more control over web browsers than other scripting languages. Many languages require large scripts to do very simple task whereas PHP can do the same in just few lines of code. PHP works very well with HTML and this is the reason the websites created by using them together are very neat in their functionality. The control over the design flow is also good. It allows user to design web pages according to exact specification.

Speed

PHP is much faster than other scripting languages. PHP 7 is double in speed from its earlier releases and it does not use much system resources in order to run. Even when it is used with other software, it does not slow down the process and retains the speed.

PHP also works well with many RDBMS (Relational Database Management System), and CMS (Content Management System) such as WordPress, Drupal, Zoomla, and other such platforms. So, using PHP for dynamic websites is a good option.

Self-Evaluation Test

Answer the following questions and then compare them to those given at the end of this chapter:

1. The three fundamental technologies given by Tim Berners-Lee are _____, _____, and _____.

2. Full form of PHP is _____ now.

Introduction to Dynamic Websites

3. Dynamic website have dynamic content which can change _____ at run time.

4. _____ is the latest version of PHP.

5. PHP is free of cost because it is an _____.

Review Questions

Answer the following questions:

1. WWW stands for:

   (a) World Wide Web-application (b) World Wide Web
   (c) Wide Web World   (d) None of them

2. HTTP stands for:

   (a) Hypertext Transfer Protocol   (b) Hyperlink Transfer Protocol
   (c) Hyper Token Transfer Protocol   (d) None of them

3. URI stands for:

   (a) Uniform Resource Identifier (b) Union Resource Identifier
   (c) Uniform Resource Identity   (d) None of them

4. Which of the following versions of PHP is the latest version?

   (a) PHP 6   (b) PHP 5
   (c) PHP 8   (d) PHP 7

Answers to Self-Evaluation Test
1. HTTP, HTML, URI, **2.** Hypertext Preprocessor, **3.** automatically, **4.** PHP 7, **5.** open source

Chapter 2

Setting Up the Development Environment

Learning Objectives

After completing this chapter, you will be able to:
- *Understand the requirements to work with PHP*
- *Understand the types of local development environment*
- *Understand the XAMPP server*
- *Understand the concept of document root*
- *Understand the concept of working remotely*
- *Understand IDE*

INTRODUCTION

To work with PHP language, a development environment is required. You can create the development environment by installing a local server in your system. The local server is used to develop and deploy the dynamic website as well as to test the website locally and for debugging. Once the website is tested locally then it is easier to ensure that the website will run properly on the web server. You can then upload the website on web server using Internet.

In this chapter, you will understand the importance of working with PHP, different types of local server environments, text editor, and IDE. You will also learn how to install XAMPP on Windows, testing the server, and working remotely which will help you to setup the development environment for PHP and MySQL.

Tip
To check the functioning of your website, make sure you have different browsers on your system such as Internet explorer, Mozilla Firefox, Opera, Safari, Google Chrome, and so on. To make a website user friendly, it should run properly on every browser, system, and mobile device.

REQUIREMENTS TO WORK WITH PHP

To work efficiently, PHP requires few important things. The following is the list of requirements to work with PHP:

PHP Enabled Server or Web Server

PHP is a server side scripting language. So it is important to have access to PHP enabled server. PHP can reflect the output only when it is running on a server. Without a server, it is not possible to check the functioning of PHP code written for a dynamic website.

Text Editor or IDE

To write a PHP code, you need a text editor or an IDE (Integrated Development Environment). You can use any text editor or IDE to work with PHP. There are many text editors such as Notepad, Notepad++, and so on, and IDEs such as PhpStorm, Sublime Text, and so on, to work with PHP.

PHP Installed

To work with PHP, install PHP on your system. The current stable release is PHP 7. PHP can be installed easily on any OS (Operating System) such as Linux, Windows, Mac OS X, and so on. PHP package can be downloaded free from *http://php.net*, according to the operating system installed on your computer.

Database Management System (MySQL)

PHP is used to create dynamic websites. Therefore, a Database Management System (DBMS), such as MySQL, is necessary which stores the data that is sent from the website. This also collects data from the website and stores in the database and then displays it on the website. MySQL is an open source Relational Database Management System (RDBMS) based on SQL (Structured Query Language).

LOCAL DEVELOPMENT ENVIRONMENT

The local development environment is the development environment created locally on the system to work efficiently with PHP. You have already learned about the requirements to work with PHP in previous section. You can setup the local development environment to work with PHP in two ways. Either you can install Apache server, PHP, and MySQL individually or there is a very simple and convenient way to install them all together in your system by installing local server environment such as LAMP, WAMP, MAMP, or XAMPP.

LAMP, WAMP, MAMP, or XAMPP are four different local server environments which have Apache server, PHP, and MySQL all together in a single package. You can download and install any of the local server in your system depending upon the Operating System (OS) you are using. But, before installing any one of them, you must know which local server environment will support your system. The description about all these environments is given next.

LAMP

LAMP stands for Linux, Apache, MySQL, and PHP. Here, Linux is the Operating System, Apache is the web server, MySQL is the Relational Database Management System, and PHP is the server side scripting language. LAMP is an open source platform which is used to setup a development environment to work with PHP only on Linux operating system. It is a solution stack (a set of software components). Therefore, after installing it no additional software is required to work with dynamic websites. Linux OS users can use LAMP to setup a local server environment.

WAMP

WAMP stands for Windows, Apache, MySQL, and PHP. Here, Windows is the Operating System, Apache is the web server, MySQL is the RDBMS, and PHP is the server side scripting language. WAMP is a set of open source applications used to setup a development environment to work with PHP only on Windows operating system. The combined usage of these programs is called server stack. Windows OS users can use WAMP to setup a local server environment.

MAMP

MAMP stands for Mac, Apache, MySQL, and PHP. Here, Mac is the Operating System, Apache is the web server, MySQL is the RDBMS, and PHP is the server side scripting language. MAMP is a package of open source applications used to setup a development environment to work with PHP only on Mac OS x. MAMP is a solution stack used to run dynamic websites on Apple Macintosh systems.

XAMPP

XAMPP stands for X-OS, Apache, MySQL, PHP, and Perl. X-OS can work on any operating system. It is most popular and preferably used local server environment as it can work on cross platforms. XAMPP can work efficiently on Mac, Windows, and Linux operating systems. Additionally, it supports two server side scripting languages (PHP and Perl).

XAMPP ON WINDOWS

There are many types of local server environment packages, but the most popular of them is XAMPP as it is easy to download and install. The steps for downloading and installing XAMPP are given next.

Downloading XAMPP on Windows

The following steps are required to download XAMPP on Windows:

1. Open *https://www.apachefriends.org* in your browser; the **XAMPP** page will be displayed, as shown in Figure 2-1.

*Figure 2-1 The **XAMPP** page*

2. Choose the latest stable release of XAMPP from the **Download** area of the **XAMPP** page, as shown in Figure 2-2; the **Download** page will be displayed, as shown in Figure 2-3.

Note

*In the **Download** page, you will find different links to download the latest version of XAMPP for different operating systems.*

Setting Up the Development Environment

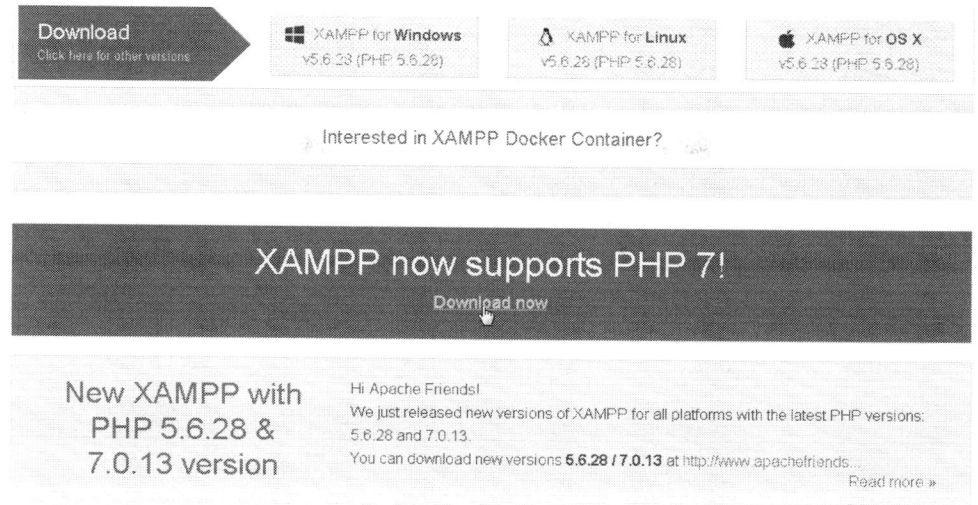

Figure 2-2 *The **Download** area with the **Download now** link*

Figure 2-3 *The **Download** page with the **Download (32 bit)** buttons*

3. For Windows operating system, choose the **Download (32 bit)** button corresponding to the **7.0.13 / PHP 7.0.13** version from the **XAMPP for Windows 5.5.38, 5.6.28 & 7.0.13** area, refer to Figure 2-3; a dialog box is displayed. In this dialog box, navigate to the desired location and choose **OK** to save the file.

Note
During the download process of XAMPP, some of the screens may change as website gets updated from time to time. In such cases, visit the site and look for the latest stable version of PHP and download it.

Installing XAMPP on Windows

The following steps are required to install XAMPP on windows:

1. Double-click on the executable file; the **Setup** dialog box of XAMPP installer is displayed, as shown in Figure 2-4.

Note
*If you are using any antivirus program or have activated **User Account Control settings** in Windows, then the **User Account Control** dialog box will be displayed. Now, you need to choose **Yes** or **OK** to continue installation; otherwise, you will be directed to the **Setup** dialog box.*

*Figure 2-4 The **Setup** dialog box of XAMPP installer*

2. Now, choose the **Next** button from the **Setup** dialog box; the **Select Components** page is displayed, as shown in Figure 2-5.

Setting Up the Development Environment

3. In this page, the check boxes are already selected. You can clear the check box corresponding to the component that is not required. But you must keep the **MySQL**, **PHP**, **Apache**, and **phpMyAdmin** check boxes selected. After selecting the components, choose the **Next** button, refer to Figure 2-5; the **Installation folder** page is displayed, as shown in Figure 2-6.

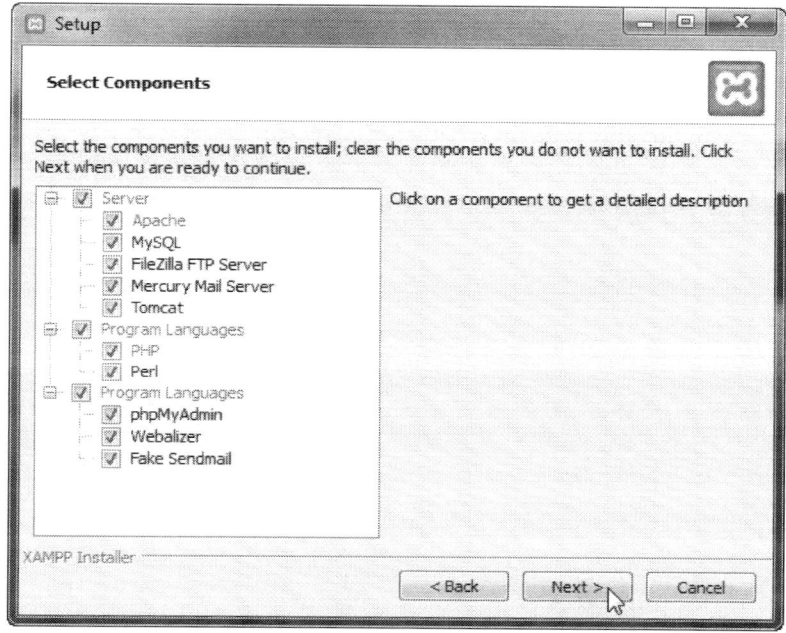

Figure 2-5 The Select Components page

4. In this page, choose the default **xampp** folder for installation, as recommended. Next, choose the **Next** button to proceed to the installation, refer to Figure 2-6; the **Bitnami for XAMPP** dialog box is displayed, as shown in Figure 2-7.

5. In this page, the **Learn more about Bitnami for XAMPP** check box is selected by default, refer to Figure 2-7. This will provide you free installers such as **WordPress**, **Joomla**, and so on. Next, choose the **Next** button; the **Ready to Install** dialog box is displayed, as shown in Figure 2-8.

6. In this page, choose the **Next** button to start the installation, refer to Figure 2-8; the **Welcome to XAMPP** dialog box is displayed, as shown in Figure 2-9. Also, the installation process will start and its progress will be displayed.

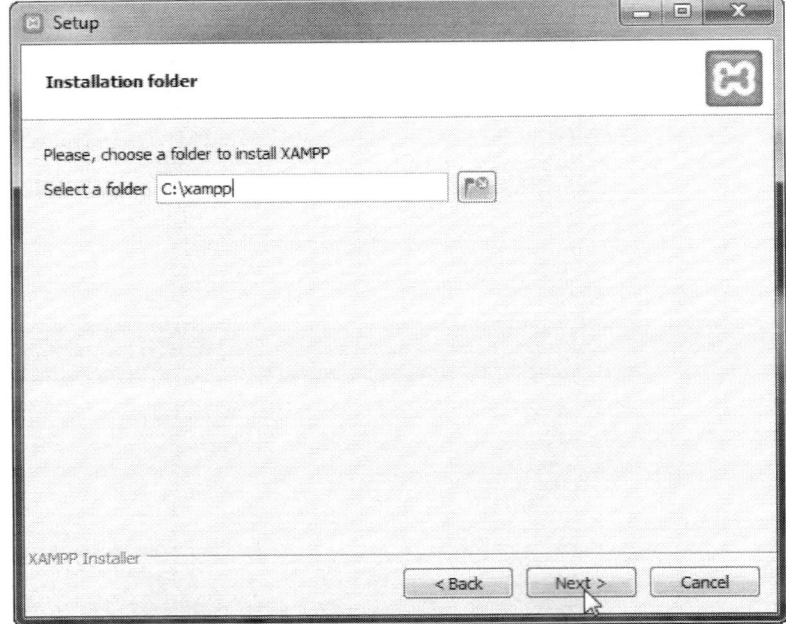

Figure 2-6 *The* **Installation folder** *page*

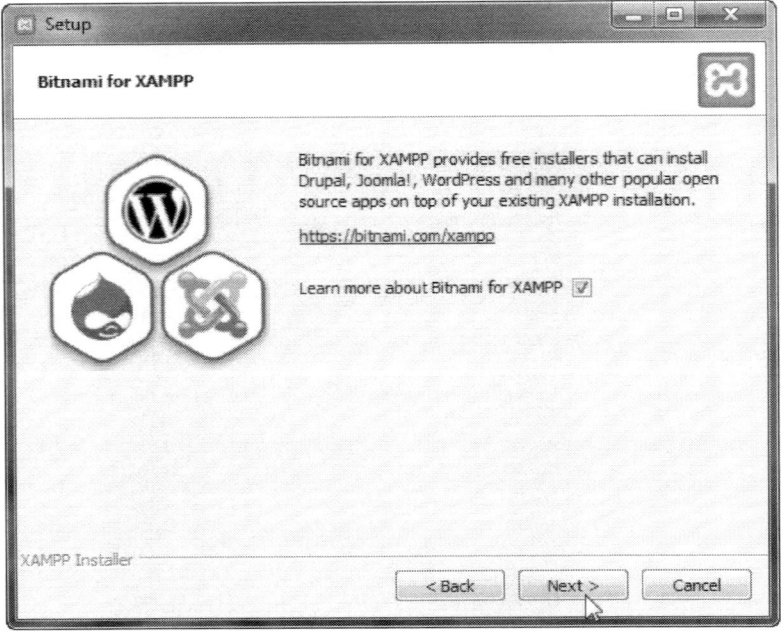

Figure 2-7 *The* **Bitnami for XAMPP** *page*

Setting Up the Development Environment

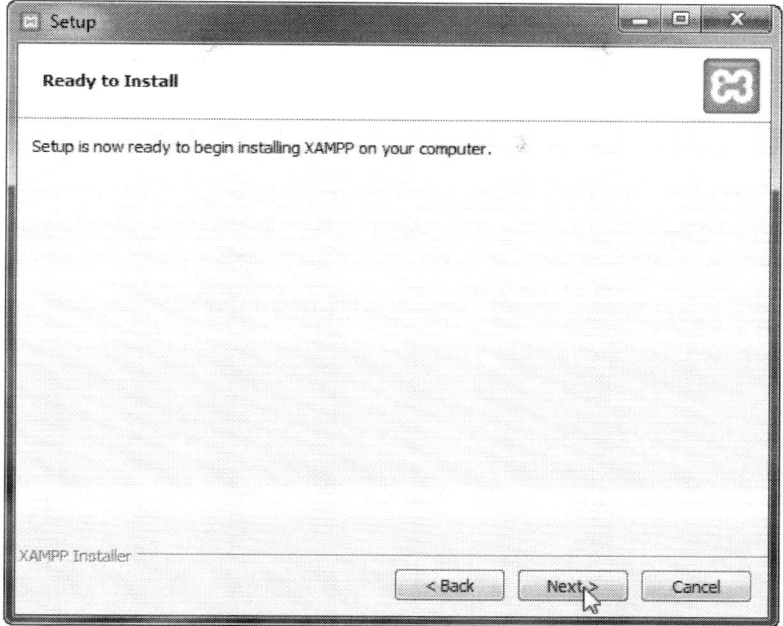

Figure 2-8 The **Ready to Install** page

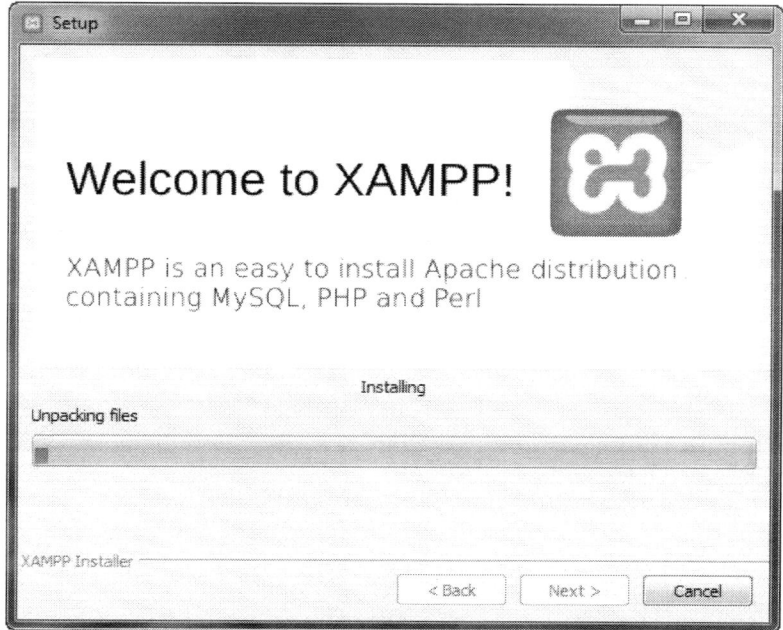

Figure 2-9 The installation in progress

7. When the installation process is complete, the **Completing the XAMPP Setup Wizard** page is displayed, as shown in Figure 2-10. In this dialog box, the **Do you want to start the Control Panel now?** check box is selected by default.

*Figure 2-10 The **Completing the XAMPP Setup Wizard** page*

8. Next, choose the **Finish** button; the installation gets completed and the **Language** dialog box is displayed, as shown in Figure 2-11.

9. In this dialog box, two radio buttons represented by Flags are displayed. To set the language, select one of the radio buttons and then choose the **Save** button; the process gets completed and the **XAMPP Control Panel** dialog box is displayed, as shown in Figure 2-12.

10. In this dialog box, choose the **Config** button at the top right corner of the window; the **Configuration of Control Panel** dialog box is displayed, as shown in Figure 2-13.

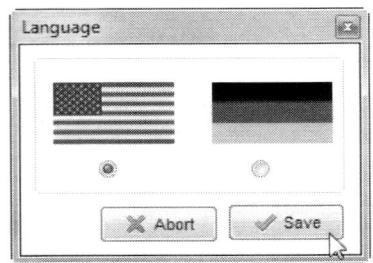

*Figure 2-11 The **Language** dialog box*

11. In this page, the default editor is set to **notepad.exe**. If you want to use any other editor, click on the folder icon corresponding to the **Editor** text box and then choose the desired editor. Next, select the **Apache** and **MySQL** check boxes from the **Autostart of modules** area; it will ensure that these modules will autostart when XAMPP is launched.

Setting Up the Development Environment

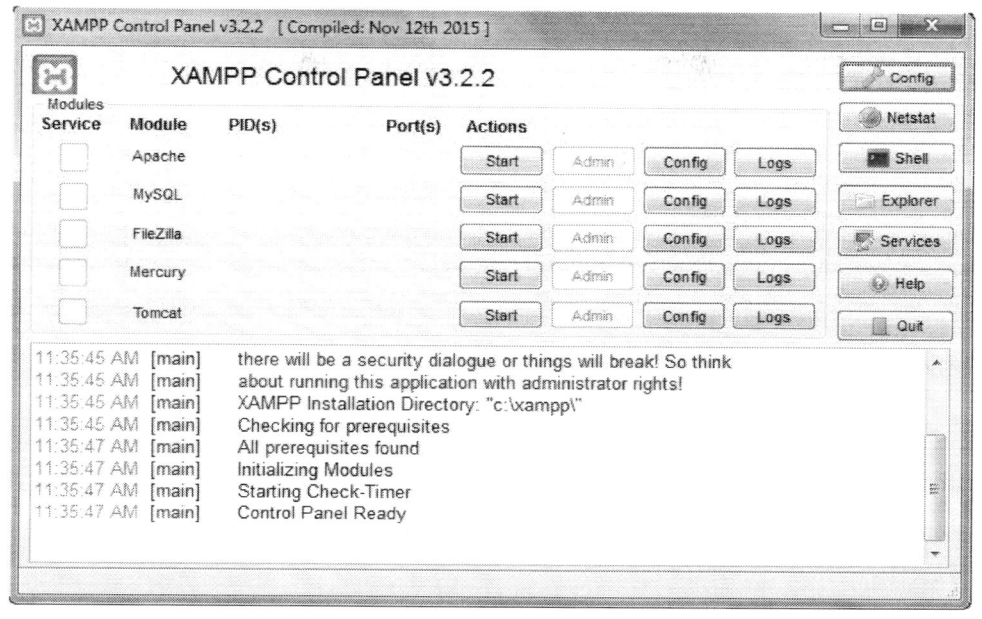

Figure 2-12 The **XAMPP Control Panel** dialog box

Figure 2-13 The **Configuration of Control Panel** dialog box

12. To alter the default port settings, choose the **Service and Port Settings** button; the **Service Settings** dialog box is displayed, as shown in Figure 2-14. By default, port assigned to **Apache** web server is 80 and for **MySQL** it is 3306. Next, choose the **Save** button; all changes are done and the **Configuration of Control Panel** dialog box re-appears. Choose the **Save** button in this dialog box; all the changes are saved and the process gets finished.

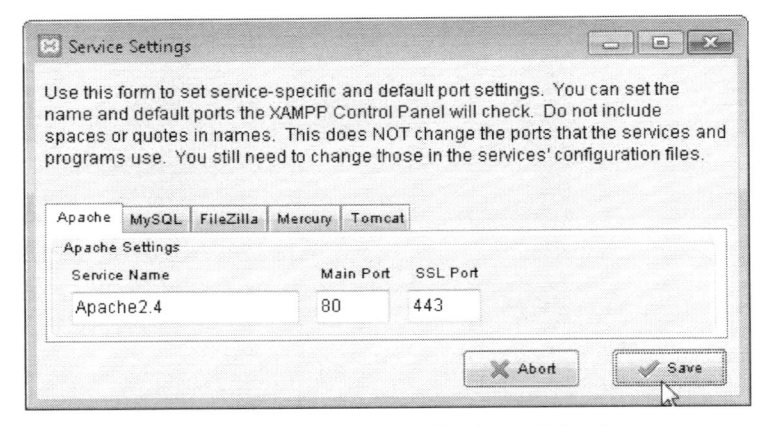

Figure 2-14 The Service Settings dialog box

Note
*Instead of autostart, you can start and stop components of XAMPP by choosing the **Start** and **Stop** buttons, respectively each time you open the **XAMPP Control Panel**, refer to Figure 2-12.*

TESTING THE LOCAL SERVER

It is important to test the local server after the installation of XAMPP so that everything works smoothly. To verify if the local server is working properly, you can try to display the default web page of XAMPP which is saved in the server document root folder.

In the address bar of your web browser, enter either of the following two URLs:

localhost
127.0.0.1

If it displays the default web page of XAMPP, as shown in Figure 2-15, it proves that the local server is working properly and your system is ready to work with PHP and MySQL, refer to Figure 2-15.

Setting Up the Development Environment 2-13

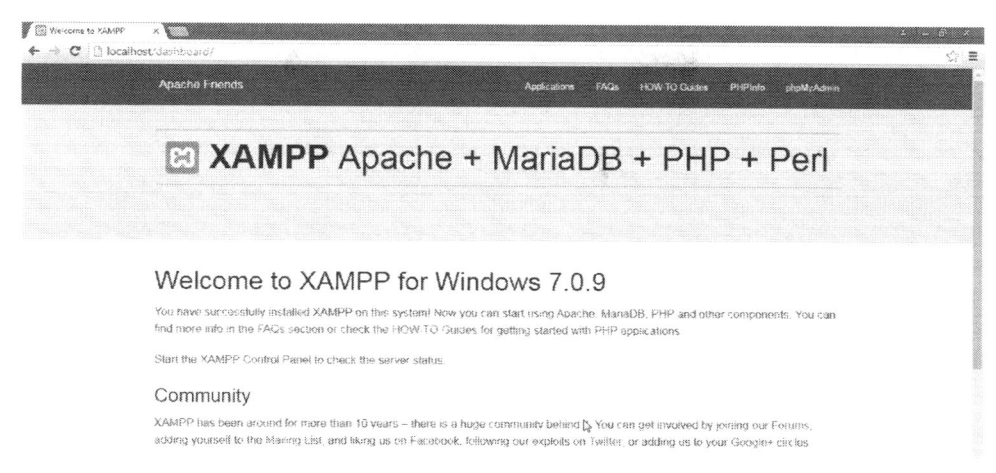

Figure 2-15 Default web page of XAMPP

Note
1. To test the local server or to run the PHP programs, it is necessary to start the Apache and MySQL through XAMPP control panel once.

2. If you choose the Apache port number other than 80 using the XAMPP control panel, then you must place a colon followed by the new port number after either of the preceding URLs. For example, if you choose port 8080 instead of 80 then you will have to enter **localhost:8080** instead of **locolhost** or **127.0.0.1** in the address bar of your web browser.

DOCUMENT ROOT

The document root is the folder or directory where you can save website files with their domain names. When a user enters a URL in the browser, they are actually accessing the document root location of your website. In order for a website to be accessible to the users, it must be saved or published to the correct directory which is the document root. The document root is different for different local servers as every host is different and consists of different sets of folders.

Accessing the Document Root in XAMPP

The document root for XAMPP is **htdocs** directory, where you will save your file to run on local server of your system. By default, XAMPP uses the following location for this directory:

C:/xampp/htdocs

In the given line, **C** is the drive, **xampp** is the main XAMPP server folder, and **htdocs** is the document root directory.

To run the program in the local server, you will have to create the PHP or HTML file. For example, create the *example.html* file and save this file in the *C:/xampp/htdocs* location. After saving the file, you will open the **XAMPP Control Panel** and start **Apache** by choosing the **Start** button, if the application is not already running. Once **Apache** gets started, open your web browser and enter the URL - *http://localhost/example.html* to run the *example.html* file. Similarly, you can run other programs on your local server by just replacing the file name *example.html* with your file name or folder name.

> **Note**
> *Once **Apache** gets started, there is no need to open the **XAMPP Control Panel** again as the local server keeps on running until you choose **Quit** in the **XAMPP Control Panel**, refer to Figure 2-12.*

WORKING REMOTELY

Working remotely means to work directly on the web server. To work remotely, you must have access to the web server already configured with MySQL and PHP. It requires high-speed Internet connection to upload files on the server. You must have correct login details to work remotely because for security reasons there may be some authentications to access server and MySQL such as password and unique id.

Working remotely is not always the best option. If all the conditions and requirements to work remotely are not appropriate then it can slow down the process of development whereas local development can be done faster with no or less upload delay. It is not even easy to access MySQL remotely. To access MySQL and create database manually, you will have to enter into your server through Telnet or SSH and set different types of permission through command lines.

Logging into a Server

To log into a server, you can use SSH. SSH stands for Secure Shell which is a network protocol that provides a secure way to access a remote computer to the administrators. The **SSH** network protocol is already available in Operating Systems such as Macintosh and Linux, but it is not available in Windows Operating System. To use SSH in Windows Operating System, you need to download and install program such as PuTTy.

PuTTY is a network file transfer application which provides the secure remote terminal to Windows Operating System where you can work with **SSH** network protocol. You can download PuTTY from *http://www.putty.org* and follow the installation process to install PuTTY on your Windows Operating System. You can then use the terminal provided by PuTTY to log in to a server using SSH as follows:

ssh loginid@server.com

In the given line, **ssh** stands for Secure Shell, **loginid** is the username, and **server.com** is the name of the server you wish to log into. After executing the given command, you will be prompted to enter password associated with the username and then you will be logged into the server.

Using FTP

FTP stands for File Transfer Protocol. It is used to transfer files between a client and a server. If you are working remotely, then you need a FTP to transfer the files from the web server to the client or from the client to the web server. You can use any FTP of your choice to perform this task.

Setting Up the Development Environment

Note

FTP and SSH are not required to work with local server.

TEXT EDITOR

A text editor is a word processing program that allows a user to open, view, write, edit, and store any text. So, to write programs in any language such as PHP, HTML, and JavaScript, you need a text editor. You can use any plain text editor or advance text editor to create programs. A plain text editor is a normal editor which does not provide huge level of text formatting. Text written in plain text editor is normal and it becomes difficult to manage the text in large program files. So, in place of plain text editors you can use advance text editors which can easily manage large program files. Advance text editors are much smarter than the normal plain text editors. It has many new features such as colored syntax highlighting, which makes the program easy to read and understand; syntax error detection, which is helpful in avoiding syntax errors; highlighting the matching pair, which is used when you want to find the matching pair of any braces or brackets, and so on.

You can choose any text editor according to your preferences. For example, you can use **Notepad++** which is an advanced text editor as compared to **Notepad** which is a plain text editor. Figure 2-16 shows the **Notepad++** editor and Figure 2-17 shows the **Notepad** editor.

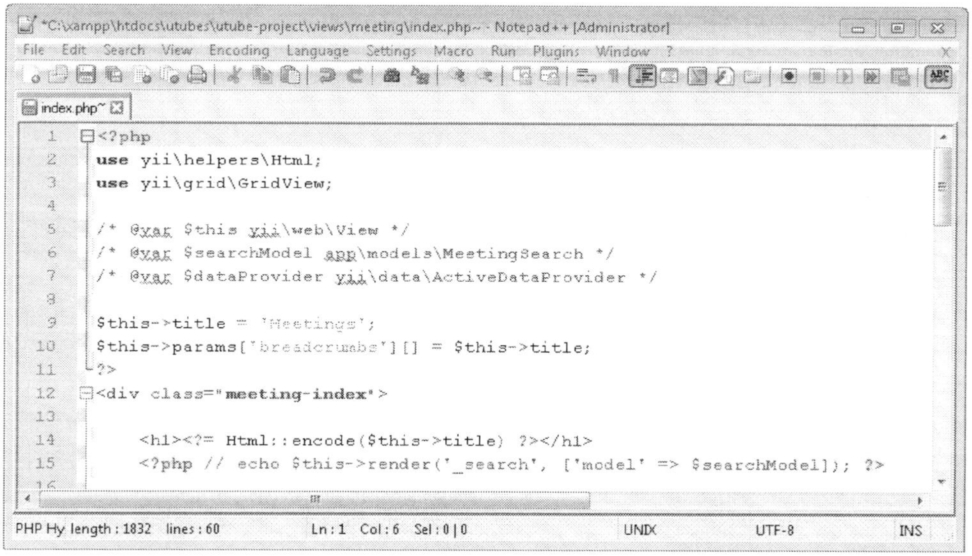

*Figure 2-16 The **Notepad++** editor*

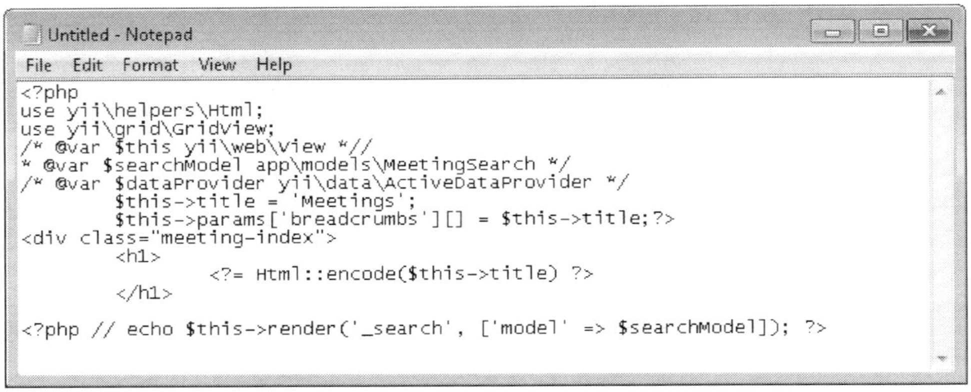

*Figure 2-17 The **Notepad** editor*

IDE

An IDE stands for Integrated Development Environment. It is also used to edit PHP programs and has much better functions than a normal text editor. In text editors, you can just write or edit the program code and to debug it, you need a compiler or some external software or program. But IDE offers many additional features such as program testing and in-editor debugging, which means you can write your code and debug it in the same program and so on. The speciality of an IDE is that it also includes all the features of an improved text editor.

The 10 most popular IDE for PHP are:

1. NetBeans
2. PhpStorm
3. Sublime Text
4. Eclipse PDT (PHP Development Tools)
5. VIM
6. Zend Studio
7. Atom
8. NuSphere
9. PHP Designer
10. Cloud 9 (cloud based programming environment)

It is your choice to work with an IDE or a text editor. As a beginner, you can go for a text editor but for professional web development, you must start with an IDE. For example, PhpStorm is an IDE. It is better than a text editor. It has many features such as syntax highlighting, in-editor debugging, SQL and Database support, and so on. Figure 2-18 shows the popular PhpStorm IDE.

Setting Up the Development Environment 2-17

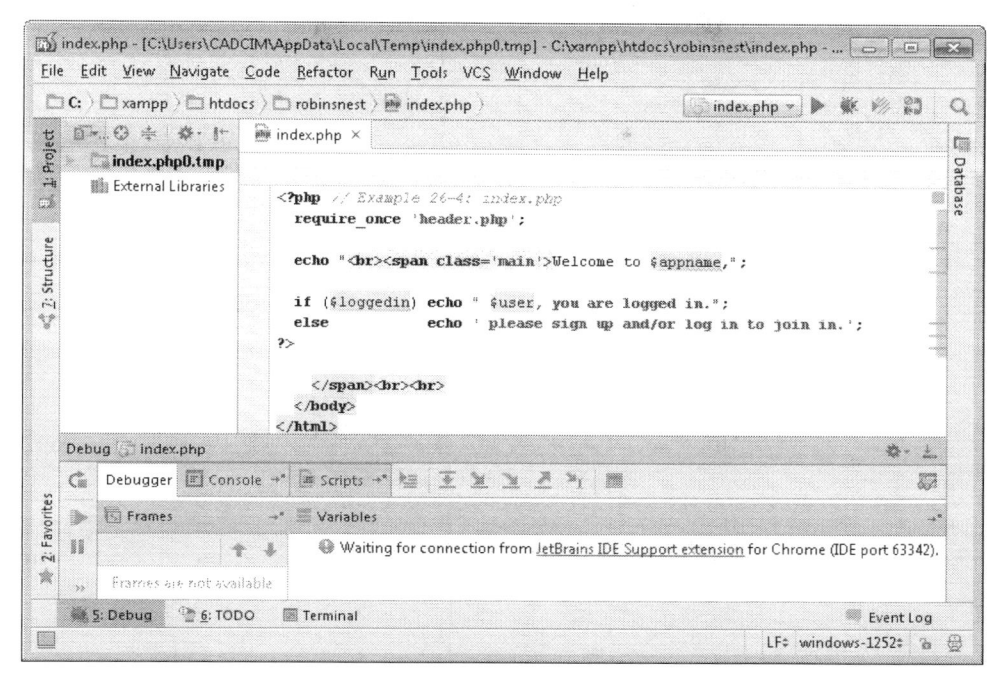

Figure 2-18 The PHPStorm IDE

Self-Evaluation Test

Answer the following questions and then compare them to those given at the end of this chapter:

1. _____ is a server side scripting language.

2. To write a PHP code, the _____ or an _____ is required.

3. The _____ is the folder or directory where you keep website files for a domain name.

4. FTP stands for _____.

5. IDE stands for _____.

Review Questions

Answer the following questions:

1. Which of the following options are the requirements to work with PHP?

    (a) Text Editor, PHP, and MySQL (b) PHP, MySQL, text editor, and web server
    (c) Server and PHP   (d) None of them

2. XAMPP stand for:

   (a) Multiple, Apache, MS-SQL, PHP, and Pearl
   (b) X-OS, Apache, MySQL, PHP, and Python
   (c) X-OS, Apache, MySQL, PHP, and Perl
   (d) X-OS, Apache, MS-SQL, PHP, and Perl

3. Which of the following options is the document root of XAMPP?

   (a) htdocs directory   (b) document directory
   (c) root directory   (d) files directory

4. FTP stands for:

   (a) File Transportation Project (b) File Transfer Protocol
   (c) File Transfer Project   (d) None of them

5. An IDE stands for:

   (a) In-built Development Environment
   (b) Inherited Development Environment
   (c) Integrated Designing Environment
   (d) Integrated Development Environment

Answers to Self-Evaluation Test
1. PHP, **2.** text editor, IDE, **3.** document root, **4.** File Transfer Protocol, **5.** Integrated Development Environment

Chapter 3

Fundamentals of PHP

Learning Objectives

After completing this chapter, you will be able to:
- *Understand the basic syntax of PHP*
- *Understand about comments*
- *Understand case sensitivity*
- *Understand echo and print statements*
- *Understand data types*
- *Understand type declaration*

INTRODUCTION

PHP stands for "Hypertext Preprocessor". It is a server-side scripting language used for developing dynamic websites. PHP and JavaScript are the languages embedded with HTML and CSS are used to develop dynamic websites. MySQL is a relational database management system and is used for data storage purposes. In this chapter, you will learn basic syntax and functionality of PHP such as comments, case sensitivity, echo and print statements, data types, and type declaration.

PHP FILE

PHP is used to develop dynamic websites. PHP code can be written in any text editor or IDE as discussed in previous chapter. PHP files can contain various other languages including PHP such as HTML, CSS, JavaScript, MySQL, and also plain text. The PHP files are saved with the extension *.php*. If you are working with the XMAPP server, you need to save these files in the *C:\xampp\htdocs* directory.

PHP is embedded with HTML code. Therefore, when a PHP file is executed on the server, it returns the plain HTML result to the browser.

> **Note**
> *You can save a file having HTML code with .html, .htm, or .php extension. But, to save a file having both HTML and PHP codes, you need to use .php extension only.*

SYNTAX OF PHP

PHP has a syntax that governs how a PHP code should be written. PHP script or code can be placed anywhere in the program according to the requirement of website.

The syntax to write a PHP script or code is as follow:

```
<?php

    //PHP Code

?>
```

In the given syntax, **<?php** is the start tag, **//PHP Code** is the one line comment which is not executed as a part of the program, and **?>** is the end/close tag. The code inside these tags will be executed.

PHP code can also start with **<?** tag instead of **<?php** tag; for example, you can write the PHP code inbetween **<?** and **?>** tags where **<?** is the start tag and **?>** is the end or close tag. But, it will not work with XML. Therefore, for the compatibility of PHP with all the scripting languages, you must write the PHP code in between **<?php** and **?>**.

COMMENTS IN PHP

Comments are the statements or lines written in between some special characters or begin with special characters. Comments are used for the reading purpose only. These lines are not considered as part of the program and ignored at the time of execution. Comments make the program more understandable and are used for the convenience of the programmer. For example, you were working on a PHP project two years ago and now you want to work on that project again, it will become difficult for you to understand the code. But if you have comments in your program, you can easily inspect the functionality of the existing code.

PHP supports C, C++, and Unix shell style comments. There are two types of comments in PHP:

1. One-line comment
2. Multiple line comment

One-Line Comment

One-line comment is a single line comment. The browser ignores the line which is commented. The basic purpose of the comment is to give a name to any part of a code, small description about code, to provide short remarks during programming, or to temporarily remove a line from a program written in PHP wherever needed. There are two ways in which you can write one-line comment in the PHP program:

1. By using pair of forward slashes(//), preceding the line.
2. By using hash(#), preceding the line.

You can use any of them to write a one-line comment.

For example:

```
<?php
    //First one-line comment in PHP.
    #Second one-line comment in PHP.
?>
```

In this example **<?php** is the start tag of PHP, **//First one-line comment in PHP** is a one-line comment, preceding with pair of forward slashes (//). Next, **#Second one-line comment in PHP** is also a one-line comment, preceding with hash(#), and **?>** is the end tag of PHP.

Multiple Line Comment

The Multiple line comment is used to comment more than one line or multiple lines. This comment is used to write a long description, a small documentation about the program, or to temporarily disable a large section of code which you do not want in your program for testing purpose or for some other reasons. Anything written in between /* and */ pair of characters is not executed as a part of the program.

For example:

```
<?php
    /* This is a multiple line comment which is
       used to comment one or more lines in the PHP code. */
?>
```

In the given example, **<?php** is the start tag of PHP and **?>** is the end tag of PHP. In the next line, **/*** is used to start a multiple line comment, ***/** is used to end the multiple line comment.

Nested multiple line comments are not possible in PHP. Nested multiple line comments mean one comment inside another comment. You cannot place opening **/*** and closing ***/** characters inside another opening **/*** and closing ***/** characters. On doing so, the program will generate an error because comment will end automatically at the first occurrence of closing ***/** character.

For example:

```
<?php
    /* This is a multiple line comment,
    /* multiple line comment ends here. */
    It will generate an error because it will not
    be able to detect the last closing characters of comment*/
?>
```

In the given example, multiple line comment is used inside another multiple line comment which is not possible in PHP. It will generate parsing error when the code is executed.

ECHO AND PRINT STATEMENTS

In PHP, you can display the output data in the browser by writing any of the two statements in your program:

1. **Echo** statement
2. **Print** statement

The **Echo** and **print** statements are almost same, but there are few differences between them which are discussed next.

Echo Statement

In PHP, the **echo** statement is used to display output data in the browser. This statement can be used with parentheses or without parentheses such as **echo()** or **echo**. This statement does not return any value which makes it faster as compared to the **print** statement. Multiple parameters can be passed to the **echo** statement, although usage of multiple parameters or arguments is rare. The echo statement starts with the keyword **echo**.

For example:

```
<?php
    echo "Welcome to CADCIM Technologies";
?>
```

In the given example, **<?php** is the start tag of PHP, **echo "Welcome to CADCIM Technologies";** is the **echo** statement which will be displayed as output in the browser, and **?>** is the closing tag of PHP.

Fundamentals of PHP

Note

To work with XAMPP and to run examples given in this book, you need to write programs in any text editor or IDE of your choice. Next, you need to save the program at the location C:\xampp\htdocs with .php extension, such as example.php.

Example 1

The following program will display the output text in the browser by using the **echo** statement. The line numbers on the right are not part of this program and are mentioned for reference only.

```
<!Doctype html>                                              1
<html>                                                       2
<head>                                                       3
<title>echo</title>                                          4
</head>                                                      5
<body>                                                       6
   <h1>First PHP program</h1>                                7
   <?php                                                     8
        echo "Cadcim Technologies";                          9
        echo "<h2>PHP echo statement</h2>";                  10
        echo "Echo ", "with ", "multiple parameters.";       11
   ?>                                                        12
</body>                                                      13
</html>                                                      14
```

Explanation

Line 1
<!Doctype html>
In this line, **<!Doctype html>** is the HTML tag used to define the version of HTML, which is HTML 5 in this case. Anything written in between **< >** (angle brackets) in HTML is known as start tag.

Line 2
<html>
In this line, **<html>** is the start tag of HTML document.

Line 3
<head>
In this line, **<head>** is the start tag of HTML. It provides the header information about the document.

Line 4
<title>echo</title>
In this line, **<title>** is the start tag and **</title>** is the end tag. Anything written between these tags is the title given to the document. In this case, **echo** is the title given to the document.

Line 5
</head>
In this line, **</head>** is the end tag of HTML. It indicates that the header information of the document ends here. Anything written between **</>** (angle brackets with a forward slash) in HTML is known as end tag.

Line 6
<body>
In this line, **<body>** is the start tag of HTML body which precedes the visible page content.

Line 7
<h1>First PHP program</h1>
In this line, **<h1>** is the start tag and **</h1>** is the end tag of HTML to define the most important heading in the HTML page. In HTML, there are six tags (from **<h1>** to **<h6>**) that are used to define headings in the HTML page. The **<h1>** tag defines the most important heading and **<h6>** defines the least important heading of the web page. This line will display the following as a heading of the web page in the browser:

First PHP program

Line 8
<?php
In this line, **<?php** is the start tag of PHP which is used to start the PHP code.

Line 9
echo "Cadcim Technologies";
In this line, **echo** is the keyword used to display the output in the browser in PHP. This line will display the following in the browser:

Cadcim Technologies

Line 10
echo "<h2>PHP echo statement</h2>";
In this line, **echo** is the keyword used to display the output in the browser in PHP. **<h2>** and **</h2>** are the start and end tags of HTML used to define the heading of the HTML code. This line will display the following in the browser:

PHP echo statement

Line 11
echo "Echo ", "with ", "multiple parameters.";
In this line, **echo** is the keyword used in PHP to display the output in the browser, but in this line, multiple parameters are passed in the single **echo** statement. This line will display the following in the browser:

Echo with multiple parameters.

Fundamentals of PHP

Line 12
```
?>
```
In this line, **?>** is the end tag of PHP which is used to end the PHP code.

Line 13
```
</body>
```
In this line, **</body>** is the end tag of HTML. It indicates that the visible page content ends here.

Line 14
```
</html>
```
In this line, **</html>** is the end tag of HTML. It indicates that the HTML document ends here.

The output of Example 1 is displayed in Figure 3-1.

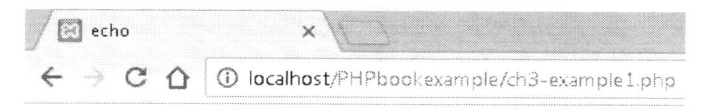

Figure 3-1 The output of Example 1

Print Statement

In PHP, the **print** statement can be used in place of the **echo** statement to display output data in the browser. This statement has a return value 1, therefore, it can be used in complex expressions where **echo** statement cannot be used. This statement can be used with parentheses or without parentheses such as **print()** or **print**. You can only pass one argument in **print** statement. This statement does not accept multiple arguments.

For example:

```
<?php
    print "Welcome to CADCIM Technologies";
?>
```

In the given example, **<?php** is the start tag of PHP, **print "Welcome to CADCIM Technologies";** is the **print** statement which will be displayed as output in the browser, and **?>** is the end tag of PHP.

Example 2

The following program will display the output text in the browser by using the **print** statement. The line numbers on the right are not the part of this program and are for reference only.

```
<!Doctype html>                                         1
<html>                                                  2
<head>                                                  3
<title>print</title>                                    4
</head>                                                 5
<body>                                                  6
    <h1>Second PHP program</h1>                         7
    <?php                                               8
         print "Cadcim Technologies";                   9
         print "<h2>PHP print statement</h2>";          10
    ?>                                                  11
</body>                                                 12
</html>                                                 13
```

Explanation
Line 9
print "Cadcim Technologies";
In this line, **print** is the keyword used to display the output in the browser in PHP. This line will display the following in the browser:

Cadcim Technologies

Line 10
print "<h2>PHP print statement</h2>";
In this line, **print** is the keyword used to display the output in the browser in PHP. The **<h2>** and **</h2>** tags are the start and end tags of HTML used to define the heading of the HTML code. This line will display the following in the browser:

PHP print statement

The output of Example 2 is displayed in Figure 3-2.

Fundamentals of PHP

> ### Second PHP program
>
> Cadcim Technologies
>
> ### PHP print statement

Figure 3-2 *The output of Example 2*

USE OF SPECIAL SYMBOLS

In PHP, some special symbols are used such as semicolon(;) and dollar sign($). They are discussed next.

Use of the ; Symbol

Every PHP command ends with a semicolon(;). It is important to place a semicolon(;) after every PHP command as it indicates that a PHP statement or command ends here. In other words, it terminates the PHP instructions. You do not need to place a semicolon at the last line of a PHP block because the closing tag of PHP block code automatically implies a semicolon.

For example:

```
<?php
    echo "This statement ends with a semicolon";
    echo "Last line of this PHP block does not need a semicolon"
?>
```

In the given example, the last statement does not contain a semicolon; still it would not throw an error as the statement is correct if it is ending with ?>. But if the end tag of PHP is missing then it will throw an error as the closing tag of PHP automatically implies a semicolon.

For example:

```
<?php
    echo "This statement ends with a semicolon";
    echo "Last line of this PHP block does not ends with a semicolon"
```

Note that this example will throw an error as ?> is missing in the code, but this will work properly if the last PHP command ends with a semicolon.

For example:

```
<?php
    echo "This statement ends with a semicolon";
```

```
echo "Last line of this PHP block needs a semicolon to avoid
error";
```

> **Tip**
> *It is a good practice to end every PHP statement or instruction with a semicolon and end PHP block with ?> tag to avoid errors.*

Use of the $ Symbol

In PHP, the **$** symbol is used for variables. All variables start with a **$** symbol because whenever **$** symbol comes across a variable, it makes the PHP parser faster and defines that any thing written after **$** symbol in PHP is a variable.

> **Note**
> *A variable is a named location where data is stored. This is a container used to store data and always starts with $ symbol. You will learn more about variables in later chapters.*

CASE SENSITIVITY

Case sensitivity means that each letter of a code or text is restricted to follow a proper case of characters whether it is uppercase (capital letter), lowercase (small letter), or both. For example, "Book" is the password set for an account. To open that account it is important to enter password correctly. If user enters "book" instead of "Book" then a message will appear informing that the password is wrong because passwords are case sensitive. In such cases, "book" and "Book" are two different words because "b" is in lowercase in first word and "B" is in uppercase in second word.

In PHP, all the classes, functions, user defined functions, and keywords such as **echo**, **if**, **else**, and so on are not case-sensitive, whereas all the variables and constants are case-sensitive.

> **Note**
> *You will learn about the classes, functions, user defined functions, variables, constants, and keywords in the later chapters.*

Example 3

The following program will display the output text in the browser by using the **echo** statement written in different cases.

```
<!Doctype html>                                        1
<html>                                                 2
<head>                                                 3
<title>Case sensitivity</title>                        4
</head>                                                5
<body>                                                 6
    <?php                                              7
        echo "<h1>echo in lowercase. </h1>";           8
        ECHO "<h2>ECHO in uppercase. </h2>";           9
        EcHo "<h3>EcHo in both case. </h3>";           10
```

```
    ?>                                                              11
</body>                                                             12
</html>                                                             13
```

Explanation
Line 8
echo "<h1>echo in lowercase. </h1>";
In this line, **echo** is the keyword used to display the output in the browser in PHP. **<h1>** and **</h1>** are the start and end tags of HTML used to define the heading of the HTML code. This line will display the following in the browser:

echo in lowercase.

Line 9
ECHO "<h2>ECHO in uppercase. </h2>";
In this line, **ECHO** is the keyword used to display the output in the browser in PHP. **<h2>** and **</h2>** are the start and end tags of HTML used to define the heading of the HTML code. This line will display the following in the browser:

ECHO in uppercase.

Line 10
EcHo "<h3>EcHo in both case. </h3>";
In this line, **EcHo** is the keyword used to display the output in the browser in PHP. **<h3>** and **</h3>** are the start and end tags of HTML used to define the heading of the HTML code. This line will display the following in the browser:

EcHo in both case.

The output of Example 3 is displayed in Figure 3-3.

Figure 3-3 The output of Example 3

DATA TYPES
While writing a program, you need to store different types of data in variables. Data type describes type of value that can be stored in a variable. Data types are used to construct the variables.

PHP stores eight types of primitive data types, which are as follows:

- String
- Integer
- Float (floating point numbers - also called double)
- Boolean
- Array
- Object
- NULL
- Resource

These eight primitive data types are grouped into three different categories:

1. Scalar data types
2. Compound data types
3. Special data types

Scalar Data Types

Scalar data types in PHP are used to represent single value. They are also known as base data types as they provide base for other data types such as array, object, and so on.

In PHP, there are four scalar data types, which are as follows:

- String
- Integer
- Float
- Boolean

String

A string is a sequence of characters where characters are same as bytes. A string can be any text written inside quotes. It can be written inside a single or a double quote. For example, "Welcome to Cadcim".

Before PHP 7, there were some restrictions in length of the string. But now in PHP 7, there are no such restrictions regarding the length of a string on 64-bit builds. On 32-bit builds and in the earlier versions, a string could be as large as up to 2GB (2147483647 bytes maximum).

Example 4

The following program will display the output text in the browser by using string data type.

```
<!Doctype html>                              1
<html>                                       2
<head>                                       3
<title>String Data type</title>              4
</head>                                      5
<body>                                       6
    <?php                                    7
```

Fundamentals of PHP

```
            $x = "Hello User!";                 8
            $y = 'It is a string.';             9
            echo $x;                           10
            echo "<br>";                       11
            echo $y;                           12
        ?>                                     13
    </body>                                    14
</html>                                        15
```

Explanation

Line 8
$x = "Hello User!";
In this line, **$x** is the variable which is holding a string type data **Hello User!**. This string type data is written inside the double quote.

Line 9
$y = 'It is a string.';
In this line, **$y** is the variable which holds a string type data **It is a string**. This string type data is written inside the single quote.

Line 10
echo $x;
In this line, **echo** will display the value of the **$x** variable which was assigned to it in Line 8. This line will display the following in the browser:

Hello User!

Line 11
echo "<br>";
In this line, **
** is the break tag of HTML used to break the line. This line does not display anything in the browser as it is used to break the line only.

Line 12
echo $y;
In this line, **echo** will display the value of the **$y** variable which was assigned to it in Line 9. This line will display the following in the browser:

It is a string.

The output of Example 4 is displayed in Figure 3-4.

Figure 3-4 The output of Example 4

Integer

The integer data type is used only for those numbers that do not contain any fractional part or decimal point. In other words, this data type is used only for signed whole numbers, either negative or positive.

Rules for integer data type are as follows:

- Data should have at least one digit.
- There cannot be a decimal point in data.
- This can be either positive or negative.
- This can be specified in three formats: decimal (10-based), hexadecimal (16-based -prefixed with 0x), or octal (8-based -prefixed with 0).

For example:

42 // decimal (10-based)
0755 // octal (8-based -prefixed with 0)
0xC4E // hexadecimal (16-based -prefixed with 0x)

In the given example, **42**, **0755**, and **0xC4e** are integer type values written in different formats as mentioned in the comments represented by double forward slash(//).

Example 5

The following program will display the output text in the browser by using integer data type.

```
<!Doctype html>                          1
<html>                                   2
<head>                                   3
<title>Integer Data type</title>         4
</head>                                  5
<body>                                   6
   <?php                                 7
        $x = 1233;                       8
        echo $x;                         9
        echo "<br>";                     10
        echo "It is an integer.";        11
   ?>                                    12
</body>                                  13
</html>                                  14
```

Explanation
Line 8
$x = 1233;
In this line, **1233** is the integer type value assigned to the **$x** variable.

Fundamentals of PHP

Line 9
echo $x;
In this line, **echo** will display the values of the **$x** variable assigned to it in Line 8. This line will display the following in the browser:

1233

The output of Example 5 is displayed in Figure 3-5.

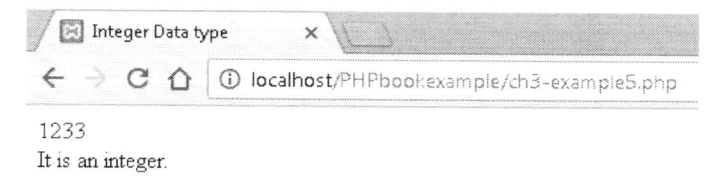

1233
It is an integer.

Figure 3-5 *The output of Example 5*

Float
The float data type is used only for those numbers that contain a decimal point or that have a fractional part. All the float, double, or real numbers are the part of float data type in PHP.

For example:

```
$x = 4.20;
```

In the given example, **$x** is the variable and 4.20 is the float type value assigned to it.

Example 6
The following program will display the output text in the browser by using the float data type. The line numbers on the right are not the part of the program and are for reference only.

```
<!Doctype html>                         1
<html>                                  2
<head>                                  3
<title>Float Data type</title>          4
</head>                                 5
<body>                                  6
   <?php                                7
        $x = 12.33;                     8
        echo $x;                        9
        echo "<br>";                    10
        echo "It is a float type.";     11
   ?>                                   12
</body>                                 13
</html>                                 14
```

Explanation
Line 8
$x = 12.33;
In this line, **12.33** is the float type value assigned to the **$x** variable.

Line 9
echo $x;
In this line, **echo** will display the value of the **$x** variable which was assigned to it in Line 8. This line will display the following in the browser:

12.33

The output of Example 6 is displayed in Figure 3-6.

Figure 3-6 The output of Example 6

Boolean
A boolean returns a true or false value. Alternatively, you can use zero to represent false and any nonzero value to represent true. Booleans are often used in conditional testing, so to check any condition, a user can use boolean.

> **Note**
> *You will learn about conditional testing in later chapter.*

For example:

```
$x = true;
$y = false;
```

In the above example, **$x** is the variable and **true** is the boolean type value assigned. Similarly, **$y** is the variable and **false** is the boolean type value assigned.

Compound Data Types
Compound data types in PHP are used for multiple items of the same type to be aggregated under a single representative entity. It is a collection of basic data types.

Fundamentals of PHP

In PHP, there are two compound data types that are as follows:

- Array
- Object

Array

In PHP, an array is the collection of data elements of the same or different types. These elements are referred by a common name and are stored in contiguous memory locations. You can refer to a particular data element in an array by using the index. The index starts from the lowest address (0) and ends at the highest address (n-1, here n specifies the total number of elements).

For example:

```
<?php
$mobile = array("Samsung", "Nexus", "iPhone");
echo "I like". $mobile[0]. "," . $mobile[1]. "and" . $mobile[2]. ".";
?>
```

In the given example, **$mobile** is a single variable which holds multiple value or elements, **array()** is the array function used to define the elements of array inside the parentheses. Here, **Samsung**, **Nexus**, and **iPhone** are the elements of the array referred by a common name **$mobile**. Next, **$mobile[0], $mobile[1]**, and **$mobile[2]** are the array index which will print the array element according to the index.

Object

An object is a data type in PHP that stores data and gives information how to process the data. An object is an instance of a class. Class serves as templates for objects and on the basis of these templates, objects are created using the **new** keyword.

An object must be explicitly declared. The declaration of an object's characteristics and behavior takes place within a class. Every object has properties and methods corresponding to those of its parent class. Objects can be manipulated independent of other objects of the same class as every object instance is completely independent.

For example:

```
$obj = new Car;
$temp= new Car('name' , 'model');
```

In the above example, **$obj** and **$temp** are declared as the objects of class **Car** by using **new** keyword. Here, **$obj** has no arguments and **$temp** has two values **name** and **model** which are passed as arguments.

Note
You will learn more about array and object in the later chapters.

Special Data Types

Special data types in PHP are of two types:

- NULL
- Resource

These types of data types are used in special cases in PHP and are discussed next.

NULL

NULL is a special data type which has only one value **NULL**. If a variable is created without a value, then the value **NULL** will be automatically assigned to the variable. You can also empty a variable by setting its value **NULL**.

For example:

```
$x;
$y = NULL;
```

In the above example, both **$x** and **$y** variables are NULL type. The **$x** variable has no value assigned to it. So by default, the **NULL** value is automatically assigned to the **$x** variable.

Example 7

The following program will display the output text in the browser by using NULL type.

```
<!Doctype html>                 1
<html>                          2
<head>                          3
<title>NULL type</title>        4
</head>                         5
<body>                          6
    <?php                       7
        $x = "Hello User";      8
        $x = null;              9
        echo $x;                10
    ?>                          11
</body>                         12
</html>                         13
```

Explanation

Line 8
$x = "Hello User";
In this line, **Hello User** is a string type value assigned to the **$x** variable.

Line 9
$x = NULL;
In this line, **NULL** is the NULL type value assigned to the **$x** variable.

Fundamentals of PHP

Line 10
echo $x;
In this line, **echo** will display value of the **$x** variable assigned in Line 9.

There will be no output of Example 7 in the browser as the value of **$x** variable has become null (empty) in Line 9.

Resource
A resource type is not an actual data type. It is a special variable which holds a reference to an external resource and therefore referred as special type. These resources are created and used by special functions. They are used to store the reference to access the resources external to PHP file. A common example of using the resource data type is a database call or database connectivity.

> **Note**
> *You will learn more about resource in later chapter.*

TYPE DECLARATION
Type declaration means specifying the expected type of data which will be stored in the variable. It is also known as type hinting. The data type of expected data can be declared during function declaration while passing the parameters to the function.

In PHP versions prior to PHP 5 version, type declaration was not possible. PHP used to set the data type of variables automatically according to the values assigned. The type declaration was introduced in PHP 5 version that allows you to set the data type of the variable. This is used to check that the value passed in the function calling is related to the required data type or not.

PHP 7 version introduces two new features for type declaration that are as follows:

1. Scalar type declaration
2. Return type declaration

Scalar Type Declaration
Scalar type declaration is introduced in PHP 7. Scalar type declaration specifies the data type of input parameters of functions used in PHP program as integer, float, string, or boolean. Keywords used for scalar type declarations are: **int** (for integers), **float** (for floating point numbers), **string** (for strings), and **bool** (for booleans). Scalar type declaration can also specify the type of array and name of an interface. Scalar type declaration helps in finding out mistakes in program by comparing the data type of values passed in the parameters with the expected data type. Scalar type declaration ensures the input consistency and easily eliminate the error in the complex programs.

Scalar type declaration can be done with any of the two modes:

1. Coercive mode(default)
2. Strict mode

Coercive Mode

Coercive mode is the default mode. This mode is selected by default in a PHP program if the mode of scalar type declaration is not specified.

For example:

```
<?php
function Cmode(int $a){
echo "integer = " .$a;
}
Cmode(12); //function call
//output: integer = 12
```

In the above example, mode of scalar type declaration is not specified. So this mode is coercive mode which is the default mode. Here, **function** is the keyword used for function in PHP, **Cmode** is the function name, and **(int $a)** is the input parameter. Inside the input parameter, **int** is the keyword used to specify that the function will accept integer type value and **$a** is the variable. When a value is passed to the function, the value will be matched with the data type passed in the input parameters of function and the output will be displayed. In this case, **12** is the integer type value passed to the function **Cmode**. So without any type conversion, the program will display the exact value **12** as output.

If the data type of value passed to the function does not match the data type in the input parameter list of function, the program will not generate an error. Due to coercive mode, the program will convert the value passed to the function into the expected data type specified in the input parameter list of function and display the output.

For example:

```
<?php
function Cmode(int $a){
echo "integer = " .$a;
echo "</br>";
}
Cmode(12.1); //function call
Cmode(True); //function call
/*output: integer = 12
         integer = 1 */
```

In the given example, **(int $a)** is the input parameter where **int** is the keyword used to specify that the function will accept integer type values. Here, **12.1** and **True** are the float and boolean type values passed to the function **Cmode**, respectively. These two values do not match with the **int** data type passed in input parameter of function. Therefore, due to the coercive mode, these values will get converted into integer type and the output will be displayed as 1 for True and 12 for 12.1.

Fundamentals of PHP

Note

*If the input parameter(s) of a function consists of **int** or **float** data type and the value passed to the function call is of **string** data type then an error will occur because the **string** data type cannot get converted into integer or float type. But, if the input parameter(s) of the function consists of **string** data type and the value passed to the function call is of integer type then it will accept integer as string.*

Strict Mode

When a developer specifies the mode of scalar type then that mode is known as strict mode. It gets enabled when developer places a single declare directive at the top of the PHP program file. This directive ensures that any function call made in the program will have to strictly follow the specified data type.

The single declare directive to be placed at the top of the program file is:

```
declare(strict_types=1);
```

For example:

```
<?php
declare(strict_types=1);
function Smode(int $a){
echo $a;
}
Smode(True); //Function call
 /* Output: Fatal error: Uncaught TypeError: Argument 1 passed to
    Smode() must be of the type integer, boolean given ..*/
```

In the above example, **declare(strict_types=1);** is the single declare directive which makes the program in strict mode. Its working is same as it is in coercive mode with only difference that it does not perform type conversion as coercive does. If the data type in input parameter of function does not match with the value passed in the function, it will throw a fatal error instead of converting it in that type. In the given example, it will throw fatal error because value passed in function **Smode** is **True** which is of boolean type and it does not match with data type **int** (keyword for integer data type) which is passed in the input parameter of the function.

Return Type Declaration

Return type declaration is also introduced in PHP 7. It specifies the type of value that a function should return. It is available in most of the popular programming languages such as C, C++, Java, and so on, but it was not available before PHP 7. Return type declaration ensures output consistency.

It works with coercive and strict mode. In coercive mode, if the value gets matched with the data type passed for return type then it will return the exact value; otherwise it will convert it into the given type and display the output. In strict mode, it will display the output only if it returns the value with the correct data type, otherwise it will throw a fatal error, specifically TypeError. To specify the return type, colon is added in front of the function input parameter and the return data type is specified next to it.

For example:

```
function returnIntValue(int $value): int {
        //block of function.
    return $value;
}
```

In the above example, **function** is the keyword used for function, **returnIntValue** is the function name, **(int $value)** is the function input parameter where **int** is the keyword used to declare the scalar type and **$value** is the variable, **:** (colon) is used before specifying the return data type, and **int** is the keyword used to return integer data type. In the block of function, **return** is the keyword used to return a value.

Self-Evaluation Test

Answer the following questions and then compare them to those given at the end of this chapter:

1. In PHP, _____ and _____ statements are used to display output data in the browser.

2. The _____ statement cannot take multiple arguments.

3. The _____ type in PHP is used to represent single value.

4. The _____ type is a number with a decimal point.

5. _____ and _____ type declarations are introduced in PHP 7.

Review Questions

Answer the following questions:

1. Which of the following options is the correct basic syntax of PHP?

    (a) `<?php`
    `        //PHP Code`
    `    ?>`

    (b) `<php`
    `        //PHP Code`
    `    ?>`

    (c) `<!--php`
    `        //PHP Code`
    `    -->`

Fundamentals of PHP

(d) ```
<php>
    //PHP Code
</php>
```

2. Which of the following symbols is used to end the PHP command?

   (a) $                      (b) *
   (c) ?                      (d) ;

3. Which of the following options is the correct example of integer data type?

   (a) 45.70             (b) TRUE
   (c) "45"               (d) 15

4. Which of the following options is the single declare directive which is placed at the top of the program file to declare the strict mode?

   (a) `declare(strict_type=1);`      (b) `declare(strict_types=1);`
   (c) `declare(strict_mode=1);`    (d) `declare(strict_types=on);`

5. **Find errors in the following blocks of source code:**

   (a) ```
   <?php
   echo "<h1>Find Error</h1>;
   echo "This","is","string","made,"with","multiple parameters.";
   ?>
   ```

   (b) ```
   <?php
   /* find an error in the multi line comment, this is line 1
       /* this is line 2, of PHP multi line comment */
           and this is line 3 where the comment ends */
   ?>
   ```

   (c) ```
   <?php
       $x = "Hello User!";
       $y = It is a string.;
       echo $x;
       echo "<br>";
       echo $y;
   ```

   (d) ```
   <?php
       $x = "Hello User!";
       $y = 'you found the error.';
       echo $x;
       echo "<br>"
       echo $y;
   ?>
   ```
   ```

(e)
```
<!doctype html>
<html>
<head>
<title> Program
<body>
    <?php
        print "Hello User";
        print "How are you";
    ?>
</body>
</html>
```

EXERCISES

Exercise 1

Write a program to display the string value "This is the String type scalar declaration" in the browser using strict mode of scalar type declaration.

Exercise 2

Write a program to display any float and integer numbers in the browser using the **echo** statement in coercive mode of scalar type declaration where input parameter function must be of float type.

Answers to Self-Evaluation Test
1. print, echo, 2. Print, 3. Scalar, **4.** Float, **5.** Scalar, return

Chapter 4

Variables, Constants, and Strings

Learning Objectives

After completing this chapter, you will be able to:
- *Use variables*
- *Understand the scope of variables*
- *Use constants*
- *Understand strings*
- *Understand the concept of escape sequence*
- *Understand different string functions*

INTRODUCTION

In the previous chapter, you learned about basic syntax and functionality of PHP. In this chapter, you will learn about the variables that stores the data, scope of variables, superglobal variables, constants, strings, and so on in detail.

VARIABLES

A variable is the container for data where data is stored in a named location. Variable always starts with a **$** (dollar) symbol followed by its name. Equal operator (**=**) is used to assign data to the variable.

For example:

```
$name = "String_Data";
```

In the given example, **$name** is the variable which is a named location to store data. **String_Data** is the string type data which is stored in the **$name** variable. In other words, assigned to the **$name** variable.

Variable Name

While naming a variable, you must follow certain rules. The rules are as follows:

1. Only alphabetic characters, both uppercase and lowercase, digits from 0 to 9, and the underscore (_) can be used.
2. Variable name can start with an alphabet or an underscore but not with a digit.
3. Variable names can not contain space. If variable name consist of more than one word, it can be separated by using _ (underscore) character or can be written in camel case instead of using space.
4. Variable names are case sensitive. For example, **$case** and **$Case** are two different variables.

The following variable names are invalid in PHP:

```
$9_count   // Variable name cannot start with a digit.
$count#    // Variable name cannot contain # (Hash symbol).
$my account // Variable name cannot have a space.
```

The following variable names are valid in PHP:

```
$count_9   //Variable name can start with alphabetic characters.
$_Account  //Variable name can start with an underscore.
$my_account //Variable name can be separated with an underscore.
$myAccount //Variable name can be written in camel case.
```

> **Note**
> *PHP has no command to declare a variable unlike other programming languages. It is created the moment any value or data is assigned to it. The assigned value can be of any type.*

Variables, Constants, and Strings 4-3

Example 1

The following program will display the output in the browser by using variables, storing different types of data. The line numbers on the right are not the part of this program and are for reference only.

```
<!Doctype html>                                     1
<html>                                              2
<head>                                              3
<title>Variable</title>                             4
</head>                                             5
<body>                                              6
<?php                                               7
    echo "<h3>String type data,for example:</h3>";  8
    $txt = "User"; //creating variable.             9
    echo "<b>Hello $txt!</b>";                     10
    echo "<h3>Integer type data,for example:</h3>"; 11
    $x = 5;                                        12
    echo "<b>$x</b>";                              13
    echo "<h3>Float type data,for example:</h3>";  14
    $y = 8.9;                                      15
    echo "<b>$y</b>"                               16
?>                                                 17
</body>                                            18
</html>                                            19
```

Explanation
Line 9
$txt = "User"; //creating variable.
In this line, **$txt** is the variable, = (equal) operator is used to assign a value to the variable, **User** is the string type data assigned to the **$txt** variable which is written inside the double quotes, and **//creating variable**. is the one-line comment.

Line 10
echo "Hello $txt!";
In this line, **echo** is the keyword used to display the output in the browser in PHP. **** and **** are the start and end tags of the HTML used to make the data written between them boldface. **$txt** is the variable which will call the value assigned to it in Line 9. This line will display the following in the browser:

Hello User!

Line 12 and Line 15
$x = 5;
$y = 8.9;
In these lines, **5** is the integer type value assigned to the **$x** variable and **8.9** is the float type value assigned to the **$y** variable.

Line 13 and Line 16
echo "$x";
echo "$y";
These lines will work the same way as Line 10 and will display the following in the browser.

5
8.9

The output of Example 1 is displayed in Figure 4-1.

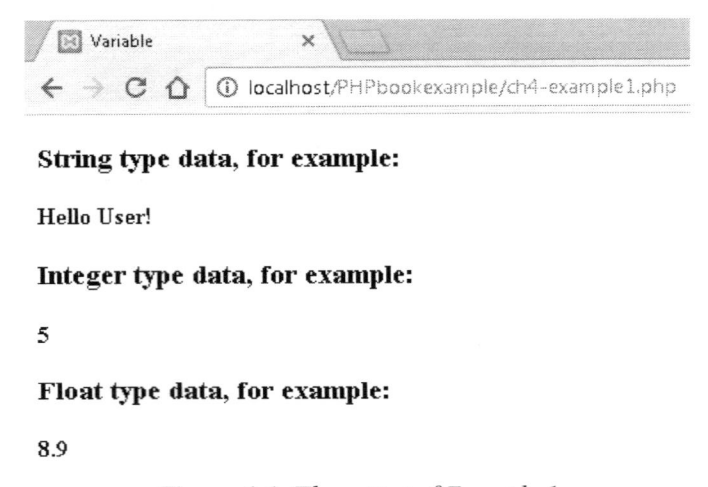

Figure 4-1 *The output of Example 1*

Note
*You can reassign the variable to another variable. For example, **$name** = **$new_name**;. In this example **$name** and **$new_name** both are variables.*

VARIABLE SCOPE
The scope of a variable refers to that part of the program within which it can be accessed and manipulated. The scope also specifies when to allocate or deallocate memory to the variable.

The scope is of the following three types:

1. Local scope
2. Global scope
3. Static scope

Local Variables
The variables that are declared inside a block of a function are known as local variables. The scope of local variable is limited to that function. In other words, these variables are accessible only within that particular block of function. It cannot be accessed outside that block of the function.

Variables, Constants, and Strings

For example:

```php
<?php
   $val = 4;
   function func_name () {
      //block of function
      $val = 0;//local variable.
         -------
         -------
   }
   func_name();
   -----------
   -----------
?>
```

In the given example, **func_name()** is a function and the **$val=0** inside this block of function is the local variable holding an integer type value 0 and can be accessed or manipulated within this function only. In this example, **$val = 4** is the global variable and cannot be accessed inside the function directly. You will learn about the function in the later chapter.

Example 2

The following program will display the output in the browser by using local variable and storing integer type data.

```
<!Doctype html>                                                       1
<html>                                                                2
<head>                                                                3
<title>Local Variable</title>                                         4
</head>                                                               5
<body>                                                                6
<?php                                                                 7
 $ls = 500;                                                           8
 function local_scope () {                                            9
 $ls = 100;//local variable.                                         10
 echo "<h2>Value of variable inside function is: $ls</h2>";          11
 }                                                                   12
 local_scope(); //function call.                                     13
 echo "<p>Value of variable outside function is: $ls</p>";           14
?>                                                                   15
</body>                                                              16
</html>                                                              17
```

Explanation
Line 8
$ls = 500;
In this line, **500** is the integer type value assigned to **$ls** variable.

Line 9
function local_scope () {
In this line, **function** is the keyword used for function, **local_scope()** is the function name, and { (open curly bracket) is used to start the block of function.

Line 10
$ls = 100;
In this line, **100** is the integer type value assigned to **$ls** variable. Here, **$ls** is a local variable as it is inside the block of function.

Line 11
echo "<h2>Value of variable inside function is: $ls</h2>";
In this line, **$ls** is the local variable which will call the value assigned to it in Line 10. This line will display the following in the browser:

Value of variable inside function is: 100

Line 12
}
In this line, **}** (closing curly bracket) is used to close the block of function.

Line 13
local_scope();
In this line, **local_scope()** is the function name through which a function is called.

Line 14
echo "<p>Value of variable outside function is: $ls</p>";
In this line, **echo** is the keyword used to display the output in the browser in PHP. **<p>** and **</p>** are the start and end tags of the HTML used to define the paragraph of the HTML code. **$ls** is the variable which will call the value assigned to it in line 8 as it can not access the variable inside the function. This line will display the following in the browser:

Value of variable outside function is: 500

The output of Example 2 is displayed in Figure 4-2.

Value of variable inside function is: 100

Value of variable outside function is: 500

Figure 4-2 *The output of Example 2*

Variables, Constants, and Strings

> **Note**
> You can have local variables with the same name in different functions because local variables can be accessed only by the function in which they are declared.

Global Variables

The variables that can be accessed and used anywhere in the program are known as global variable. The memory is allocated to this variable when the program execution begins and deallocated after the program terminates normally. To access the global variable outside the function, there is no requirement for declaring the variable to be global. But to access global variable inside a function, it must be explicitly declared to be global. It can be done by placing **GLOBAL** or **global** keyword in front of the variable that is inside the block of function.

For example:

```php
<?php
    $val = 10;//global variable.
    function func_name () {
       //block of function.
     GLOBAL $val;//global variable explicitly declared.
         -------
         -------
    }
    func_name();
    -----------
    -----------
?>
```

In the given example, **$val = 10;** is the global variable holding an integer value **10**. **func_name()** is a function and the **$val** inside this block of function is also global variable as **GLOBAL** keyword is placed before the **$val**. These global variables can be accessed or manipulated from anywhere in the program.

Example 3

The following program will display the output in the browser by using global variable, storing integer type of data, and can be accessed from anywhere in the program.

```
<!Doctype html>                                          1
<html>                                                   2
<head>                                                   3
<title>Local Variable</title>                            4
</head>                                                  5
<body>                                                   6
<?php                                                    7
    $x = 5; //global variable.                           8
    $y = 10; //global variable.                          9
    $z = 15; //global variable.                         10
```

```
        $sum = 12; //global variable.                              11
    function globalFunc() {                                        12
        GLOBAL $x, $y, $z, $sum; //global variable.                13
        echo "<p>Variable x inside function is: $x</p>";           14
        echo "<p>Variable y inside function is: $y</p>";           15
        $sum = $z + $x;  //value of $sum will change.              16
    }                                                              17
    globalFunc();  // function calling.                            18
    echo "<p>Variable x outside function is: $x</p>";              19
    echo "<p>Variable sum outside function is: $sum</p>";          20
    ?>                                                             21
    </body>                                                        22
    </html>                                                        23
```

Explanation
Line 8 to Line 11
$x = 5;
$y = 10;
$z = 15;
$sum = 12;
In these lines, **5**, **10**, **15**, and **12** are the integer type values assigned to the **$x, $y, $z,** and **$sum**, respectively. These variables are global variable as they are declared outside the function and do not require to be explicitly declared global.

Line 13
GLOBAL $x, $y, $z, $sum;
In this line, **$x, $y, $z,** and **$sum** are the global variables as **GLOBAL** keyword is placed before them to explicitly declare them global because they are inside the function **globalFunc()**. These global variables can be accessed or manipulated from anywhere in the program.

Line 14 and Line 15
echo "<p>Variable x inside function is: $x</p>";
echo "<p>Variable y inside function is: $y</p>";
In these lines, **$x** and **$y** variables will call the value assigned to them outside the function in Line 8 and Line 9 as they are global variables. These lines will display the following in the browser:

Variable x inside function is: 5
Variable y inside function is: 10

Line 16
$sum = $z + $x;
In this line, **$sum** is the global variable. **$z** and **$x** are also the global variables which hold **15** and **5** integer type values, respectively, and + (addition) is the arithmetic operator which will do the sum of **$z** and **$x** and the resultant value 20 will get assigned to **$sum** with the help of assignment operator (=).

Note that you will learn about different operators later in this chapter.

Variables, Constants, and Strings

Line 19 and Line 20
echo "<p>Variable x outside function is: $x</p>";
echo "<p>Variable sum outside function is: $sum</p>";
In these lines, **$x** will call the value 5, assigned to it in Line 8, outside the function. But **$sum** will not call the value 12, assigned to it in Line 11, because its value got changed inside the function **globalFunc()**. As **$sum** is a global variable and can be accessed from anywhere in the program, it will call the value 20 assigned to it in Line 16. These lines will display the following in the browser:

Variable x outside function is: 5
Variable sum outside function is: 20

The output of Example 3 is displayed in Figure 4-3.

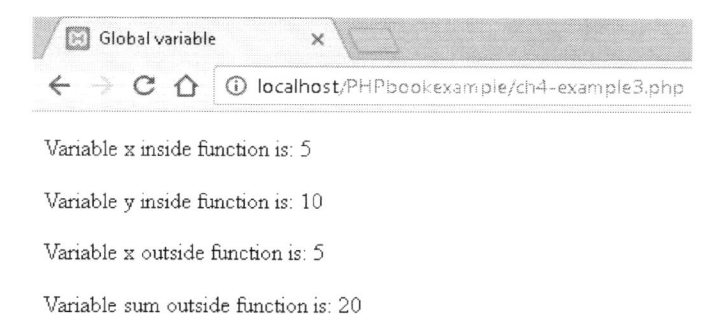

Figure 4-3 The output of Example 3

Static Variables

The variables that hold the values even after the function exits are known as static variables. When a function is executed, its variables get destroyed. But if you need that value again for further job, you will not be able to get it back until you use the static variable. Generally, the variable declared inside the functions holds its initial value, it will not be able to hold the updated value once the function exits. So, in case of multiple calls, it will always display the initial value of that variable instead of the updated or latest value. To get that updated value, static variables are used.

A static variable is declared by using **STATIC** or **static** keyword which is placed in front of the variable that is inside the block of function. It holds the updated value of the variables even if the function exits. If a function is called multiple time, it will display the updated or latest value every time.

For example:

```
<?php
    function func_name () {
      //block of function.
    static $val = 5;//static variable.
        -------
        -------
```

```
        }
            func_name();
            func_name();
            func_name();
            -----------
            -----------
?>
```

In the given example, **func_name()** is a function and the **$val** inside this block of function is a static variable as **static** keyword is placed before the **$val** which holds the integer value **5**. This static variable can hold the latest or updated value of the variable even after function gets exit.

Example 4

The following program will display the output in the browser by using static variable, storing integer type of data which can hold latest value of variable.

```
<!Doctype html>                                                        1
<html>                                                                 2
<head>                                                                 3
<title>Static Variable</title>                                         4
</head>                                                                5
<body>                                                                 6
<?php                                                                  7
    function normalFunc() {                                            8
        $p = 7;//local variable.                                       9
        $q = 3;//local variable.                                       10
        $p = $q + $p;                                                  11
    echo "<p>Latest value of local variable p is: $p </p>";            12
}                                                                      13
function staticFunc() {                                                14
    static $x = 5; //static variable.                                  15
        $y = 4;                                                        16
        $x = $y + $x;                                                  17
    echo "<p>Latest value of static variable x in is:$x </p>";         18
}                                                                      19
normalFunc();//function calling.                                       20
normalFunc();//function calling.                                       21
normalFunc();//function calling.                                       22
echo "<br>";                                                           23
staticFunc();//function calling.                                       24
staticFunc();//function calling.                                       25
staticFunc();//function calling.                                       26
?>                                                                     27
</body>                                                                28
</html>                                                                29
```

Variables, Constants, and Strings 4-11

Explanation
Line 9 and Line 10
$p = 7;
$q = 3;
In these lines, **7** and **3** are the integer type values assigned to the **$p** and **$q**, respectively. These variables are local variables as they are declared inside the block of function **normalFunc()**.

Line 12
echo "<p>Latest value of local variable p is: $p</p>";
In this line, **$p** will call the value 10, assigned to it in line 11. As **normalFunc()** function is called 3 times from Line 20 to Line 22, it will display the **echo** statement 3 times in the browser. But the value of **$p** will be same for all three as local variables do not hold the updated value. This line will display the following in the browser:

Latest value of local variable p is: 10

Line 15 to Line 16
static $x = 5;
$y = 4;
In these lines, **$x** is static variable as the **static** keyword is placed before it and it holds the integer value 5. **$y** is the local variable which holds integer value 4. These both variables are declared inside the block of the **staticFunc()** function.

Line 17
$x = $y + $x;
In this line, **$x** and **$y** are the local variables that hold the value 5 and 4, respectively which were declared in Line 15 and Line 16. **+** (addition) is the arithmetic operator which will do the sum of **$y** and **$x** and the resultant value 9 will get assigned to **$x** with the help of assignment operator (**=**). But this value will get updated as **$x** is a static variable, the resultant value will get updated whenever **staticFunc()** function is called.

Line 18
echo "<p>Latest value of static variable x is: $x</p>";
In this line, **$x** will call the value 9 assigned to it in Line 17. As the **staticFunc()** function is called 3 times from Line 24 to Line 26, it will display the **echo** statement 3 times in the browser. But the value of **$x** will be updated every time the call is made as it is static variable and it holds the updated value. This line will display the following 3 statements in the browser:

Latest value of static variable x is: 9
Latest value of static variable x is: 13
Latest value of static variable x is: 17

The output of Example 4 is displayed in Figure 4-4.

Latest value of local variable p is: 10

Latest value of local variable p is: 10

Latest value of local variable p is: 10

Latest value of static variable x in is: 9

Latest value of static variable x in is: 13

Latest value of static variable x in is: 17

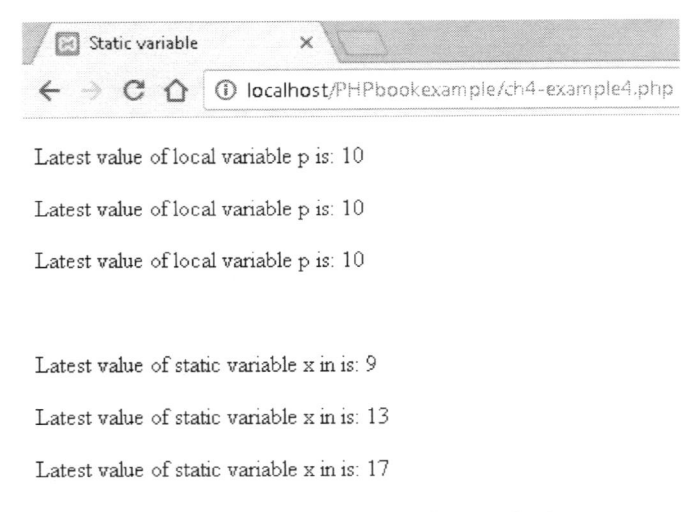

Figure 4-4 The output of Example 4

SUPERGLOBAL VARIABLES

The variables that are predefined in PHP are known as superglobals. They are built-in variables which can be accessed from any part of the program such as functions, classes, and so on. In short, they are always available for all the scopes as its global and does not require any keyword to declare it global explicitly. These superglobals are used to get the information of current program and its environment. Table 4-1 shows the list of superglobal variables with their description.

Table 4-1 Superglobals and their description

Superglobal	Description
$GLOBALS	It contains all the variables that are defined in the global scope. PHP stores all the global variables in an array with the help of **$GLOBALS**[name of the variable]. For example, **$GLOBALS['p'] = $GLOBALS['q'] + $GLOBALS['r'];**
$_SERVER	It contains information such as headers, paths, and script locations. The entries stored in the array of **$_SERVER** superglobal variable are created by the web server.
$_POST	It contains variables that are passed to the current script through the HTTP POST method.
$_GET	It contains the query string variable that is sent with the URL through the HTTP GET method.
$_COOKIE	It contains variables passed to the current script through the HTTP Cookies.

Variables, Constants, and Strings 4-13

$_SESSION	It sets the session variables that are available to the current script.
$_REQUEST	It contains the contents of **$_GET**, **$_POST**, and **$_COOKIE** that are passed by the browser.
$_FILES	It contains an array of items uploaded to the current script through the HTTP POST method.
$_ENV	It contains variables passed to the current script through the environment method.

Note

You will learn more about superglobals in later chapters as superglobal variables are the part of arrays.

CONSTANTS

A constant is an identifier or a name for a value which will remain fixed throughout the program or script. By default, it is case sensitive and is always written in uppercase. A constant name must start with a letter or an underscore.

Constant Name

While naming a constant, you must follow certain rules. The rules are as follows:

1. Only alphabetic characters, digits from 0 to 9, and the underscore (_) can be used.
2. Constant name can start with an alphabet or an underscore but not with a digit.
3. Constant names can not contain space. If constant name consist of more than one word, it can be separated by using _ (underscore) character.
4. Constant names are case sensitive. It should be written in uppercase. For example, VALUE.

The following constant names are invalid in PHP:

```
9_COUNT // Constant name cannot start with a digit.
COUNT# // Constant name cannot contain #(hash symbol).
```

The following constant names are valid in PHP:

```
COUNT_9 // Constant name can start with alphabetic characters.
_ACCOUNT // Constant name can start with an underscore.
MY_ACCOUNT // Constant name can be separated with an underscore.
ACCOUNT // Constant name must be written in uppercase.
```

Syntax of Constant

Constants are defined by using the **define()** function. It accepts two or three arguments as per the requirement of developer. To use the value of a constant, you will specify its name wherever required in the program.

For example:

```
define("NAME", "Value"); //two arguments.
//or
define("NAME", "Value", case-insensitive);//three arguments.
```

In the given example, **define()** is the function used to define constant, **NAME** is the constant name, **Value** is the value of the constant. The value of constant can be integer, boolean, string, float, NULL, or array type. Here, **case-insensitive** is the third argument which is optional because by default it is **false**, but it can be set to **true** for using constant name in any case (lowercase and uppercase).

Example 5

The following program will display the output in the browser by using static variable and storing integer type of data which can hold latest value of variable.

```
<!Doctype html>                                          1
<html>                                                   2
<head>                                                   3
<title>Constants</title>                                 4
</head>                                                  5
<body>                                                   6
<?php                                                    7
   define("HELLO", "Hello User!!");                      8
        echo HELLO; // outputs "HELLO User!!"            9
        echo "<br>";                                    10
   define("STR", "Repeat", true);                       11
        echo STR; // outputs "Repeat"                   12
        echo "<br>";                                    13
        echo str; // outputs "Repeat"                   14
        echo "<br>";                                    15
// Works in PHP 7                                       16
   define('VERSION', array(                             17
        'Array type value cannot be used in PHP 4.',    18
        'Array type value cannot be used in PHP 5.',    19
        'Array type value can be used in PHP 7.'        20
        ));                                             21
echo VERSION[2];                                        22
?>                                                      23
</body>                                                 24
</html>                                                 25
```

Explanation
Line 8
define ("HELLO", "Hello User!!");
In this line, **define()** is the function used to define constant, **HELLO** is the constant name, and **Hello User!!** is the string type value of the constant.

Variables, Constants, and Strings

4-15

Line 9
echo HELLO;
In this line, **HELLO** is the name of the constant which is used to display the value of constant using **echo** statement. This line will display the following in the browser:

Hello User!!

Line 11
define ("STR", "Repeat", true);
In this line, **define()** is the function used to define constant, **STR** is the constant name, **Repeat** is the string type value of the constant, and **true** specifies that the constant name can be used in any case (lowercase and uppercase) which means it can be case-insensitive. This line will display the following in the browser:

Repeat
Repeat

Line 12 and Line 14
echo STR;
echo str;
In these lines, **STR** and **str** both are the name of constant defined in Line 11. Both the lines will give the same value because they both are same constant name written in different case as its case-insensitivity is defined **true** in Line 11.

Line 17 to Line 21
define ('VERSION', array(
        'Array type value cannot be used in PHP 4.' ,
        'Array type value cannot be used in PHP 5.'
        'Array type value can be used in PHP 7.'
        ));
In these lines, **define()** is the function used to define constant, **VERSION** is the constant name, and **array** is the keyword used to define array where its elements are written inside its parentheses. Array defined here is the value of the constant. You will learn more about arrays in later chapter.

Line 22
echo VERSION[2];
In this line, **VERSION** is the constant name defined in Line 17 and **2** is the array index which will call the 3rd element of array as array index starts from 0. Array index is written between square brackets. This line will display the following in the browser:

Array type value can be used in PHP 7.

The output of Example 5 is displayed in Figure 4-5.

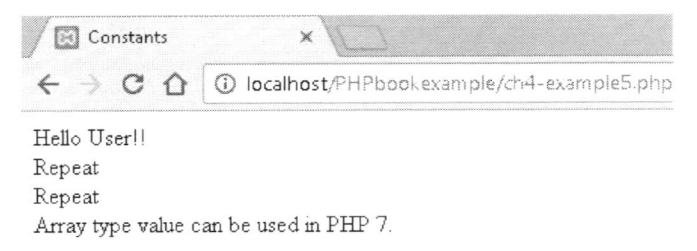

Figure 4-5 The output of Example 5

> **Note**
> *Array type value for a constant is only valid in PHP 7, earlier versions of PHP does not support array type constant value.*

constant() Function

In the last example, you have directly used constant name to return or display the value of a constant. You can also do the same by using the **constant()** function.

For example:

```
<?php
   define ("NAME" , "Value");
   echo constant ("NAME");
?>
```

In the given example, **define()** is the function used to define constant, **NAME** is the constant name, and **Value** is the value of the constant which can be of integer, boolean, string, float, or NULL type. Next, **constant()** is the function used to return constant value where **NAME** is the constant name whose value is to be returned.

> **Note**
> *The constant() function cannot return array type value of a constant in any PHP version including PHP 7.*

If you do not know that the constant is stored in a variable or it is returned by a function then you can use the **constant()** function to retrieve the value of the constant. It can obtain the constant value dynamically by using the constant name. The **constant()** function also works in the class constant. You will learn more about class constant in a later chapter.

Magic Constants

There are some special constants in PHP known as magic constants. They are predefined and change their values depending upon where they are used. Magic constant name starts with the double underscore and ends with the same. They are case-insensitive, for example, __LINE__ and __line__ , both are valid magic constants and perform same task. You can use them directly wherever required.

Variables, Constants, and Strings

For example:

```php
<?php
    echo __line__;
    echo "it is using" . __FILE__ . " file";
?>
```

In the given example, **__line__** and **__FILE__** are the magic constants. Here **__line__** will display the current line number of the program file and **__FILE__** will display the complete file path of current file including file name.

There are 8 magical constants in PHP. Table 4-2 shows the list of magical constants with their description.

Table 4-2 Magical constants and their description

Name	Description
__LINE__	It will display the current line number of program file.
__FILE__	It will display the complete path of the current file with the file name. If written inside an include statement then path with the name of the file included will be displayed or returned.
__DIR__	It will return the directory (path of file without its name) of the file.
__FUNCTION__	It will return the function name.
__CLASS__	It will return the class name.
__TRAIT__	It will return the trait name. If declared in namespace, it will return both.
__METHOD__	It will return the method name.
__NAMESPACE__	It will return the name of the current namespace.

Note
You will learn more about functions, methods, and classes in later chapters.

STRING

String is the sequence of characters written inside the quotation mark, for example, "I am string". You have used strings in many examples before. There are two types of strings and are discussed next.

Types of String

There are two types of strings supported by PHP which are as follows:

1. Single-quoted string.
2. Double-quoted string.

Single-Quoted String

To display the exact string that has some special characters, single quotation mark is used which is known as single-quoted string. For example, if you want to display **$var** then you will have to write it inside the single quotes because every variable starts with dollar sign ($) in PHP. It is possible that instead of displaying it, browser may read it as a variable.

For example:

```
<?php
    $var = 30; //Line 1
    echo 'Variable starts with $ for example, $var.'; //Line 2
?>
//output: Variable starts with $ for example, $var.
```

In the given example, **$var** in Line 1 is the variable having integer type value **30**. In Line 2, string is written inside the single quotes which will display the each character of the string exactly by using **echo** statement. In Line 2, **$var** inside the quotation mark is not treated as variable, it is treated as string.

Double-Quoted String

String written inside the double quotes are known as double-quoted string. It does not display the string having some special characters which are used for some functionality in PHP. Instead of displaying it as string, it performs the function for the purpose they are used in PHP. For example, if you want to use **$var** as variable to display the value of it in string, you will write it inside the double quotes. It will act as variable instead of string and will display its value.

For example:

```
<?php
    $var = 30; //Line 1
    echo "This month have $var days." //Line 2
?>
//output: This month have 30 days.
```

In the given example, **$var** in Line 1 is the variable having integer type value **30**. In Line 2, string is written inside the double quotes which will display the string by using the **echo** statement. In Line 2, **$var** inside the quotation mark is treated as variable which is used to display the value of variable in the string.

Example 6

The following program will display the output in the browser by using single-quoted and double-quoted strings.

```
<!Doctype html>                                                     1
<html>                                                              2
<head>                                                              3
```

Variables, Constants, and Strings   4-19

```
        <title>String type</title>                          4
    </head>                                                 5
    <body>                                                  6
        <?php                                               7
        $value = 100;                                       8
        echo 'Dollar sign ($) is used to start the variable 9
        followed by its name for example: $value';
        echo "<br>";                                       10
        echo "The value of the variable is $value.";       11
        ?>                                                 12
    </body>                                                13
</html>                                                    14
```

Explanation
Line 8
$value = 100;
In this line, **100** is the integer type data assigned to **$value** variable.

Line 9
echo 'Dollar sign ($) is used to start the variable followed by its name for example: $value';
In this line, the string is written inside the single quotes to display the exact string. So, here **$value** is not considered as variable and therefore, instead of displaying the value of variable, it will display **$value** as string. This line will display the following in the browser:

Dollar sign ($) is used to start the variable followed by its name for example: $value

Line 11
echo "The value of the variable is $value.";
In this line, the string is written inside the double quotes. So, here **$value** will be considered as variable and it will display the value of variable instead of displaying **$value** as string. This line will display the following in the browser:

The value of the variable is 100.

The output of Example 6 is displayed in Figure 4-6.

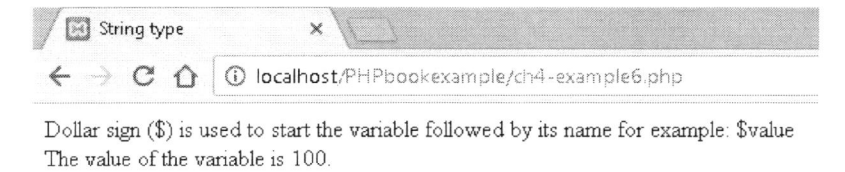

Figure 4-6 *The output of Example 6*

String Concatenation Operator

String concatenation operator is used to join two or more strings stored in different variables. In short, Concatenation(.) operator is used to concatenate two strings.

For example:

```
<?php
    $str1= "Hello User! "; //Line 1
    $str2= "How are you?"; //Line 2
    echo $str1 . $str2; //Line 3
?>
//output: Hello User! How are you?
```

In the given example, **$str1** and **$str2** in Line 1 and Line 2 are two variables that are holding string type data. In Line 3, concatenation(.) operator is used between **$str1** and **$str2** in the echo statement to concatenate the two strings.

Example 7

The following program will display the concatenation of multiple strings in the browser by using string concatenation operator.

```
<!Doctype html>                                              1
<html>                                                       2
<head>                                                       3
    <title>String Concatenation</title>                      4
</head>                                                      5
<body>                                                       6
    <?php                                                    7
        $h = "Hello";                                        8
        $u = $h . " User! "; //String concatenation          9
        $user = "Welcome to CADCIM";                        10
        $tech = " Technologies";                            11
        echo $u;                                            12
        echo "<br>";                                        13
        echo $h . "!!" . " " . $user . $tech ;              14
    ?>                                                      15
</body>                                                     16
</html>                                                     17
```

Explanation
Line 8
$h = "Hello";
In this line, **Hello** is the string type data assigned to the **$h** variable.

Variables, Constants, and Strings

Line 9
$u = $h . " User! ";
In this line, concatenation(.) is the string concatenation operator which is used here to concatenate **$h** and **User!**. Here **$h** is the variable which is already holding a data defined in Line 8 and **User!** is the string type data. **$u** is a variable that is holding the concatenated string.

Line 10 and Line 11
$user = "Welcome to CADCIM";
$tech = " Technologies";
In these lines, **Welcome to CADCIM** and **Technologies** are the string type data assigned to the **$user** and **$tech**, respectively.

Line 14
echo $h . "!!" . " " . $user . $tech ;
In this line, **$h**, **$user**, and **$tech** are the variables which will call the value assigned to them in Line 8, Line 10, and Line 11, respectively. These multiple variables are concatenated with **!!** and blank space strings written inside the double quotation marks. Here, concatenation(.) is the string concatenation operator. This line will display the following in the browser:

Hello!! Welcome to CADCIM Technologies

The output of Example 7 is displayed in Figure 4-7.

Figure 4-7 The output of Example 7

ESCAPE SEQUENCE

Escape sequence is a sequence of characters that are used to send a command to a device or a program. These characters are preceded by a backslash (\ ) which is called an escape character. These characters are not only used for text formatting but they also serve a special purpose. For example, **\n** is used for next line. Table 4-3 shows the list of escape sequences used in PHP.

Table 4-3 Escape sequence and their description

Escape Sequence	Description
\n	Insert a new line.
\r	Insert a carriage return.
\t	Insert a tab.
\$	Insert a dollar sign.
\"	Insert a double quote.
\'	Insert a single quote.
\\	Insert a backslash.

Example 8

The following program will display the output strings in the browser by using escape sequence.

```
<!Doctype html>                                                 1
<html>                                                          2
<head>                                                          3
    <title>Escape sequence</title>                              4
</head>                                                         5
<body>                                                          6
    <?php                                                       7
        echo "<pre>CADCIM\tTechnologies</pre>";                 8
        echo "<pre>CADCIM\nTechnologies</pre>";                 9
        echo "\"CADCIM Technologies\"";                        10
        echo '\'CADCIM Technologies\' ';                       12
        echo "<br>";                                           13
        echo "\\CADCIM Technologies\\";                        14
        echo "<br>";                                           15
        echo "Example of variable is \$cadcim ";               16
    ?>                                                         17
</body>                                                        18
</html>                                                        19
```

Note
/n, /t, and /r are the escape sequences whose outputs are not visible in the browser. It is because HTML code uses lots of tab and browser understands that they are not meant to be displayed. To display the output of these escape sequence, use the <pre> tag or inspect the browser page to see correct indentation.

Explanation
Line 8
echo "<pre>CADCIM\tTechnologies</pre>";
In this line, **<pre>** is the start tag and **</pre>** is the end tag of HTML which defines the

Variables, Constants, and Strings 4-23

preformatted text in HTML. Here, the string consist of **\t** which is escape sequence used for inserting tab. This line will display the following in the browser:

CADCIM   Technologies

Line 9
echo "<pre>CADCIM\nTechnologies</pre>";
In this line, the string consist of **\n** which is escape sequence used for inserting new line. This line will display the following in the browser:

CADCIM
Technologies

Line 10
echo "\"CADCIM Technologies\"";
In this line, the string consist of **\"** which is escape sequence used for inserting double quotation mark. This line will display the following in the browser:

"CADCIM Technologies"

Line 12
echo '\'CADCIM Technologies\' ';
In this line, the string consist of **\'** which is escape sequence used for inserting single quotation mark. Here, the string is written inside the single quotes because **\'** works only inside the single quotation marks. This line will display the following in the browser:

'CADCIM Technologies'

Line 14
echo '\\CADCIM Technologies\\';
In this line, the string consist of **** which is escape sequence used for inserting backward slash. This line will display the following in the browser:

\CADCIM Technologies\

Line 16
echo "Example of variables is \$cadcim";
In this line, the string consist of **\$** which is escape sequence used for inserting dollar sign. This line will display the following in the browser:

Example of variables is $cadcim

The output of Example 8 is displayed in Figure 4-8.

```
                    CADCIM  Technologies

                    CADCIM
                    Technologies

                    "CADCIM Technologies"
                    'CADCIM Technologies'
                    \CADCIM Technologies\
                    Example of variable is $cadcim
```

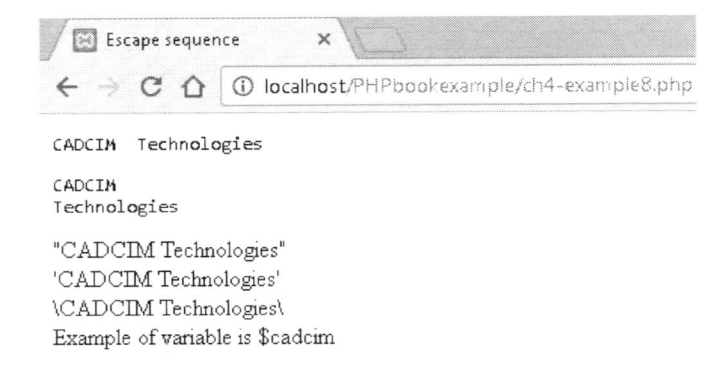

Figure 4-8 The output of Example 8

STRING FUNCTIONS

There are many string functions in PHP. These functions are used to manipulate strings in different ways. Some of the string functions are discussed next.

strtolower()

The **strtolower()** is a string function which is used to convert any string, written inside its parameter, to lowercase. The syntax for **strtolower()** is as follows:

```
strtolower("String");
```

In the given syntax, **strtolower()** is the function used to convert a string to lowercase. Here, **String** can be any word or sentence written inside the parameter of function that is to be converted in lowercase.

For example:

```
<?php
    echo strtolower("Hello USER!!");
?>
    //output : hello user!!
```

In the given example, **strtolower()** is a string function which will change the string **Hello USER!!** into lowercase.

strtoupper()

The **strtoupper()** is a string function which is used to convert any string, written inside its parameter, to uppercase. The syntax for **strtoupper()** is as follows:

```
strtoupper("string");
```

In the given syntax, **strtoupper()** is the function used to convert a string to uppercase. Here, **string** can be any word or sentence written inside the parameter of function that is to be converted in uppercase.

For example:

```
<?php
   echo strtoupper("Hello user!!");
?>
 //output : HELLO USER!!
```

In the given example, **strtoupper()** is a string function which will change the string **Hello user!!** into uppercase.

strlen()

The **strlen()** is a string function which returns length of any string written inside its parameter. It starts from 1 and also counts blank space. The syntax for **strlen()** is as follows:

```
strlen("String-length");
```

In the given syntax, **strlen()** is the function used to return a length of a string. Here, this function will return the length of **String-length** which can be any string written inside the parameter of function.

For example:

```
<?php
   echo strlen("Hello user, count my length.");
?>
   //output : 28
```

In the given example, **strlen()** is a string function which will return the length of string **Hello user, count my length.** and displays the output 28 .

str_word_count()

The **str_word_count()** is a string function which is used to count the number of words in any string written inside its parameter. The syntax for **str_word_count()** is as follows:

```
str_word_count("string",return,"char");
```

In the given syntax, **str_word_count()** is the function used to count the number of words in a string. A **string** can be any string written inside the parameter of function. Here, **return** and **char** are optional parameters. A **return** specifies the return value of the function. It can have 3 possible values. The default value of **return** is 0 which returns the number of words in a string, 1 returns the array with its value or words in string, and 2 returns an array with position of the word in the string and value where value is the actual word. A **char** can be any special character that is to be considered as a word or string.

For example:

```php
<?php
   echo str_word_count("Hello, count the words");
?>
 //output : 4
```

In the given example, **str_word_count()** is a string function which will count the number of words in the string **Hello, count the words** and display the output 4.

strrev()

The **strrev()** is a string function which is used to reverse any string written inside its parenthesis. The syntax for **strrev()** is as follows:

```
strrev("string");
```

In the given syntax, **strrev()** is the function used to reverse a string. Here, **string** can be any word or sentence written inside the parameter of function that is to be reversed.

For example:

```php
<?php
   echo strrev("Hello User!!");
?>
 //output : !!resU olleH
```

In the given example, **strtoupper()** is a string function which will reverse the string **Hello user!!** and display output !!resU olleH.

str_replace()

The **str_replace()** is a string function which is used to replace some characters with some other characters in any string written inside its parameter. The syntax for **str_replace()** is as follows:

```
str_replace("find-word", "replace-word","String", var-count);
```

In the given syntax, **str_replace()** is the function used to replace some characters with some other characters in a string. Here, **find-word** specifies the character or word that is to be replaced. A **replace-word** specifies the word or character which will take place of the **find-word**. A **string** specifies the string or array string where the replacement will take place. A **var-count** is the variable that counts the number of replacements in a string, it is optional.

For example:

```php
<?php
   echo str_replace("Hello","Welcome","Try to replace the word - Hello");
?>
```

Variables, Constants, and Strings

```
//output :Try to replace the word - Welcome
```

In the given example, **str_replace()** is a string function which will replace the word **Hello** with **Welcome** in the string **Try to replace the word - Hello** and display the **Try to replace the word - Welcome**.

substr_compare()

The **substr_compare()** is a string function which is used to compare two strings written inside its parameter from a specified start point. The syntax for **substr_compare()** is as follows:

```
substr_compare("string1","string2",startpoint,length,case-sens);
```

In the given syntax, **str_compare()** is the function used to compare two strings. A **string1** is a first string which will be compared with **string2** which is second string. A **startpoint** is the point or position of string from where comparison will be started. If **startpoint** is positive number, it will start comparison from starting of the string and if it is negative number, it will start from end of the string. Here, **length** and **case-sens** are optional. The **length** specifies the point till where the string should be compared. The **case-sens** specifies whether case-sensitivity must be considered or not. It can have 2 possible values. FALSE is the default value of **case-sens** which represents case-sensitive while TRUE represents case-insensitive.

The **substr_compare()** returns the numerical value as output in the browser. If the two string **string1** and **string2** are equal, it will return 0. If **string1** is less then **string2**, it will return a negative number and if **string1** is greater than **string2**, it will return number greater than 0.

For example:

```
<?php
    echo substr_compare("Hello User","Hello User",0);
?>
 //output : 0
```

In the given example, **substr_compare()** is a string function which will compare **Hello User**, which is string 1, with **Hello User** string 2. It will display the output 0.

Self-Evaluation Test

Answer the following questions and then compare them to those given at the end of this chapter:

1. A _____ is the container for data where data is stored in a named location.

2. The variables that are declared inside a block of function are known as _____.

3. The variables that are predefined in PHP are known as _____.

4. A _____ is the identifier for a value which will remain fixed throughout the program.

5. A _____ is the sequence of characters written inside the quotation mark.

Review Questions

Answer the following questions:

1. Which of the following options is the valid variable in PHP?

   (a) $15_Var (b) $_Var
   (c) Var   (d) $Var_#

2. Which of the following variables is declared inside the block of function?

   (a) Global variable   (b) Local variable
   (c) Superglobal variable (d) Static variable

3. Which of the following options is the identifier or name for a value which will remain fixed throughout the program?

   (a) Variable   (b) String
   (c) Static variable (d) Constant

4. Which of the following magic constants display the current line number of program file?

   (a) __LINE__ (b) __DIR__
   (c) __FILE__ (d) __TRAIT__

5. Which of the following escape sequences is used to insert a tab?

   (a) \n (b) \tab
   (c) \t (d) \?

6. Which of the following functions is used to reverse any string written inside its parenthesis?

   (a) **strlen()**   (b) **strrev()**
   (c) **str_replace()** (d) **str_word_count()**

7. Find errors in the following source codes:

   (a)
   ```
   <?php
        echo __line_;
        echo "it is accessing" . __FILE__ . "file";
   ?>
   ```

(b)
```php
<?php
    $str1= "Hello";
    $str2= "user";
    echo $str1 $str2;
?>
```

(c)
```php
<?php
    echo str_re_place("replace", "Welcome" "Try to replace");
?>
```

(d)
```php
<?php
    echo strev("Hello User!!");
?>
```

(e)
```
<!doctype html>
<html>
<head>
<title> String function </title>
</head>
<body>
    <?php
        echo substr_compare("Hello World","Hello World");
    ?>
</body>
</html>
```

EXERCISES

Exercise 1

Write a program to display the string "The $value will give 7 as output" in the browser, using escape sequence.

Exercise 2

Write a program to convert the string "Hello user i am in Uppercase" to uppercase, using string function.

Answers to Self-Evaluation Test

1. variable, **2.** local variables, **3.** superglobals, **4.** constant, **5.** string

Chapter 5

Operators

Learning Objectives
After completing this chapter, you will be able to:
- *Understand concept of operators*
- *Use arithmetic operators*
- *Use assignment operators*
- *Use bitwise operators*
- *Use comparison operators*
- *Use increment/decrement operators*
- *Use string operators*
- *Use array operators*
- *Use conditional operator*
- *Use null coalescing operator*
- *Understand the concept of operators precedence and associativity*

INTRODUCTION

In this chapter, you will learn about various types of operators used in PHP. An operator is a symbol that performs an operation. You will also learn about operators precedence along with their associativity.

OPERATORS

Operators are the symbols that are used when an operation is performed on variables or constants. PHP provides a variety of operators divided into different categories as follows:

a. Arithmetic operators
b. Assignment operators
c. Bitwise operators
d. Comparison operators
e. Logical operators
f. Increment or decrement operators
g. String operators
h. Array operators
i. Conditional operator
j. Null coalescing operator
k. Type operator

Arithmetic Operator

Operators that are used in mathematical expressions are known as arithmetic operators. Table 5-1 lists all arithmetic operators used in PHP.

Table 5-1 Arithmetic operators with their syntax

Operator	Description	Syntax
+	Addition	$var1 = $var2 + $var3
-	Subtraction	$var1 = $var2 - $var3
*	Multiplication	$var1 = $var2 * $var3
/	Division	$var1 = $var2 / $var3
%	Modulus Operator gives remainder	$var1 = $var2 % $var3
**	Exponentiation	$var1 = $var2 ** $var3

Note

*The exponentiation operator returns the result of the **$var2** raise to the power **$var3**. For example, 5 is assigned to **$var2** and 2 is assigned to **$var3** so it will be represented as 5 raise to the power 2 (5^2) and returns 25 as output.*

Example 1

The following program will perform addition, subtraction, multiplication, division, modulus, and exponentiation operations on two numbers using arithmetic operators and display the resultant values in the browser.

```
<!Doctype html>                                          1
<html>                                                   2
<head>                                                   3
<title>Arithmetic Operators</title>                      4
</head>                                                  5
<body>                                                   6
<?php                                                    7
$val1 = 6;                                               8
$val2 = 3;                                               9
$sum = $val1 + $val2;   //addition                       10
$sub = $val1 - $val2;   //subtraction                    11
$mul = $val1 * $val2;   //multiplication                 12
$div = $val1 / $val2;   //division                       13
$rem = $val1 % $val2;   //modulus                        14
$exp = $val1 ** $val2; //exponentiation                  15
echo "<p>Value of \$val1 is <b>$val1</b></p>";           16
echo "<p>Value of \$val2 is <b>$val2</b></p>";           17
echo "<p>The addition of two numbers is <b>$sum</b></p>"; 18
echo "<p>The subtraction of two numbers is <b>$sub</b></p>"; 19
echo "<p>The multiplication of two numbers is <b>$mul</b>  20
</p>";
echo "<p>The division of two numbers is <b>$div</b></p>"; 21
echo "<p>The modulus(remainder) of two numbers is <b>$rem</b> 22
</p>";
echo "<p>The exponentiation of two numbers is <b>$exp</b>   23
</p>";
?>                                                       24
</body>                                                  25
</html>                                                  26
```

Explanation

Line 8 and Line 9

$val1 = 6;

$val2 = 3;

In these lines, **6** and **3** are the integer type values assigned to the **$val1** and **$val2** variables, respectively.

Line 10

$sum = $val1 + $val2;

In this line, the value 6 of the **$val1** variable is added to the value 3 of the **$val2** variable. Next, the resultant value 9 is assigned to the **$sum** variable.

Line 11
$sub = $val1 - $val2;
In this line, the value 3 of the **$val2** variable is subtracted from the value 6 of the **$val1** variable. Next, the resultant value 3 is assigned to the **$sub** variable.

Line 12
$mul = $val1 * $val2;
In this line, the value 6 of the **$val1** variable is multiplied by the value 3 of the **$val2** variable. Next, the resultant value 18 is assigned to the **$mul** variable.

Line 13
$div = $val1 / $val2;
In this line, the value 6 of the **$val1** variable is divided by the value 3 of the **$val2** variable. Next, the resultant value 2 which represents the quotient is assigned to the **$div** variable.

Line 14
$rem = $val1 % $val2;
In this line, the value 6 of the **$val1** variable is divided by the value 3 of the **$val2** variable. Next, the resultant value 0 which represents the remainder is assigned to the **$rem** variable.

Line 15
$exp = $val1 ** $val2;
In this line, exponential operator (******) is used between **$val1** and **$val2** variables. The value 6 of the **$val1** variable and the value 3 of the **$val2** variable are represented as **$val1** raise to the power **$val2** that is 6^3. It will return value 216 as a resultant which is assigned to the **$exp** variable.

Line 16
echo "<p>Value of \\$val1 is $val1</p>";
This line will display the following in the browser:

Value of $val is 6

The working of Lines 17 to 23 is same as Line 16.

The output of Example 1 is displayed in Figure 5-1.

```
                    Arithmetic Operators    ×
                ← → C ⌂   ⓘ localhost/PHPbookexample/ch5-example1.php

            Value of $val1 is 6

            Value of $val2 is 3

            The addition of two numbers is 9

            The subtraction of two numbers is 3

            The multiplication of two numbers is 18

            The division of two numbers is 2

            The modulus(remainder) of two numbers is 0

            The exponentiation of two numbers is 216
```

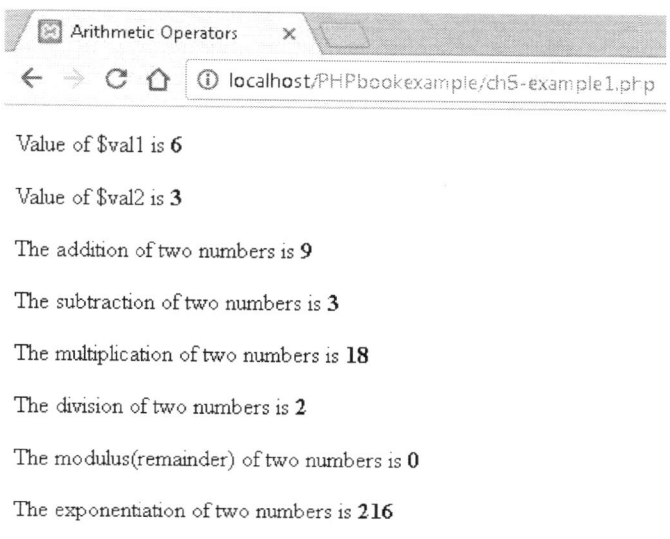

Figure 5-1 *The output of Example 1*

Assignment Operators

Assignment operators are used to assign value to a variable. These operators can be categorized as follows:

    a. Basic assignment operator
    b. Combined assignment operators

Basic Assignment Operator

Basic assignment operator is denoted by equal (=) symbol which is used to assign value to a variable. The syntax for using the assignment operator is as follows:

```
$variable = value;
```

In this syntax, the **value** on the right of the assignment operator (=) is assigned to the **$variable** variable on the left of the assignment operator. The left value should always be a variable. The right value can be a variable, a constant, or a result of any given operation.

You can also use the assignment operator (=) for multiple assignments. Its syntax is as follows:

```
$var1 = $var2 = $var3 = val;
```

In the given syntax, the value represented by **val** is assigned to all the three **$var1**, **$var2**, and **$var3** variables. The assignment operator is evaluated from right to left. For example, **$var1 = $var2 = $var3 = 5;** would assign 5 to **$var3**, then **$var3** to **$var2**, and then **$var2** to **$var1**.

Combined Assignment Operators

Combined assignment operators are a combination of two operators: first that specifies the operation to be performed and the second is the assignment operator. Compound assignment operators are also known as Short hand assignment operators. Table 5-2 shows a list of compound assignment operators with their syntax.

Table 5-2 Combined assignment operators and their syntax

Operator	Description	Syntax	Equivalent Expression
+=	Addition assignment operator adds right operand to the left operand and assigns result to the left operand.	$var1+=$var2;	$var1=$var1+$var2;
-=	Subtraction assignment operator subtracts right operand from the left operand and assigns result to the left operand.	$var1-=$var2;	$var1=$var1-$var2;
*=	Multiplication assignment operator multiplies right operand to the left operand and assigns result to the left operand.	$var1*=$var2;	$var1=$var1*$var2;
/=	Division assignment operator divides left operand with the right operand and assigns result to the left operand.	$var1/=$var2;	$var1=$var1/$var2;
%=	Modulus assignment operator takes modulus using left and right operands and assigns result to the left operand.	$var1%=$var2;	$var1=$var1%$var2;
**=	Exponentiation assignment operator performs operation between left operand and right operand and assigns result to the left operand.	$var1**=$var2;	$var1=$var1**$var2;

In the syntax shown in Table 5-2, first the given operation is performed on **$var1** and **$var2** variables. Next, the resultant value is assigned back to **$var1**. For example, to add **4** to the value of the **$a** variable and again assign the resultant value to **$a** variable, use the following statement:

```
$a=2;
$a+=4; //it will function as 2+4=6
```

You can also perform the same operation in the following way:

```
$a = $a + 4 ;
```

Example 2

The following program will apply combined assignment operations on the given values and display the resultant values in the browser.

```
<!Doctype html>
<html>
<head>
<title>Arithmetic Operators</title>
</head>
<body>
<?php
$val1 = 8;    //basic assignment operator
$val2 = 12;
$val3 = 6;
$val4 = 16;
$val5 = 10;
$val6 = 5;
$val1 += 5;   //addition assignment operator
$val2 -= 4;   //subtraction assignment operator
$val3 *= 6;   //multiplication assignment operator
$val4 /= 4;   //division assignment operator
$val5 %= 8;   //modulus assignment operator
$val6 **= 4;  //exponentiation assignment operator
echo "<p>The output using addition assignment operator is <b>$val1</b></p>";
echo "<p>The output using subtraction assignment operator is <b>$val2</b></p>";
echo "<p>The output using multiplication assignment operator is <b>$val3</b></p>";
echo "<p>The output using division assignment operator is <b>$val4</b></p>";
echo "<p>The output using modulus assignment operator is <b>$val5</b></p>";
echo "<p>The output using exponentiation assignment operator is <b>$val6</b></p>";
?>
</body>
</html>
```

Explanation

Line 8 to Line 13
$val1 = 8;
$val2 = 12;
$val3 = 6;
$val4 = 16;

$val5 = 10;
$val6 = 5;
In these lines, **8**, **12**, **6**, **16**, **10**, and **5** integer type values are assigned to the **$val1**, **$val2**, **$val3**, **$val4**, **$val5**, and **$val6** variables, respectively, by using basic assignment operator.

Line 14
$val1 += 5;
In this line, addition assignment operator (**+=**) is applied between **$val1** variable and **5**. The value 8 assigned to the **$val1** variable in Line 8 is added with the integer type number **5** and then the resultant value 13 is assigned to the **$val1** variable.

Line 15
$val2 -= 4;
In this line, subtraction assignment operator (**-=**) is applied between **$val2** variable and **4**. The integer type number **4** is subtracted from the value 12 assigned to the **$val12** variable in Line 9 and then the resultant value 8 is assigned to the **$val2** variable.

Line 16
$val3 *= 6;
In this line, multiplication assignment operator (***=**) is applied between **$val3** variable and **6**. The value 6 assigned to the **$val3** variable in Line 10 is multiplied with the integer type number **6** and then the resultant value 36 is assigned to the **$val3** variable.

Line 17
$val4 /= 4
In this line, division assignment operator (**/=**) is applied between **$val4** variable and **4**. The value 16 assigned to the **$val4** variable in Line 11 is divided with the integer type number **4** and then the resultant value 4, which represents the quotient, is assigned to the **$val4** variable.

Line 18
$val5 %= 8;
In this line, modulus assignment operator (**%=**) is applied between **$val5** variable and **8**. The value 10 assigned to the **$val5** variable in Line 12 is divided with the integer type number **8** and then the resultant value 2, which represents the remainder, is assigned to the **$val5** variable.

Line 19
$val6 **= 4;
In this line, exponential assignment operator (****=**) is applied between **$val6** variable and **4**. The value 5 assigned to the **$val6** variable in Line 13 and the integer type number **4** are represented as **$val6** raise to the power **4** (5^4). It will return the value 625 as a resultant which is assigned to the **$val6** variable.

Line 20
echo "<p>The output using addition assignment operator is $val1</p>";
This line will display the following in the browser:

The output using addition assignment operator is 13

Operators

The working of Lines 21 to 25 is same as Line 20.

The output of Example 2 is displayed in Figure 5-2.

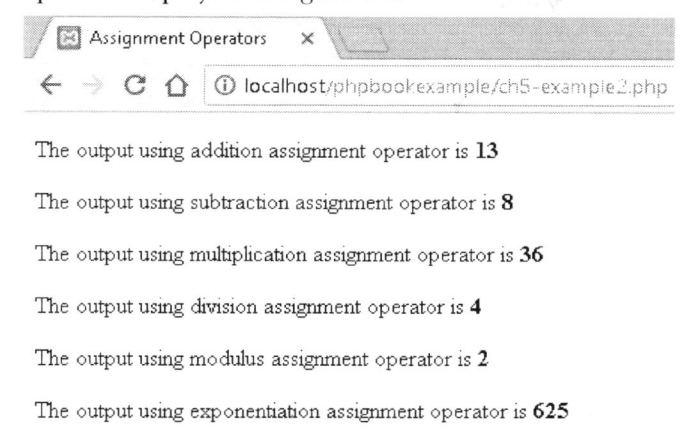

Figure 5-2 *The output of Example 2*

Bitwise Operator

Data is stored in the memory of computer in binary code (0 and 1). For example, 3 byte is stored in the memory of computer as 00000011. To operate or manipulate these bits individually, PHP provides some operators known as bitwise operators. Bitwise operators are used to operate on single bits of an operand. These operators are mostly applied on the integer data type but can also be applied on the string data type. Table 5-3 shows a list of bitwise operators.

Table 5-3 *Bitwise operators*

Operator	Operation
&	Bitwise AND
|	Bitwise OR
~	Bitwise Compliment
^	Bitwise XOR
<<	Left Shift
>>	Right Shift

These operators are the least commonly used operators. Some of the bitwise operators are categorized under bitwise logical operators and are discussed next.

The Bitwise AND (&) Operator

The bitwise AND (&) operator comes under the category of bitwise logical operators. If both the variables(operands) contain value 1 then the & operator will produce bit 1 as the result. And, if one or both the variables contain value 0 then the & operator will produce 0 as the result. The syntax for using the & operator is as follows:

```
$operand1 & $operand2;
```

For example, if you use the AND (&) operator with two variables holding 23 and 15 as respective values, the output given will be 7, as given next.

```
   00010111 //Bits representing the value 23
&  00001111 //Bits representing the value 15
   --------
   00000111 //Bits representing the value 7
```

The Bitwise OR (|) Operator

The bitwise OR (|) operator also comes under the category of bitwise logical operators. If one or both the variables(operands) contain value 1 then the | operator will produce bit 1 as the result. And, if both the variables contain 0 then the | operator will produce 0 as the result.
The syntax for using the | operator is as follows:

```
$operand1 | $operand2;
```

For example, if you use the OR (|) operator with two variables holding 23 and 15 as respective values, the output given will be 31, as given next.

```
   00010111 //Bits representing the value 23
|  00001111 //Bits representing the value 15
   --------
   00011111 //Bits representing the value 31
```

The Bitwise Compliment (~) Operator

The bitwise compliment (~) operator also comes under the category of bitwise logical operators. The ~ operator inverts all bits of its variable(operand); for example, 0 becomes 1 and 1 becomes 0. This operator is also known as the bitwise unary NOT operator. The syntax for using the compliment (~) operator is as follows:

```
~ $variable;
```

For example:

```
$a = 3;
$b = ~$a;
```

In the above example, 3 is assigned to the **$a** variable as an initial value which is stored in the computer's memory as 00000011. In the next statement, ~ operator is used with the **$a** variable. This operator inverts all the bits 00000011 of the value 3 into 11111100. Then, the resultant value is assigned to the **$b** variable.

The Bitwise Exclusive OR (^) Operator

The bitwise exclusive OR (^) or XOR operator also comes under the category of bitwise logical operators. The ^ operator produces bit 1 as the result, only when one of the variables (operand)

Operators

contain value 1. Otherwise, it produces bit 0 as the result. The syntax for using the ^ operator is as follows:

```
$operand1 ^ $operand2;
```

For example, you can use the XOR (^) operator with two variables holding the 23 and 15 as respective values, the output given will be 24, as given next.

```
  00010111 //Bits representing the value 23
^ 00001111 //Bits representing the value 15
  --------
  00011000 //Bits representing the value 24
```

Table 5-4 represents all (~, &, |, and ^) bitwise logical operators.

Table 5-4 Bitwise logical operators

X	Y	X&Y	X|Y	X^Y	~X
0	0	0	1	0	1
0	1	0	1	1	1
1	0	0	1	1	0
1	1	1	0	0	0

Other than the bitwise logical operators, the following operators are also available:

The Left Shift (<<) Operator

The left shift (<<) operator is used to shift all the bits of an operand in the left for specified number of times. The syntax for using the left shift operator is as follows:

```
$var << num;
```

In the given syntax, **num** represents the number of times you want to perform the left shift operation on the bits of a value assigned to **$var** variable.

For example:

```
$a = 17;
$b = $a<<2;
```

The above example operates in the following way:

```
00010001 //Bits representing the value 17 assigned to $a
```

When the << operator operates on the given bits for the first time, the left most bit (0 bit) is lost and all other bits shifts in left. The bit pattern that is produced after the first step is as follows:

```
00100010 //Bits representing the value 34
```

In the second step, the same process is repeated as in the first step and the bit pattern which is produced after the second step is assigned to **$b** variable as follows:

    01000100 //Bits representing the value 68

The Right Shift (>>) Operator
The right shift (**>>**) operator is used to shift all the bits of an operand in the right for specified number of times. The syntax for using the right shift operator is as follows:

    $var >> num

In the above syntax, **num** represents the number of times you want to perform the right shift operation on all the bits of a value assigned to **$var** variable.

For example:

    $a = 17;
    $b = $a>>2;

The above example operates in the following way:

    00010001 //Bits representing the value 17 assigned to $a

When the **>>** operator operates on the given bits for the first time, the right most bit (1 bit) is lost and all other bits shifts in right. The bit pattern which is produced after the first step is as follows:

    00001000 //Bits representing the value 8

In the second step, the same process is repeated and the bit pattern which is produced after the second step is assigned to **$b** variable as follows:

    00000100 //Bits representing the value 4

Example 3
The following program will apply all the bitwise operations on the given values and display the resultant values in the browser.

```
<!Doctype html>                                 1
<html>                                          2
<head>                                          3
<title>Bitwise Operators</title>                4
</head>                                         5
<body>                                          6
<?php                                           7
    $val1 = 15;                                 8
    $val2 = 10;                                 9
```

Operators

```
                echo "Value of \$val1 is $val1";               10
                echo "</br>";                                  11
                echo "Value of \$val2 is $val2";               12
                echo "</br>";                                  13
                echo "<h3> Result of Bitwise Operations</h3>"; 14
                echo "\$val1 & \$val2 = ";                     15
                echo  $val1 & $val2 ;                          16
                echo "</br>";                                  17
                echo "\$val1 | \$val2 = ";                     18
                echo  $val1 | $val2 ;                          19
                echo "</br>";                                  20
                echo "~\$val1 = ";                             21
                echo  ~$val1;                                  22
                echo "</br>";                                  23
                echo "\$val1 ^ \$val2 = ";                     24
                echo  $val1 ^ $val2 ;                          25
                echo "</br>";                                  26
                echo "\$val1>>2 = ";                           27
                echo  $val1>>2 ;                               28
                echo "</br>";                                  29
                echo "\$val1<<2 = ";                           30
                echo  $val1<<2 ;                               31
    ?>                                                         32
    </body>                                                    33
    </html>                                                    34
```

Explanation

Line 16
echo $val1 & $val2 ;
In this line, **&** is the bitwise AND operator between **$val1** and **$val2** variables and performs the bitwise AND operation. The resultant value is then displayed in the browser.

Line 19
echo $val1 | $val2 ;
In this line, **|** is the bitwise OR operator between **$val1** and **$val2** variables and performs the bitwise OR operation. The resultant value is then displayed in the browser.

Line 22
echo ~$val1;
In this line, **~** is the bitwise compliment operator that performs bitwise compliment operation on **$val1** variable and the resultant value is then displayed in the browser.

Line 25
echo $val1 ^ $val2 ;
In this line, **^** is the bitwise XOR operator between **$val1** and **$val2** variables and performs the bitwise XOR operation. The resultant value is then displayed in the browser.

Line 28
echo $val1>>2 ;
In this line, **>>** is the bitwise right shift operator that will shift all the bits of **$val1** variable twice towards right. In this process the right most bits are lost and the resultant value is displayed in the browser.

Line 31
echo $val1<<2 ;
In this line, **<<** is the bitwise left shift operator that will shift all the bits of **$val1** variable twice towards left. In this process the left most bits are lost and the resultant value is displayed in the browser.

The output of Example 3 is displayed in Figure 5-3.

Value of $val1 is 15
Value of $val2 is 10

Result of Bitwise Operations

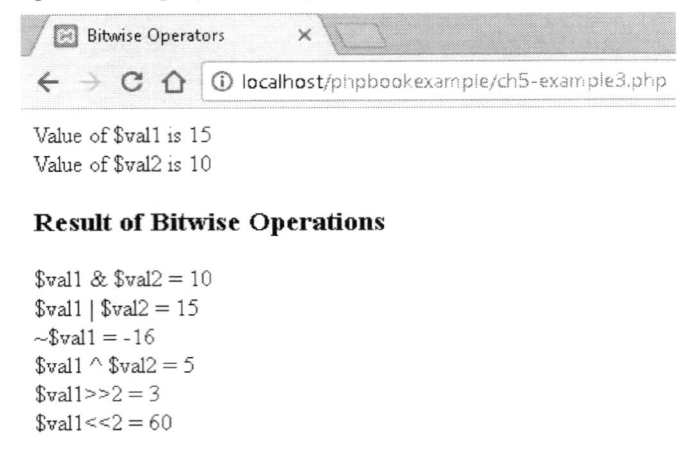

$val1 & $val2 = 10
$val1 | $val2 = 15
~$val1 = -16
$val1 ^ $val2 = 5
$val1>>2 = 3
$val1<<2 = 60

Figure 5-3 The output of Example 3

Comparison Operators

The comparison operators are used to determine relationship between two values assigned to the variables and this operation is known as relational or comparison expression. The outcome of the operation is a boolean value, either **true** or **false**. Only spaceship operator returns an integer value between -1 to 1. Table 5-5 shows the list of comparison operators and their syntax.

Operators

Table 5-5 Comparison operators and their syntax

Operator	Operation	Syntax
==	Equal	$var1 == $var2
===	Identical	$var1 === $var2
!=	Not equal	$var1 != $var2
<>	Not equal	$var1 <> $var2
!==	Non-identical	$var1 !== $var2
<	Less than	$var1 < $var2
>	Greater than	$var1 > $var2
<=	Less than or equal to	$var1 <= $var2
>=	Greater than or equal to	$var1 >= $var2
<=>	Spaceship	$var1 <=> $var2

In the syntax shown in Table 5-5, the comparison operators checks the relation between the two variables, **$var1** and **$var2**. If the values of **$var1** and **$var2** variables satisfy the condition then the outcome of this operation will be **true**. Otherwise, it will be **false**.

The Equal(==) Operator

The equal(==) operator is used to compare equality between the values of two variables. It will return **true** if the value of two variables is equal or same. Otherwise, it will return **false**.

For example:

```
<?php
$var1 = 10;
$var2 = "10";
echo $var1 == $var2;
?>
```

In the given example, **10** is the integer type value assigned to the **$var1** variable and **10** is the string type value assigned to the **$var2** variable. The equality comparison between **$var1** and **$var2** is done with == operator. It will check the values of both variables and will return **true** because both variables have same value as **10**. It will display 1(for **true**) in the browser.

> **Note**
> *The equal(==) operator does not consider the data type of the values assigned to the variables. It only compares the value of the variables.*

The Identical(===) Operator

The identical(===) operator is used to compare the equality between the values of two variables including the data type. It will return **true** if the value and the data type of the two variables are same. Otherwise, it will return **false**.

For example:

```php
<?php
$var1 = 10;
$var2 = "10";
echo $var1 === $var2;
?>
```

In the given example, **10** is the integer type value assigned to the **$var1** variable and **10** is the string type value assigned to the **$var2** variable. The identical comparison between **$var1** and **$var2** is done with === operator. It will check the value and data type of both the variables. Next, it will return **false** because both the variables have same value (**10**) but different data types.

The Not equal(!= and <>) Operators

The != and <> both are not equal operators. Their working is opposite of the equal operator. These operators are used to compare inequality between the values of two variables. The not operator will return **true** if the value of the two variables is not same. Otherwise, it will return **false**.

For example:

```php
<?php
$var1 = 10;
$var2 = 9;
echo $var1 != $var2; //echo $var1 <> $var2;
?>
```

In the given example, **10** and **9** are the integer type values assigned to the **$var1** and **$var2** variables. The inequality comparison between **$var1** and **$var2** is done with != operator. This operator will check the value of both the variables. Next, it will return **true** because both the variables have the different values **10** and **9** which are not equal. The commented line contains <> operator which will work same as != operator, you can use any of them.

The Non-identical(!==) Operator

The non-identical(!==) operator is used to compare the inequality between the values of two variables including the data type. It will return **true** if the value or the data type of the two variables is different. Otherwise, it will return **false**.

For example:

```php
<?php
$var1 = 10;
$var2 = "10";
echo $var1 !== $var2;
?>
```

In the given example, **10** is the integer type value assigned to the **$var1** variable and **10** is the string type value assigned to the **$var2** variable. The non-identical comparison between **$var1**

Operators

and **$var2** is done with **!==** operator. It will check the value and data type of both the variables and will return true because both the variables have same value (**10**) but different data types.

The Spaceship(<=>) Operator

The spaceship(**<=>**) operator is introduced in PHP 7 and is used to compare values of two variables but not their data types. It can also compare two numbers or strings directly without assigning them to the variable. It will return **0** if the values of the two variables are equal or same. It will return **1** if the value on the left side of **<=>** operator is greater than on the right side and will return **-1** if the value on the right side of **<=>** operator is greater than on the left side.

For example:

```
<?php
$var1 = 10;              //Line 1
$var2 = "10";            //Line 2
echo $var1 <=> $var2;    //Line 3
echo "y" <=> "y";        //Line 4
echo 5 <=> 4;            //Line 5
echo 3 <=> 10;           //Line 6
?>
```

In the given example, **10** is the integer type value assigned to the **$var1** variable and **10** is the string type value assigned to the **$var2** variable. In Line 3, the comparison between **$var1** and **$var2** is done with **<=>** operator. It will check the values of both variables and will return **0** because both variables have the same value **10**. In Line 4, comparison is done between two strings that has the same value **y**, here also the value returned will be **0**. In Line 5, comparison is done between two integer type numbers 5 and 4 with **<=>** operator and will return **1** because 5 on the left is greater than 4 on the right of the spaceship operator. In Line 6, comparison is done between 3 and 10 with **<=>** operator and will return **-1** because 3 on the left is smaller than 10 on the right of the spaceship operator.

Logical Operators

Logical operators are used to compare two or more relational expressions (statements that contain comparison operator) in a single statement and the outcome of this operation is a boolean value, either **true** or **false**. Table 5-6 shows a list of the logical operators.

Table 5-6 The logical operators

Operator	Operation
and	Logical AND operator
or	Logical OR operator
xor	Logical XOR operator
&&	Logical AND operator
||	Logical OR operator
!	Logical NOT operator

The Logical AND(and / &&) Operators

The logical AND(**and** / **&&**) operator is used to compare two or more comparison expressions. It will return **true** if the outcome of all the given expressions are **true**, otherwise it will return **false**. It is mostly used in control structures in which the final outcome is based on the outcome of two or more than two conditions. The syntax for using the logical AND(**and** / **&&**) operators is as follows:

```
comp_exp and comp_exprs
comp_exp && comp_exprs
```

In the given syntax, **comp_exp** and **comp_exprs** are two different comparison expressions. In the first syntax, **and** operator is used between the comparison expressions. In the second syntax, the **&&** operator is used between the comparison expressions. You can use any of the given syntax to perform logical AND (**and** / **&&**) operation.

For example:

```
$var1==$var2 && $var3==$var4
```

In the given example, **$var1**, **$var2**, **$var3**, and **$var4** are the variables. Here, **$var1==$var2** and **$var3==$var4** are the comparison expressions. The **&&** operator is the logical AND operator used between these variables for comparison. If both the comparison expressions will return **true** only then the AND operation return **true** and display the output in the browser. Otherwise, it will return **false**.

> **Note**
> *You will learn about control structures in the later chapter.*

The Logical OR(or / ||) Operator

The logical OR(**or** / **||**) operator is used to compare two or more comparison expressions. It will return **true** if the outcome of any or all of the given expressions is **true**. Otherwise, it returns **false**. It is mostly used in control flow statements in which the final outcome is based on the outcome of two or more than two conditions. The syntax for using the logical OR(**or** / **||**) operators is as follows:

```
comp_exp or comp_exprs
comp_exp || comp_exprs
```

In the given syntax, **comp_exp** and **comp_exprs** are different comparison expressions. In the first syntax, **or** operator is used between the comparison expressions. In the second syntax, **||** operator is used between the comparison expressions. You can use any of the given syntax to perform logical OR(**or** / **||**) operation.

For example:

```
$var1==$var2 || $var3==$var4
```

Operators

In the given example, **$var1**, **$var2**, **$var3**, and **$var4** are the variables. Here, **$var1==$var2** and **$var3==$var4** are the comparison expressions. The **||** operator is the logical OR operator used between the comparison expressions for comparison. If any of the comparison expressions or both comparison expressions return **true** then the OR operation will return **true** and display the output in the browser otherwise it will return **false**.

The Logical XOR(xor) Operator

The logical XOR(**xor**) operator is used to compare two or more comparison expressions. It will return **true** if the outcome of any one of the given expressions is **true**. If the outcome of all the expressions are same that is either all true or all false then it returns **false**. It is also mostly used in control flow statements in which the final outcome is based on the outcome of two or more than two conditions. The syntax for using the logical XOR(**xor**) operators is as follows:

```
comp_exp xor comp_exprs
```

In the given syntax, **comp_exp** and **comp_exprs** are different comparison expressions. The **xor** operator is used between the comparison expressions. You can use the given syntax for performing logical XOR(**xor**) operation.

For example:

```
$var1==$var2 xor $var3==$var4
```

In the given example, **$var1**, **$var2**, **$var3**, and **$var4** are the variables. Here, **$var1==$var2** and **$var3==$var4** are comparison expressions. The **xor** operator is the logical XOR operator used between them for comparison. If any of the comparison expressions returns **true** then the XOR operation will return **true** and display the output in the browser. Otherwise, it will return **false**.

The Logical NOT(!) Operator

The logical NOT(**!**) operator is used to check whether the given comparison expression returns **true** or **false**. It will return **true** if the outcome of the given expressions is **false**. Otherwise, it will return **false**. In short, it inverts the outcome of the comparison operator. It is also mostly used in control flow statements. The syntax for using the logical NOT(**!**) operator is as follows:

```
!(comp_exprs)
```

In the given syntax, **comp_exprs** is the comparison expression prefixed by NOT(**!**) operator. You can use the given syntax to perform logical NOT(**!**) operation.

For example:

```
!($var1==$var2)
```

In the given example, **$var1** and **$var2** are the variables. Here, **$var1==$var2** is the comparison expression prefixed by **!** operator. The **==** (equal to) operator is used to check the equality between the two variables, **$var1** and **$var2**. If the outcome of the given comparison expression (**$var1==$var2**) will return **false** then the NOT(**!**) operation will return **true** and display the output in the browser. Otherwise, it will return **false**.

In Table 5-7, you will observe that the **&&/and** operator will return **true** only when both the operands are **true**, otherwise it will return **false**. The **||** operator on the other hand returns **true** even if any one or both the operands are **true**. The **xor** operator returns **true** only if any of the one operand is **true**. The **!** operator returns **true** if the given operator is **false** otherwise it returns **false**.

Table 5-7 The Truth Table of logical operators

X	Y	X && Y / X and Y	X||Y / X or Y	X xor Y	!X
false	false	false	false	false	true
false	true	false	true	true	true
true	false	false	true	true	false
true	true	true	true	false	false

The Increment(++) or Decrement(--) Operators

The increment(**++**) operator is used to increase the value of its operand by 1 and the decrement(**--**) operator is used to decrease the value of its operand by one.

You can use these operators in two notations which are as follows:

a. Postfix notation
b. Prefix notation

The Postfix Notation

In postfix notation, the increment or decrement operator is used after the variable (operand). The syntax for using the postfix increment and decrement operators is as follows:

```
$var1++; //increment
$var1--; //decrement
```

In this syntax, the increment and decrement operators (**++** and **--**) are used after the variable(operand) **$var1**. First, it will return **$var1** and then it will increase or decrease the value of the variable **$var1** by 1.

If the postfix notation is used in an expression then the value of variable on the right of the assignment (=) operator is assigned to the variable on the left of the assignment (=) operator. Next, the value of the variable will be incremented or decremented by one.

For example:

```
$y = $x--;
```

In the given example, first the value of the **$x** variable is assigned to the **$y** variable and then it is decreased by one.

Operators

The following two statements produce the same result as produced by the **y = x--;** statement given in the previous example.

```
$y = $x;
$x = $x-1;
```

The Prefix Notation

In prefix notation, the increment or decrement operator is used before the variable (operand). The syntax for using the prefix operator is as follows:

```
++$var1;
--$var1;
```

In the above syntax, the increment and decrement operators (**++** and **--**) are used before the **$var1** variable. First, it will increase or decrease the value of the **$var1** variable by one and then will return **$var1**.

If the prefix notation is used in an expression then first the value of the variable on the right of the assignment(**=**) operator is incremented or decremented by one and then it is assigned to the variable on the left of the assignment(**=**) operator.

For example:

```
$y = --$x;
```

In the above example, first the value of the **$x** variable is decreased by one and then it is assigned to the **$y** variable.

The following two statements produce the same result as was produced by the **y = --x;** statement given in the previous example.

```
$x = $x-1;
$y = $x;
```

Example 4

The following program will increment the value of a variable, assign the resultant value to variable, and then display the output in the browser.

```
<!Doctype html>                                  1
<html>                                           2
<head>                                           3
<title>Increment Operator</title>                4
</head>                                          5
<body>                                           6
<?php                                            7
    $val1 = 50;                                  8
    $val2 = $val1++;                             9
    $val3 = ++$val1;                            10
```

```
        $val4 = 99;                                          11
            echo "<p>Value of \$val2 is: $val2</p>";         12
            echo "<p>Value of \$val1 is: $val1</p>";         13
            echo "<p>Value of \$val3 is: $val3</p>";         14
            echo "Value of \$val4 is: " . ++$val4;           15
    ?>                                                       16
    </body>                                                  17
    </html>                                                  18
```

Explanation

Line 9
$val2 = $val1++;
In this line, the value **50** of **$val1** variable is assigned to **$val2** variable. So first, it will return **50**. Next, the value of **$val1** variable is incremented by 1 and it becomes 51.

Line 10
$val3 = ++$val1;
In this line, the value 51(value incremented in Line 9) of **$val1** variable is incremented by 1 and it becomes 52. Next, it is assigned to **$val3** variable.

Line 12
echo "<p>Value of \$val2 is: $val2</p>";
This line will display the following on the screen:

Value of $val2 is: 50

Line 13
echo "<p>Value of \$val1 is: $val1</p>";
In this line, **$val1** variable will return the finally incremented value instead of the initial value of **$val1** variable. This line will display the following on the screen:

Value of $val1 is: 52

Line 14
echo "<p>Value of \$val3 is: $val3</p>";
This line will display the following on the screen:

Value of $val3 is: 52

Line 15
echo "Value of \$val4 is: " . ++$val4;
In this line, ++**$val4** is incrementing the value **99** of **$val4** variable by 1 and it becomes 100. This line will display the following on the screen:

Value of $val4 is: 100

The output of Example 4 is displayed in Figure 5-4.

Value of $val2 is: 50

Value of $val1 is: 52

Value of $val3 is: 52

Value of $val4 is: 100

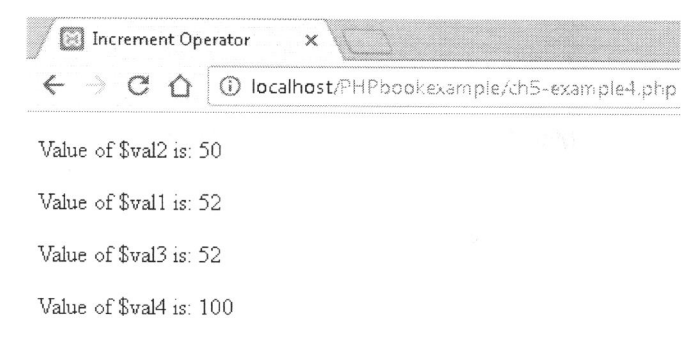

Figure 5-4 The output of Example 4

The String Operators

In PHP, there are two string operators that are used only on string type data. Table 5-8 lists the string operators that are used in PHP.

Table 5-8 The string operators

Operator	Operations	Syntax
.	Concatenation	$var1.$var2
.=	Concatenation assignment	$var1.=$var2

Concatenation Assignment Operator

String concatenation assignment(**.=**) operator is used to join two or more strings stored in different variables. In the concatenation assignment syntax given in Table 5-8, first the concatenation operation is performed on the **$var1** and **$var2** variables. Next, the resultant value is assigned back to **$var1**.

For example:

```
<?php
   $str1= "Hello! "; //Line 1
   $str2= "How are you?"; //Line 2
   $str1.= $str2;      //Line 3
   echo $str1;         //Line 4
?>
//output: Hello! How are you?
```

In the given example, **$str1** and **$str2** in Line 1 and Line 2 are two variables that are holding string type data. In Line 3, concatenation assignment(**.=**) operator is used between **$str1** and **$str2**. First, it will concatenate the two strings **Hello!** and **How are you?** that are stored in the **$str1** and **$str2** variables. Next, the resultant string(Hello! How are you?) is assigned back to **$str1** variable. In Line 4, the **echo** statement will display the concatenated string stored in **$str1** variable.

> **Note**
> *You have already learned about concatenation(.) operator in previous chapter.*

The Array Operators

The array operators are very similar to the comparison operators. The only difference between them is that the functionality of these operators changes slightly while working with array. Table 5-9 lists all the array operators that are used in PHP.

Table 5-9 The array operators

Operator	Operation	Syntax
+	Union	$var1 + $var2
==	Equality	$var1 == $var2
===	Identity	$var1 === $var2
!=	Inequality	$var1 != $var2
<>	Inequality	$var1 <> $var2
!==	Non-identity	$var1 !== $var2

In the syntax shown in the Table 5-9, the array operators are used to check relation between **$var1** and **$var2** variables that hold array type values. If the values of variables satisfy the condition then the outcome of the operation is **true** otherwise it is **false**. But, only in case of union operation the **+** operator does not check the relation between two variables. The array operators are discussed next.

The Union(+) Operator

The **+** operator works as addition operator for integer type values. But in case of array type values, it works as a union operator. The union (**+**) operator joins arrays and returns all the common and unique values in the arrays. It means that the values which exist in both the arrays are not repeated. According to the syntax (**$var1 + $var2**) given in Table 5-9, all the common and unique values of **$var1** and **$var2** array variables are returned.

The Equality(==) Operator

The equality(**==**) operator checks the equality between the values of two arrays. It is same as equal(**==**) operator. It will return **true** if the values of two arrays are equal or same otherwise it will return **false**.

The Identity(===) Operator

The identity(**===**) operator checks the equality between the values of two arrays including their order, index, and the data type. It will return **true** if the value, order, and the data type of the two arrays are same, otherwise will return **false**.

The Inequality(!= / <>) Operator

The **!=** and **<>** both are Inequality operators. Their working is opposite of the equality operator. They are used to check the inequality between the values of two arrays. It will return **true** if the values of two arrays are not same, otherwise will return **false**.

Operators

The Non-identity(!==) Operator

The non-identical(!==) operator checks the inequality between the values of two arrays including their order, index, and the data type. It will return **true** if the values, order, or the data type of the two arrays are different, otherwise will return **false**.

> **Note**
> *The array operators are explained with programming examples in Chapter 8.*

The Conditional(? :) Operator

The conditional(? :) operator is also known as the ternary operator. It works on three expressions where first expression is a conditional expression. If the first expression is **true** then it will return the second expression. If the first expression is **false**, it will return third expression. It is a conditional operator that provides a shorter syntax for the **if-else** statement (discussed later in this book). The syntax for using the conditional operator(?:) is as follows:

```
conditional_expression ? expression_1 : expression_2;
```

In the given syntax, if the condition specified by **conditional_expression** is **true**, it will return **expression_1**, otherwise it will return **expression_2**.

The short-hand syntax for conditional operator(?:) is as follows:

```
conditional_expression ?: expression_2;
```

In the given syntax, if the condition specified by **conditional_expression** is **true**, it will return **conditional_expression**, otherwise it will return **expression_2**.

> **Note**
> *It is recommended that you should avoid nesting of conditional(?:) operator (using the operator more than once in a statement). In such cases, PHP statements become complicated and return undesired output. Although it can be avoided by proper formatting of the nested statement using parentheses, it still will create complications in your PHP code.*

Null Coalescing(??) Operator

In PHP 7, the null coalescing(??) operator has been introduced to overcome the drawback of conditional(?:) operator. The null coalescing(??) operator is used to check if a value is assigned to a variable or not and also if the assigned value is **NULL** or not. This operator will perform an in-line comparison and will return first expression if a value associated with the first expression does exist and is not **NULL**. Otherwise, it will return second expression or string. The null coalescing(??) operator can be nested easily and gives the desired result. The syntax for using the null coalescing(??) operator is as follows:

```
expression_1 ?? expression_2;
```

In the given syntax, if the **expression_1** is not **NULL** and has a value, it will return **expression_1**, otherwise it will return **expression_2**.

The given null coalescing(**??**) operator syntax is similar to the Conditional operator(**?:**) syntax as follows:

```
expression_1 ? expression_1 : expression_2;
```

Both the syntax will return same output.

The syntax for nesting the null coalescing(**??**) operator is as follows:

```
expression_1 ?? expression_2 ?? expression_3 ?? expression_n;
```

In the given syntax, if the **expression_1** is not **NULL** and has a value, it will return **expression_1**, otherwise it will return **expression_2** and skip the remaining expressions. If **expression_2** is also **NULL**, it will return **expression_3** and skip the last expression. If **expression_3** is also **NULL** then it will return **expression_n**.

For example:

```
<?php
    $var1 = null;
    $var2 = null;
    $var3 = 11;
    $var4 = 22;
    echo $var1 ?? $var2 ?? $var3 ?? $var4; // display 11
?>
```

In the given example, the **NULL** values are assigned to the **$var1** and **$var2** variables. The integer type values **11** and **22** are assigned to **$var3** and **$var4** variables, respectively. In the **echo** statement, nested null coalescing(**??**) operators are used. So, it will return **11** which is assigned to **$var3** because **$var1** and **$var2** has **null** values and it will skip **$var4**.

> **Note**
> The **instanceof** operator is a type operator. You will learn about the **instanceof** operator later in the book.

OPERATOR PRECEDENCE

The operator precedence determines the order of execution of operators. An operator with a high precedence is used before an operator with a low precedence.

For example:

```
$x= $a+$b*$c ;
```

The multiplication operator (*****) has a higher precedence than the addition (**+**) and assignment operators (**=**). Therefore, in the given example, first the value of the **$b** variable is multiplied by the value of **$c** variable and then the resultant value is added to the **$a** variable (because the addition operator has a higher precedence than the assignment operator). Next, the resultant value of the expression **$a+$b*$c** is assigned to the **$x** variable.

OPERATOR ASSOCIATIVITY

When two or more operators have same precedence in an expression, the order in which the operation is performed is defined as the associativity of an operator. The following are the two types of associativity:

a. Left to Right
b. Right to Left

Left to Right Associativity

In the left to right associativity, all the operations are performed from left to right.

For example:

```
$x=$a+$b+$c;
```

In this example, the addition operator performs left to right associativity. So, the value of **$a** variable is added to the value of **$b** variable and then the resultant value is added to the value of the **$c** variable.

Right to Left Associativity

In the right to left associativity, all the operations are performed from right to left.

For example:

```
x+=y;
```

In this example, the addition assignment operator performs right to left associativity. So, the value of **$y** variable is added to the value of **$x** variable and then the resultant value is assigned back to **$x** variable.

Table 5-10 shows all the operators, their precedence, and their associativity in high to low precedence order. In this table, R to L is used for Right to Left associativity and L to R is used for Left to Right associativity.

Table 5-10 The operator precedence and their associativity

Precedence	Operator	Operation	Associativity
1	()	Parentheses	Non-associative
2	**	Arithmetic	R to L
3	++ -- ~ (int) (float) (string) (array) (object) (bool)	Increment/Decrement, bitwise, and types	R to L
4	instanceof	Types	Non-associative
5	!	Logical	R to L
6	* / %	Arithmetic	L to R
7	+ - .	Arithmetic and string	L to R
8	<< >>	Bitwise	L to R
9	< <= > >=	Comparison	Non-associative
10	== != === !== <> <=>	Comparison	Non-associative
11	&	Bitwise	L to R
12	^	Bitwise	L to R
13	|	Bitwise	L to R
14	&&	Logical	L to R
15	||	Logical	L to R
16	??	Null coalescing	R to L
17	? :	Conditional	
18	= += -= *= **= /= .= %= &= |= ^= <<= >>=	Assignment	R to L
19	and	Logical	L to R
20	xor	Logical	L to R
21	or	Logical	L to R

Self-Evaluation Test

Answer the following questions and then compare them to those given at the end of this chapter:

1. Operators that are used in mathematical expressions are known as _____.

2. A _____ operator returns the remainder after the division of two numbers.

3. The _____ operator is used to increase the value of its operand by one.

Operators

4. The _____ operators are used to determine the relationship between two expressions.

5. The _____ and _____ operators are introduced in PHP 7.

6. The modulus operator (%) returns the remainder after the division of two numbers. (T/F)

7. The equality operator (==) is same as the assignment operator (=). (T/F)

Review Questions

Answer the following questions:

1. Which of the following operators is used in mathematical expressions?

   (a) Bitwise operators
   (c) Arithmetic operators
   (b) Assignment operators
   (d) Comparison operators

2. Which of the following operators is used to compare the equality between the values of two variables?

   (a) ===
   (c) !=
   (b) =
   (d) ==

3. Which of the following operators is used to compare the values of two variables excluding their data type?

   (a) <=>
   (c) >=
   (b) <=
   (d) <>

4. Which of the following operators is introduced to overcome the drawback of conditional operator?

   (a) ||
   (c) ?:
   (b) &&
   (d) ??

5. Find errors in the following source codes:

   (a)
   ```
   <?php
       $val1 = 7;
       $val2 = 4;
       $div = $val1 / $val2;
       $rem = $val1 % $val2;
       $exp = $val1 *** $val2;
       echo "<p>The division is <b>$div</b></p>";
       echo "<p>The modulus(remainder)is <b>$rem</b></p>";
       echo "<p>The exponentiation is <b>$exp</b></p>";
   ?>
   ```

(b) ```php
<?php
    $val1 = 6;
    $val2 = 10;
    $val3 = 5;
    $val1 /= 4;
    $val2 =% 8;
    $val3 *= 4;
    echo "<p>The division is $val1</p>";
    echo "<p>The modulus is $val2</p>";
    echo "<p>The multiplication is $val3</p>";
?>
```

(c) ```php
<?php
    $var1 = 9;
    $var2 = "9";
    echo $var1 <=> $var2;
    echo "<br>";
    echo "x" <==> "x";
?>
```

(d) ```php
<?php
    $var1 = null;
    $var2 = 11;
    $var3 = 15;
    echo $var1 ? $var2 ?? $var3;
?>
```

# EXERCISE

## Exercise 1

Write a program to compare two integer type values 50 and 100 stored in a variable using various comparison operators.

**Answers to Self-Evaluation Test**

**1.** arithmetic operators, **2.** %, **3.** ++, **4.** comparison, **5.** spaceship, null coalescing, **6.** T, **7.** F
```

Chapter 6

Control Structures

Learning Objectives

After completing this chapter, you will be able to:
- *Understand the flowchart*
- *Use the if control structure*
- *Use the if-else control structure*
- *Use the if-elseif control structure*
- *Use the switch control structure*
- *Use the while loop*
- *Use the do-while loop*
- *Use the for loop*
- *Use jump statements*

INTRODUCTION

The programs that you have studied in earlier chapters consist of some statements in which inputs are processed and then result is displayed based on the calculations done in the program. But practically, you may need to take decisions and control the flow of program using some control structures. These control structures can be better understood using the flowcharts. In PHP, various control structures such as **if, for, do-while**, and so on are used to control the program flow. In this chapter, you will learn about the flowchart and the control structures in detail.

Before learning about the control structures, you need to learn about the flowcharts.

FLOWCHART

A flowchart is a graphical representation of steps that constitute a program. It shows how the control moves in a program. A flowchart is drawn using some special symbols which are discussed next.

Oval
The oval symbol, as shown in Figure 6-1, represents the start and end of the program.

Rectangle
The rectangle symbol, as shown in Figure 6-2, represents the process box in which certain actions such as calculations are performed.

Diamond
The diamond symbol, as shown in Figure 6-3, represents the decision box in which a particular condition is checked and on the basis of results, a path is selected from multiple paths.

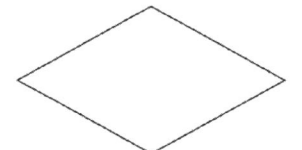

Figure 6-1 An oval symbol   *Figure 6-2* A rectangle symbol   *Figure 6-3* A diamond symbol

Arrow
The arrow symbols, as shown in Figure 6-4, represent the path through which the control passes from one symbol to another symbol. In a flowchart, the control is passed from left to right or from up to down.

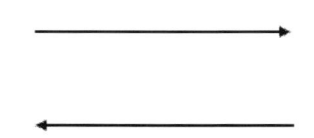

Figure 6-4 The arrow symbols

Parallelogram
The parallelogram symbol, as shown in Figure 6-5, represents the input or the output box.

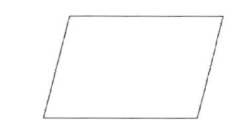

Figure 6-5 A parallelogram symbol

CONTROL STRUCTURES

The control structures are used to alter the flow of execution in a program based on a particular condition. PHP provides control structures or control statements that specify the order of the execution of the statements. The control structures are divided into the following three categories:

    a. Conditional control structure
    b. Iteration or Loop control structure
    c. Jump statements

Conditional Control Structure

A conditional control structure contains one or more conditional expressions and based on the result, the block of code associated with it will be executed or skipped. If conditional expression is found to be true then the next block of statements will be executed otherwise the statement after the block will be executed, if the condition is found to be false. Note that in conditional control structure, the associated code is executed only once. PHP supports various conditional control structures that are as follows:

    a. if control structure
    b. if-else control structure
    c. elseif control structure
    d. switch control structure

The if Control Structure

The **if** control structure is a single path statement which means it will execute a statement or a block of statements only if the condition is true. The syntax for the **if** statement is as follows:

```
if(condition or expression)
statement1;
```

In this syntax, the condition or expression can be true or false. If the condition or expression is true, **statement1** will be executed otherwise the control will be transferred to the next statement after the **if** block, as shown in Figure 6-6.

For example:

```
<?php
   $b=55;
   $a=43;
   if($b>$a)
   echo "b is greater than a";
   echo "bye";
?>
```

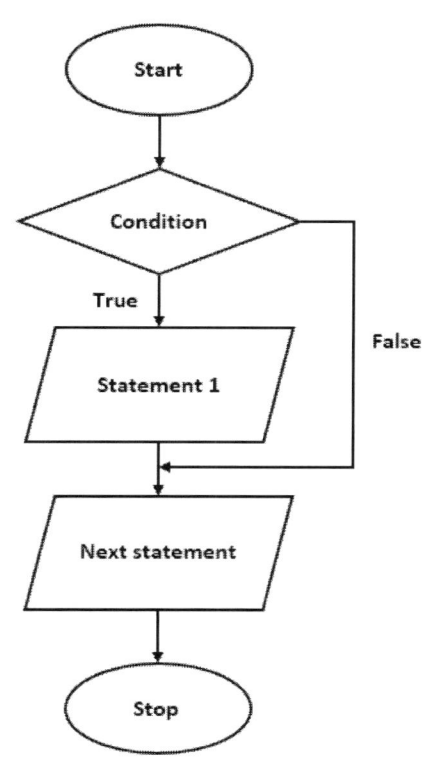

Figure 6-6 Flowchart of the if statement

In the given example, first the condition **$b>$a** (value of the variable a is greater than the value of the variable b) will be checked. If the condition returns true then all the statements next to the **if** condition will be executed. But if the condition returns false then the statement **echo "b is greater than a";** next to the **if** condition will be skipped and control will be transferred to the next statement and the statement **echo "bye";** will be executed.

In case, if the condition is true and there are more than one statement that must be executed, then the statements should be grouped together inside curly braces ({}). The syntax for the **if** control structure is as follows:

```
if(condition or expression)
{
statement 1;
statement 2;
____-
____-
statement n;
}
```

In this syntax, all the statements from 1 to n will be executed, if the condition or expression within the **if** statement is true otherwise they will not be executed and the control will be transferred to the next statement after the **if** block.

For example:

```
<?php
        $a = 10;
        $b = 11;
        if($a>$b)
        {
                echo "a is greater than b";
                echo "you got the result";
        }
        echo "b is greater than a";
?>
```

In the given example, first the condition **$a>$b** (value of the variable a is greater than the value of the variable b) will be checked. If the condition returns true then all the next statements inside and outside the **if** block will be executed. But, if the condition returns false then the statement inside the **if** block will be skipped and control will be transferred to the next statement outside the **if** block and the statement **echo "b is greater than a"** will be executed.

> **Note**
> *The statements enclosed in the curly braces are known as block of statements. The control structure block starts with a open curly bracket ({) and ends with a closing curly bracket (}).*

Control Structures

Example 1

The following program will illustrate the use of the **if** statement. The program will assess the performance of a sales executive and calculate the salary according to the performance based on sales target. Finally, the program will display the salary in the browser.

```
<!Doctype html>                                                 1
<html>                                                          2
<head>                                                          3
<title>If statements</title>                                    4
</head>                                                         5
<body>                                                          6
<?php                                                           7
   $salary = 25000;                                             8
   $incentive = 1000;                                           9
   $sales = 18000;                                             10
   $target = 15000;                                            11
   if( $sales>=$target)                                        12
    {                                                          13
         echo "You have achieved the target.";                 14
         echo "<br>";                                          15
         echo "You will get the salary with incentive.";       16
         echo "<br>";                                          17
         $salary = $salary+$incentive;                         18
    }                                                          19
         echo "Salary = $salary" ;                             20
         echo "<br>";                                          21
?>                                                             22
</body>                                                        23
</html>                                                        24
```

Explanation
Line 12
if($sales>=$target)
In this line, first the conditional expression is checked, whether the value 18000 of the variable **$sales** is greater than or equal to the value 15000 of the variable **$target**. Here, this condition will return true and all the statements that are inside and outside the **if** block (from Line 13 to Line 21) will be executed. But, if the conditional expression **$sales>=$target** returns false then the control will be transferred to the next statement (Line 20) immediately after the **if** block.

Line 13
{
This line indicates the start of the **if** block.

Line 14
echo "You have achieved the target";
This line will display the following in the browser:

You have achieved the target

Line 18
$salary = $salary+$incentive;
In this line, the value 25000 of the variable **$salary** will be added to the value 1000 of the variable **$incentive** and the resultant value 26000 will be assigned back to the variable **$salary**.

Line 19
}
This line indicates the end of the **if** block.

Line 20
echo "Salary = $salary" ;
According to the **if** condition this line will display the following in the browser:

Salary = 26000

The output of Example 1 is displayed in Figure 6-7.

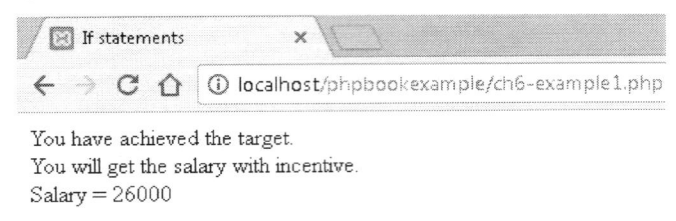

Figure 6-7 The output of Example 1

The if-else Control Structure

The **if-else** control structure is a dual path control structure which routes the flow of execution in two different paths. The path selection is based on the result of a particular condition. The **if-else** statement works in such a way that if the condition given within the **if** statement is true, the statements associated with the **if** block will be executed. Otherwise, the **if** block will be skipped and the statements associated with the **else** block will be executed. The syntax for the **if-else** control structure is as follows:

```
if(conditional_expression)
{
statement 1;
statement 2;
}
else
{
statement 3;
statement 4;
}
```

In the given syntax, if the given **conditional_expression** is true, the statements 1 and 2 which are associated with the **if** block, will be executed and the **else** block will be skipped. Otherwise, the **if** block will be skipped and the statements 3 and 4 which are associated with the **else** block, will be executed, refer to Figure 6-8 for the **if-else** flowchart.

Control Structures

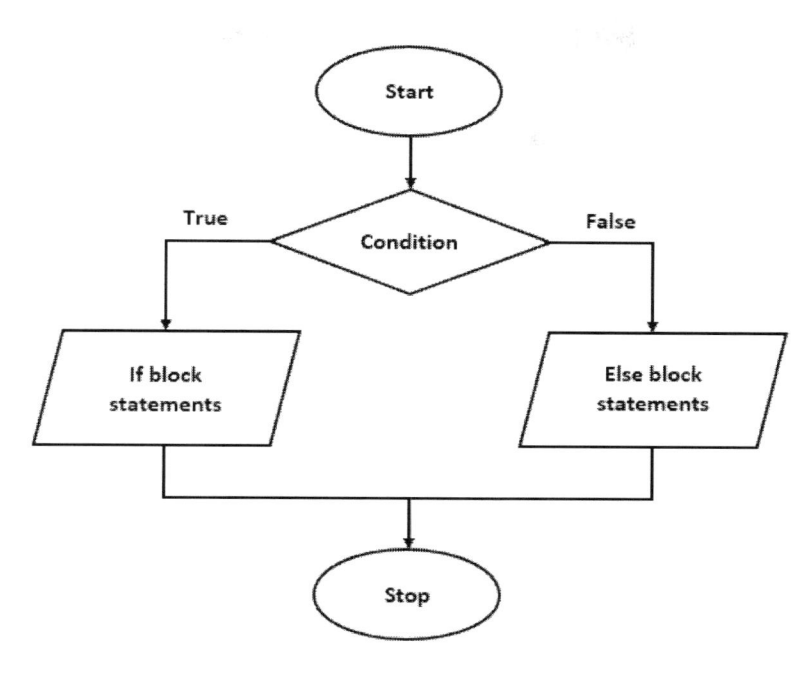

*Figure 6-8 Flowchart of the **if-else** statement*

For example:

```php
<?php
    $a = 10 ;
    $b = 11;
        if ($a>$b)
        {
            echo "a is greater";
            echo "b is smaller";
        }
        else
        {
            echo "b is greater";
            echo "a is smaller";
        }
?>
```

In the given example, if the value of the variable **$a** is greater than the value of the variable **$b**, the statements: **echo "a is greater";** and **echo "b is smaller";** associated with the **if** block will be executed. Otherwise, the **if** block will be skipped and the statements: **echo "b is greater";** and **echo "a is smaller";** associated with the **else** block will be executed.

Example 2

The following program will illustrate the use of the **if-else** statement. The program will assess the performance of a sales executive and calculate the salary according to the performance based on sales target. Finally, the program will display the salary in the browser.

```
<!Doctype html>                                              1
<html>                                                       2
<head>                                                       3
<title>if-else statements</title>                            4
</head>                                                      5
<body>                                                       6
<?php                                                        7
    $salary = 25000;                                         8
    $incentives = 1000;                                      9
    $sales = 10000;                                          10
    $target = 15000;                                         11
        if($sales>=$target)                                  12
            {                                                13
                echo "You have achieved the target.";        14
                echo "<br>";                                 15
                $salary = $salary+$incentives;               16
                echo "Salary = $salary" ;                    17
            }                                                18
        else                                                 19
            {                                                20
                echo "You have not achieved the target.";    21
                echo "<br>" ;                                22
                echo "Salary = $salary" ;                    23
            }                                                24
?>                                                           25
</body>                                                      26
</html>                                                      27
```

Explanation
Line 12
if($sales>=$target)
In this line, first the conditional expression is checked, whether the value 10000 of the variable **$sales** is greater than or equal to the value 15000 of the variable **$target**. Here, this condition will return false. The control will be transferred outside the **if** block and the statements (from Line 21 to Line 23) associated with **else** block will be executed.

Line 13
{
This line indicates the start of the **if** block.

Control Structures   6-9

Line 14
echo "You have achieved the target";
This line will display the following in the browser:

You have achieved the target

Line 16
$salary = $salary+$incentives;
In this line, the value 25000 of the variable **$salary** will be added to the value 1000 of the variable **$incentives** and the resultant value 26000 will be assigned back to the variable **$salary**.

Line 17
echo "Salary = $salary" ;
This line will display the following in the browser:

Salary = 26000

Line 18
}
This line indicates the end of the **if** block.

Line 19
else
The control will be transferred to this line when the condition given in the **if** statement becomes false. When the control transfers to this line, the statements (from Line 21 to 23) associated with the **else** block are executed.

Line 20
{
This line indicates the start of the **else** block.

Line 21
echo "You have not achieved the target";
This line will display the following in the browser:

You have not achieved the target

Line 23
echo "Salary = $salary" ;
This line will display the following in the browser:

Salary = 25000

Line 24
}
This line indicates the end of the **else** block.

The output of Example 2 is displayed in Figure 6-9.

You have not achieved the target.
Salary = 25000

Figure 6-9 *The output of Example 2*

The elseif Control Structure

The **elseif** control structure is a conditional control structure that is used when you want to verify more than one condition. The syntax for the **elseif** statement is as follows:

```
if(conditional_expression1)
{
    statements;
}
elseif(conditional_expression2)
{
    statements;
}
elseif(conditional_expression3)
{
    statements;
}
else
{
    statements;
}
```

In the given syntax, the **conditional_expression1** of **if** statement will be evaluated first. In this case, if it returns true, the statements associated with the **if** block will be executed. Otherwise, the control will be transferred to the next **elseif** statement and the **conditional_expression2** will be evaluated. Again, if it returns true, the statements associated with the **elseif** block will be executed. Otherwise, the control will be transferred to the next **elseif** statement. This process will continue until a conditional expression evaluates to true. If each and every conditional expression evaluates to false then the **else** block will be executed (if it exists). Otherwise, the control will be transferred to the next statement immediate after the **if-elseif** statement, refer to Figure 6-10.

> **Note**
> *The **elseif** and **else if** can be considered same in one condition where the block of statements associated with them is written inside the curly braces({}). If you are using colon(:) instead of curly braces (an alternative method discussed later in this chapter) then in that case the **elseif** statement, program will work fine but the **else if** statement program will throw an error.*

Control Structures

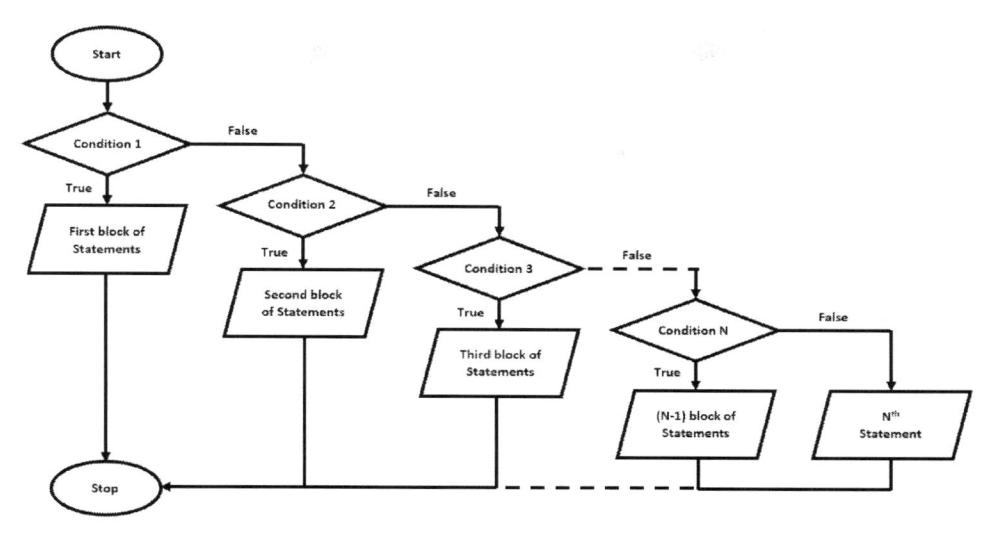

Figure 6-10 Flowchart of the *if-elseif* statements

For example:

```php
<?php
   $sales= 10000;
   $target= 20000;
        if($sales>$target)
            {
                echo "Excellent Performance";
            }
        elseif($sales==$target)
            {
                echo "Good Performance";
            }
        elseif($sales<$target)
            {
                echo "Bad Performance";
            }
        else
            {
                echo "Terminated";
            }
?>
//output: Bad Performance
```

In the given example, if the conditional expression **$sales>$target** of **if** statement evaluates to true, the statement associated with the **if** block will be executed. Otherwise, the next conditional expression **$sales==$target** of the **elseif** statement will be evaluated. If it evaluates to true, the statement associated with the **elseif** block will be executed. Otherwise, the control will be transferred to the next **elseif** statement and the conditional expression **$sales<$target** will be evaluated. If none of the conditions evaluates to true, the control will be transferred to the **else** statement and the statement associated with it will be executed.

Example 3

The following program illustrates the use of the **if-elseif** statement. The program will calculate the grade according to the points scored by a student in the examination and display the result in the browser.

```
<!Doctype html>                                              1
<html>                                                       2
<head>                                                       3
<title>elseif statements</title>                             4
</head>                                                      5
<body>                                                       6
<?php                                                        7
    $total_points=75;                                        8
    if($total_points>=90)                                    9
        {                                                   10
            echo "Grade A";                                 11
            echo "<br>";                                    12
            echo "You scored $total_points points";         13
            echo "<br>";                                    14
            echo "Excellent Performance";                   15
        }                                                   16
    elseif($total_points>=80)                               17
        {                                                   18
            echo "Grade B";                                 19
            echo "<br>";                                    20
            echo "You scored $total_points points";         21
            echo "<br>";                                    22
            echo "Good Performance";                        23
        }                                                   24
    elseif($total_points>=70)                               25
        {                                                   26
            echo "Grade C";                                 27
            echo "<br>";                                    28
            echo "You scored $total_points points";         29
            echo "<br>";                                    30
            echo "Average Performance" ;                    31
        }                                                   32
    else                                                    33
        {                                                   34
            echo "You scored $total_points points";         35
            echo "<br>";                                    36
            echo "Bad Performance";                         37
        }                                                   38
?>                                                          39
```

Control Structures

```
        </body>                                          40
        </html>                                          41
```

Explanation
Line 9
if($total_points>=90)
In this line, the conditional expression **$total_points>=90** will be evaluated. This conditional expression returns false because 75 is less than 90. Now, the **if** block (from Line 11 to Line 15) will be skipped and the control will be transferred to the **elseif** statement (Line 17).

Line 17
elseif($total_points>=80)
In this line, the conditional expression **$total_points>=80** will be evaluated. This conditional expression will return false because 75 is less than 80. Now, the **elseif** block (from Line 19 to Line 23) will be skipped and the control will be transferred to the next **elseif** statement (Line 25).

Line 25
elseif($total_points>=70)
In this line, the conditional expression **$total_points>=70** will be evaluated. This conditional expression will return true because 75 is greater than 70. Now, the statements (from Line 27 to 31) associated with the **elseif** block will be executed.

Line 33
else
If none of the conditional expressions evaluates to true then the control will be transferred to this **else** statement. In this case, it will get skipped because the **elseif** statement (Line 25) has already returned true.

The output of Example 3 is displayed in Figure 6-11.

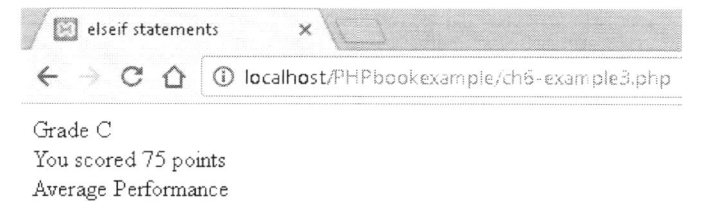

Figure 6-11 The output of Example 3

The switch Control Structure
The **switch** control structure is a selection or a case control structure. The **switch** statement makes it possible for the parser to transfer the control to different statements within the **switch** body depending on the value of a variable or expression. In a **switch** control structure, the flow of execution is controlled by the value of the variable or expression. This variable or expression is known as the control variable. In the same **switch** body, two **case** constants cannot have identical values. Also, the **case** constant values are case-sensitive. The syntax for using the **switch** statement is as follows:

```
switch(value or expression)
{
   case 1:
         statement1;
         break;
   case 2:
         statement2;
         break;
   ----------;
   ----------;
   ----------;
   case N:
         statement3;
         break;
   default:
         statement;
}
```

In the given syntax, the value or expression given in the **switch** statement represents a control variable. The **switch** statement works in such a way that the value of the control variable is matched with all values in the **case** statements, one by one. If match is found, the statement associated with that particular **case** will be executed. If no match is found, the statements associated with the **default** case will be executed (if it exists). The **break** statement which is used inside the **switch** body is a jump statement. When a **break** statement is encountered inside a **switch** body, the control is transferred to the statement that is immediately after the **switch** body refer to Figure 6-12. You will learn more about the jump statements later in this chapter.

For example:

```
<?php
   $month="MAR";
   switch($month)
{
   case 1:
         echo "JANUARY";
         break;
   case 2:
         echo "FEBRUARY";
         break;
   case 'MAR':
         echo "MARCH";
         break;
   default:
         echo "Cannot fetch the month";
}
?>
```

Control Structures 6-15

In this example, value **MAR** is assigned to the variable **$month** which is treated as a control variable. In the first step, the value of the control variable **$month** is compared with the first **case** that has literal value 1. Here, no match is found. Now, the control is transferred to the next **case** statement and again the value of the control variable **$month** is compared with the second **case** that has literal value 2. This process is repeated until no match or the **default** case is found. While repeating this process, a match is found in the **case** that has literal value **MAR** and the statement associated with it, **echo "MARCH";** is executed. Next, the control is transferred to the statement which is immediately after the **switch** body.

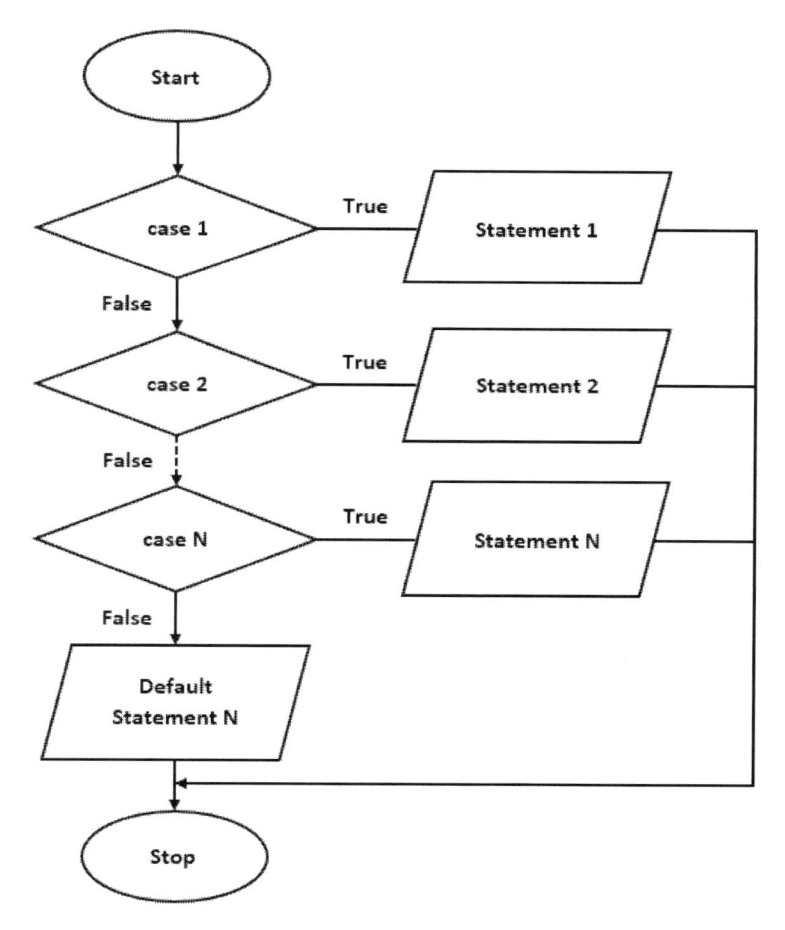

*Figure 6-12 Flowchart of the **switch** statement*

Example 4

The following program illustrates the use of the **switch** statement. The program will display the day of a week in the browser based on the value given in the program.

```
<!Doctype html>                                                 1
<html>                                                          2
<head>                                                          3
```

```
          <title>switch statement</title>                    4
        </head>                                              5
        <body>                                               6
        <?php                                                7
           $day=5;                                           8
           switch ($day)                                     9
                 {                                          10
                 case 1:                                    11
                     echo "Monday";                         12
                     break;                                 13
                 case 2:                                    14
                     echo "Tuesday";                        15
                     break;                                 16
                 case 3:                                    17
                     echo "Wednesday";                      18
                     break;                                 19
                 case 4:                                    20
                     echo "Thursday";                       21
                     break;                                 22
                 case 5:                                    23
                     echo "Friday";                         24
                     break;                                 25
                 case 6:                                    26
                     echo "Saturday";                       27
                     break;                                 28
                 default:                                   29
                     echo "Sunday";                         30
                 }                                          31
        ?>                                                  32
        </body>                                             33
        </html>                                             34
```

Explanation
Line 9
switch ($day)
In this line, the value of the variable **$day** is passed as a parameter to the **switch** statement. Here, the variable **$day** is treated as a control variable and its value will be compared with all the literal values of **case**.

Line 10
{
This line indicates the start of the **switch** body.

Line 11
case 1:
In this line, first the value of the control variable **$day** will be compared with the literal value **1**. If match is found, the control will be transferred to the next line (Line 12). But in this case, as no match is found, the control will be transferred to the next case statement (Line 14).

Control Structures

Line 12
echo "Monday";
This line will display the following in the browser:

Monday

Line 13
break;
The **break** statement is a jump statement which transfers the control outside the **switch** body. If **break** statement is not used in the **switch** body, all cases from the matched statements including the **default** one will be executed.

The working of Lines 14 to 22 is same as the working of Lines 11 to 13.

Line 23
case 5:
Again in this line, the value of the control variable **$day** will be compared with the literal value **5**. Here, match is found and the control will be transferred to the next line (Line 24).

Line 24
echo "Friday";
This line will display the following in the browser:

Friday

Lines 29 and 30
default:
echo "Sunday";
These lines contain the **default** case. This case will be executed only when no match is found in all other cases.

The output of Example 4 is displayed in Figure 6-13.

Figure 6-13 The output of Example 4

Iteration or Loop Control Structure

Loops are used to repeat a particular block of code for a certain number of times. In PHP, the iteration statements or loop statements are used to repeat a particular set of instructions until the termination condition is met. It means that the block of code is repeated when the condition is true. If the condition is false, the loop ends and the control is transferred to the next statement immediately after the loop. The loop structure consists of three expressions: initialization, condition, and increment or decrement. These expressions are discussed next.

Initialization Expression

The initialization expression executes only once at the start of the loop. It is used to set the initial value of the loop control variable such as **$x=1**.

Condition Expression

The condition expression is evaluated every time before the execution of the body of the loop. The execution of the body of the loop depends on the condition whether it is true or false. If the condition is true, the body of the loop will be executed. Otherwise, it will be skipped and the control will be transferred to the next instruction after the loop.

Increment or Decrement Expression

The increment or decrement expression updates the variables that control the condition statement. It is used to increase or decrease the value of the loop control variable by one. This expression is always executed after the statements in the body of the loop has been executed.

In PHP, there are four types of iteration or loop control structure, and they are as follows:

a. while loop
b. do-while loop
c. for loop
d. foreach loop

The while Loop

The **while** loop is an entry controlled loop where the condition is evaluated at the start and the statements associated with it will continue executing and repeating until the condition becomes false. The syntax for using the **while** loop is as follows:

```
initialization;
while(condition)
{
statements;
increment/decrement;
}
```

In the given syntax, the initialization part of the loop is executed. It sets the value of the loop control variable which acts as a counter that controls the loop. Next, **while** is a keyword and the condition given in the **while** statement is evaluated. It evaluates to either true or false. Till the condition evaluates to true, the statements in the **while** block will be executed repeatedly. Otherwise, the loop terminates. After executing the statements in the **while** block, the control will be transferred to the increment or decrement part. It will increment or decrement the value of the control variable by one. Next, again the conditional expression will be evaluated. This process will be repeated until the conditional expression evaluates to false, refer to Figure 6-14.

Control Structures

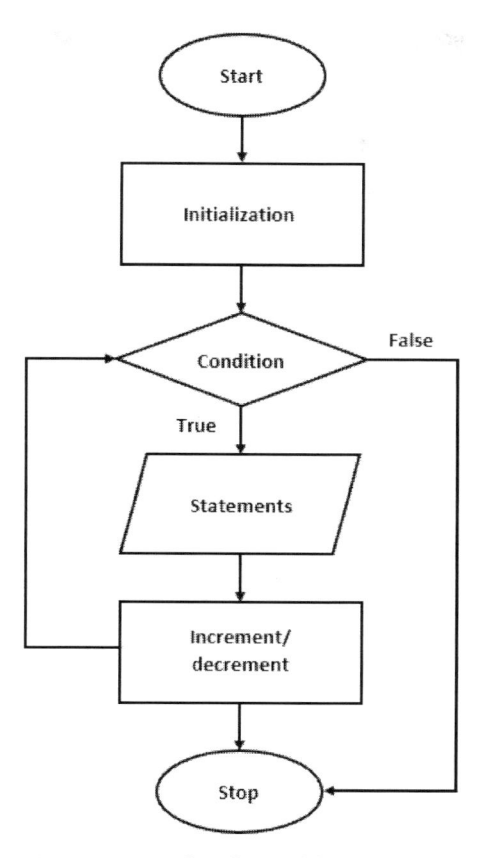

*Figure 6-14 Flowchart of the **while** loop*

For example:

```
<?php
    $count=1;
    while ($count<=5)
        {
            echo "The count is: $count <br>";
            $count++;
        }
?>
```

In the given example, the variable **$count** is treated as a loop control variable and 1 is assigned as an initial value to it. This variable acts as a counter and controls the entire loop. Next, the conditional expression **$count<=5** will be evaluated. If it evaluates to true, the body of the loop will be executed. Otherwise, the body of the loop will be skipped. After executing the statement in the **while** block, the control will be transferred to the increment part **$count++** which will increment the value of the control variable by one. Next, the condition will be evaluated. This process will be repeated until the value of the variable **$count** becomes less than or equal to the value 5.

Example 5

The following program illustrates the use of the **while** statement. The program will compare two variables and display the value of both the variables until they are equal.

```
<!Doctype html>                                  1
<html>                                           2
<head>                                           3
<title>while loop</title>                        4
</head>                                          5
<body>                                           6
<?php                                            7
        $a=5;                                    8
        $b=1;                                    9
        while($a>$b)                            10
          {                                     11
                echo "a = $a ,  b = $b <br>";   12
                $b++;                           13
          }                                     14
                echo "a and b are equal";       15
?>                                              16
</body>                                         17
</html>                                         18
```

Explanation
Line 8 and Line 9
$a=5;
$b=1;
In these lines, 5 and 1 are integer type values initially assigned to **$a** and **$b** variables, respectively.

Line 10
while($a>$b)
In this line, the conditional expression **$a>$b** will be evaluated repeatedly until it evaluates to false. When the conditional expression evaluates to true, the body of the loop (Line 12 and Line 13) will be executed. Otherwise, the control will be transferred to the next statement (Line 15) which is immediately after the body of the loop.

Line 11
{
This line indicates the start of the body of the **while** loop.

Line 12
**echo "a = $a , b = $b
";**
This line will display the following in the browser:

a= 5, b= 1

Control Structures

> **Note**
> In Line 12, while the body of the **while** loop executes repeatedly, the value of the variable **$b** keeps on changing.

Line 13
$b++;
In this line, the **++** (postfix increment) operator is used. This operator will increment the value of the variable **$b** while the body of the **while** loop executes repeatedly. After the execution of each loop, the value of the variable **$b** will be incremented by one.

Line 14
}
This line indicates the end of the body of the **while** loop.

Line 15
echo "a and b are equal";
When the conditional expression given in the **while** statement evaluates to false, the control will be transferred to this line and it will display the following in the browser:

a and b are equal

The output of Example 5 is displayed in Figure 6-15.

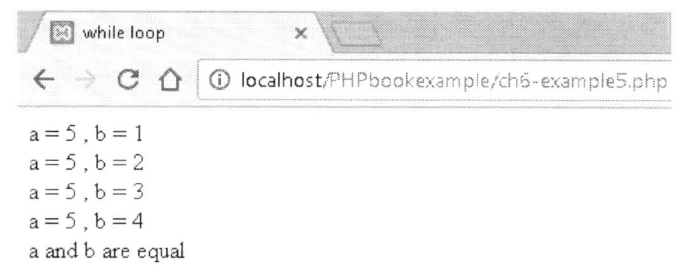

Figure 6-15 The output of Example 5

The do-while Loop

In the **while** loop, first the conditional expression is evaluated and if it evaluates to true, only then the body of the loop is executed. Otherwise, the body of the loop is skipped. But, sometimes it is required that the body of the loop must execute at least once, and then the conditional expression should be evaluated. For this, PHP provides a loop statement which is known as the **do-while** loop. In the **do-while** loop, the body of the loop will be executed at least once, and then the conditional expression will be evaluated. The syntax for using the **do-while** loop is as follows:

```
initialization;
do
{
statements;
increment/decrement;
}
while (condition);
```

> **Note**
> *In the **do-while** loop, the **while** statement should be terminated with a semicolon (;).*

In the given syntax, the initialization part of the loop is executed. It sets the value of the loop control variable which acts as a counter that controls the loop. Next, **do** is a keyword and statements in the **do** block will execute at least once. After executing the statements in the **do** block, the control will be transferred to the increment or decrement part. It will increment or decrement the value of the control variable by one. Next, **while** is a keyword and the condition given in the **while** statement is evaluated. If it evaluates to true, the **do** block will execute again. Otherwise, the loop will terminate and the control will be transferred to the next statement which is immediately after the **do-while** loop, refer to Figure 6-16.

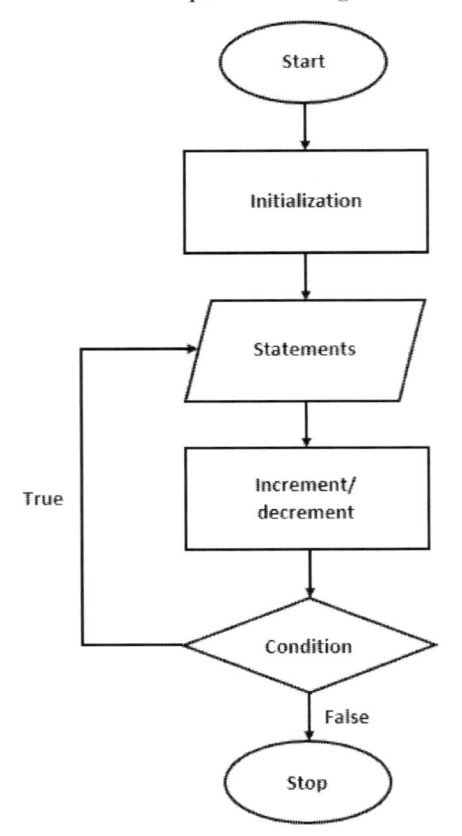

*Figure 6-16 Flowchart of the **do-while** loop*

For example:

```
<?php
    $count=1;
    do
    {
        echo "The count is: $count <br>";
```

Control Structures

```
                $count++;
        }
        while ($count<=5);
?>
```

In the given example, the variable **$count** is treated as a loop control variable and 1 is assigned as an initial value to it. This variable acts as a counter and controls the entire loop. Next, the statement in the **do** block will be executed at least once. After executing the statement in the **do** block, the control will be transferred to the increment part **$count++** which will increment the value of the control variable by one. Next, the condition given in the **while** statement, **$count<=5** will be evaluated. If it evaluates to true, the body of the loop will be executed again. Otherwise, the body of the loop will be skipped. This process will be repeated until the value of the variable count becomes less than or equal to the value 5.

Example 6

The following program illustrates the use of the **do-while** statement. The program will compare two variables and display the value of both the variables until they are equal.

```
<!Doctype html>                                         1
<html>                                                  2
<head>                                                  3
<title>do-while loop</title>                            4
</head>                                                 5
<body>                                                  6
<?php                                                   7
        $a=5;                                           8
        $b=1;                                           9
        do                                              10
         {                                              11
                echo "a = $a , b = $b <br>";            12
                $b++;                                   13
         }                                              14
                while($a>$b);                           15
                echo "a and b are equal";               16
?>                                                      17
</body>                                                 18
</html>                                                 19
```

Explanation

The working of the given program is the same as the previous programming example except that here the body of the **do-while** loop (Line 12 and Line 13) must be executed at least once. Next, the condition **$a>$b** given in the **while** statement will be evaluated. If the condition evaluates to true, the body of the loop will be executed again. Otherwise, the loop will be terminated.

The output of Example 6 is displayed in Figure 6-17.

```
a = 5 , b = 1
a = 5 , b = 2
a = 5 , b = 3
a = 5 , b = 4
a and b are equal
```

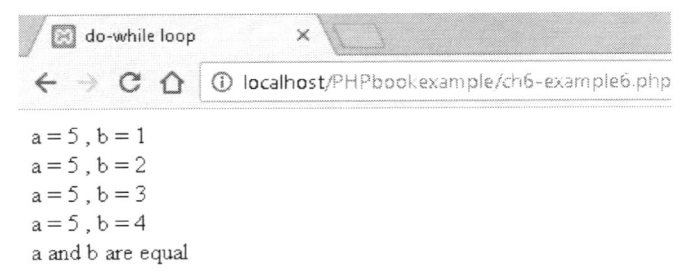

Figure 6-17 *The output of Example 6*

The for Loop

The **for** loop is also an iteration control structure that is used to execute a particular block of code for a specific number of times. The **for** loop is mostly used when you know the number of times the body of the loop will be executed. The **for** loop is easy to understand because all control elements (initialization, condition, and increment or decrement) are placed together. The syntax for using the **for** loop is as follows:

```
for(initialization; condition; increment or decrement)
```

In the given syntax, **for** is a keyword and initialization, condition, and increment or decrement are the control expressions. Initialization is the first statement inside the **for** loop parentheses. In initialization part, counter variable is assigned by an initial value. It is the control variable of the loop. Next, condition is the second expression inside the **for** loop parentheses. It is an expression that should evaluate to either true or false. If it evaluates to true, the **for** loop is evaluated one more time. If it evaluates to false, the **for** loop is not executed anymore, and execution jumps to the first statement after the body of the **for** loop. The third expression in the **for** loop is the increment or decrement. It executes after each iteration of the **for** loop. It will increment or decrement the value of the variable by one, refer to Figure 6-18. These three expressions must be separated by a semicolon (;).

For example:

```
for($i=0; $i<5; $i++)
{
body of the for loop;
}
```

In the given example, the variable **$i** is treated as a loop control variable and 0 is assigned as an initial value. This variable acts as a counter and controls the entire loop. This initialization part is executed only once. Next, the conditional expression **$i<5** will be evaluated. If it evaluates to true, the body of the loop will be executed. Otherwise, the body of the loop will be skipped. After executing the body of the loop, the control will be transferred to the increment part **$i++** which will increment the value of the control variable **$i** by one. The conditional expression will be evaluated again. This process will be repeated until the value of variable **$i** becomes less than 5. It will be evaluated 5 times.

Control Structures

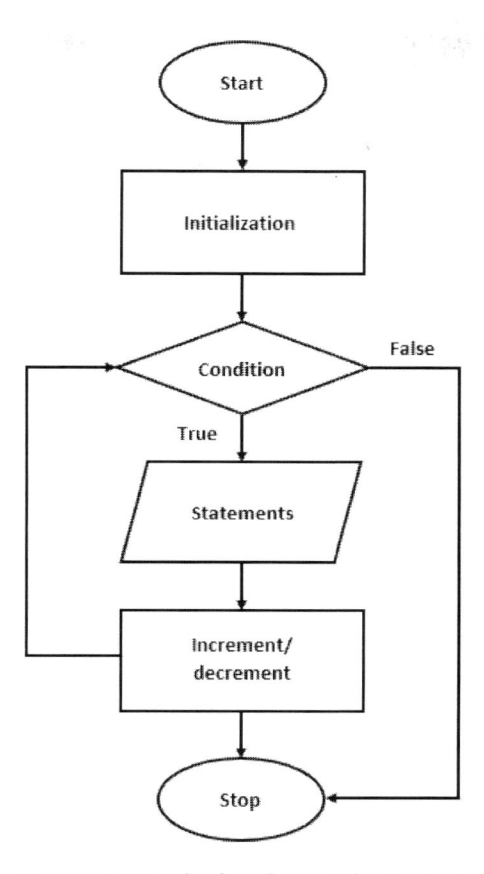

Figure 6-18 The flowchart of the **for** loop

Example 7

The following program illustrates the use of the **for** loop. The program will calculate the multiples of a given number and display them in the browser.

```
<!Doctype html>                                                 1
<html>                                                          2
<head>                                                          3
<title>for loop</title>                                         4
</head>                                                         5
<body>                                                          6
<?php                                                           7
    $num=8;                                                     8
    echo "The multiplication table of $num is as follows:<br>"; 9
    for( $i=1; $i<=10; $i++)                                    10
        {                                                       11
            $mul = $num*$i;                                     12
```

```
            echo "$num  *  $i  =  $mul <br>";          13
        }                                              14
    ?>                                                 15
    </body>                                            16
</html>                                                17
```

Explanation
Line 9
**echo "The multiplication table of $num is as follows:
";**
This line will display the following in the browser:

The multiplication table of 8 is as follows:

Line 10
for($i=1; $i<=10; $i++)
This line contains the **for** loop. In this line, the variable **$i** (loop control variable) is initialized to 1 and the condition **$i<=10** will be checked. If the condition is true, the body of the loop will be executed and the control will be transferred to Line 13. This process will be repeated till the condition is true. When the condition becomes false, the loop will terminate.

Line 12
$mul = $num*$i;
In this line, the value of the variable **$num** is multiplied by the value of variable **$i** and the resultant value will be assigned to the variable **$mul**.

Line 13
**echo "$num * $i = $mul
";**
This line will display the following in the browser:

8 * 1 = 8

> **Note**
> In Line 13, the value of the variable **$i** will be increased by 1 in each iteration.

The output of Example 7 is displayed in Figure 6-19.

Control Structures

```
The multiplication table of 8 is as follows:
8 * 1 = 8
8 * 2 = 16
8 * 3 = 24
8 * 4 = 32
8 * 5 = 40
8 * 6 = 48
8 * 7 = 56
8 * 8 = 64
8 * 9 = 72
8 * 10 = 80
```

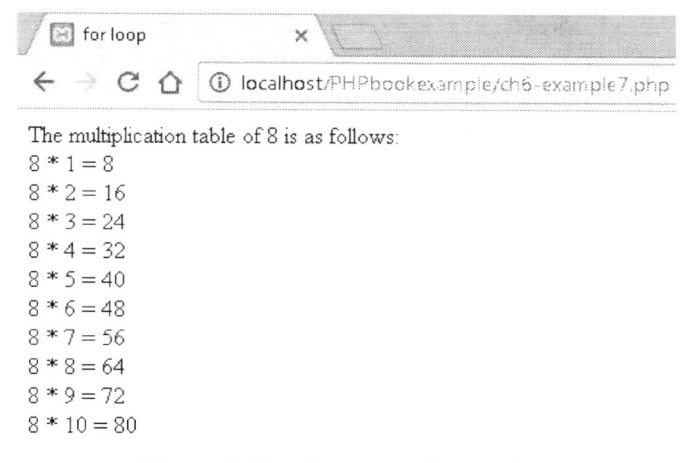

Figure 6-19 The output of Example 7

Note
The **foreach** loop is an iteration control structure. You will learn about the **foreach** loop in Chapter 8.

The Jump Statements

The jump statements are used to skip a part of the loop or other statement and transfer the control to another statement. When a jump statement is encountered within a block, it transfers the control unconditionally to some other part in a program. PHP supports the following four jump statements:

a. break
b. continue
c. goto
d. return

The break Statement

The **break** statement is used to skip the nearest enclosing loop control structures such as **for**, **foreach**, **while**, and **do-while** or the **switch** control structure. Whenever a **break** statement is encountered within the body of the loop or **switch** statement, the body of the statement terminates and the control is transferred to the next immediate statement after the loop or the **switch** control structure. The syntax for using the **break** statement is as follows:

Example 8

The following program illustrates the use of the **break** statement. The program will create the Fibonacci series and also display the resultant series in the browser.

```
<!Doctype html>                                 1
<html>                                          2
<head>                                          3
<title>break statement</title>                  4
```

```
        </head>                                  5
        <body>                                   6
        <?php                                    7
           $a=0;                                 8
           $b=1;                                 9
           $c=0;                                10
           $i=0;                                11
           echo "$a <br>";                      12
           echo "$b <br>";                      13
           while($c<=4000)                      14
                {                               15
                     $c=$a+$b;                  16
                     echo "$c <br>";            17
                     $a=$b;                     18
                     $b=$c;                     19
                     $i++;                      20
                if($i==10)                      21
                     break;                     22
                }                               23
           echo "Exit from the loop";           24
        ?>                                      25
        </body>                                 26
        </html>                                 27
```

Explanation

Line 14
while($c<=4000)
This line contains the **while** statement. In this line, first the conditional expression **$c<=4000** will be evaluated. If it evaluates to true, the statements (from Line 16 to Line 22) associated with the **while** loop will be executed. Otherwise, the loop will terminate and the control will be transferred to Line 24 which is immediately after the **while** loop.

Line 16
$c=$a+$b;
In this line, the value of the variable **$a** will be added to the value of the variable **$b**. Next, the resultant value will be assigned to the variable **$c**.

Line 17
**echo "$c
";**
This line will display the value of the variable **$c** in the browser.

Line 18 and Line 19
$a=$b;
$b=$c;
In these lines, the value of the variable **$b** will be assigned to the variable **$a** and the value of the variable **$c** will be assigned to the variable **$b**.

Control Structures

Line 20
$i++;
In this line, the variable **$i** is treated as a counter variable which is increased by 1 every time the body of the loop is executed.

Line 21
if($i==10)
In this line, the conditional expression **$i==10** will be evaluated. If it evaluates to true, the control will be transferred to Line 22. Otherwise, Line 22 will be skipped.

Line 22
break;
This line will be executed when the conditional expression given in Line 21 evaluates to true. When this **break** statement is executed, the control will be transferred outside the **while** loop. As a result, the control will be transferred to Line 24.

Line 24
echo "Exit from the loop";
This line will display the following in the browser:

Exit from the loop

The output of Example 8 is displayed in Figure 6-20.

```
0
1
1
2
3
5
8
13
21
34
55
89
Exit from the loop
```

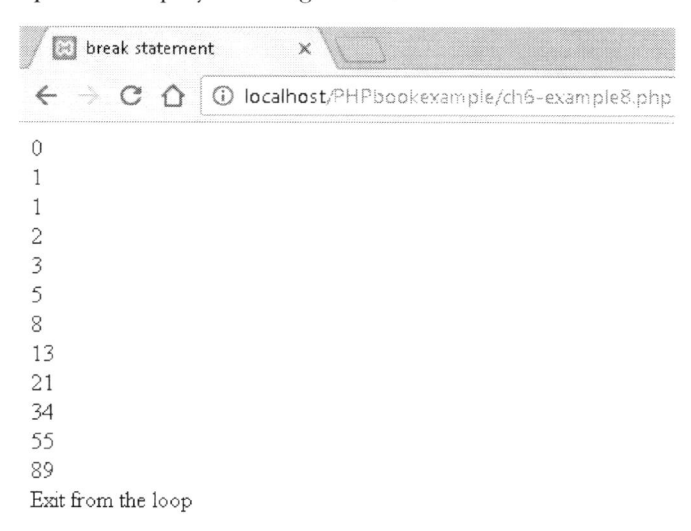

Figure 6-20 *The output of Example 8*

Note
You can nest different control structures together in a program. It means you can use a control structure inside another control structure and it is known as nested control structure.

In the previous section, you learned that the **break** statement is used to jump outside the nearest enclosing control structure or to exit from the current structure. You can also use the **break** statement to jump outside the nested enclosing control structure. You can do it by passing numeric argument with the **break** statement which tells to jump out of given numbers of nested control structure. The default numeric value for **break** statement is 1. So you can also use **break 1** in place of **break** to jump out of the nearest enclosing control structure. You can use **break 2** to jump out of second nearest control structure and so on for further nested control structures.

> **Note**
> *You cannot pass 0 or variables as argument with the **break** statement because PHP 5.4 version has invalidated these arguments.*

Example 9

The following program illustrates the use of the numeric arguments with the **break** statement inside the nested control structure and display the output in the browser.

```
<!Doctype html>                                                         1
<html>                                                                  2
<head>                                                                  3
<title>break numeric statement</title>                                  4
</head>                                                                 5
<body>                                                                  6
<?php                                                                   7
   $nest = 0;                                                           8
   while (++$nest)                                                      9
    {                                                                  10
      switch ($nest)                                                   11
       {                                                               12
         case 2:                                                       13
             echo "<b>case 2</b> statement  <br>";                     14
             break 1;  /* Exit only the switch. */                     15
         case 4:                                                       16
             echo "<b>case 4</b> statement <br>";                      17
             break ;  /* Exit only the switch. */                      18
         case 6:                                                       19
             echo "<b>case 6</b> statement <br>";                      20
             break 2; /* Exit the switch and the while. */             21
         case 8:                                                       22
             echo "<b>case 8</b> statement <br>";                      23
             break;                                                    24
         case 10:                                                      25
             echo "<b>case 10</b> statement <br>";                     26
             break ;                                                   27
         default:                                                      28
             break;                                                    29
        }                                                              30
    }                                                                  31
      echo "OUT OF THE NESTED CONTROL STRUCTURE";                      32
```

Control Structures

```
?>                                                          33
</body>                                                     34
</html>                                                     35
```

Explanation

Line 9
while (++$nest)
This line contains the **while** statement. In this line, the conditional expression **++$nest** will be evaluated and treated as a counter variable which is increased by 1 every time the body of the loop (from Line 10 to Line 31) is executed.

Line 11
switch ($nest)
In this line, the value of the variable **$nest** is passed in the parentheses with the **switch** keyword. This **switch** statement is nested inside the body of **while** loop. Here, the variable **$nest** is treated as a control variable and its value will be compared with all the **case** literal values.

Line 13
case 2:
In this line, first the value of the control variable **$nest** will be compared with the **case** literal value 2. Here, the match is found and the control will be transferred to the next line (Line 14).

Line 14
**echo "case 2 statement
";**
This line will display the following in the browser:

case 2 statement

Line 15
break 1;
The **break 1** statement is a jump statement. As **1** is the numeric argument passed with the **break** statement, it will make the program jump out of one control structure which is the nearest enclosing structure. So, the **break 1** statement will transfer the control outside the **switch** body.

> **Note**
> If **break 1** or **break** statement is not used in the **switch** body then all cases starting from the matched statement (case) including the **default** statement (case) will be executed.

The working of Lines 16 to 18 is the same as the working of Lines 13 to 15 where **break 1** and **break** statement works exactly same.

Line 19
case 6:
Again in this line, the value of the control variable **$nest** will be compared with the **case** literal value 6. Here, match is found and the control will be transferred to the next line (Line 20).

Line 20
**echo "case 6 statement
";**
This line will display the following in the browser:

case 6 statement

Line 21
break 2;
The **break 2** statement is a jump statement. As **2** is the numeric argument passed with the **break** statement, it will make the program jump out of two control structures that are **switch** statement and **while** loop. So, the **break 2** statement will skip rest of the statements (from Line 22 to Line 29) that are after its occurrence and transfer the control to Line 32 outside the **while** body.

Line 32
echo "OUT OF THE NESTED CONTROL STRUCTURE";
This line will display the following in the browser:

OUT OF THE NESTED CONTROL STRUCTURE

The output of Example 9 is displayed in Figure 6-21.

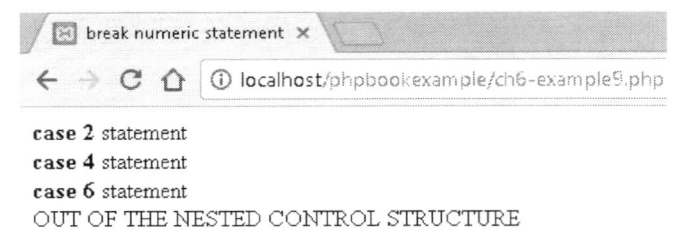

Figure 6-21 The output of Example 9

The continue Statement

The **continue** statement is similar to the **break** statement with the only difference that instead of exiting from the loop, the **continue** statement transfers the control back to the top of the current loop for the next iteration. The **continue** statement is used in those cases where you want an early iteration of the loop. When the **continue** statement is encountered inside the block of code, it will skip the remaining part (statements which are immediately after the continue statement) of that particular block. The syntax for using the **continue** statement is as follows:

```
continue;
```

For example:

```
<?
   for($i=0;$i<=10;$i++)
       {
           echo "statement 1 <br>";
           if($i==5)
```

Control Structures

```
                continue;
        echo "statement 2 <br>";
    }
?>
```

In this example, when the value of the variable **$i** will be equal to five, the **continue** statement will be executed. The **echo "statement 2
";** statement will be skipped and the control will be transferred back to the increment part of the **for** statement for the next iteration.

Example 10

The following program illustrates the use of the **continue** statement. The program will display all odd numbers from 1 to 20 in the browser.

```
<!Doctype html>                                         1
<html>                                                  2
<head>                                                  3
<title>continue statement</title>                       4
</head>                                                 5
<body>                                                  6
<?php                                                   7
    echo "Odd numbers from 1 to 20: <br>";              8
        for($i=1; $i<=20; $i++)                         9
        {                                               10
            if($i%2==0)                                 11
            continue;                                   12
            echo "$i <br>";                             13
        }                                               14
?>                                                      15
</body>                                                 16
</html>                                                 17
```

Explanation
Line 11
if($i%2==0)
In this line, the **%** (modulus) operator returns the remainder after dividing the value of the variable **$i** with the value 2. If the remainder value is equal to 0, the control will be transferred to the next line (Line 12). Otherwise, the control will be transferred to Line 13.

Line 12
continue;
This line will execute when the condition given in the **if** statement evaluates to true. When the **continue** statement is executed, the control will be transferred to the increment part of the loop and the next iteration will continue.

Line 13
**echo "$i
";**
This line will display the value of the variable **$i** in the browser when the condition given in the **if** statement evaluates to false.

The output of Example 10 is displayed in Figure 6-22.

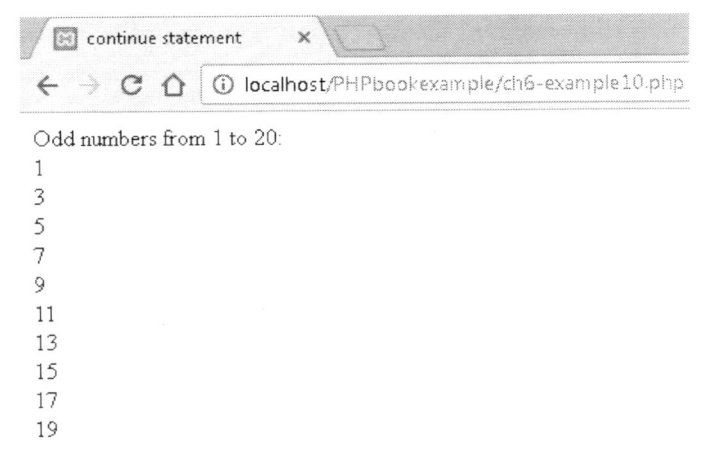

Figure 6-22 The output of Example 10

You can also pass numeric arguments in the **continue** statement just like the **break** statement. The default numeric value for the **continue** statement is 1. So you can also use **continue 1** in place of **continue** to transfers the control back to the top of the current control structure for the next iteration. In case of nested control structure, you can use **continue 2** to transfer the control back to the second nearest control structure for the next iteration and so on for further nested control structures.

The goto Statement

The **goto** statement allows the program control to jump unconditionally to another part of the program which is associated with the named label. A label is an identifier followed by a colon (:). The syntax is as follows:

```
goto label;
```

In the given syntax, the label is a valid identifier which represents a name that points to a particular block of code. When the **goto** statement is executed, the control will be transferred outside that particular block to the block of label. To name a block, put a label followed by a colon at the beginning of the block.

For example:

```
greater:   //label
{
----------;
----------;
if(conditional expression)
goto greater;
----------;
----------;
}
```

Control Structures

In the given example, **greater** represents a label. The curly braces {} indicate the start and the end of the named block. In this block, if the given conditional expression evaluates to true, the control will be transferred to the next statement which is a labeled **goto** statement.

> **Note**
> *The **goto** statement can be used to jump out of any nearest enclosing control structure other than the **switch** control structure and any loop control structure. You can also not jump out of a function or method. To transfer the control to any label through the **goto** statement, the specified label must be in the same file.*

Example 11

The following program illustrates the use of the **goto** statement. The program will terminate the execution of the loop when the value of the control variable will be equal to five. It will display the output in the browser.

```
<!Doctype html>                                 1
<html>                                          2
<head>                                          3
<title>goto statement</title>                   4
</head>                                         5
<body>                                          6
<?php                                           7
   for($i=1;$i<=10;$i++)                        8
        {                                       9
            if($i==5)                          10
            goto stop;                         11
            echo "The value of i is: $i <br>"; 12
        }                                      13
   stop:                                       14
        echo "Label is encountered";           15
?>                                             16
</body>                                        17
</html>                                        18
```

Explanation
Line 8
for($i=1;$i<=10;$i++)
In this line, the variable **$i** is initialized to 1 and the condition **$i<=10** is checked. If the condition is true, the body of the loop will be executed and the control will be transferred to Line 10. Otherwise, the body of the loop will be skipped.

Line 10
if($i==5)
In this line, the value of variable **$i** is checked to see if it is equal to five. If this condition is true, the control is transferred to the next line (Line 11) which is a **goto** statement. Otherwise the control is transferred to the Line 12.

Line 11
goto stop;
In this line, **stop** is used as a label with the **goto** statement. When this statement is executed, the control will be transferred to the statement (Line 15) associated with the label.

Line 14
stop:
In this line, **stop** is a named label.

Line 15
echo "Label is encountered";
This line will display the following in the browser:

Label is encountered

The output of Example 11 is displayed in Figure 6-23.

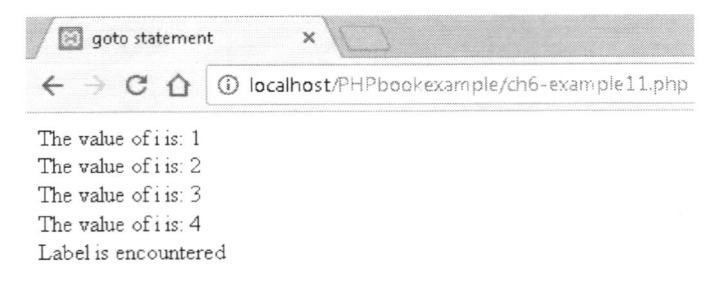

Figure 6-23 The output of Example 11

The return Statement

The **return** statement is another type of jump statement that terminates the execution of a function and the control returns to the calling function. Next, the execution begins from the statement that immediately follows the call in the calling function. The syntax for using the **return** statement is as follows:

```
return expression;
```

In the given syntax, the expression represents some values that will be returned by the **return** statement.

You will learn more about the working of the **return** statement in the later chapters.

ALTERNATE SYNTAX FOR CONTROL STRUCTURES

There are also alternate syntax that can be used for some of the control structures that you have already learned in previous sections. The control structures that have alternate syntax are as follows:

a. if
b. if-else

Control Structures

    c. elseif
    d. for
    e. foreach
    f. while
    g. switch

The basic format of alternate syntax for every control structure mentioned in this section is the same as discussed earlier. The only difference in the syntax is that the opening curly braces({) and closing curly braces(}) of the basic syntax will get replaced. The opening curly braces({) is replaced by a colon(:). The closing curly braces(}) is replaced by **endif;**, **endfor;**, **endforeach;**, **endwhile;**, or **endswitch;** depending on the control structure. The alternate syntax for various control structures are discussed next.

Alternate Syntax for if Structure

The alternate syntax for **if** structure is as follows:

```
if (condition or expression):
   Statement 1;
   Statement 2;
   ---------
   ---------
   Statement n;
endif;
```

In the given syntax, all the statements from 1 to n will be executed, if the condition or expression within the **if** statement is true. Otherwise, they will not be executed and the control will be transferred to the next statement after the **if** block. Here, the **if** block starts with colon (:) and ends with **endif;**.

For example:

```
<?
   $s = 20;
   $m = 21;
      if($s>$m):
            echo "s is greater than m";
            echo "you got the result";
      endif;
            echo "m is greater than s";
?>
```

In the given example, first the condition **$s>$m**(value of the variable s is greater than the value of the variable m) will be checked. If the condition returns true then both the next statements inside the **if** block will be executed. But if the condition returns false then the statement inside the **if** block will be skipped and control will be transferred to the next statement outside the **if** block and the statement **echo "m is greater than s"** will be executed.

Alternate Syntax for the if-else and if-elseif Structures

The alternate syntax for the **if-else** control structure is as follows:

```
if(conditional_expression):
    statement 1;
    statement 2;
else:
    statement 3;
    statement 4;
endif;
```

The working of the given alternate syntax of the **if-else** control structure is same as the basic syntax of it that you have learned in previous sections. In the alternate syntax, the **if** and **else** blocks start with colon(:) and end with **endif;**.

For example:

```
<?php
    $s = 20;
    $m = 21;
        if ($s>$m):
            echo "s is greater <br>";
            echo "m is smaller ";
        else:
            echo "m is greater <br>";
            echo "s is smaller";
        endif;
?>
```

In the given example, if the value of the variable **$s** is greater than the value of the variable **$m**, the statements: **echo "s is greater";** and **echo "m is smaller";** associated with the **if** block will be executed. Otherwise, the **if** block will be skipped and the statements: **echo "m is greater";** and **echo "s is smaller";** associated with the **else** block will be executed.

The alternate syntax for the **if-elseif** control structure is as follows:

```
if(conditional_expression1):
    statements;
elseif(conditional_expression2):
    statements;
elseif(conditional_expression3):
    statements;
else:
    statements;
endif;
```

Control Structures

The working of the given alternate syntax of the **if-elseif** control structure is same as the basic syntax of it that you have learned in previous sections. In the alternate syntax, the **if** and **elseif** blocks start with colon(**:**) and end with **endif;**.

For example:

```php
<?php
    $sales= 20000;
    $target= 30000;
        if($sales>$target):
                    echo "Excellent Performance";
        elseif($sales==$target):
                    echo "Good Performance";
        elseif($sales<$target):
                    echo "Bad Performance";
        else:
                    echo "Terminated";
        endif;
?>
//output: Bad Performance
```

In the given example, if the conditional expression **$sales>$target** of **if** statement evaluates to true, the statement associated with the **if** block will be executed. Otherwise, the next conditional expression **$sales==$target** of **elseif** statement will be evaluated. If it evaluates to true, the statement associated with the **elseif** block will be executed. Otherwise, the control will be transferred to the next **elseif** statement and the conditional expression **$sales<$target** will be evaluated. If none of the conditions evaluates to true, the control will be transferred to the **else** statement and the statement associated with it will be executed.

Alternate Syntax of the while and for loop Control Structures

The alternate syntax of the **while** loop control structure is as follows:

```
initialization;
while(condition):
statements;
increment/decrement;
endwhile;
```

The working of the given alternate syntax of **while** loop control structure is same as the basic syntax of it that you have learned in previous sections. In the alternate syntax, the block of the **while** loop starts with colon(**:**) and ends with **endwhile;**.

For example:

```php
<?php
    $numb=1;
```

```
            while ($numb<=10):
                    echo "The number is: $numb <br>";
                    $numb++;
            endwhile;
?>
```

In the given example, the variable **$numb** is treated as a loop control variable and 1 is assigned as an initial value to it. This variable acts as a counter and controls the entire loop. Next, the conditional expression **$numb<=10** will be evaluated. If it evaluates to true, the body of the loop will be executed. Otherwise, the body of the loop will be skipped. After executing the statement in the **while** block, the control will be transferred to the increment part **$numb++**, which will increment the value of the control variable by one. The condition will again be evaluated. This process will be repeated until the value of the variable **$numb** becomes less than or equal to the value 10.

The alternate syntax of the **for** loop control structure is as follows:

```
for(initialization; condition; increment or decrement):
   statements;
endfor;
```

The working of the given alternate syntax of **for** loop control structure is the same as the basic syntax of it that you have learned in previous sections. In the alternate syntax, the block of the **for** loop starts with colon(**:**) and ends with **endfor;**.

Alternate Syntax for the switch Structure

The alternate syntax for the **switch** structure is as follows:

```
switch(value or expression):
   case 1:
         statement1;
         break;
   case 2:
         statement2;
         break;
   ---------;
   ---------;
   ---------;
   case N:
         statementn;
         break;
   default:
         statement;
endswitch;
```

The working of the given alternate syntax of **switch** control structure is same as the basic syntax of it that you have learned in previous sections. In the alternate syntax, the block of the **switch** statements start with colon(**:**) and end with **endswitch;**.

Control Structures

For example:

```php
<?php
   $year=3;
   switch($year):
   case 1:
        echo "1 year experience";
        break;
   case 2:
        echo "2 years experience";
        break;
   case 3:
        echo "3 years experience";
        break;
   default:
        echo "Not eligible for this job";
   endswitch;
?>
```

In this example, value 3 is assigned to variable **$year** which is treated as a control variable. In the first step, the value of the control variable **$year** is compared with the first **case** that has literal value **1**. Here, no match is found. Now, the control is transferred to the next **case** statement and again the value of the control variable **$year** is compared with the second **case** that has literal value **2**. This process is repeated until no match or the **default** case is found. While repeating this process, a match is found in **case** that has the literal value **3** and the statement associated with it, **echo "3 years experience";** is executed. Next, the control is transferred to the statement, which is immediately after the **switch** body.

LOGICAL OPERATORS

You have already learned about the logical operators in the earlier chapters. In this section, you will learn about the usage of logical operators with the help of a programming example. The syntax for the logical AND (**and** / **&&**) operator is as follows:

```
comp_exp1 and comp_exp2
comp_exp1 && comp_exp2
```

In the given syntax, if both the expressions, comp_exp1 and comp_exp2 are true, the operator will return true, otherwise false.

The syntax for the logical OR (**or**/**||**) operator is as follows:

```
comp_exp1 or comp_exp2
comp_exp1 || comp_exp2
```

In the given syntax, if either of the comp_exp1 and comp_exp2 is true, the operator will return true, otherwise false.

The syntax for the logical NOT(!) operator is as follows:

```
!(expression)
```

In this syntax, if the expression is true, the operator will return false. If the expression is false, the operator will return true. This operator reverses the resultant value of the expression.

Example 12

The following program illustrates the use of the logical operator along with the **if-elseif** statement. The program will compare the age of a football candidate and display the output in the browser based on the condition satisfied.

```
<!Doctype html>                                              1
<html>                                                       2
<head>                                                       3
<title>logical operators</title>                             4
</head>                                                      5
<body>                                                       6
<?php                                                        7
    $age=23;                                                 8
    echo "Your age is $age. <br>";                           9
    if(($age>=10) && ($age<=17))                            10
    {                                                       11
        echo "You are eligible for <b>under 18</b>          12
        football team.<br>";
    }                                                       13
    elseif(($age>=18) && ($age<=28))                        14
    {                                                       15
        echo "You are eligible for <b>senior</b> football   16
        team. <br>";
    }                                                       17
    else                                                    18
    {                                                       19
        echo "You are not eligible for any football team."; 20
    }                                                       21
?>                                                          22
</body>                                                     23
</html>                                                     24
```

Explanation
Line 10
if(($age>=10) && ($age<=17))
In this line, the logical AND(**&&**) operator is used. If both the conditional expressions **$age>=10** and **$age<=17** given in the statement are true, the control will be transferred to Line 12. Otherwise, the **if** block (from Line 11 to Line 13) will be skipped and the control will be transferred to the **elseif** statement (Line 14).

Control Structures

Line 14
elseif(($age>=18) && ($age<=28))
In this line, if both the conditional expressions **$age>=18** and **$age<=28** given in the statement are true, the control will be transferred to line 16. Otherwise, the **elseif** block (from Line 15 to Line 17) will be skipped and the control will be transferred to the next **else** statement (Line 18). But here, it will return true.

Line 18
else
If none of the conditional expressions evaluates to true then the control will be transferred to the **else** statement. In this case, it will get skipped because the **elseif** statement (Line 14) have already returned true.

The output of Example 12 is displayed in Figure 6-24.

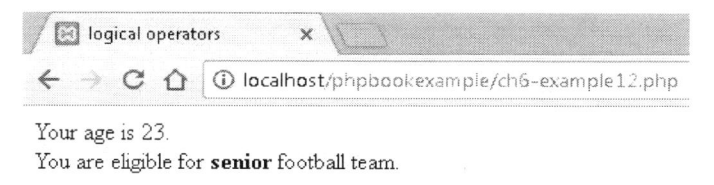

Figure 6-24 The output of Example 12

Self-Evaluation Test

Answer the following questions and then compare them to those given at the end of this chapter:

1. A _____ is a graphical representation of the steps that constitute a program.

2. The _____ control structure is a single path statement.

3. The _____ control structure is a dual path control structure which routes the flow of execution in two different paths.

4. The _____ control structure is a selection or a case control structure.

5. The **for** loop is used when you know the number of times the body of a loop will be executed. (T/F)

6. The **while** loop is an entry controlled loop where the condition is evaluated at the end. (T/F)

7. The **break** statement transfers the control back to the start of a loop. (T/F)

8. In the **do-while** loop, the body of the loop is executed at least once. (T/F)

Review Questions

Answer the following questions:

1. Which of the following control structure is a dual path control structure which routes the flow of execution in two different paths.?

   (a) **if** control structure
   (b) **switch** control structure
   (c) **if-else** control structure
   (d) **while** control structure

2. In which of the following loop, the body of the loop will be executed at least once?

   (a) **do-while** loop
   (b) **while** loop
   (c) **for** loop
   (d) none of them

3. Which of the following statement transfers the control back to the start of the loop?

   (a) **continue** statement
   (b) **return** statement
   (c) **break** statement
   (d) **goto** statement

4. Which of the following statement allows the program control to jump unconditionally to another part of the program which is associated with the named label?

   (a) **return** statement
   (b) **break** statement
   (c) **goto** statement
   (d) **continue** statement

5. Find errors in the following source codes:

   (a)
   ```php
   <?php
        $sales = 20000;
        $target = 15000;
        if($sales>=$target)
             {
                  echo "You have achieved the target";
             }
        else
             {
             echo "You have not achieved the target";
   ?>
   ```

   (b)
   ```php
   <?php
        $a=5;
        $b=1;
        while $a>$b
             {
                  echo "a = $a ,  b = $b <br>";
                  $b++;
             }
   ```

```
            echo "a and b are equal";
    ?>
```

(c)
```
<?php
    $a=5;
    $b=1;
        do
        {
            echo "a = $a , b = $b <br>";
            $b++;
        }
        while($a>$b)
            echo "a and b are equal";
?>
```

(d)
```
<?php
$num=5;
echo "The multiplication table of $num is as follows:<br>";
    for( $i=1 $i<=10; $i++)
        {
            $mul = $num*$i;
            echo "$num * $i = $mul <br>";
        }
?>
```

EXERCISES

Exercise 1

Using the **if-else** statement, write a program to find whether 53 is even or odd number.

Exercise 2

Write a program to find the square of the first ten natural numbers using the **for** loop.

Answers to Self-Evaluation Test

1. flowchart, 2. if, 3. if-else, 4. switch, 5. T, 6. F, 7. F, 8. T

Chapter 7

Functions, Classes, and Objects

Learning Objectives

After completing this chapter, you will be able to:
- *Understand the functions*
- *Use the file inclusion statements*
- *Understand the concept of classes*
- *Use the methods and properties*
- *Understand the concept of objects*
- *Use the constructor and destructor*
- *Understand the concept of inheritance*
- *Use the parent and final keywords*
- *Use the instanceof operator*
- *Understand the concept of interface*
- *Understand the concept of anonymous class*

INTRODUCTION

All the programs that you have studied in the earlier chapters consist of a limited number of statements. Large programs, however, consist of many statements which make the program complex and difficult to understand. You can divide a large program into small groups of statements known as function to remove the program complexity. In case of Object-Oriented Programming (OOP), the data is treated as the most critical element of the program and the primary focus is on the data and not on the procedures. Therefore, in OOP, the programs are implemented using classes, methods, and objects. In this chapter, you will learn about functions, classes, objects, methods, inheritance, constructors, destructor, and so on.

FUNCTIONS

A function is a group of statements that perform a specific task and can be used multiple times in a program. A function has a name and it returns a value. It may also have a list of arguments and it gets executed when a call is made. If a function consists of an argument then a value can be passed to that argument at the time of function calling.

There are two types of functions in PHP which are as follows:

1. User Defined Functions
2. In-built Functions

These functions are discussed next.

User Defined Functions

PHP provides you more than a thousand in-built functions which can be directly used in a program as required. Other than these in-built functions, you can create user defined functions and name them.

Creating User Defined Functions

The syntax for creating a user defined function is as follows:

```
function Func_name($arguments){
   //statements
}
```

In the given syntax, **function** is the keyword used to create or declare function. The **Func_name** represents the name of function used as a reference in the program. The Parentheses (open and close bracket ( )) after the function name are required. Here, **$arguments** represents the arguments or input parameters of the function which are passed inside the parentheses of the function. But, these arguments are optional. The function block starts with open curly bracket ({) and ends with a closing curly bracket (}) and the function statements are written inside the block of function.

For example:

```
<?php
   function cadcim(){
```

Functions, Classes, and Objects

```
            echo "Welcome to CADCIM" ;
                    }
    cadcim(); //function calling
?>
// output: Welcome to CADCIM
```

In the given example, **function** is the keyword used to declare function. **cadcim()** is the function name with no input parameters passed inside the parentheses. When the function is called by its name, it displays the statement written inside the function block in the browser.

You can also pass input parameters to the function if required in the program.

For example:

```
<?php
    function bookname($book){
        echo "$book" ;
                }
    bookname("Introducing PHP/MySQl");
?>
//output: Introducing PHP/MySQl
```

In the given example, **function** is the keyword used to declare function in PHP, **bookname** is the function name, and **$book** is the input parameter passed to the function **bookname**. When some value is passed to the function, it will get assigned to the input parameter **$book** of the function and output will be displayed using the **echo** statement. In this case, **Introducing PHP/MySQL** is the value passed to the function **bookname()** so it will get assigned to **$book** and will be displayed as output.

Function Name

The function name is used as reference in the program. It can be used multiple times to call the same function if required in the program.

While naming a function, you must follow certain rules. The rules are as follows:

1. Only alphabetic characters, both uppercase and lowercase, digits from 0 to 9, and the underscore (_) can be used.
2. Function name can start with an alphabet or an underscore but not with a digit.
3. Function names are case insensitive. For example, case, CASE, and Case, all three will be treated as name of a single function.

The following function names are invalid in PHP:

```
9_Count() // Function name cannot start with a digit.
COUNT#() // Function name cannot contain #(hash symbol).
```

The following function names are valid in PHP:

```
COUNT_9() // Function name can start with alphabetic characters.
_ACCOUNT() // Function name can start with an underscore.
Account() // Function name is case insensitive.
```

> **Tip**
> *It is recommended to name the function according to its functionality rather than random names. It will make your code more clear.*

Function Arguments

The function arguments are used to pass information to the function. You can pass one or more arguments in a single function according to the requirement of the program. The arguments or input parameters of function are passed inside the parentheses just after the function name. The function arguments work like a variable inside the function.

For example:

```
<?php
   function family($fname, $age, $hobby) {
        echo "$fname is $age years old.<br>";
        echo "He loves playing $hobby.<br>";
   }
        family("John", 40, "football");//function call
?>
```

In the given example, **family($fname, $age, $hobby)** is a function created by using the **function** keyword. Here, **family** is the function name and **$fname, $age,** and **$hobby** are multiple arguments passed to the function and are separated by comma. At the time of function call, some values are passed to the function which gets assigned to the input parameters **$fname, $age,** and **$hobby** of the function.

> **Note**
> *A function can be called multiple times by passing different values to it. If you call a function without passing any value then it takes the default value.*

Example 1

The following program will illustrate the use of the function by passing multiple arguments to it. In this program, function is called multiple times and the output is displayed in the browser.

```
<!Doctype html>                                                 1
<html>                                                          2
<head>                                                          3
<title>Function with multiple arguments</title>                 4
</head>                                                         5
<body>                                                          6
<?php                                                           7
```

Functions, Classes, and Objects

```
function player($fname="Smith", $age=16, $team="Not eligible")     8
{                                                                   9
   if($age<18)                                                     10
    {                                                              11
      echo "$fname you are $age years old.<br>";                   12
      echo "Your age is below 18. You are $team to play <br>";     13
      echo "<br>";                                                 14
    }                                                              15
   elseif($age==18)                                                16
    {                                                              17
      echo "$fname your age is $age.<br>";                         18
      echo "You will play in team $team.<br>";                     19
      echo "<br>";                                                 20
    }                                                              21
elseif($age==19)                                                   22
    {                                                              23
      echo "$fname your age is $age.<br>";                         24
      echo "You will play in team $team.<br>";                     25
      echo "<br>";                                                 26
    }                                                              27
else                                                               28
    {                                                              29
      echo "$fname players above the age 19 will play in team      30
      $team<br>";                                                  31
      echo "<br>";                                                 32
    }                                                              33
}                                                                  34
player("John", 18, "A");                                           35
player("Justin", 19, "B");                                         36
player("All", 40, "C");                                            37
player();                                                          38
?>                                                                 39
</body>                                                            40
</html>                                                            41
```

Explanation
Line 8
function player($fname="Smith", $age=16, $team="Not eligible")
In this line, **function** is the keyword used to create a function. **player** is the function name and **($fname="Smith", $age=16, $team="Not eligible")** are multiple arguments separated by comma, passed to the function inside the parentheses. Here, each argument in the function is assigned a default value.

Line 35
player("John", 18, "A");
In this line, **Player** is the function name and **John, 18,** and **A** are the values passed to the function. Here, this line will call the function and the values passed here will get assigned to

the arguments of the function **Player**, declared in Line 8. Now, this line will display the current assigned values instead of the default values in the output.

The working of Line 36 and Line 37 is similar to Line 35.

Line 38
player();
In this line, **player()** is the function name by which function is called. In this function, no value is passed inside the parentheses. Therefore, it will call the function and display the default values assigned to the arguments of the function **player** in Line 8.

The output of Example 1 is displayed in Figure 7-1.

John your age is 18.
You will play in team A.

Justin your age is 19.
You will play in team B.

All players above the age 19 will play in team C

Smith you are 16 years old.
Your age is below 18. You are Not eligible to play

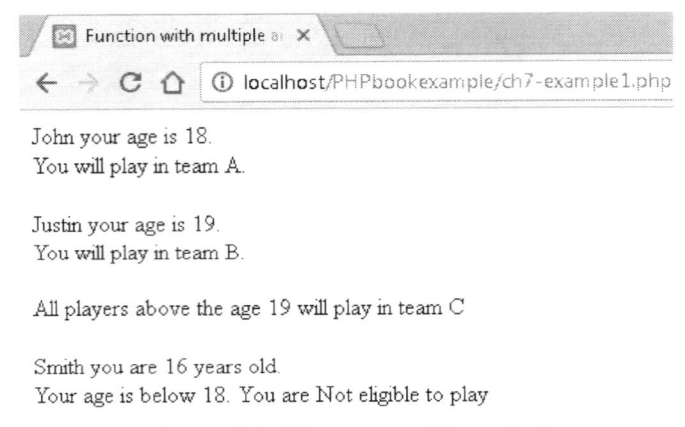

Figure 7-1 The output of Example 1

Function Return Value

You have already learned about **return** statement in the previous chapter. The **return** statement is used to return a function value.

For example:

```
<?php
    function mul($p, $q) {
    $r = $p * $q;
    return $r;
    }
    echo "5 * 10 = " . mul(5,10) . "<br>";
    echo "7 * 13 = " . mul(7,13) . "<br>";
?>
```

In the given example, **function** is the keyword used to create a function and **mul** is the function name. Here, **$p** and **$q** are the two arguments passed to the function. In this function, multiplication operation is performed between **$p** and **$q** variables and the resultant value gets assigned to the **$r** variable. Next, the **return** statement will return the resultant value which is assigned to the **$r** variable at the time of function call.

Dynamic Function Call

In PHP, it is possible to dynamically call a function by assigning the function name as a string to the variables. These variables will behave exactly same as the function assigned to them. Therefore, to call a function dynamically instead of the function name, you can use the variable name with parentheses.

For example:

```
<?php
    function dynamicFunc() {
        echo "It is a string <br>";
    }
    $func_var = "dynamicFunc";
    $func_var();
?>
```

In this example, **dynamicFunc()** is the function which consist of an **echo** statement inside its block. Here, **$func_var** is the variable which holds **dynamicFunc** (function name) as string type value. Now, **$func_var** variable will behave exactly same as the **dynamicFunc()** function. Therefore, you can use **$func_var** variable as a **$func_var()** function to dynamically call the **dynamicFunc()** function.

In-built Functions

There are many in-built functions in PHP. These in-built functions are pre-defined and can be used directly in the program. You have already learned some in-built string functions in the previous chapters. In this section, you will learn more about the in-built PHP functions which are discussed next.

date()

The PHP **date()** function is used to display current date and time. The syntax for the **date()** function is as follows:

```
date(format,timestamp);
```

In the given syntax, **date()** is the in-built function name for date. Inside the parentheses of date function, **format** represents different formats for date and **timestamp** is an optional parameter. The **date()** function displays the current time, if **timestamp** is not specified.

For example:

```
<?php
   echo "Current Date in Format 1 is" . date("Y/m/d") . "<br>";
   echo "Current Date in Format 1 is" . date("Y.m.d") . "<br>";
   echo "Current Date in Format 1 is" . date("Y-m-d") . "<br>";
   echo "Current day is" . date("l") . "<br>";
   echo "Current time is" . date("h:i:sa");
?>
```

In the given example, **date()** is the function used to display current date. Here, **y/m/d**, **y.m.d**, and **y-m-d** are the 3 different date formats defined inside the parentheses of **date()** function, where **y** represents the year (in 4 digit), **m** represents the month (from 01 to 12), **d** represents the date (from 01 to 31), and **l** represents the day of week. The **h:i:sa** is the time format to display current time, where **h** represents the 12 hour format of an hour, **i** represents minutes, **s** represents the seconds and **a** represents the ante meridiem (am) or post meridiem (pm).

var_dump()
The **var_dump()** function is used to display the variable related information including the data type of the value assigned to the variable. The syntax of **var_dump()** is as follows:

```
var_dump($var);
```

In the given syntax, **var_dump()** is the function used to get the details of a variable and **$var** can be any variable whose detail is to be displayed in the browser.

Example 2

The following program will illustrate the use of the **var_dump()** function. In this program, different values will be assigned to the variables and the output is displayed in the browser.

```
<!Doctype html>                              1
<html>                                        2
<head>                                        3
<title>Var_dump function</title>              4
</head>                                       5
<body>                                        6
<?php                                         7
   $value1=508;                               8
   $value2="Hello";                           9
   $value3=698.99;                           10
   $value4=true;                             11
   $value5="num123";                         12
   echo var_dump($value1)."<br>";            13
   echo var_dump($value2)."<br>";            14
   echo var_dump($value3)."<br>";            15
   echo var_dump($value4)."<br>";            16
   echo var_dump($value5)."<br>";            17
?>                                           18
</body>                                      19
</html>                                      20
```

Explanation
Line 13
**echo var_dump($value1)."
";**
In this line, **var_dump()** is the function used to display variable related information. Here, the

var_dump() function will display the data type and value of the **$value1** variable. This line will display the following in the browser:

int(508)

The working of lines 14 to 17 is similar to Line 13.

The output of Example 2 is displayed in Figure 7-2.

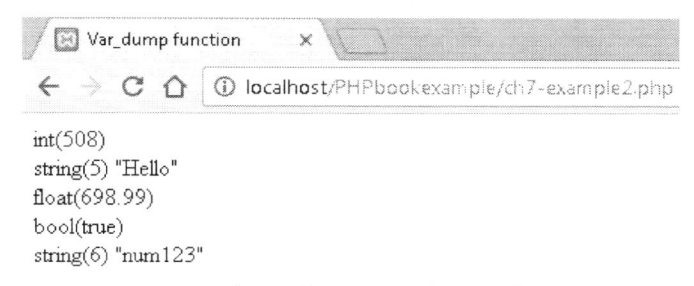

Figure 7-2 The output of Example 2

CSPRNG FUNCTIONS

The CSPRNG functions are introduced in PHP 7. Here, CSPRNG stands for Cryptographically Secure Pseudo-Random Number Generator. It consists of following two functions:

a. **random_bytes()**
b. **random_int()**

They are used to generate cryptographically secure integers and strings in a cross platform way. These CSPRNG functions are discussed next.

random_bytes()

The **random_bytes()** function is used to generate cryptographically secure pseudo-random bytes in PHP. It means this function is used to convert the information provided by the coder or user into randomly generated bytes to secure the information or data. The **random_bytes()** function is used to generate keys or initialization vectors. The syntax of the **random_bytes()** function is as follows:

```
string random_bytes ( int $length )
```

In the given syntax, **random_bytes()** is an in-built **string** type function used to generate random string. Inside the parentheses of this function, integer type variable **$length** is passed. This function will convert the integer value assigned to the **$length** variable into random string and return the requested number of the random string.

Example 3

The following program will illustrate the use of **random_bytes()** and **bin2hex()** functions. In this program, random string will be generated and converted into hexadecimal form and the output is displayed in the browser.

```
<!Doctype html>                                              1
<html>                                                       2
<head>                                                       3
<title>Random bytes</title>                                  4
</head>                                                      5
<body>                                                       6
<?php                                                        7
     $string= random_bytes(11);                              8
     print("Random string generated is ");                   9
     print ($string);                                       10
     print("<br>Binary to hex conversion value for this     11
              randomly generated string is ");
     print(bin2hex($string));                               12
?>                                                          13
</body>                                                     14
</html>                                                     15
```

Explanation
Line 8
$string= random_bytes(11);
In this line, **random_bytes()** is the function assigned to the **$string** variable. Inside the parentheses of function, 11 is the integer type value. This value will get converted into random string using the **random_bytes()** function.

Line 12
print(bin2hex($string));
In this line, **print** is the statement used to display the output in the browser. Inside the parentheses of **print** statement, **bin2hex()** function is passed. This function is used to convert binary data into hexadecimal data. Here, **$string** is the variable passed inside the parentheses of **bin2hex()** function. The value of **$string** variable will convert into hexadecimal form.

The output of Example 3 is displayed in Figure 7-3.

Figure 7-3 The output of Example 3

Functions, Classes, and Objects

random_int()

The **random_int()** function is used to generate cryptographically secure pseudo-random integers in PHP. It means this function is used to convert the information provided by the coder or user into randomly generated integers to secure the information or data. The **random_int()** function is used where unbiased results are critical. The syntax of **random_int()** function is as follows:

```
int random_int ( int $min , int $max )
```

In the given syntax, **random_int()** is an in-built **int** type function used to generate random integers. Inside the parentheses of this function, integer type variables **$min** and **$max** are passed. Here, **$min** variable will hold minimum value and **$max** variable will hold maximum value. This function will return the random integer value in between the **$min** and **$max** values.

Example 4

The following program will illustrate the use of **random_int()** function. In this program, random integers will be generated and the output is displayed in the browser.

```
<!Doctype html>                                              1
<html>                                                       2
<head>                                                       3
<title>Random integer</title>                                4
</head>                                                      5
<body>                                                       6
<?php                                                        7
    $min_value= -1000;                                       8
    $max_value= 100;                                         9
    print("Random generated first integer is ");            10
    print(random_int(1000 , 3000));                         11
    print("<br>Random generated second integer is ");       12
    print(random_int($min_value , $max_value));             13
?>                                                          14
</body>                                                     15
</html>                                                     16
```

Explanation
Line 11
print (random_int(1000 , 3000));
In this line, **random_int()** is the function. Inside the parentheses of function, 1000 and 3000 are the minimum and maximum integer type values passed, respectively. The **random_int()** function will generate the random integer value whose range will be between 1000 to 3000.

The working of Line 13 is similar to Line 11.

The output of Example 4 is displayed in Figure 7-4.

Random generated first integer is 1332
Random generated second integer is -565

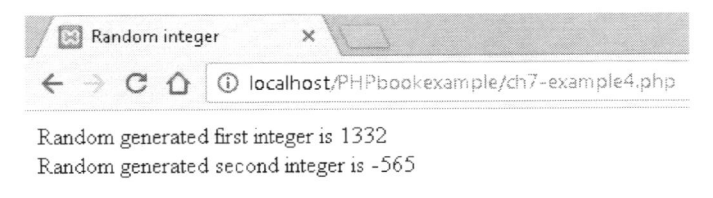

Figure 7-4 The output of Example 4

FILE INCLUSION STATEMENTS

File inclusion statements are used to include any functions, HTML code, or PHP code saved in another file in the current PHP file. There are two types of file inclusion statements as follows:

a. **include** statement
b. **require** statement

The **include** and **require** statements are discussed next.

The include Statement

The **include** statement is used when the current PHP file requires the content of another PHP file in it. The advantage of the **include** statement is that it loads the total content of a given file in the current file in just one line of code. There is no need to copy paste the entire code in the current file. The disadvantage of this statement is that if it does not find the included file which is essential for the specified task, it will still execute the program. The syntax of **include** statement is as follows:

```
include 'file_name.extension';
```

In the given syntax, **include** is the keyword used to include a required file. The **file_name.extension** is the required file which is to be included in the current file.

For example:

```
<?php
        include 'example.php';
        // PHP code
?>
```

In the given example, **include** is the keyword used to include **example.php** file in the current program.

The require Statement

The working of the **require** statement is same as of the **include** statement with the only difference that if the required file is missing, it will not execute the program. So if it is important to include

Functions, Classes, and Objects

a file in the program, it is better to use the **require** statement in place of the **include** statement. The syntax of the **require** statement is as follows:

```
require 'file_name.extension';
```

In the given syntax, **require** is the keyword used to include a required file. The **file_name.extension** is the required file which is to be included in the current file.

Example 5

The following program will illustrate the use of the **include** and **require** statements. In this program, two files are included and the output is displayed in the browser.

The *header.php* file for inclusion.

```
<?php                                           1
    echo "<p><b>Hello User</b></p>"             2
?>                                              3
```

The *footer.php* file for inclusion.

```
<?php                                                          1
    echo "<p>Copyright &copy;".date("Y")." CADCIM</p>"         2
?>                                                             3
```

The *ch7-example5.php* program file will include the two files: *header.php* and *footer.php*.

```
<!Doctype html>                                              1
<html>                                                       2
<head>                                                       3
<title>File inclusion</title>                                4
</head>                                                      5
<body>                                                       6
<?php                                                        7
    include 'header.php';                                    8
        echo "This is the PHP code";                         9
        echo "<br> It includes 2 external files as follows:";  10
        echo "<br>1. header.php";                            11
        echo "<br>2. footer.php";                            12
    require 'footer.php';                                    13
?>                                                           14
</body>                                                      15
</html>                                                      16
```

Explanation (Footer.php)
Line 2
echo "<p><b>Copyright ©".date("Y"). " Cadcim</b></p>";
In this line, **©** is the HTML keyword to draw the copyright symbol in the browser, **date()**

is the function used to display the current date, inside the parentheses of function, **"Y"** displays the current year.

Explanation (ch7-example5.php)
Line 8
include 'header.php';
In this line, **include** is the keyword used to load all the content of the given file in the current file. Here, **header.php** file is the required file which is included.

Line 13
require 'footer.php';
In this line, **require** is the keyword used to load all the content of required file in the current file. Here, **footer.php** file is the required file which is included.

The output of Example 5 is displayed in Figure 7-5.

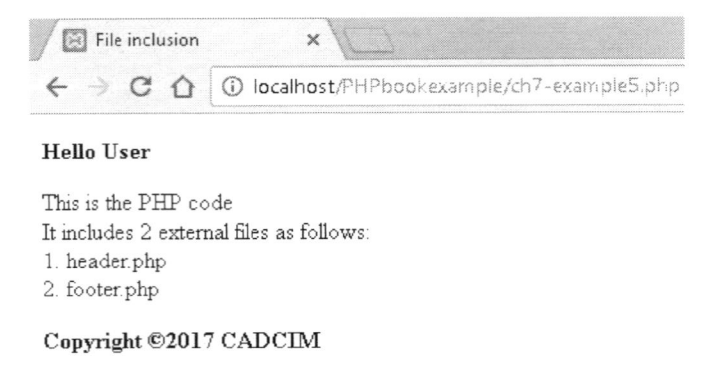

Figure 7-5 The output of Example 5

CLASSES
A class is an user-defined data type and is a collection of data and methods (functions). It acts as a blueprint or prototype in the creation of objects. These objects are known as the instances of a class having specific data type. The data in a class specifies the nature of a class, whereas the methods(functions) are used to operate on the data inside a class. Both the data and methods are known as the members of a class. The motive behind using a class is to encapsulate the data and methods into a single unit so that the data members can be accessed only through a well-defined interface. This process is known as data hiding.

Declaring a Class
A class is declared by using the **class** keyword with the class name. The class name should be a valid identifier. The class definition consists of data members and methods. The syntax for declaring a class is as follows:

```
class class_name
{
    // property(variable) declaration
        ----------;
        ----------;
```

```
        //method(function) declaration;
        {
                //body of method
                ----------;
                ----------;
        }
}
```

In the given syntax, the declaration of the class begins with the **class** keyword followed by a **class_name** which is an identifier given by the programmer to specify the name of the class. The body of the class is enclosed within the curly braces {}.

The functions used in a class are known as methods and the variables used in a class are known as properties.

Property and Method Scope

The property and method scope specifies the visibility of the properties or the methods of a class. There are three keywords used to specify the visibility of method and function which are:

a. **public**
b. **protected**
c. **private**

You can use any of the three keywords to specify the visibility of the properties and methods. These keywords are discussed next.

public

The **public** methods or properties of a class can be accessed by the members of the same class and by the members of the other classes. So it means the method or the property declared as **public** can be accessed from anywhere in the program.

The syntax for declaring **public** property is as follows:

```
public $variable = 'string';
```

In the given syntax, the **$variable** is the property which is declared as public by prefixing it with the **public** keyword. This specifies that the **$variable** property can be accessed from anywhere in the program.

The syntax for declaring **public** method is as follows:

```
public function MyFunc() { }
```

In the given syntax, the **MyFunc()** is the method which is declared as public by prefixing it with the **public** keyword. This specifies that the **MyFunc()** method can be accessed from anywhere in the program.

protected

The **protected** methods or the properties of a class can be accessed by members of the same class and by the inheriting classes.

The syntax for declaring the **protected** property is as follows:

```
protected $variable = 'string';
```

In the given syntax, **$variable** is the property which is declared as protected by prefixing it with the **protected** keyword. This specifies that the **$variable** property can be accessed from the same class or by the inheriting classes in the program.

The syntax for declaring the **protected** method is as follows:

```
protected function MyFunc() { }
```

In the given syntax, **MyFunc()** is the method which is declared as protected by prefixing it with the **protected** keyword. This specifies that the **MyFunc()** method can be accessed from the same class or by the inheriting classes in the program.

> **Note**
> *You will learn about inheritance later in this chapter.*

private

The **private** methods or the properties of a class can only be accessed by the members of the same class.

The syntax for declaring the **private** property is as follows:

```
private $variable = 'string';
```

In the given syntax, **$variable** is the property which is declared as private by prefixing it with **private** keyword. This specifies that the **$variable** property can be accessed only by the members of the same class.

The syntax for declaring **public** method is as follows:

```
public function MyFunc() { }
```

In the given syntax, **MyFunc()** is the method which is declared as private by prefixing it with the **private** keyword. This specifies that the **MyFunc()** method can be accessed only by the members of the same class.

OBJECTS

In object-oriented programming, a problem is divided into certain basic entities called objects. In this type of programming, all communication is carried out between the objects. When a program is executed, the objects interact with each other by sending messages. The objects contain the data and the functions that can be used to manipulate data.

An object is defined as an instance or a physical instantiation of a class. It is also known as a living entity within a program. When an object is created within a class, it maintains its own copy of instance variables that are defined inside the class. A class provides certain attributes and each object can have different values for those attributes. Therefore, each object of a class is uniquely identified.

Creating an Object

After the declaration of a class, you can create the objects of that class by using the class name with the **new** keyword. The syntax of creating an object is as follows:

```
$obj = new class_name;
```

In the given syntax, **class_name** represents the name of the class. The object is created by assigning the **class_name** prefixed with the **new** keyword to the **$obj** variable. After the assignment of **new class_name**, the variable **$obj** acts as the object of the specified class. So here, **$obj** represents an object of **class_name** class.

Accessing Members Using Objects

The **objects** are used to access the members of a class using arrow operator (**->**). The syntax for accessing a member using **objects** is as follows:

```
$obj->member;
```

In the given syntax, **$obj** is representing an object. The arrow operator (**->**) is used with the object to access the member. Here, **member** can be a property or a method of the class.

The syntax to access the property of the class is as follows:

```
$obj->prop; //line 1
$obj->prop = "value"; //line 2
```

There are two syntax to access the property of a class. In the line 1, **$obj** represents the object and **prop** represents the property name without **$** (dollar) sign. This syntax is used if a value is already assigned to the property. In the other case, the second syntax is used which is line 2 where value is assigned while accessing the property.

Example 6

The following program will illustrate the use of **class** and **object**. In this program, the values of the properties are accessed using the objects of a class and the output is displayed in the browser.

```
<!Doctype html>                                                     1
<html>                                                              2
<head>                                                              3
```

```
<title>Accessing property</title>                              4
</head>                                                         5
<body>                                                          6
<?php                                                           7
   class prop                                                   8
   {                                                            9
     public $property = "The value of \$property is accessed   10
                        by using \$var object";
     public $property2;                                        11
   }                                                           12
   $var = new prop;                                            13
   $var2 = new prop;                                           14
   echo $var->property;                                        15
   echo "<br>";                                                16
   echo $var2->property2 = "The value of \$property2 is        17
                        by accessed using \$var2 object";
?>                                                             18
</body>                                                        19
</html>                                                        20
```

Explanation

Line 8
class prop
In this line, **class** is the keyword and **prop** is the name of the class.

Line 9
{
This line indicates the start of the body of the **prop** class.

Line 10
public $property = "The value of \$property is accessed by using \$var object";
In this line, **$property** is the property which is declared as public by prefixing it with **public** keyword. This specifies that the **$property** property can be accessed from any part of the program. The **$property** property holds a string type value.

Line 11
public $property2;
In this line, **$property2** is the property which is declared as public by prefixing it with **public** keyword. This specifies that the **$property2** property can be accessed from any part of the program. Here, no value is assigned to this property.

Line 12
}
This line indicates the end of the body of the **prop** class.

Line 13 and Line 14
$var = new prop;

Functions, Classes, and Objects

$var2 = new prop;

In these lines, the **$var** and **$var2** are the objects of the **prop** class created by using the **new** keyword.

Line 15
echo $var->property;
In this line, **property** is the property name without the **$** sign. This property is accessed by using the **$var** object with the arrow operator (**->**).

This line will display the following in the browser:

The value of $property is accessed by using $var object

Line 17
echo $var2->property2 = "The value of \$property2 is accessed by using \$var2 object";
In this line, **property2** is the property name without the **$** sign. This property is accessed by using the **$var2** object with the arrow operator (**->**). Here, the value is assigned to the **$property2** property at the time of accessing the property.

This line will display the following in the browser:

The value of $property2 is accessed by using $var2 object

The output of Example 6 is displayed in Figure 7-6.

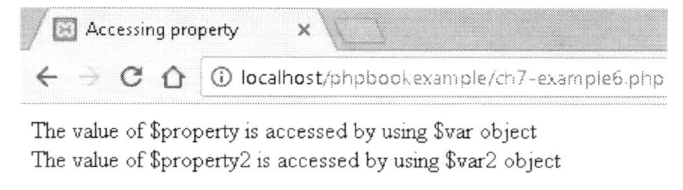

Figure 7-6 The output of Example 6

The syntax to access the method of the class is as follows:

```
$obj->method();
```

In the given syntax, **$obj** represents the object and **method()** represents the method. The arrow operator (**->**) is used with the object to access the method.

For example:

```
<?php
    class world
    {
        function user()
        {
            echo "Hello User!";
        }
```

```
            }
        $var = new world;
        $var->user();
?>
```

In the given example, **$var** is the object and **user()** is the method. The **$var** object is used with the arrow operator (**->**) to access the **user()** method.

OBJECT CLONING

Every object is uniquely identified in PHP. But if we create a copy of an object then its properties also get completely copied by its reference. For example, if object1 is copied to object2 then they get linked. Whenever there will be change in the value of any linked object that is either object1 or object2, the same result will be displayed in the other. Therefore through copying object the same output can get generated for multiple objects. This can be avoided by cloning an object instead of copying an object.

Cloning an object creates copy of an object without referencing the main object. This means that any change in the value of one object will not affect the value of another object. The clone of an object is created by using the **clone** keyword.

The syntax of an object cloning is as follows:

```
$CopyOfObject = clone $object;
```

In the given syntax, **$object** is the main object which will get copied to **$CopyOfObject** by using **clone** keyword. Here, **$CopyOfObject** represents another object.

Example 7

The following program will illustrate object cloning in PHP. In this program, an object is copied directly and by using the **clone** keyword and the output is displayed in the browser.

```
<!Doctype html>                                      1
<html>                                               2
<head>                                               3
<title>Object cloning</title>                        4
</head>                                              5
<body>                                               6
<?php                                                7
    class object_cloning                             8
    {                                                9
        public $gesture;                            10
    }                                               11
    $var = new object_cloning;                      12
    $var->gesture = "Hello main object";            13
    $var2 = $var; //copy of object                  14
    $var2->gesture = "Hello copy object";           15
```

Functions, Classes, and Objects 7-21

```
            $var3 = clone $var; //clone of object              16
            $var3->gesture = "Hello clone object";             17
            echo "orignal value of main-object is <b>Hello main 18
                object</b>.<br>";
            echo "orignal value of copy-object is <b>Hello copy 19
                object</b>. <br>";
            echo "orignal value of clone-object is <b>Hello clone 20
                object</b>. <br>";
            echo "<b> Values:</b> <br>";                       21
            echo "main-object = <b>" .$var->gesture."</b><br>"; 22
            echo "copy-object = <b>" .$var2->gesture."</b><br>"; 23
            echo "clone-object = <b>" .$var3->gesture."</b><br>"; 24
        ?>                                                     25
    </body>                                                    26
</html>                                                        27
```

Explanation
Line 11
public $gesture;
In this line, **$gesture** is the property which is declared as public by prefixing it with **public** keyword. This specifies that the **$gesture** property can be accessed from any part of the program. Here, no value is assigned to this property.

Line 12
$var = new object_cloning;
In this line, **$var** is an object of class **object_cloning** created by using the **new** keyword.

Line 13
$var->gesture = "Hello main object";
In this line, **gesture** is the property name without the **$** sign. This property is accessed by using the **$var** object with the arrow operator (**->**). Here, the value is assigned to the **$gesture** property at the time of accessing the property.

Line 14
$var2 = $var;
In this line, **$var2** is an object which will copy **$var** object by its reference.

Line 15
$var2->gesture = "Hello copy object";
In this line, **gesture** is the property name without the **$** sign. This property is accessed by using the **$var2** object with the arrow operator (**->**). Here, the value is assigned to the **$gesture** property at the time of accessing the property.

Line 16
$var3 = clone $var;
In this line, **$var3** is an object which will copy **$var** object by using **clone** keyword.

Line 17
$var3->gesture = "Hello clone object";
In this line, **gesture** is the property name without the **$** sign. This property is accessed by using the **$var3** object with the arrow operator (**->**). Here, the value is assigned to the **$gesture** property at the time of accessing the property.

The output of Example 7 is displayed in Figure 7-7.

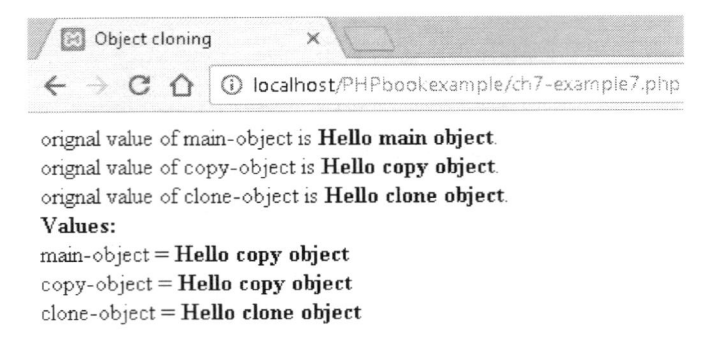

Figure 7-7 The output of Example 7

CONSTRUCTOR

A constructor is a special method (function) used to initialize the objects of a class. You can pass multiple parameters in the constructor while creating a new object. The **__construct()** method is the in-built constructor method of a class. The syntax of constructor is as follows:

```
class Class_name {
    function __construct() {
                    //body of constructor method
                    }
                }
```

In the given syntax, **Class_name** represents the name of class, **function** is the keyword used to create method, and **__construct()** is the constructor method of the **class_name** class.

> **Note**
> In the past, the name of constructor was the same as the name of class. This old format is deprecated in PHP 7. Now, the standard name of constructor is **__construct()**.

DESTRUCTOR

A destructor is also a special method used to destroy the objects that have been initialized by a constructor and are no longer required. The **__destruct()** method is the in-built destructor method of a class. The syntax of destructor is as follows:

```
class Class_name {
    function __construct()
            {
                    //body of constructor method
```

Functions, Classes, and Objects

```
        }
function __destruct()
        {
                //body of destruct method
        }
    }
```

In the given syntax, **Class_name** represents the name of class and **function** is the keyword used to create method. Here, **__construct()** is the constructor method and **__destruct()** is the destructor method of the **class_name** class.

Example 8

The following program will illustrate the use of constructor and destructor. The program will create and destroy two objects of a class and the output is displayed in the browser.

```
<!Doctype html>                                          1
<html>                                                   2
<head>                                                   3
<title>Constructor and Destructor</title>                4
</head>                                                  5
<body>                                                   6
<?php                                                    7
    class objects                                        8
        {                                                9
            public $val = "Object";                     10
            public function __construct($val)           11
            {                                           12
                echo "Object is created<br>";           13
                $this->val = $val;                      14
            }                                           15
            public function __destruct()                16
            {                                           17
                echo "Object is destroyed<br>";         18
            }                                           19
        }                                               20
    $new_val = new objects("Object");                   21
    echo $new_val->val. " is alive <br>";               22
?>                                                      23
</body>                                                 24
</html>                                                 25
```

Explanation
Line 11
public $val = "Object";
In this line, **Object** is a string type value assigned to the **$val** property (variable) and the property is declared as public by using the **public** keyword.

Line 12
public function __construct($val)
In this line, **function** is the keyword used to create method and **__construct($val)** is the parameterized constructor method of the **objects** class. Here, **$val** is the parameter passed inside the parentheses of constructor **__construct()**. It will initialize the object of **objects** class.

Line 14
$this->val = $val;
In this line, **$this** is the pre-defined variable used to access the current object. The **val** is the property name without the **$** sign and **$val** property is assigned to it. After the execution of this line, the control will be passed to Line 21 and Line 22.

Line 16
public function __destruct()
In this line, **function** is the keyword used to create method and **__destruct()** is the destructor method of the **objects** class which will destroy the object. It will be executed in the end when object initialized by a constructor is no longer required.

Line 21
$new_val = new objects("Object");
In this line, the **$new_val** is an object of class **objects** created by using the **new** keyword. Here, **Object** is the value passed to the object created.

Line 22
**echo $new_val->val. " is alive
" ;**
In this line, **val** is the property name without the **$** sign. The **$val** property is accessed by using the **$new_val** object with the arrow operator (**->**).

This line will display the following in the browser:

Object is alive

The output of Example 8 is displayed in Figure 7-8.

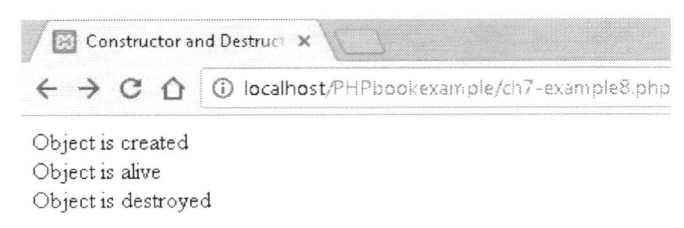

Figure 7-8 The output of Example 8

CLASS CONSTANT
The working of class constant is same as the constant which you learned in the previous chapter with the only difference that the constant in the class is declared using the **const** keyword instead of **define()** function. The scope of class constant is limited to the class in which it is declared.

Functions, Classes, and Objects

The syntax of class constant is as follows:

```
class Class_name
{
    const NAME = 'value';
}
```

In the given syntax, **const** is the keyword used to define constant inside the class, **NAME** represents the constant name, and **value** is the value of the constant. The value of constant can be an integer, boolean, string, float, NULL, or an array type.

The name of the class followed by double colon(::) also known as scope resolution operator along with the name of the class constant is used to return the class constant value outside the class.

For example:

```
<?php
    class Const_class
        {
            const HELLO = 'Hello User';
        }
    echo Const_class::HELLO;
?>
```

In the given example, **Const_class** is the class name. Inside the class, a constant is defined by using the **const** keyword along with constant name **HELLO**. The value assigned to constant is **Hello User**. The **echo** statement is used to display the constant value where **Const_class::HELLO** is used to return the value of constant.

To return the value of constant inside the class, the keyword **self** is used followed by scope resolution(::) operator and class constant name. For example, **self::const_name;** where **const_name** is the class constant name.

STATIC METHODS AND PROPERTIES

Declaring a method or property of a class as static makes them accessible directly without creating or instantiating an object of that class. You can create static methods and properties by using the **static** keyword. By default, the visibility of static methods and properties is public. The static methods and properties are linked to the class in which it is declared. The value of static property can be changed multiple times in a program. But in a constant property, the value remains fixed throughout the program if once defined for a particular property.

The syntax of static property is as follows:

```
public static $static_property;
```

In the given syntax, **public** is the keyword which is used to define the visibility of the property to be public. **$static_property** is the property which is declared as static property by using the **static** keyword.

The name of the class followed by the scope resolution operator(::) along with the name of the property is used to call the static property outside the class.

For example:

```
class prop
{
   public static $var = 5; //Static variable or property
}
echo prop::$var;
```

In the given example, **public** is the keyword used to define the visibility of the property to be public. **$var** is the property which is declared as static property by using the **static** keyword inside the class **prop** holding integer type value 5. The **prop::$var** is used to call the static property where **prop** is the class name followed by scope resolution operator(::) along with **$var** static property.

To call the value of static property inside the class, the keyword **self** is used followed by scope resolution operator(::) and static property name. For example, **self::$var;** where **$var** is the static property.

The syntax of static method is as follows:

```
public static function static_method()
        {
                // body of method or function
        }
```

In the given syntax, **public** is the keyword used to define the visibility of the method to be public. The **static_method()** is the method which is declared as static method by using the **static** keyword.

The name of the class followed by the scope resolution operator(::) along with the name of the method is used to call the static method outside the class.

For example:

```
<?php
class func
{
   static function test($var1 , $var2)
   {
        echo "$var1  $var2";
   }
}
func::test("Hello" , "User");
?>
```

Functions, Classes, and Objects

In the given example, **function** is the keyword used to create method in the class. The **test($var1, $var2)** is the parameterized method which is declared as static method by using the **static** keyword. Here, **$var1** and **$var2** are the two parameters passed inside the static method. By default, the visibility of the method is public as it is not declared in the example. The **func::test("Hello" , "User");** is used to call the static method where **func** is the class name followed by scope resolution operator(::) along with static method **test()**. Here, the two values **Hello** and **User** are passed to the method.

To call the value of static method inside the class, the keyword **self** is used followed by scope resolution operator(::) and static method name. For example, **self::test();** where **test()** is the static method.

Example 9

The following program will define class constant, static methods, and static properties. It will also call them inside as well as outside the class and the output is displayed in the browser.

```
<!Doctype html>                                              1
<html>                                                       2
<head>                                                       3
<title>Class constant and static</title>                     4
</head>                                                      5
<body>                                                       6
<?php                                                        7
    class const_static                                       8
    {                                                        9
            const FIRST_CONST = "Hello User";               10
            const SECOND_CONST = 10;                        11
            static $var = 5;                                12
            static $var2 = "The output is displayed";       13
        public static function test($var1 , $var2)          14
        {                                                   15
            echo "$var1  $var2 <br>";                       16
        }                                                   17
        static function test2()                             18
        {                                                   19
            echo "Welcome to CADCIM Technologies <br>";     20
        }                                                   21
        function showConstant()                             22
        {                                                   23
            echo self::FIRST_CONST . "<br>";                24
            self::test2();                                  25
            echo self::$var2 . "<br>";                      26
        }                                                   27
    }                                                       28
    $class = new const_static;                              29
    $class->showConstant();                                 30
    const_static::test("The integer" , "values are:");      31
```

```
            echo const_static::$var . "<br>";     // returns 5            32
            echo const_static::SECOND_CONST. "<br>";   // returns 10      33
            const_static::$var = 20;    // now equals 20                  34
            echo const_static::$var. "<br>";                              35
    ?>                                                                    36
    </body>                                                               37
    </html>                                                               38
```

Explanation
Line 10
const FIRST_CONST = "Hello User";
In this line, **const** is the keyword used to declare the constant inside the class, **FIRST_CONST** is the class constant name which holds the string type value **Hello User**. This value will remain constant throughout the program.

Line 11
const SECOND_CONST = 10;
In this line, **const** is the keyword used to declare the constant inside the class, **SECOND_CONST** is the class constant name which holds the integer type value 10. This value will remain constant throughout the program.

Line 12
static $var = 5;
In this line, **$var** is the method declared as static method using the **static** keyword. It holds integer type value 5 which can be changed if required.

Line 13
static $var2 = "The output is displayed";
In this line, **$var2** is the method declared as static method using the **static** keyword. It holds string type value **The output is displayed** which can be changed if required.

Line 14
public static function test($var1 , $var2)
In this line, **function** is the keyword used to create method in the class. The **test($var1, $var2)** is the parameterized method which is declared as static method by using the **static** keyword. Here, **$var1** and **$var2** are the two parameters passed inside the static method. Here, **public** is the keyword used to define the visibility of the method to be public.

Line 18
static function test2()
In this line, **function** is the keyword used to create method in the class. **test2()** is the method which is declared as static method by using the **static** keyword. Here, by default the visibility of the method is public as it is not declared.

Line 22
function showConstant()
In this line, **ShowConstant()** is the method of **const_static** class which is created by using **function** keyword.

Functions, Classes, and Objects

7-29

Line 24
echo self::FIRST_CONST . "<br>";
In this line, **echo** statement is used to display the value of class constant. **self::FIRST_CONST** is used to call the value of class constant defined in Line 10. Here, **self** is the keyword used to call the class constant inside the class followed by the scope resolution operator (::) and class constant name **FIRST_CONST**.

This line will display the following in the browser:

Hello User

Line 25
self::test2();
In this line, **self::test2();** is used to call the static method declared in Line 18. Here, **self** is the keyword used to call the static method inside the class followed by the scope resolution operator (::) and static method name **test2()**.

Line 26
echo self::$var2 . "<br>";
In this line, **self::$var2** is used to display the value of static **$var2** property that is defined in Line 13 inside the **const_static** class. Here, **self** is the keyword used to call the static property inside the class followed by the scope resolution operator (::) and static **$var2** property name.

This line will display the following in the browser:

The output is displayed

Line 29
$class = new const_static;
In this line, **$class** is the object of class **const_static** created by using the **new** keyword.

Line 30
$class->showConstant();
In this line, **$class** is the object and **showConstant()** is the method. The **$class** object is used with the arrow operator (**->**) to access the **showConstant()** method declared in Line 22.

Line 31
const_static::test("The integer" , "values are:");
In this line, **const_static** is the class name followed by **::** operator and **test()** method. It will call the static method **test()** of class **const_static** declared in Line 14. Here, two string type values are passed to the **test()** method.

Line 32
echo const_static::$var . "<br>";
In this line, **echo** statement is used to display the value of static property declared inside the class **const_static**. The **const_static::$var** is used to call the value of static property defined in Line 13. Here, **const_static** is the class name used to call the static property outside the class followed by the scope resolution operator (::) and static property name **$var2**.

This line will display the following in the browser:

5

Line 33
echo const_static::SECOND_CONST . "<br>";
In this line, **echo** statement is used to display the value of class constant. The **const_static::SECOND_CONST** is used to call the value of class constant defined in Line 11. Here, **const_static** is the keyword used to call the class constant outside the class followed by the scope resolution operator (**::**) and class constant name **SECOND_CONST**.

This line will display the following in the browser:

10

The output of Example 9 is displayed in Figure 7-9.

Figure 7-9 The output of Example 9

INHERITANCE

Different kind of objects often have certain amount of properties in common. Inheritance is a key feature of object oriented programming. It gives you the benefit of reusing methods and properties of a class and therefore, it reduces the lines of code in a PHP program. Inheritance is the process by which one object can acquire the properties of another object.

Technically, inheritance is a technique of deriving new class from an existing class by reusing the features (properties and methods) of the existing class in that new class. In addition to the inherited features, new class can also have some additional new features.

The class that inherits the property and methods of another class is known as derived class. The derived class is also known as sub class or child class and the class from which the derive class is derived is known as super class or base class or parent class.

The **extends** keyword is used to perform inheritance in PHP. In inheritance, the child class can only inherit all the public and protected features (methods and properties) of the parent class. But, it cannot inherit the private methods and properties of the parent class.

Functions, Classes, and Objects

The syntax of inheritance in PHP is as follows:

```
class Parent {
  // The body of Parent class
}

class Child extends Parent {
  // The body of derived class
}
```

In the given syntax, **Parent** represents the name of the base class, **Child** represents the name of the derived class. Here, the class **Child** is derived from base class **Parent** by using the **extends** keyword. The class **Child** will inherit all the non-private methods and the properties of base class **Parent**.

Example 10

The following program will illustrate the use of inheritance. The program will calculate the area of a rectangle and the output is displayed in the browser.

```
<!Doctype html>                                                 1
<html>                                                          2
<head>                                                          3
<title>Inheritance</title>                                      4
</head>                                                         5
<body>                                                          6
<?php                                                           7
    class Rectangle {                                           8
        public $length;                                         9
        public $width;                                          10
        public function __construct($length, $width)            11
        {                                                       12
            $this->length = $length;                            13
            $this->width = $width;                              14
        }                                                       15
    }                                                           16
    class rect_area extends Rectangle {                         17
        public function GetArea()                               18
        {                                                       19
            return $this->length * $this->width;                20
        }                                                       21
    }                                                           22
    $res = new rect_area(10, 5);                                23
echo 'The length of rectangle is <b>'.$res->length.'</b><br>';  24
echo 'The width of rectangle is <b>'.$res->width.'</b><br>';    25
echo 'Area of rectangle is <b>'.$res->GetArea().'</b><br>';     26
?>                                                              27
</body>                                                         28
</html>                                                         29
```

Explanation

Line 11

public function __construct($length, $width)

In this line, **__construct($val)** is the parameterized constructor method of the class **Rectangle**. Here, **$length** and **$width** are the parameters passed inside the parentheses of constructor **__construct()**. It will initialize the object of class **Rectangle**.

Line 13 and Line 14

$this->length = $length;
$this->width = $width;

In these lines, **$this** is the pre-defined variable used to access the current object. The **length** and **width** are the name of the properties without the **$** sign and in this case, **$length** and **$width** properties are assigned to these objects, respectively.

Line 17

class rect_area extends Rectangle {

In this line, **rect_area** is the derived class name which is derived from the **Rectangle** parent class by using the **extends** keyword. Here, **rect_area** class will inherit all the public methods and properties of **Rectangle** class.

Lines 18 to 21

public function GetArea()
{
    return $this->length * $this->width;
}

These lines contain the definition of the method **GetArea()** of class **rect_area**. In the body of the method, the public properties **$length** and **$width** of the base class **Rectangle** is accessed directly through **$this** keyword. The multiplication operation is performed between both the properties. After multiplication, the resultant value is returned with the help of **return** keyword.

Line 23

$res = new rect_area(10, 5);

In this line, **$res** is the instance of class **rect_area**. The class **rect_area** can access the methods and properties of class **Rectangle**. So the two integer values 10 and 5 passed inside the parentheses of class **rect_area** are assigned to **$length** and **$width** properties of class **Rectangle** at the time of instantiation.

The output of Example 10 is displayed in Figure 7-10.

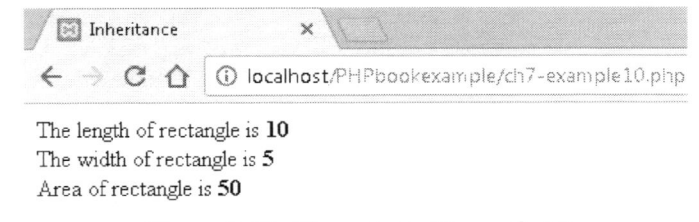

Figure 7-10 The output of Example 10

The parent Keyword

To call the value of static method of parent class inside the child class, the keyword **parent** is used followed by the scope resolution operator(::) and static method name. For example, **parent::test();** where **test()** is the static method of parent class. The working of **parent** keyword is exactly same as **self** keyword with the only difference that it call the methods and properties of base class.

The **parent** keyword can also be used to differentiate between constructors of parent and child class. To call the constructor of parent class, the **parent** keyword can be used in a similar way as discussed before. For example, **parent::__construct();** where **__construct** is the constructor of parent class.

If a parent class and derived class both have the methods with same name then that method gets overridden. In such cases, to call the method of parent class, **parent** keyword is used which is followed by the scope resolution operator(::) and the name of the parent class method. Whereas **self** keyword is used to call the method of the existing class.

Example 11

The following program will illustrate the use of inheritance with **parent** keyword. The program will prevent overriding of method and constructor with the help of **parent** keyword and the output is displayed in the browser.

```
<!Doctype html>                                                          1
<html>                                                                   2
<head>                                                                   3
<title>parent keyword</title>                                            4
</head>                                                                  5
<body>                                                                   6
<?php                                                                    7
class A {                                                                8
function __construct()                                                   9
 {                                                                      10
  print "I am output of <b>parent class</b> constructor.<br>";          11
 }                                                                      12
function Samefunc()                                                     13
 {                                                                      14
   echo "I am output of method <b>Samefunc()</b>                        15
   of parent class <b>A</b>.<br>";
 }                                                                      16
}                                                                       17
class B extends A {                                                     18
function __construct()                                                  19
 {                                                                      20
   parent::__construct();                                               21
   print "I am output of <b>child class</b> constructor.<br>";          22
 }                                                                      23
function Samefunc()                                                     24
 {                                                                      25
```

```
        echo "I am output of method <b>Samefunc()</b>           26
        of child class <b>B</b>.<br>";
        parent::Samefunc();                                      27
    }                                                            28
}                                                                29
$b = new B;                                                      30
$b->Samefunc();                                                  31
?>                                                               32
</body>                                                          33
</html>                                                          34
```

Explanation

Line 18
class B extends A {
In this line, **B** is the derived class name which is derived from the **A** parent class by using the **extends** keyword. Here, class **B** will inherit all the public methods and properties of class **A**.

Lines 19 to 23
function __construct()
{
       parent::__construct();
       **print " I am output of child class constructor.
";**
}
These lines define the constructor **__construct()** of class **B**. In the body of constructor, the **parent::__construct();** is calling the constructor of parent class **A** declared in Line 9 by using the keyword **parent** followed by **::** operator and constructor name **__construct()**. Here, the use of **parent** keyword is preventing the overriding of constructors. So, this function will execute both the **print** statements of class **A** and class **B** constructors.

Lines 24 to 28
function Samefunc()
{
   echo "I am output of method Samefunc() of child class B.
";
   parent::Samefunc();
}
These lines define the method **Samefunc()** of class **B**. In the body of the method, the **parent::Samefunc();** is calling the method of parent class **A** declared in Line 13 by using the keyword **parent** followed by **::** operator and method name **Samefunc()**. Here, the use of **parent** keyword is preventing the overriding of methods. So this function will execute both the **echo** statement of class **A** and class **B** method **Samefunc()** when the object of class **B** will be called in Line 31.

Line 30
$b = new B;
In this line, the **$b** is an object of class **B** created by using the **new** keyword.

Functions, Classes, and Objects

Line 31
$b->Samefunc();
In this line, object **$b** is calling the **Samefunc()** method of **B** class which in turn will call the **Samefunc()** method of **A** class because **B** class has inherited all the methods of **A** class.

The output of Example 11 is displayed in Figure 7-11.

I am output of **parent class** constructor.
I am output of **child class** constructor.
I am output of method **Samefunc()** of child class **B**.
I am output of method **Samefunc()** of parent class **A**.

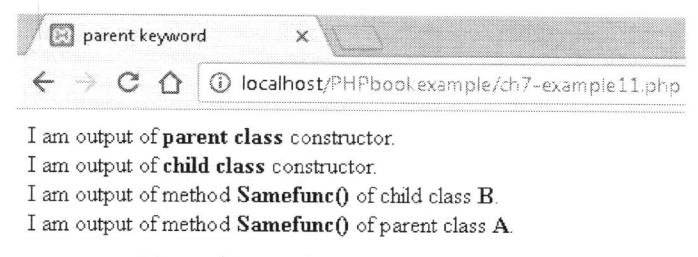

Figure 7-11 *The output of Example 11*

The final Keyword

The **final** keyword can be prefixed with the method of base class to prevent overriding of the method in derived class. It is also known as final method. The syntax of final method is as follows:

```
class Base_cl
{
   final function unique()
   {
        //Body of final method
   }
}
```

In the given syntax, **unique()** represents the method of base class **Base_cl**. The **final** keyword is used to prevent the overriding of method **unique()**.

After using the **final** keyword with the method declared in the base class if the method in derived class is declared with the same name, it will throw an error.

You can also declare a base class as final class to prevent overriding of the methods declared in the base class by prefixing the class with **final** keyword. In this case, there is no need to separately specify the method of base class to be the final method.

The syntax of final class is as follows:

```
final class Base_cl
{
    function unique()
    {
        //Body of method
    }
    function unique2()
```

```
        {
            //Body of method.
        }
}
```

In the given syntax, **unique()** and **unique2()** represent the methods of base class **Base_cl**. The **final** keyword is used to prevent the overriding of methods **unique()** and **unique2()** of class **Base_cl**.

After using the **final** keyword with the base class, if the method in the derived class is declared with the name same as one of the methods in the base class then it will throw an error.

Example 12

The following program will illustrate the use of inheritance with the **final** keyword. The program will prevent overriding of method with the help of **final** keyword and the output is displayed in the browser.

```
<!Doctype html>                                                        1
<html>                                                                 2
<head>                                                                 3
<title>final keyword</title>                                           4
</head>                                                                5
<body>                                                                 6
<?php                                                                  7
    class A {                                                          8
function __construct()                                                 9
{                                                                      10
  print "I am output of <b>parent class</b> constructor.<br>";         11
}                                                                      12
final function Samefunc()                                              13
{                                                                      14
   echo "I am output of method <b>Samefunc()</b>                       15
   of parent class <b>A</b>.<br>";
}                                                                      16
}                                                                      17
class B extends A {                                                    18
function __construct()                                                 19
{                                                                      20
   parent::__construct();                                              21
   print "I am output of <b>child class</b> constructor.<br>";         22
}                                                                      23
function Samefunc()                                                    24
{                                                                      25
   echo "I am output of method <b>Samefunc()</b>                       26
   of child class <b>B</b>.<br>";
   parent::Samefunc();                                                 27
}                                                                      28
}                                                                      29
```

Functions, Classes, and Objects

```
$b = new B;
$b->Samefunc();
?>
</body>
</html>
```
30
31
32
33
34

Explanation

The working of this program is the same as the previous programming example (Example 11) except that in Line 13 the **final** keyword is used with the method **samefunc()** of parent class **A**. So this method cannot override in child class **B**. This example will output error displaying the following message in the browser:

Fatal error: Cannot override final method A::Samefunc() in C:\xampp\htdocs\PHPbookexample\ch7-example12.php on line 33

The output of Example 12 is displayed in Figure 7-12.

Figure 7-12 The output of Example 12

The instanceof Operator

Before using any object, the **instanceof** operator can be used to check whether an object is an instance of the specified class or subclass. If the object is of the specified class, then the **instanceof** operator evaluates to true otherwise the result is false.

The syntax for the **instanceof** operator is as follows:

```
$object_name instanceof class_name
```

In the given syntax, **$object_name** represents the object name. The **instanceof** is the operator and the **class_name** is the name of class whose instance is to be checked.

Example 13

The following program will check whether the object is an instance of the class by using the **instanceof** operator and the output is displayed in the browser.

```
<!Doctype html>
<html>
<head>
<title>instanceof operator</title>
</head>
<body>
<?php
```
1
2
3
4
5
6
7

```
            class firstClass                                 8
            {                                                9
                //Body of class firstClass                  10
            }                                               11
            class secondClass extends firstClass            12
            {                                               13
                //Body of class secondClass                 14
            }                                               15
        $a = new secondClass;                               16
        var_dump($a instanceof secondClass);                17
        var_dump($a instanceof firstClass);                 18
        var_dump(!($a instanceof firstClass));              19
    ?>                                                      20
    </body>                                                 21
    </html>                                                 22
```

Explanation
Line 17
var_dump($a instanceof secondClass);
In this line, the **instanceof** operator is checking whether the **$a** object is an instance of the class **secondClass**.

This line will display the following in the browser:

bool(true)

The working of Line 18 and Line 19 is same as Line 17.

The output of Example 13 is displayed in Figure 7-13.

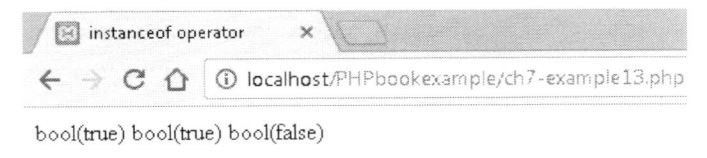

bool(true) bool(true) bool(false)

Figure 7-13 The output of Example 13

INTERFACE
An interface is a blueprint of a class. It is very much similar to the class but it contains only abstract method. An abstract method is a method that is declared but contains no implementation. In other words, an interface defines the task to be performed by the class but it does not specify the procedure to perform it. The interface may also contain constants but it does not contain any constructor because it cannot be instantiated. Interfaces can only be implemented by classes or can be extended by other interfaces. A single interface can be implemented by any number of classes and vice-versa. This means a class can implement multiple interfaces.

Declaring an Interface

You can declare an interface in the same way as you define a class except that you need to use the **interface** keyword in the definition statement, as shown in the following syntax:

```
interface interface_name
{
    public function();
    public function();
    -------
    -------
}
```

In this syntax, the declaration of interface begins with the keyword **interface** followed by the **interface_name** which is an identifier given by the programmer to specify the name of the interface. Here, **public** specifies the scope of the method. The scope of the method defined inside the interface body must be public. The methods inside an interface end with a semicolon and contain no implementation.

For example:

```
interface demo
{
    public function show( );
    public function sqr( );
}
```

In the given example, the **interface** is the keyword used to declare the interface and **demo** is the interface name. The interface **demo** contains two methods, **show()** and **sqr()** which are declared as **public**. The methods of the interface are not defined in the body of the interface.

Implementing an Interface

Once an interface has been declared, other classes can implement that interface by using the **implements** keyword in the class declaration statement. The syntax for implementing an interface is as follows:

```
class class_name [extends superclass] implements interface_name
{
    //Body of the class
}
```

In the given syntax, the class represented by **class_name** implements the interface that is represented by **interface_name**. If a class implements an interface, all methods declared inside the interface should be implemented by the class. Here, **extends superclass** is optional where **extends** is the keyword used to inherit the parent class and **superclass** represents the parent class.

A class can also implement more than one interface by using comma to separate the list of interfaces. The syntax for implementing more than one interfaces is as follows:

```
class class_name implements interface1, interface2, interfaceN
{
    //Body of the class
}
```

In the given syntax, **interface1**, **interface2**, and **interfaceN** represent the names of different interfaces in a program which can be implemented by a class.

> **Note**
> *A class cannot perform multiple inheritance. It means that a single class cannot inherit multiple classes. In PHP, multiple inheritance is possible only by using interface. This means a class can inherit multiple interfaces but not multiple classes.*

Extending an Interface

In this chapter, you have learned about inheritance. A class inherits the characteristics of another class. In the same way, the concept of inheritance can be applied on interfaces also. An interface can inherit the characteristics of another interface using the **extends** keyword. When an interface is implemented by a class and the interface inherits another interface, the class must provide the implementation for all methods of all interfaces that are inherited.

For example:

```
interface A
{
public function method1( );
}
interface B extends A
{
public function method2( );
}
class demo implements B
{
    public function method1( )
    {
            ----------;
            ----------;
    }
    public void method2( )
    {
            ----------;
            ----------;
    }
}
```

Functions, Classes, and Objects

In the given example, the interface **A** contains only one method **method1()** and the interface **B** also contains only one method **method2()**. Here, the interface **B** inherits the characteristics of the interface **A** by using the **extends** keyword and the class **demo** implements it. In this way, inside the demo class, both the methods, **method1( )** and **method2( )**, of the interfaces **A** and **B** are defined.

Example 14

The following program illustrates the use of extended interface. The program will perform certain mathematical operations on the given values and the output is displayed in the browser.

```php
<!Doctype html>                                              1
<html>                                                       2
<head>                                                       3
<title>extend and implement interface</title>                4
</head>                                                      5
<body>                                                       6
<?php                                                        7
   interface mathematical                                    8
     {                                                       9
        public function mul($num1, $num2);                  10
     }                                                      11
   interface remainder extends mathematical                 12
     {                                                      13
        public function rem($a, $b);                        14
     }                                                      15
   class Extend_interface implements remainder              16
     {                                                      17
        public $a, $b, $num1, $num2 ;                       18
        public function mul($num1, $num2)                   19
     {                                                      20
        $this->num1 = $num1;                                21
        $this->num2 = $num2;                                22
     }                                                      23
   public function rem($a, $b)                              24
     {                                                      26
        $this->a = $a;                                      27
        $this->b = $b;                                      28
     }                                                      29
   public function result()                                 30
    {                                                       31
     echo "The multiplication is: <b>".($this->num1 *       32
     $this->num2). "</b><br>";
     echo "The remainder is: <b>".($this->a % $this->b).   33
     "</b><br>";
    }                                                       34
  }                                                         35
  $res_obj1 = new Extend_interface;                         36
```

```
$res_obj1->mul(8 , 7);                          37
$res_obj1->rem(10 , 8);                         38
return $res_obj1->result();                     39
?>                                              40
</body>                                         41
</html>                                         42
```

Explanation

Lines 8
interface mathematical
In this line, **mathematical** is defined as an interface using the keyword **interface**.

Line 10
public function mul($num1, $num2);
This line contains the declaration part of the method **mul()** where **$num1** and **$num2** are the two parameters passed inside the parentheses of the method **mul()**. This method is declared inside the **mathematical** interface. The implementation part of this method will be defined by the class that implements the **mathematical** interface.

Line 12
interface remainder extends mathematical
In this line, **remainder** is defined as an interface by using the keyword **interface**. Also, it inherits another interface **mathematical** by using keyword **extends**.

Line 14
public function rem($a, $b);
This line contains the declaration part of the **rem()** method where **$a** and **$b** are the two parameters passed inside the parentheses of the method **rem()**. This method is declared inside the **remainder** interface. Therefore, it will be implemented by the class that implements the **remainder** interface.

Line 16
class Extend_interface implements remainder
In this line, the class **Extend_interface** implements the interface **remainder** by using the keyword **implements**. This class can implement all methods of both the interfaces, **remainder** and **mathematical**.

Lines 19 to 23
public function mul($num1, $num2)
 {
            $this->num1 = $num1;
            $this->num2 = $num2;
 }
These lines contain the implementation of the method **mul()** of the interface **mathematical**. Inside the body of method, **$this** is the pre-defined variable used to access the current object. Here, **num1** and **num2** are the property names without the $ sign, and **$num1** and **$num2** properties are assigned to them, respectively.

Lines 24 to 29
public function rem($a, $b)
{
        $this->a = $a;
        $this->b = $b;
}

These lines contain the implementation of the method **rem()** of the interface **remainder**. Inside the body of method, **$this** is the pre-defined variable used to access the current object. Here, **a** and **b** are the properties name without the **$** sign, and **$a** and **$b** properties are assigned to them, respectively.

Lines 30 to 34
public function result()
{
        echo "The multiplication is: " .($this->num1 * $this->num2)."
";
        echo "The remainder is: ".($this->a % $this->b). "<br>";
}

These lines contain the declaration of the method **result()** of the class **Extend_interface**. Inside the body of method, the public properties **$num1** and **$num2** of the interface **mathematical** are accessed directly through the **$this** keyword. The multiplication operation is performed between both the properties. And, the public properties **$a** and **$b** of the interface **remainder** are accessed directly through **$this** keyword. The remainder operation is performed between both the properties.

The output of Example 14 is displayed in Figure 7-14.

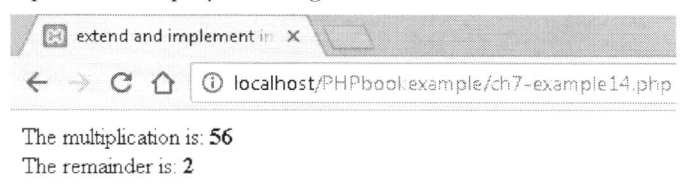

Figure 7-14 The output of Example 14

ANONYMOUS CLASS

When a class is declared without a class name, it is known as anonymous class. It is useful to create an object without creating a normal class. Anonymous class is introduced in PHP 7. It can be defined by using keyword **new class**. Anonymous class features are very similar to normal class. It can implement interfaces, extend classes, use constructor, and so on.

If you nest anonymous class inside the outer class (normal class) then the anonymous class cannot access any private or protected methods and properties of the outer class directly. The anonymous class can access the private properties of the outer class by using constructors. And it can also access the protected properties or methods of the outer class by extending the outer class.

Example 15

The following program illustrates the use of anonymous class. The program will perform the addition operation on 3 numbers by accessing the private and protected properties and methods of outer class inside the anonymous class and display the output in the browser.

```
<!Doctype html>                                                     1
<html>                                                              2
<head>                                                              3
<title>Anonymous class</title>                                      4
</head>                                                             5
<body>                                                              6
<?php                                                               7
class Normal                                                        8
{                                                                   9
   private $property = 20;                                         10
   protected $property2 = 30;                                      11
   protected function number()                                     12
   {                                                               13
       return 100;                                                 14
   }                                                               15
   public function anoy_func()                                     16
   {                                                               17
       return new class($this->property) extends Normal {          18
           private $property3;                                     19
           public function __construct($property)                  20
           {                                                       21
               $this->property3 = $property;                       22
           }                                                       23
       public function sum()                                       24
       { echo "The sum is ";                                       25
   return $this->property2 + $this->property3 + $this->number();   26
           }                                                       27
       };                                                          28
   }                                                               29
}                                                                  30
echo (new Normal)->anoy_func()->sum();                             31
?>                                                                 32
</body>                                                            33
</html>                                                            34
```

Explanation
Line 18
return new class($this->property) extends Normal {
In this line, the function **anoy_func()** declared in Line 16 is returning an anonymous class. Here, **new class** is the keyword used to create anonymous class. The anonymous class is extending the outer class **Normal** to access the protected property **$property2** and protected method **number()** in anonymous class.

Line 20
public function __construct($property)
In this line, the private property **$property** declared in Line 10 of outer class **Normal** is accessed by using constructor **__construct()** inside the anonymous class.

Line 31
echo (new Normal)->anoy_func()->sum();
In this line, the object of class **Normal** is called directly by using the **new** keyword which is further calling the functions **anoy_funct()** and **sum()** of anonymous class to display the result. This line will display the following in the browser:

The sum is 150

The output of Example 15 is displayed in Figure 7-15.

Figure 7-15 The output of Example 15

Self-Evaluation Test

Answer the following questions and then compare them to those given at the end of this chapter:

1. A _____ is a group of statements that perform a specific task and can be used multiple times in a program.

2. Function _____ are used to pass information to the function.

3. The _____ function is used to display the variable related information.

4. The _____ stands for Cryptographically Secure Pseudo-Random Number Generator.

5. The property and method scope specifies the _____ of the properties or the methods of a class.

6. The **random_int()** function is used to generate cryptographically secure pseudo-random bytes in PHP. (T/F)

7. A constructor is a special method which is used to initialize the objects of a class. (T/F)

8. A class can implement only one interface. (T/F)

9. An anonymous class is declared without a class name. (T/F)

Review Questions

Answer the following questions:

1. Function name can start with which of the following options?

    (a) Only an alphabet
    (b) Only an underscore
    (c) Only digits
    (d) an alphabet or an underscore

2. Which of the following is the correct function name?

    (a) _aBC12()   (b) 2cOUNT()
    (c) Hello#()   (d) 4hEllo_1()

3. Which of the following functions is used to display the variable related information including its data type?

    (a) **var_data()**   (b) **var_detail()**
    (c) **var_dump()**   (d) **var_info()**

4. Which of the following functions is used to generate cryptographically secure pseudo-random bytes in PHP?

    (a) **random_int()**   (b) **secure_byte()**
    (c) **random_bytes()**   (d) **crypt_dara()**

5. Which of the following is a collection of data and methods?

    (a) class   (b) function
    (c) constructor   (d) destructor

6. The **private** methods or the properties of a class can be accessed by the members of:

    (a) same class and other classes (b) same class
    (c) other classes   (d) inherited class

7. Which of the following is known as living entity within a program?

    (a) Class   (b) Properties
    (c) Methods   (d) Object

8. Which of the following keywords is used to call the value of static method of parent class inside the child class?

    (a) **parent**   (b) **self**
    (c) **friend**   (d) **final**

EXERCISES

Exercise 1

Write a program to calculate the area of a square using inheritance.

Exercise 2

Write a program to add and subtract two numbers by implementing and extending the interface.

Answers to Self-Evaluation Test
1. function, **2.** arguments, **3. var_dump()**, **4.** CSPRNG, **5.** visibility, **6.** F, **7.** T, **8.** F, **9.** T

Chapter 8

Arrays

Learning Objectives
After completing this chapter, you will be able to:
- *Understand array and array types*
- *Understand foreach loop*
- *Understand print_r() function*
- *Understand array functions*
- *Understand array operators*

INTRODUCTION

In the earlier chapters, you have used arrays in some programs. In this chapter, you will learn about arrays and their types in detail. You will also learn about **foreach** loop, array functions, and so on in detail.

ARRAYS

A variable stores single data at one time. Therefore, to store multiple data, you need to define multiple variables. But, this method is very time consuming and makes the program lengthy. Therefore, to minimize the program size, you can use arrays. In PHP, an array is a data type that can hold multiple data in a single variable. An array assigns index to every data stored in it. You can refer to a particular data element in an array by using the index. The index starts from the lowest address (0) and ends at the highest address (n-1). Here n specifies the total number of elements. Various types of arrays are discussed next.

Indexed Array

An indexed array consist of numeric keys also known as index. By default, indexed array starts with 0 index. The index of an indexed array sets automatically but you can also set it manually. The indexed array is also known as numeric array.

The syntax for declaring an indexed array is as follows:

```
$array_name = array(list of array elements);
```

In the given syntax, **$array_name** represents the name of an array variable and **array()** is the array function used to define the elements of an array inside the parentheses.

For example:

```
$new = array(100,200,300);
```

In the given example, **100**, **200**, and **300** are the array elements referred by a common array name **$new.**

In PHP 5.4 version, a short hand operator to create an array was introduced. The short hand syntax for declaring an indexed array is as follows:

```
$array_name = [list of array elements] //replaced array()with[]
```

This given short hand syntax of indexed array is exactly same as the previous syntax with the only difference that **[ ]** is used instead of **array()** to declare array elements inside it.

For example:

```
$new = [100,200,300];
```

The working of given example is the same as the previous example with the only difference that in this given example, [] are used to define the array elements.

Arrays

The syntax to generate index of indexed array manually is as follows:

```
$array_name[index number]= "element";
```

In the given syntax, **$array_name[ ]** represents the array variable which is used to define array index inside the pair of square bracket. Here, **index number** is a numeric value which represents index of an element set manually.

For example:

```
$set_index[0]= 100;
$set_index[2]= 300;
$set_index[1]= 200;
```

In the given example, **$set_index[0]** is an array variable which is holding an integer type value **100** and its index position is set manually to 0. Similarly, **300** and **200** are at index position 2 and 1, respectively.

There is also an alternate method to set the index value of array elements manually which is given next:

```
$array_name = array(
    index0 => element1,
    index1 => element2,
    index2 => element3,
    -----
    -----
);
```

In the given syntax, **index0**, **index1**, and **index2** represent the numeric index position of the array elements. An index number is assigned to the element by using the **=>** operator.

For example:

```
$set_idx = array(
                0 => 100,
                2 => 200,
                1 => 300
            );
```

In the given example, **$set_idx** is the name of an array variable. Here, **100** is the integer type value and its index position is set manually to 0 by using the **=>** operator. Similarly, **200** and **300** are set to index position 2 and 1, respectively.

An indexed array can accept any number of arguments separated by a comma inside the function **array()**. There are many ways to declare indexed array. You can use any of the given syntaxes to create indexed array.

After allocating memory to an array, you can access any of its elements by using the index value. The syntax for accessing an element of an array is as follows:

```
$arr_name[index value];
```

In the given syntax, **$arr_name** specifies the array and the **index value** specifies the index position where the element is stored. The **index value** can be from 0 to n-1. Here, n specifies the total number of elements in the array.

For example:

```
echo  even_numbers[4];
```

In the given example, the element stored at the index **4** is accessed and displayed as output in the browser.

Example 1

The following program illustrates the use of an indexed array. The program will create an indexed array, define index of some of its elements, and display the output in the browser by accessing the array elements using the **for** loop.

```
<!Doctype html>                                              1
<html>                                                       2
<head>                                                       3
<title>Indexed Array</title>                                 4
</head>                                                      5
<body>                                                       6
<?php                                                        7
    $idx =[                                                  8
          "PHP",                                             9
          "PHP/FI",                                         10
          "PHP 3",                                          11
          "PHP 4",                                          12
          5 => "PHP 7" ,                                    13
          4 => "PHP 5" ,                                    14
          ];                                                15
        for ($a = 0; $a < 5; ++$a)                          16
        echo "At index $a : its $idx[$a]. <br>";            17
    echo "The latest PHP version is $idx[5]";               18
?>                                                          19
</body>                                                     20
</html>                                                     21
```

Explanation
Line 8
$idx =[
In this line, **$idx** is the name of an array variable. Here, [is the start point of array short hand operator [ ] where the array elements are declared.

Line 9 to Line 12
"PHP",
"PHP/FI",
"PHP 3",
"PHP 4",
In these lines, **PHP, PHP/FI, PHP 3**, and **PHP 4** are the string type array elements separated by a comma. The index of these elements are assigned automatically starting from 0 to 3.

Line 13 to Line 14
5 => "PHP 7",
4 => "PHP 5",
In these lines, **PHP 7** is the string type element and its index position is set manually to **5** by using the => operator. Similarly, **PHP 5** is set to index position **4**.

Line 15
];
In this line,] is the end point of array short hand operator [ ] where the declaration of **$idx** array elements end.

Line 16
for ($a = 0; $a < 5; ++$a)
This line contains the **for** loop. In this line, the variable **$a** (loop control variable) is initialized to 0 and the condition **$a<5** will be checked. If the condition is true, the body of the loop will be executed and the control will be transferred to Line 17. This process will be repeated till the condition is true. When the condition becomes false, the loop will terminate and the control will be transferred to Line 18.

The output of Example 1 is displayed in Figure 8-1.

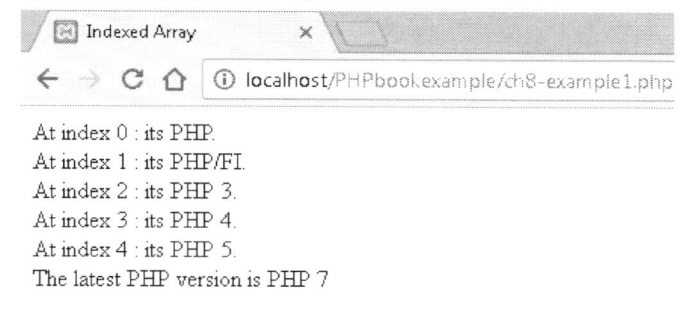

Figure 8-1 The output of Example 1

Example 2

The following program illustrates the use of an indexed array. The program will calculate average of 52, 56, and 82, and display the output in the browser.

```
<!Doctype html>                                                 1
<html>                                                          2
<head>                                                          3
```

```
<title>Avg of array elements</title>                     4
</head>                                                  5
<body>                                                   6
<?php                                                    7
    $numbers = array(52, 56, 82);                        8
    $avrg = 0;                                           9
        for ( $i=0; $i<3; $i++)                         10
        {                                               11
            $avrg= $avrg + $numbers[$i];                12
        }                                               13
    $avrg = $avrg/3;                                    14
    echo "Average is: $avrg" ;                          15
?>                                                      16
</body>                                                 17
</html>                                                 18
```

Explanation
Line 8
$numbers = array(52, 56, 82);
In this line, **52, 56**, and **82** are the array elements of the array **$numbers** declared inside the array function **array()**.

Line 9
$avrg = 0;
In this line, **0** is the integer type value assigned to the variable **$avrg**.

Line 12
$avrg= $avrg + $numbers[$i];
In this line, the value of the variable **$avrg** will be added to the index value of array **$numbers**. Next, the resultant value will be assigned back to the variable **$avrg**.

Line 14
$avrg = $avrg/3;
In this line, the final value of the variable **$avrg** will be divided by the integer value **3**. Next, the resultant value will be assigned back to the variable **$avrg**.

Line 15
echo "Average is: $avrg" ;
This line will display the following in the browser:

Average is: 63.333333333333

The output of Example 2 is displayed in Figure 8-2.

Average is: 63.333333333333

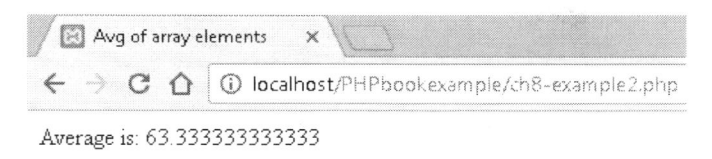

Figure 8-2 *The output of Example 2*

Associative Array

An associative array consists of named keys also known as named index. The functionality of associative array is similar to indexed array but they are different in terms of index. The associative array uses string type index whereas indexed array uses integer type index. An associative array is used when there is difficulty in memorizing the numeric index of every element in the array. The named index makes it easier to memorize and refer the elements of the array.

The syntax for declaring an associative array is as follows:

```
$array_name["index_name"]= "element";
```

In the given syntax, **$array_name[ ]** represents the array variable which is used to define array index inside the pair of square bracket. Here, **index_name** is a string value which represents named index of an element set manually.

For example:

```
$set_index["First"]= 1000;
$set_index["Second"]= 500;
$set_index["Third"]= 200;
```

In the given example, **$set_index["First"]** is an array variable which is holding an integer value **1000** and its index name is set manually to **First**. Similarly **500** and **200** is at named index position **Second** and **Third**, respectively.

The alternate syntax to generate index of associative array is as follows:

```
$array_name = array(
    "idx_name1" => element1,
    "idx_name2" => element2,
    "idx_name3" => element3,
    -----
    -----
);
```

In the given syntax, **idx_name1**, **idx_name2**, and **idx_name3** represent the named index position of the array elements. An index name is assigned to the element by using the **=>** operator.

For example:

```
$set_idx = array(
                "First" => 100,
                "Second" => 200,
                "Third" => 300
            );
```

In the given example, 100 is the integer value and its named index position is set to **First** by using the **=>** operator. Similarly, **200** and **300** is set to named index position **Second** and **Third**, respectively.

> **Note**
> *You can use both numeric index and named index together in an array as the functionality of indexed and associative array is same.*

Example 3

The following program illustrates the use of an associative and indexed array together. The program will create an array, define index of some of its elements, and display the output in the browser.

```
<!Doctype html>                                               1
<html>                                                        2
<head>                                                        3
<title> Associative and Indexed Array</title>                 4
</head>                                                       5
<body>                                                        6
<?php                                                         7
    $sal = array("Jack"=>350000,                              8
                "Sam"=>450000,                                9
                "Elle"=>200000,                              10
                 500000,                                     11
                 600000);                                    12
        echo "<h1> Employees Salary </h1>";                  13
        echo "Jack salary is ".$sal["Jack"]."<br/>";         14
        echo "Sam salary is ".$sal["Sam"]."<br/>";           15
        echo "Elle salary is ".$sal["Elle"]."<br/>";         16
        echo "John salary is ".$sal[0]."<br/>";              17
        echo "Lornado salary is ".$sal[1]."<br/>";           18
?>                                                           19
</body>                                                      20
</html>                                                      21
```

Explanation
Line 8 to 12
$sal = array("Jack"=>350000,
       "Sam"=>450000,
       "Elle"=>200000,

```
                    500000,
                    600000);
```

In these lines, **$sal** is an array name. Here, Line 8 to Line 10 are using associative array indexing where **350000** is the integer type value and its named index position is set manually to Jack by using the **=>** operator. Similarly, **450000** and **200000** are set to named index position **Sam** and **Elle**, respectively. Next, in Line 11 and Line 12 numeric array indexing is done where numeric index is generated automatically. Here, **500000** and **600000** are integer type elements having 0 and 1 index, respectively.

The output of Example 3 is displayed in Figure 8-3.

Figure 8-3 The output of Example 3

Multidimensional Array

An array of arrays is known as multidimensional array. The arrays used in the examples of this chapter till now were one dimensional arrays. These arrays are independent which means they do not contain any other array inside them. But multidimensional array contains one or more arrays inside an array. A two-dimensional array is the simplest type of multidimensional array. The syntax for declaring a two-dimensional array is as follows:

```
$array_name = array(
                    array(list of array elements ),
                    array(list of array elements ),
                    array(list of array elements ),
                    -------
                    -------
                );
```

In the given syntax, there are multiple **array()** functions inside the main **array()** function which means that the given syntax is a two-dimensional array as it contains two levels of **array()** function where main **array()** function is first level and the sub **array()** functions inside the main **array()** function represents the second level.

For example:

```
$flowers = array(
                array("rose", 10 , 15),
```

```
            array("lily", 8 , 25),
            array("orchid", 20 , 7),
            array("lotus", 10, 8),
);
```

In the given example, **$flowers** is an array variable holding two-dimensional array. There are four **array()** functions having list of different elements. These **array()** functions are inside the main **array()** function of array **$flowers**. This array indicates that there are 4 rows and 3 columns in a two-dimensional array.

In a two-dimensional array, the index consists of two values. One value specifies the row number and the other value specifies the column number in that particular row. The syntax to access the element of a two-dimensional array is as follows:

```
$array_name[row][coloumn]
```

For example, you may want to access the data element which is stored in the second column of the first row in the array **$flowers**. You can access the given element by specifying the following index values:

```
$flowers[1][2]
```

Figure 8-4 represents a two-dimensional array which contains 4 rows and 3 columns.

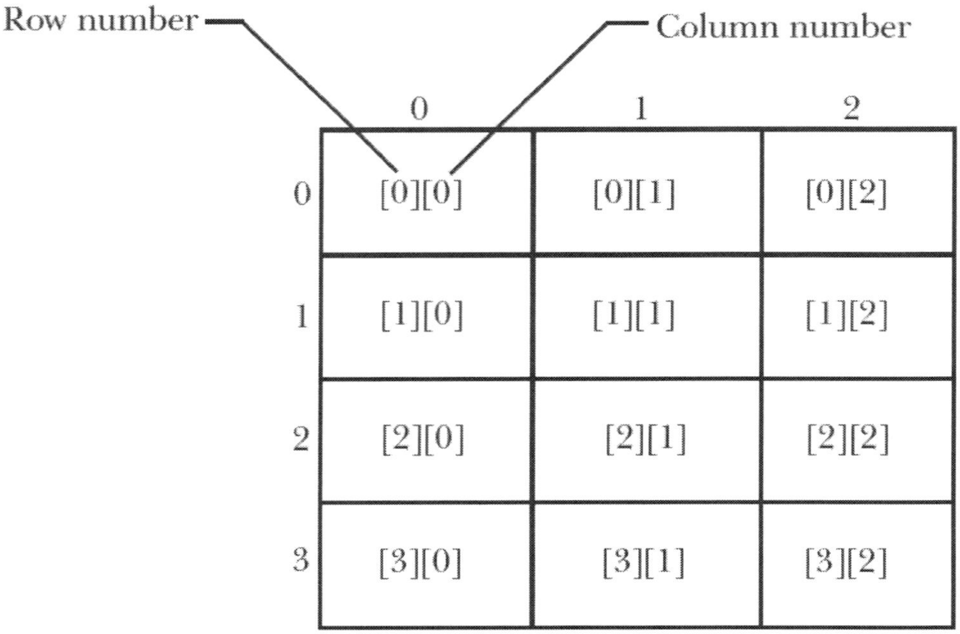

	0	1	2
0	[0][0]	[0][1]	[0][2]
1	[1][0]	[1][1]	[1][2]
2	[2][0]	[2][1]	[2][2]
3	[3][0]	[3][1]	[3][2]

Row number points to [0][0]; Column number points to [0][1].

Figure 8-4 *Representation of two-dimensional array*

Example 4

The following program illustrates the use of two-dimensional indexed array. The program will create a two-dimensional array and display the output in the browser by using the **echo** statement and the **for** loop.

```
<!Doctype html>                                                    1
<html>                                                             2
<head>                                                             3
<title> Two-dimensional Array</title>                              4
</head>                                                            5
<body>                                                             6
<?php                                                              7
   $subject = array(                                               8
              array("Maths", 2 , 15),                              9
              array("English", 1 , 25),                           10
              array("Science", 2 , 40)                            11
         );                                                       12
echo "<h1>Subjects</h1>";                                         13
   echo "<b>".$subject[0][0]."</b>: Per day <b>"                  14
   .$subject[0][1]."</b> hour class, Total no. of chapters:<b>"
   .$subject[0][2]."</b><br />";
   echo "<b>".$subject[1][0]."</b> : Per day <b>"                 15
   .$subject[1][1]."</b> hour class, Total no. of chapters:<b>"
   .$subject[1][2]."</b><br />";
   echo "<b>".$subject[2][0]."</b>: Per day <b>"                  16
   .$subject[2][1]."</b> hour class, Total no. of chapters:<b>"
   .$subject[2][2]."</b><br />";
echo "<h1>Using loops to display array elements</h1>";            17
echo "<ol>";                                                      18
for ($row = 0; $row < 3; $row++)                                  19
{                                                                 20
   echo "<li><b>The row number $row</b>";                         21
   echo "<ul>";                                                   22
  for ($col = 0; $col < 3; $col++)                                23
     {                                                            24
        echo "<li>".$subject[$row][$col]."</li>";                 25
     }                                                            26
   echo "</ul>";                                                  27
   echo "</li>";                                                  28
}                                                                 29
echo "</ol>";                                                     30
?>                                                                31
</body>                                                           32
</html>                                                           33
```

Explanation
Line 8 to 12
$subject = array(
    array("Maths", 2 , 15),
    array("English", 1 , 25),
    array("Science", 2 , 40)
  );

In these lines, **$subject** is an array variable which is holding two-dimensional array. There are three **array()** functions having list of different elements. These **array()** functions are inside the main **array()** function of array **$subject**. So, this is a two-dimensional array with 3 rows and 3 columns.

Line 14
echo "\<b\>".$subject[0][0]."\</b\>: Per day \<b\>".$subject[0][1]."\</b\> hour class, Total no. of chapters: \<b\>".$subject[0][2]."\</b\>\<br /\>";
In this line, **$subject[0][0]** is accessing the data element which is stored in the zeroth column of zeroth row in the two-dimensional **$subject** array. Similarly, **$subject[0][1]** is accessing the data element which is stored in the first column of zeroth row in the **$subject** array and **$subject[0][2]** is accessing the data element which is stored in the second column of zeroth row in the array **$subject**. This line will display the following in the browser:

Maths: Per day 2 hour class, Total no. of chapters: 15

The working of Line 15 and Line 16 is same as Line 14.

Line 18
echo "\<ol\>";
In this line, **\<ol\>** is the start tag of HTML which defines the start of the ordered list. It displays the numeric order of the list provided inside the **\<li\>** tag of the ordered list in HTML code.

Line 19
for ($row = 0; $row < 3; $row++)
In this line, the **for** loop is used to check iterations of rows of the **$subject** array. The number of iterations of this loop are equal to the number of rows. In this program, the number of rows are 3. So, this loop will be executed 3 times. In each iteration, it will initialize the **array()** function of each row which are the elements of the main **array()** function. In the first iteration, it will initialize the **array()** function of row 0, in the second iteration, the **array()** function of row 1, and in the third iteration, the **array()** function of row 2.

Line 21
echo "\<li\>\<b\>The row number $row\</b\>";
In this line, **\<li\>** is the start tag of HTML which defines the list of elements in the ordered list. This line will be executed until the iteration of the **for** loop in Line 19 comes to an end.

Arrays

Line 22
echo "<ul>";
In this line, **<ul>** is the start tag of HTML which defines the start of the unordered list. It displays the unordered list provided inside the **<li>** tag of the unordered list in HTML code. This line will be executed until the iteration of the **for** loop in Line 19 comes to an end.

Line 23
for ($col = 0; $col < 3; $col++)
In this line, the **for** loop is nested inside another **for** loop defined in Line 19. When the condition given in line 19 is true, the control will be transferred to this line. The **for** loop in the given line (Line 23) is used for columns and is repeated thrice because the number of columns in a row is 3. In each iteration, it will initialize one element in each column.

Line 25
echo "<li>".$subject[$row][$col]."</li>";
In this line, **<li>** and **</li>** are the start and end tags of HTML which define the list of elements in the unordered list. This line will be executed until the iteration of **for** loop in Line 23 comes to an end.

Line 27
echo "</ul>";
In this line, **</ul>** is the end tag of HTML which defines the end of unordered list.

Line 28
echo "</li>";
In this line, **</li>** is the end tag of HTML which defines the end of list element.

Line 30
echo "</ol>";
In this line, **</ol>** is the end tag of HTML which defines the end of ordered list.

The **for** loops given in lines 19 and 23 are used to display the values stored in the array at different locations.

The output of Example 4 is displayed in Figure 8-5.

Subjects

Maths: Per day **2** hour class, Total no. of chapters: **15**
English : Per day **1** hour class, Total no. of chapters: **25**
Science: Per day **2** hour class, Total no. of chapters: **40**

Using loops to display array elements

1. **The row number 0**
   - Maths
   - 2
   - 15
2. **The row number 1**
   - English
   - 1
   - 25
3. **The row number 2**
   - Science
   - 2
   - 40

Figure 8-5 *The output of Example 4*

A multidimensional array can also have a three-dimensional array. The syntax for declaring a three-dimensional array is as follows:

```
$array_name = array(
                array(
                    array(list of array elements ),
                    array(list of array elements ),
                    -------
                ),
                array(
                    array(list of array elements ),
                    array(list of array elements ),
                    -------
                ),
                --------
                --------
            );
```

In the given syntax, there is one main **array()** function which further has multiple major **array()** functions. These major **array()** functions further consist of multiple **array()** functions each with

Arrays

a list of array elements. The given syntax represents three-dimensional array containing three levels of **array()** functions. Here, every major **array()** function is considered as a layer of the three-dimensional array.

The multidimensional array can have multiple levels of **array()** functions. You can create multidimensional array by adding the levels of **array()** function to the syntax of two-dimensional or three-dimensional array.

In a three-dimensional array, the index consists of three values. The first value specifies the layer number, second value specifies the row number in that particular layer, and the third value specifies the column number in that particular row. The syntax to access the element of a three-dimensional array is as follows:

```
$array_name[layer][[row][coloumn]
```

Example 5

The following program illustrates the use of three-dimensional indexed array. The program will create the three-dimensional array of PHP versions and display the output in the browser by using the **for** loop.

```
<!Doctype html>                                                    1
<html>                                                             2
<head>                                                             3
<title> Three-dimensional Array</title>                            4
</head>                                                            5
<body>                                                             6
<?php                                                              7
   $Version = array(                                               8
                 array(                                            9
                     array("PHP", 1),                             10
                     array("PHP/FI", 2),                          11
                     array("PHP3", 3)                             12
                 ),                                               13
                 array(                                           14
                     array("PHP4", 4),                            15
                     array("PHP5", 5),                            16
                     array("PHP7", 7)                             17
                 ),                                               18
              );                                                  19
   echo "<ul>";                                                   20
   for ( $layer = 0; $layer < 2; $layer++ )                       21
   {                                                              22
    echo "<li>The <b>layer</b> number <b>$layer</b>";             23
    echo "<ul>";                                                  24
      for ( $row = 0; $row < 3; $row++ )                          25
      {                                                           26
         echo "<li>The <b>row</b> number <b>$row</b>";            27
```

```
            echo "<ul>";                                          28
              for ( $col = 0; $col < 2; $col++ )                  29
              {                                                   30
                echo "<li>".$Version[$layer][$row][$col]."</li>"; 31
              }                                                   32
            echo "</ul>";                                         33
            echo "</li>";                                         34
        }                                                         35
        echo "</ul>";                                             36
        echo "</li>";                                             37
    }                                                             38
    echo "</ul>";                                                 39
    ?>                                                            40
    </body>                                                       41
    </html>                                                       42
```

Explanation

Line 8 to 19
$Version = array(
        array(
            array("PHP", 1),
            array("PHP/FI", 2),
            array("PHP3", 3)
        ),
        array(
            array("PHP4", 4),
            array("PHP5", 5),
            array("PHP7", 7)
        ),
);

In these lines, **$Version** is an array variable which is holding three-dimensional array. There is one main **array()** function which further has two major **array()** functions. These major **array()** functions further consist of three **array()** functions each with a list of array elements. Here, the array **$Version** consist of two layers (major **array()** functions). Each layer consist of three rows and each row in a layer consist of two columns.

Line 21
for ($layer = 0; $layer < 2; $layer++)
In this line, the **for** loop is used to check the iterations of layers of the array **$Version**[ ] [ ] [ ]. The number of iterations of this loop are equal to the number of layers. In this program, the number of layers are 2. So, this loop will be executed 2 times. In each iteration, it will initialize the **array()** functions of each layer which are the elements of the main **array()** function. In the first iteration, it will initialize the **array()** functions of layer 0 and in the second iteration, **array()** function of layer 1.

Arrays

Line 25
for ($row = 0; $row < 3; $row++)
In this line, the **for** loop is nested inside another **for** loop which is defined in Line 21. When the condition given in Line 21 is true, the control will be transferred to this line. The number of iterations of this loop are equal to the number of rows. In this program, the number of rows are 3. So, this loop will be executed 3 times. In each iteration, it will initialize the **array()** function of each row which are the elements of major **array()** function. In the first iteration, it will initialize the **array()** function of row 0, in the second iteration, **array()** function of row 1, and in the third iteration, **array()** function of row 2.

Line 29
for ($col = 0; $col < 2; $col++)
In this line, the **for** loop is nested inside another **for** loop which is defined in Line 25. When the condition given in Line 25 is true, the control will be transferred to this line. This **for** loop is used for columns and is repeated twice because the number of columns in a row is 2. In each iteration, it will initialize one element in each column.

Line 31
echo "<li>".$Version[$layer][$row][$col]."</li>";
In this line, **$Version[$layer][$row][$col]** will access the data element which is stored in the **$col** column of the **$row** row in the **$layer** layer of the three-dimensional array **$Version**. Here, the value of **$layer**, **$row**, and **$col** is set according to the associated **for** loops.

The output of Example 5 is displayed in Figure 8-6.

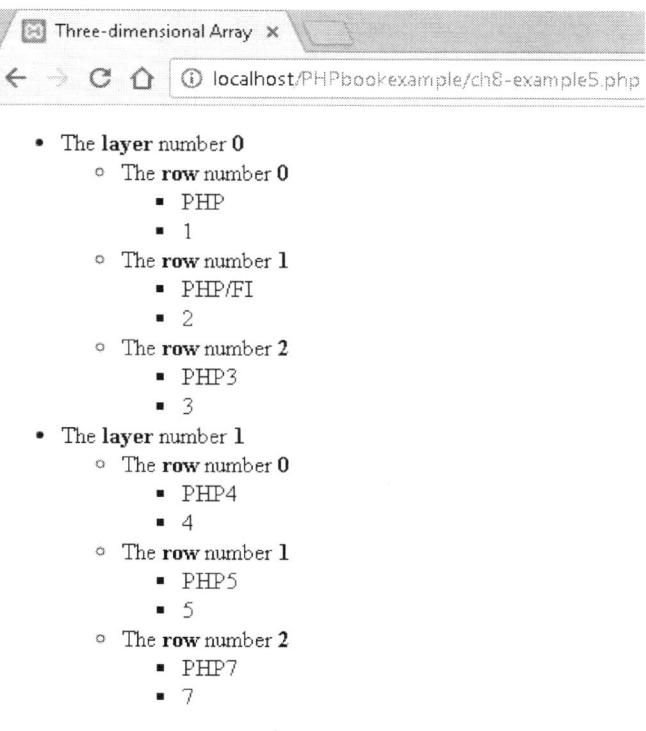

- The **layer** number 0
  - The **row** number 0
    - PHP
    - 1
  - The **row** number 1
    - PHP/FI
    - 2
  - The **row** number 2
    - PHP3
    - 3
- The **layer** number 1
  - The **row** number 0
    - PHP4
    - 4
  - The **row** number 1
    - PHP5
    - 5
  - The **row** number 2
    - PHP7
    - 7

Figure 8-6 *The output of Example 5*

Example 6

The following program illustrates the use of multidimensional associative array. The program will create a multidimensional array of students result and display the output in the browser by using the **echo** statement.

```
<!Doctype html>
<html>
<head>
<title>Multidimensional Array</title>
</head>
<body>
<?php
    $result = array(
        "Tom" => array (
                    "english" => 50,
                    "maths" => 80,
                    "science" => 70
                ),
        "John" => array (
                    "english" => 70,
                    "maths" => 90,
                    "science" => 80
                ),
        "Larry" => array (
                    "english" => 80,
                    "maths" => 70,
                    "science" => 60
                ),
        "Harry" => array (
                    "english" => 80,
                    "maths" => 77,
                    "science" => 88
                )
    );
    echo "Marks for Tom in English : ";
    echo "<b>".$result["Tom"]["english"]."</b><br>";
    echo "Marks for John in Maths : ";
    echo "<b>".$result["John"]["maths"]."</b><br>";
    echo "Marks for Larry in Science : ";
    echo "<b>".$result["Larry"]["science"]."</b><br>";
    echo "Marks for Harry in English : ";
    echo "<b>".$result["Harry"]["english"]."</b><br>";
?>
</body>
</html>
```

Arrays

Explanation
Line 8 to 29
```
$result = array(
        "Tom" => array (
                            "english" => 50,
                            "maths" => 80,
                            "science" => 70
                    ),
        "John" => array (
                            "english" => 70,
                            "maths" => 90,
                            "science" => 80
                    ),
        "Larry" => array (
                            "english" => 80,
                            "maths" => 70,
                            "science" => 60
                    ),
        "Harry" => array (
                            "english" => 80,
                            "maths" => 77,
                            "science" => 88
                    )
);
```

In these lines, **$result** is an array variable which is holding multidimensional array. There is one main **array()** function which further has four **array()** functions as its elements. These four **array()** functions has name index. Further, these functions consist of three array elements each. Every element of a row have name index. Here, the array **$result** consist of four rows and each row consist of three columns.

Line 31
echo "".$result["Tom"]["english"] . "<br>";
In this line, **$result['Tom']['english']** is accessing the data element which is stored in the column **english** of row **Tom** in the multidimensional array **$result**.

The working of Line 33, Line 35 and Line 37 is same as Line 31.

The output of Example 6 is displayed in Figure 8-7.

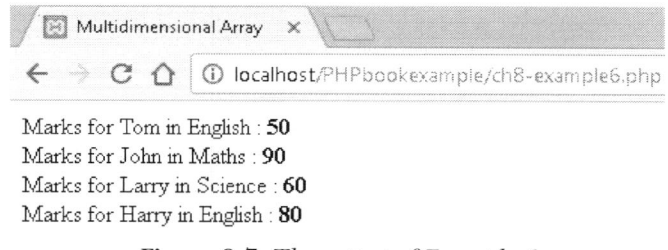

Figure 8-7 The output of Example 6

THE foreach LOOP

The **foreach** loop is a special **for** loop. The **foreach** loop is used to make iteration over a collection of objects such as arrays. It works only on arrays and objects. The syntax for using the **foreach** loop for an array is as follows:

```
foreach ($array_name as $value)
```

In the given syntax, **foreach** is a keyword which is used to define the **foreach** loop. Here, **$array_name** represents the array variable in which array is stored and **$value** represents a variable which will hold the values of array elements. On each iteration of **foreach** loop, the value of the element of an array **$array_name** is assigned to the variable **$value**. This process will be repeated until every element of an array **$array_name** is assigned to the variable **$value**.

Example 7

The following program illustrates the use of **foreach** loop for an indexed array. The program will calculate the sum of 52, 56, and 82, and display the output in the browser.

```
<!Doctype html>                                          1
<html>                                                   2
<head>                                                   3
<title>The foreach loop</title>                          4
</head>                                                  5
<body>                                                   6
<?php                                                    7
   $numbers = array(52, 56, 82);                         8
        foreach ($numbers as $num)                       9
            {                                           10
                 echo " The number is $num <br>";       11
            }                                           12
   $sum = 0;                                            13
   for ( $i=0; $i<3; $i++)                              14
   {                                                    15
        $sum= $sum + $numbers[$i];                      16
   }                                                    17
 echo "Sum of the 3 numbers is: $sum" ;                 18
?>                                                      19
</body>                                                 20
</html>                                                 21
```

Explanation
Line 9
foreach ($numbers as $num)
In this line, **foreach** is a keyword used to define the **foreach** loop. Here, **$numbers** is the array variable in which array is stored and **$num** is a variable. On each iteration of **foreach** loop, the value of the element of an array **$numbers** is assigned to the variable **$num** by using the keyword **as**. The **foreach** loop executes until every element of an array **$numbers** is assigned to variable **$num**.

Arrays

Line 11
**echo " The number is $num
";**
In this line, **$num** is the variable which is temporarily holding the values of the elements of an array **$numbers**.

The output of Example 7 is displayed in Figure 8-8.

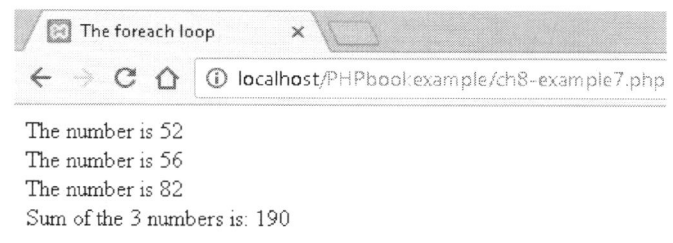

Figure 8-8 The output of Example 7

An array pointer is a variable that holds the memory address of an array. But the pointer can only hold the starting address (address of the first element) of an array. So, in order to traverse through all the array elements **foreach** loop is used.

In prior versions of PHP, the pointer points to the next element of an array that becomes the current element of that array because the internal array pointer of an array keep on incrementing by one, in every iteration of the **foreach** loop. But now in PHP 7, the internal array pointer is no more used. This means inside the **foreach** loop, the pointer will point to the next element that is assigned to a variable. But in the actual array, the pointer will always point to the first element of that array. Whereas prior to PHP 7 the current element kept on incrementing in actual array also.

Example 8

The following program illustrates the use of the **foreach** loop. The program will display the array elements and current element of an indexed array as output in the browser.

```
<!Doctype html>                                             1
<html>                                                      2
<head>                                                      3
<title>PHP 7 foreach loop</title>                           4
</head>                                                     5
<body>                                                      6
<?php                                                       7
    $numbers = array(42, 66, 72);                           8
       foreach ($numbers as $var)                           9
          {                                                10
              echo " The element assigned to variable      11
              <b>\$var</b> is: <b>$var</b> <br>";
              echo "The current element in actual array    12
```

```
                    <b>\$numbers</b> is: <b>".(current($numbers)).
              "</b><br>";
              echo "<br>";                                           13
        }                                                            14
?>                                                                   15
</body>                                                              16
</html>                                                              17
```

Explanation
Line 9
foreach ($numbers as $var)
In this line, **foreach** is a keyword used to define the **foreach** loop. Here, **$numbers** is the array variable in which array is stored and **$var** is a variable. On each iteration of the **foreach** loop, the value of the element of an array **$numbers** is assigned to the variable **$var** by using the keyword **as**. The **foreach** loop executes until every element of an array **$numbers** is assigned to variable **$var**.

Line 11
**echo " The element assigned to variable \$var is: $var
";**
In this line, **$var** is the variable which is temporarily holding the values of the elements of an array **$numbers**.

Line 12
echo "the current element in actual array \$numbers is: " . (current($numbers)). "<br>";
In this line, **current()** is an array function used to display the current element of an array. Here, the current element of an array **$number** will not change in any iteration of the **foreach** loop. The current element for this line will always be 42. This line will display the following in the browser:

The current element in actual array $numbers is: 42

The output of Example 8 is displayed in Figure 8-9.

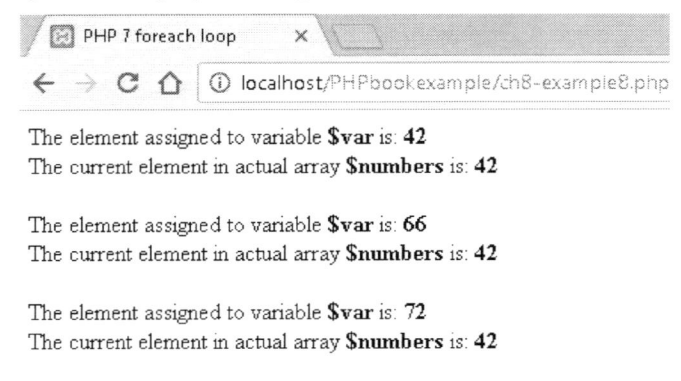

Figure 8-9 *The output of Example 8*

Arrays

The alternate syntax for using the **foreach** loop for an array is as follows:

```
foreach(array_name as $key => $value)
```

In the given syntax, **foreach** is a keyword used to define **foreach** loop. Here, **$array_name** represents the array variable in which array is stored, **$key** represents a variable for named index or numeric index of array elements and **$value** represents a variable which will hold the values of array elements. On each iteration of the **foreach** loop, the value of the element of an array **$array_name** is assigned to the variable **$value** through the index variable **$key**. This process will be repeated until every element of the array **$array_name** is assigned to the variable **$value**.

Example 9

The following program illustrates the use of the **foreach** loop in an associative array. The program will display the array elements with their index as output in the browser.

```
<!Doctype html>                                                        1
<html>                                                                 2
<head>                                                                 3
<title>The foreach loop</title>                                        4
</head>                                                                5
<body>                                                                 6
<?php                                                                  7
    $ele = array("first"=>"value1","second"=>"value2",                 8
    "third"=>"value3");
    foreach($ele as  $idx => $val)                                     9
    {                                                                  10
     echo "The element <b>$val</b> is at <b>$idx</b> index<br>";       11
    }                                                                  12
?>                                                                     13
</body>                                                                14
</html>                                                                15
```

Explanation
Line 8
$ele = array("first"=>"value1","second"=>"value2", "third"=>"value3");
In this line, **$ele** is an array variable that holds multiple array elements. Here, **value1** is the string type element and its named index position is **first**. Similarly, **value2** and **value3** are set to named index position **second** and **third**, respectively. These elements are declared inside the array function **array()**.

Line 9
foreach($ele as $idx => $val)
In this line, **foreach** is a keyword used to define **foreach** loop. Here, **$ele** is the array variable in which array is stored, **$idx** is a variable for named index of array elements and **$val** is a variable which will hold the values of array elements. On each iteration of **foreach** loop, the value of the element of the **$ele** array is assigned to the **$val** variable through the index **$idx** variable. This process will be repeated until every element of the **$ele** array is assigned to the **$val** variable.

The output of Example 9 is displayed in Figure 8-10.

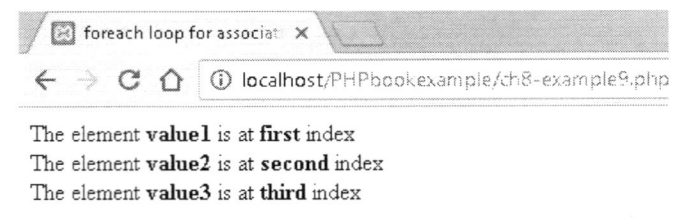

Figure 8-10 The output of Example 9

THE print_r() FUNCTION

The **print_r()** function will print the value of a variable declared inside its parentheses in human readable format. This means human can easily read the values of variables provided by the function **print_r()**. If the variable is holding a string, float, or an integer type value then the function **print_r()** will print their values. If the variable is holding an array then the function **print_r()** will print its keys (index position) and elements, including its notations. If the variable is holding a boolean type value then it will display 1 for **true** and no output for **false**.

The syntax of **print_r()** is as follows:

```
print_r ($var , return_boolean)
```

In the given syntax, **print_r()** is the function used to get the value of a variable in a human readable format and **$var** represents the variable name whose value is to be displayed in the browser. Here, **return_boolean** is optional which represents the return value. It can be set to **true** or **false** (boolean values), by default it is **false**. To store the value of **print_r()** in a variable, you can use the optional parameter **return_boolean**. If it is set to **true**, it will return the output of the function **print_r()** instead of just printing it. This means that in case of **true**, the **print_r()** value will be returned only if the variable which is holding the **print_r()** value is accessed.

Example 10

The following program will illustrate the use of **print_r()** and **var_dump()** functions. In this program, different values will be assigned to the variables and the output is displayed in the browser.

```
<!Doctype html>                                          1
<html>                                                   2
<head>                                                   3
<title>The print_r()function</title>                     4
</head>                                                  5
<body>                                                   6
<?php                                                    7
   $value1 = 508;                                        8
   $value2 = "Hello";                                    9
   $value3 = 698.99;                                    10
```

Arrays

```
        $value4 = "num123";                                    11
        $value5 = true;                                        12
        $value6 = array("Subj1"=>"Physics","Subj2"=>           13
                "Chemistry","Hour"=>array(2,1,3,8));
        $value7 = array(28, 86, 92, 100 , 121);                14
        $value8 = array(28, 86, 92);                           15
        print_r($value1);                                      16
        echo"<br>";                                            17
        print_r($value2);                                      18
        echo"<br>";                                            19
        print_r($value3);                                      20
        echo"<br>";                                            21
        print_r($value4);                                      22
        echo"<br>";                                            23
        print_r($value5);                                      24
        echo"<br>";                                            25
        print_r($value6);                                      26
        echo"<br>";                                            27
        var_dump($value6);                                     28
        echo"<br>";                                            29
        print_r($value7, true);                                30
        echo"<br>";                                            31
        $return = print_r($value8, true);                      32
        echo $return;                                          33
    ?>                                                         34
    </body>                                                    35
</html>                                                        36
```

Explanation

Line 16
print_r($value1);
In this line, the **print_r()** function will display the value of the **$value1** variable. This line will display the following in the browser:

508

The working of Line 18, Line 20 and Line 22 is same as Line 8.

Line 24
print_r($value5);
In this line, the function **print_r()** will display 1 as the output for variable **$value5** because variable **$value5** is holding a boolean type value **true** which is declared in Line 12. This line will display the following in the browser:

1

Line 26
print_r($value6);
In this line, the function **print_r()** will display keys (index position) and elements, including notations for variable **$value5**. Because variable **$value5** is holding an array which is declared in Line 13. This line will display the following in the browser:

Array ([Subj1] => Physics [Subj2] => Chemistry [Hour] => Array ([0] => 2 [1] => 1 [2] => 3 [3] => 8))

Line 28
var_dump($value6);
In this line, **var_dump()** is the function used to display the variable related information. Here, as compared to **print_r()** function, the **var_dump()** function will not only display the keys, elements, and notation of an array, it will also display the data types and the length of each element of the **$value6** variable. This line will display the following in the browser:

array(3) { ["Subj1"]=> string(7) "Physics" ["Subj2"]=> string(9) "Chemistry" ["Hour"]=> array(4) { [0]=> int(2) [1]=> int(1) [2]=> int(3) [3]=> int(8) } }

Line 30
print_r($value7, true);
In this line, the function **print_r()** will display nothing as the second parameter passed to the function **print_r()** is **true**. It will return the value of variable **$value7** only if the value of this **print_r()** function will be assigned to another variable or if the second parameter will be changed to **false**.

Line 32
$return = print_r($value8, true);
In this line, the function **print_r()** will assign the value of variable **$value8** to the variable **$return**.

Line 33
echo $return;
This line will return the keys, elements, and notations for variable **$return** because **$return** variable is holding a function **print_r()** which was assigned to it in Line 32. This line will display the following in the browser:

Array ([0] => 28 [1] => 86 [2] => 92)

The output of Example 10 is displayed in Figure 8-11.

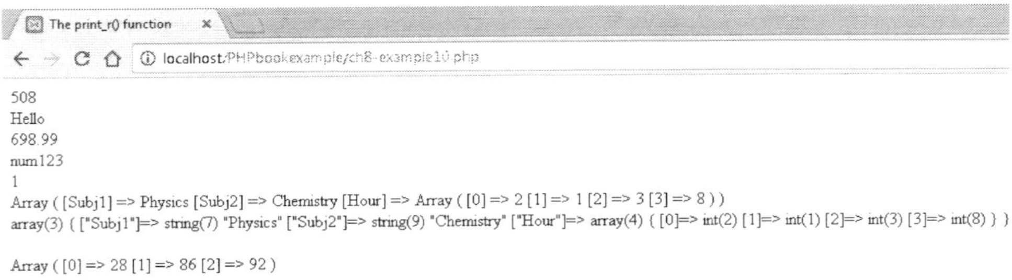

Figure 8-11 *The output of Example 10*

ARRAY FUNCTIONS

You have already learned about some in-built functions in the previous chapters. In this section, you will learn in-built array functions of PHP. which

sort()

The **sort()** is an array function used to sort the array elements in ascending order. It does not maintain the associated index of the array elements. This means the index of the array elements get changed according to the sorting of the array. The syntax of **sort()** is as follows:

```
sort($array_name,sortingtype);
```

In the given syntax, **sort()** is the array function, **$array_name** represents the array variable which holds an array and **sortingtype** is an optional parameter which represents the type of sorting that is to be performed on an array. Table 8-1 shows the list of **sortingtype** options.

Table 8-1 Sorting types and their description

Number	String	Description
0	SORT_REGULAR	Compares elements normally.
1	SORT_NUMERIC	Compares elements numerically.
2	SORT_STRING	Compares elements as strings.
3	SORT_LOCALE_STRING	Compares elements as strings based on current locale.
4	SORT_NATURAL	Compares elements as strings using natural ordering.
5	SORT_FLAG_CASE	Can be combined with SORT_STRING or SORT_NATURAL to sort strings case-insensitively by using bitwise OR.

Note

*You can either use number or string for **sortingtype** on the basis of the type of comparison required at the time of sorting from Table 8-1.*

For example:

```
<?php
    $Name = array("Jessica", "Angelina", "John", "Harry");
    sort($Name);
        foreach ($Name as $key => $val) {
        echo "Name[" . $key . "] = " . $val . "\n <br>";
        }
?>
    /* output:
        Name[0] = Angelina
        Name[1] = Harry
```

```
            Name[2] = Jessica
            Name[3] = John    */
```

In the given example, **sort($Name)** is the function used for array sorting and **$Name** is the array variable which holds an array. The output of the given example will be sorted. All the elements of array **$Name** will be arranged in alphabetical order and accordingly, their index will also get changed.

asort()

The **asort()** is an array function used to sort the array elements in ascending order by maintaining their associated index. This means the index of the array elements does not change. The syntax of **asort()** is as follows:

```
asort($array_name,sortingtype);
```

In the given syntax, **asort()** is the array function, **$array_name** represents the array variable which holds an array and **sortingtype** is an optional parameter which represents the type of sorting that is to be performed on an array, refer to Table 8-1.

For example:

```
<?php
    $Name = array("Jessica", "Angelina", "John", "Harry");
    asort($Name);
        foreach ($Name as $key => $val) {
        echo "Name[" . $key . "] = " . $val . "\n <br>";
        }
?>
    /* output:
        Name[1] = Angelina
        Name[3] = Harry
        Name[0] = Jessica
        Name[2] = John    */
```

In the given example, **asort($Name)** is the function used for array sorting and **$Name** is the array variable which holds an array. The output of the given example will be sorted. All the elements of array **$Name** will be arranged in alphabetical order but their index will remain the same.

arsort()

The **arsort()** is an array function used to sort the array elements in descending order by maintaining their associated index. This means the index of the array elements does not change. The syntax of **arsort()** is as follows:

```
arsort($array_name,sortingtype);
```

In the given syntax, **arsort()** is the array function, **$array_name** represents the array variable which holds an array and **sortingtype** is an optional parameter which represents the type of sorting is to be performed in an array, refer to Table 8-1.

Arrays

For example:

```php
<?php
   $Name = array("Jessica", "Angelina", "John", "Harry");
   arsort($Name);
       foreach ($Name as $key => $val) {
       echo "Name[" . $key . "] = " . $val . "<br>";
       }
?>
   /* output:
       Name[2] = John
       Name[0] = Jessica
       Name[3] = Harry
       Name[1] = Angelina    */
```

In the given example, **arsort($Name)** is the function used for array sorting in descending order and **$Name** is the array variable which holds an array. The output of the given example will be sorted. All the elements of array **$Name** will be arranged in reverse alphabetical order but their index will remain the same.

ksort()

The **ksort()** is an array function used to sort the array in ascending order according to the array index instead of array elements. The syntax of **ksort()** is as follows:

```
ksort($array_name,sortingtype);
```

In the given syntax, **ksort()** is the array function, **$array_name** represents the array variable which holds an array and **sortingtype** is an optional parameter which represents the type of sorting that is to be performed on an array, refer Table 8-1.

For example:

```php
<?php
   $Name=array("Q"=>"Jessica","S"=>"Angelina","P"=>"John",
   "R"=>"Harry");
   ksort($Name);
   foreach($Name as $k => $val)
   {
       echo "Index = " . $k . ", Element = " . $val . "<br>";
   }
   /* output:
       Index = P, Element = John
       Index = Q, Element = Jessica
       Index = R, Element = Harry
       Index = S, Element = Angelina    */
```

In the given example, **ksort($Name)** is the function used for array sorting in ascending order according to the array index and **$Name** is the array variable which holds an array. The output of the given example will be sorted according to the array index. All the elements of array **$Name** will be arranged according to the alphabetical order of their index.

krsort()

The **krsort()** is an array function used to sort the array in descending order, according to the array index instead of array elements. The syntax of **krsort()** is as follows:

```
krsort($array_name,sortingtype);
```

In the given syntax, **krsort()** is the array function, **$array_name** represents the array variable which holds an array and **sortingtype** is an optional parameter which represents the type of sorting that is to be performed on an array, refer to Table 8-1.

For example:

```
<?php
   $Name=array("Q"=>"Jessica","S"=>"Angelina","P"=>"John",
   "R"=>"Harry");
   krsort($Name);
   foreach($Name as $k => $val)
   {
         echo "Index = " . $k . ", Element = " . $val . "<br>";
   }
   /* output:
         Index = S, Element = Angelina
         Index = R, Element = Harry
         Index = Q, Element = Jessica
         Index = P, Element = John       */
```

In the given example, **krsort($Name)** is the function used for array sorting in descending order of the array index and **$Name** is the array variable which holds an array. The output of the given example will be sorted according to the array index. All the elements of array **$Name** will be arranged according to the descending alphabetical order of index.

Example 11

The following program will illustrate the use of **sort()**, **asort()**, **arsort()**, and **ksort()** functions. The program will display the sorted array elements with their index as output in the browser.

```
<!Doctype html>                                      1
<html>                                               2
<head>                                               3
<title>Array sorting function</title>                4
</head>                                              5
<body>                                               6
```

Arrays

```php
<?php                                                               7
  echo "<h3>sort()</h3>";                                           8
  $Number=array("Q"=>4,"S"=>1,"P"=>3,"R"=>2);                       9
  sort($Number);                                                    10
  foreach ($Number as $k => $val)                                   11
  {                                                                 12
     echo "Index = " . $k . ", Element = " . $val . "<br>";         13
  }                                                                 14
  echo "<h3>asort()</h3>";                                          15
  $Number=array("Q"=>4,"S"=>1,"P"=>3,"R"=>2);                       16
  asort($Number);                                                   17
  foreach ($Number as $k => $val)                                   18
  {                                                                 19
     echo "Index = " . $k . ", Element = " . $val . "<br>";         20
  }                                                                 21
  echo "<h3>arsort()</h3>";                                         22
  $Number=array("Q"=>4,"S"=>1,"P"=>3,"R"=>2);                       23
  arsort($Number);                                                  24
  foreach ($Number as $k => $val)                                   25
  {                                                                 26
     echo "Index = " . $k . ", Element = " . $val . "<br>";         27
  }                                                                 28
  echo "<h3>ksort()</h3>";                                          29
  $Number=array("Q"=>4,"S"=>1,"P"=>3,"R"=>2);                       30
  ksort($Number);                                                   31
  foreach($Number as $k => $val)                                    32
  {                                                                 33
     echo "Index = " . $k . ", Element = " . $val . "<br>";         34
  }                                                                 35
?>                                                                  36
</body>                                                             37
</html>                                                             38
```

Explanation

Line 10
sort($Number);
In this line, **sort($Number)** is an array function used to sort the array elements in ascending order. It does not maintain the associated index of the array elements. Here, **$Number** is the array variable which holds an array. All the elements of array **$Number** will be arranged in numerical order and their index will also get changed accordingly.

Line 17
asort($Number);
In this line, **asort($Number)** is an array function used to sort the array elements in ascending order. It maintains the associated index of the array elements. Here, **$Number** is the array variable which holds an array. All the elements of array **$Number** will be arranged in numerical order and their index will not get changed.

Line 24
arsort($Number);
In this line, **arsort($Number)** is an array function used to sort the array elements in descending order. It maintains the associated index of the array elements. Here, **$Number** is the array variable which holds an array. All the elements of array **$Number** will be arranged in descending numerical order and their index will not get changed.

Line 31
ksort($Number);
In this line, **ksort($Number)** is an array function used to sort the array elements in ascending order according to the index of array elements. Here, **$Number** is the array variable which holds an array. All the elements of array **$Number** will be arranged according to the alphabetical order of their index.

The output of Example 11 is displayed in Figure 8-12.

sort()

Index = 0, Element = 1
Index = 1, Element = 2
Index = 2, Element = 3
Index = 3, Element = 4

asort()

Index = S, Element = 1
Index = R, Element = 2
Index = P, Element = 3
Index = Q, Element = 4

arsort()

Index = Q, Element = 4
Index = P, Element = 3
Index = R, Element = 2
Index = S, Element = 1

ksort()

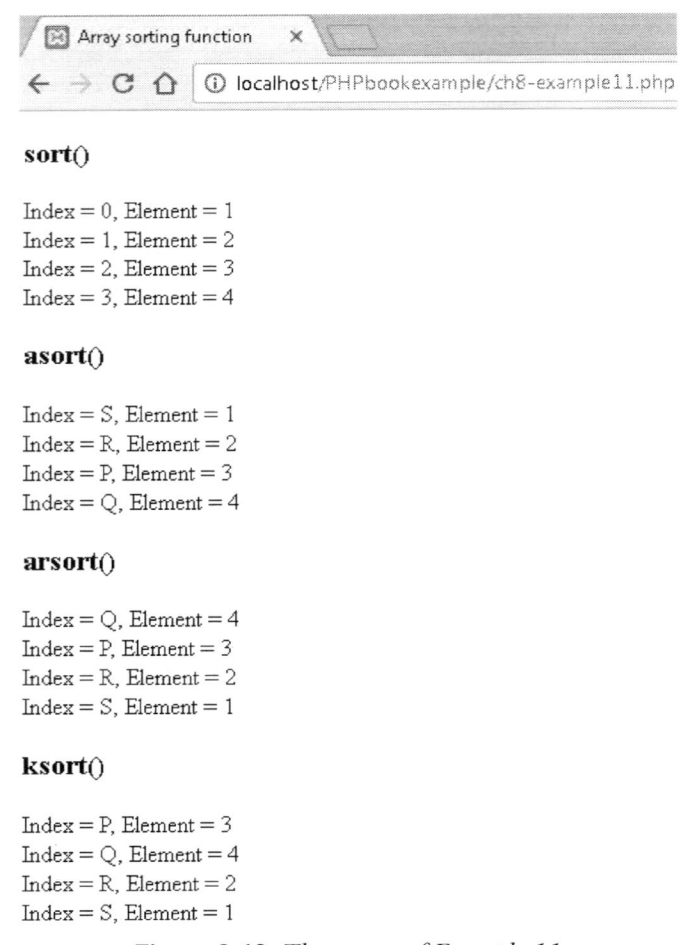

Index = P, Element = 3
Index = Q, Element = 4
Index = R, Element = 2
Index = S, Element = 1

Figure 8-12 The output of Example 11

Arrays

count()

The **count()** is an array function used to count the total number of array elements in an array. The syntax of **count()** is as follows:

```
count($array_name,mode);
```

In the given syntax, **count( )** is the array function, **$array_name** represents the array variable which holds an array, and **mode** represents the mode of element counting which is optional. The two possible values of **mode** are **1** and **0** where **0** is the default value that does not count every element of multidimensional array and **1** is the recursive mode that counts every element of multidimensional array.

Example 12

The following program illustrates the use of array function **count()**. The program will count the elements of the multidimensional array and display the output in the browser by using the **echo** statement.

```
<!Doctype html>                                                  1
<html>                                                           2
<head>                                                           3
<title>count() function</title>                                  4
</head>                                                          5
<body>                                                           6
<?php                                                            7
    $result = array(                                             8
        "Tom" => array (                                         9
                        "english" => 50,                        10
                        "maths" => 80,                          11
                        "science" => 70                         12
                       ),                                       13
        "John" => array (                                       14
                        "english" => 70,                        15
                        "maths" => 90,                          16
                        "science" => 80                         17
                       ),                                       18
        "Larry" => array (                                      19
                        "english" => 80,                        20
                        "maths" => 70,                          21
                        "science" => 60                         22
                       ),                                       23
        "Harry" => array (                                      24
                        "english" => 80,                        25
                        "maths" => 77,                          26
                        "science" => 88                         27
                       )                                        28
    );                                                          29
echo "<b>Normal count : " . count($result)."</b><br>";          30
```

```
echo "<b>Recursive count : " . count($result,1)."</b>";     31
?>                                                           32
</body>                                                      33
</html>                                                      34
```

Explanation
Line 30
echo "Normal count : " . count($result). "<br>";
In this line, **count($result)** is an array function used to count the array elements normally. This means the **count()** function will not count all the element of **$result** multidimensional array. This line will display the following in the browser:

Normal count   : 4

Line 31
echo "Recursive count : " . count($result,1)."";
In this line, **count($result,1)** is an array function used to count the array elements recursively. Here, **$result** is an array variable and **1** is the **mode** which means the **count()** function will count all the element of **$result** multidimensional array. This line will display the following in the browser:

Recursive count : 16

The output of Example 12 is displayed in Figure 8-13.

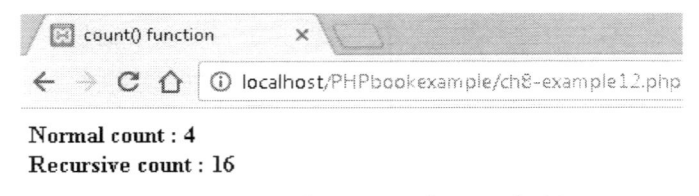

Figure 8-13 The output of Example 12

compact()
The **compact()** is an array function used to create an array from variables. The syntax of **compact()** is as follows:

```
compact("variable1","variable2",$array_name,...)
```

In the given syntax, **compact( )** is the array function used to create an array by passing different variable names as parameters. Here, **variable1** and **variable2** represent variable name without $ sign written inside the double quotes. You can also pass array variable inside the **compact()** function with $ sign without any qoutes. Here, **$array_name** represents array variable.

> **Note**
> *If the parameter passed inside the function **compact()** is not an array name or variable then the function **compact()** will skip that parameter.*

Example 13

The following program illustrates the use of array function **compact()**. The program will create an array from different variables by using function **compact()** and display the output in the browser.

```
<!Doctype html>                                          1
<html>                                                   2
<head>                                                   3
<title>compact() function</title>                        4
</head>                                                  5
<body>                                                   6
<?php                                                    7
    $Name = "Mike";                                      8
    $place = "London";                                   9
    $age = "21";                                        10
        $detail = array("Name", "place");               11
        $output = compact($detail,"birthdate","age");   12
        print_r($output);                               13
?>                                                      14
</body>                                                 15
</html>                                                 16
```

Explanation
Line 11
$detail = array("Name", "place");
In this line, **$detail** is an array variable which is holding an **array()**. Here, **Name** and **place** are the variable names declared in Line 8 and Line 9, respectively. These variable names are passed inside the **array()** as array elements without **$** sign.

Line 12
$output = compact($detail,"birthdate", "age");
In this line, **$output** is a variable that holds the values returned by the function **compact()**. Here, **compact()** is the function used to create an array by converting variable name into index of an array elements and variable values into array elements. **$detail** is an array variable declared in Line 11, **birthdate** is neither an array nor a variable so this will be skipped by the **compact()** function, and **age** is the variable name declared in Line 10.

The output of Example 13 is displayed in Figure 8-14.

Array ([Name] => Mike [place] => London [age] => 21)

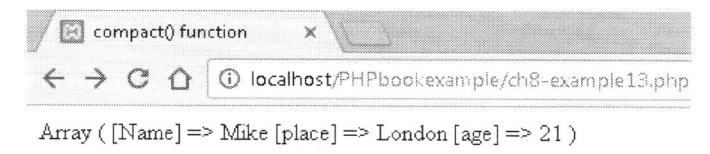

Figure 8-14 *The output of Example 13*

explode()

The **explode()** is an array function used to create an array from a string separated by a single character. The syntax of **explode()** is as follows:

```
explode(separator,string,limit)
```

In the given syntax, **explode( )** is an array function used to create an array by passing a string as parameters to the function **explode( )**. Here, **separator** represents any single character which will work as a separator to break the string and it cannot be blank. The **string** represents the string that is to be converted into array, and the **limit** represents an optional parameter which is used to set the limit of elements in the array.

If the value passed in place of **limit** will be greater than **0** then that value will be the maximum limit of an array element. If the value passed in place of **limit** will be less than **0** then that value will be subtracted from the total number of elements and remaining elements will be displayed. If the value passed in place of **limit** will be equal to **0** then only 1 element will be displayed in the array, and if the **limit** is not passed in the function **explode()** then all the possible elements are displayed in the array.

Example 14

The following program illustrates the use of array function **explode()**. The program will create an array from a string by using the function **explode()** and display the output in the browser.

```
<!Doctype html>                                              1
<html>                                                       2
<head>                                                       3
<title>compact() function</title>                            4
</head>                                                      5
<body>                                                       6
<?php                                                        7
    $fruits = "Apple,Mango,Pineapple,Grapes,Strawberry";     8
        print_r(explode(",",$fruits,0));                     9
        print "<br>";                                        10
        print_r(explode(",",$fruits,4));                     11
        print "<br>";                                        12
        print_r(explode(",",$fruits));                       13
        print "<br>";                                        14
        print_r(explode(",",$fruits,-3));                    15
?>                                                           16
</body>                                                      17
</html>                                                      18
```

Explanation
Line 8
$fruits = "Apple,Mango,Pineapple,Grapes,Strawberry";
In this line, **$fruit** is a variable which holds a string type data.

Arrays 8-37

Line 9
print_r(explode(",",$fruits,0));
In this line, **explode()** is the function used to create an array from a string. Here, comma(,) is the separator of the string. **$fruit** is the string type variable which is declared in Line 8, and **0** is the limit which will only display one element in the array. This line will display the following in the browser:

Array ([0] => Apple,Mango,Pineapple,Grapes,Strawberry)

Line 11
print_r(explode(",",$fruits,4));
In this line, the limit is set to **4** which will display maximum four elements in the array. This line will display the following in the browser:

Array ([0] => Apple [1] => Mango [2] => Pineapple [3] => Grapes,Strawberry)

Line 13
print_r(explode(",",$fruits));
In this line, no limit is passed inside the function **explode()**. Therefore, it will display all the elements in the array. In this case, it will display five elements. This line will display the following in the browser:

Array ([0] => Apple [1] => Mango [2] => Pineapple [3] => Grapes [4] => Strawberry)

Line 15
print_r(explode(",",$fruits,-3));
In this line, the limit is set to **-3** which will display maximum two elements out of five elements in the array. This line will display the following in the browser:

Array ([0] => Apple [1] => Mango)

The output of Example 14 is displayed in Figure 8-15.

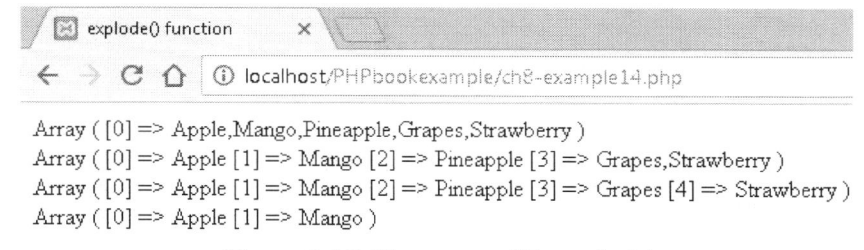

Figure 8-15 The output of Example 14

CONDITIONAL TESTING USING ARRAY OPERATORS
Conditional testing means to check whether the given condition is true or false where true and false are boolean type values. You have already learned about conditional control structure in chapter 6. The conditional control structure performs conditional testing. In this section, you will perform conditional testing between two or more arrays by using various array operators. You have already learned about array operators in Chapter 5.

Example 15

The following program illustrates the use of boolean data type in conditional testing by using array operators. The program will check the given condition and return the boolean value. It will also perform array union and display the output in the browser.

```
<!Doctype html>                                                   1
<html>                                                            2
<head>                                                            3
<title>Conditional testing</title>                                4
</head>                                                           5
<body>                                                            6
<?php                                                             7
$a = array("Apple","Mango","Pineapple","Grapes","Strawberry");    8
$b = array("Q"=>1,"S"=>2,"P"=>3,"R"=>4);                          9
$c = array("Q"=>1,"S"=>2,"P"=>3,"R"=>4);                         10
$d = array("U"=>1,"V"=>2,"W"=>3,"X"=>4);                         11
print_r($a + $b);                                                12
echo"<br>";                                                      13
    var_dump($a == $b);                                          14
    echo"<br>";                                                  15
    var_dump($b == $c);                                          16
    echo"<br>";                                                  17
    var_dump($b === $c);                                         18
    echo"<br>";                                                  19
    var_dump($c === $d);                                         20
    echo"<br>";                                                  21
    var_dump($a != $b);                                          22
    echo"<br>";                                                  23
    var_dump($b != $c);                                          24
    echo"<br>";                                                  25
    var_dump($b !== $c);                                         26
    echo"<br>";                                                  27
    var_dump($c !== $d);                                         28
?>                                                               29
</body>                                                          30
</html>                                                          31
```

Explanation
Line 12
print_r($a + $b);
In this line, Union operator (**+**) is used in between two array variables **$a** and **$b**. Here, the + operator will join both the arrays stored in variables **$a** and **$b**. This line will display the following in the browser:

Array ([0] => Apple [1] => Mango [2] => Pineapple [3] => Grapes [4] => Strawberry [Q] => 1 [S] => 2 [P] => 3 [R] => 4)

Arrays

Line 14
var_dump($a == $b);
In this line, the equality comparison is performed between **$a** and **$b** by using the == operator. It will compare the equality between the array elements of two variables **$a** and **$b**. Here, the elements of both the arrays do not match, therefore, it will return **false**. This line will display the following in the browser:

bool(false)

Line 16
var_dump($b == $c);
In this line, the equality comparison is performed between **$b** and **$c** by using the == operator. It will compare the equality between the array elements of two variables **$b** and **$c**. Here, the elements of both the arrays match, therefore, it will return **true**. This line will display the following in the browser:

bool(true)

Line 18
var_dump($b === $c);
In this line, === operator is used to compare the equality between the array elements of two variables **$b** and **$c** including their order, index and the data type. Here, the elements, order, index, and data type of both the arrays match, therefore, it will return **true**. This line will display the following in the browser:

bool(true)

Line 20
var_dump($c === $d);
In this line, === operator is used to compare the equality between the array elements of two variables **$c** and **$d** including their order, index and the data type. Here, the elements, order, and data type of both the arrays match, but their indexes do not match, therefore, it will return **false**. This line will display the following in the browser:

bool(false)

Line 22
var_dump($a != $b);
In this line, the inequality comparison is performed between **$a** and **$b** by using the != operator. It will compare the inequality between the array elements of two variables **$a** and **$b**. Here, the elements of both the arrays do not match, therefore, it will return **true**. This line will display the following in the browser:

bool(true)

Line 24
var_dump($b != $c);
In this line, the inequality comparison is performed between **$b** and **$c** by using **!=** operator. It will compare the inequality between the array elements of two variables **$b** and **$c**. Here, the elements of both the arrays do match, therefore, it will return **false**. This line will display the following in the browser:

bool(false)

Line 26
var_dump($b !== $c);
In this line, the **!==** operator is used to compare the inequality between the array elements of two variables **$b** and **$c** including their order, index, and the data type. Here, the elements, order, index, and data type of both the arrays do match, therefore, it will return **false**. This line will display the following in the browser:

bool(false)

Line 28
var_dump($c !== $d);
In this line, **!==** operator is used to compare the equality between the array elements of two variables **$c** and **$d** including their order, index, and the data type. Here, the elements, order, and data type of both the arrays match with each other but their indexes does not match, therefore, it will return **true**. This line will display the following in the browser:

bool(true)

The output of Example 15 is displayed in Figure 8-16.

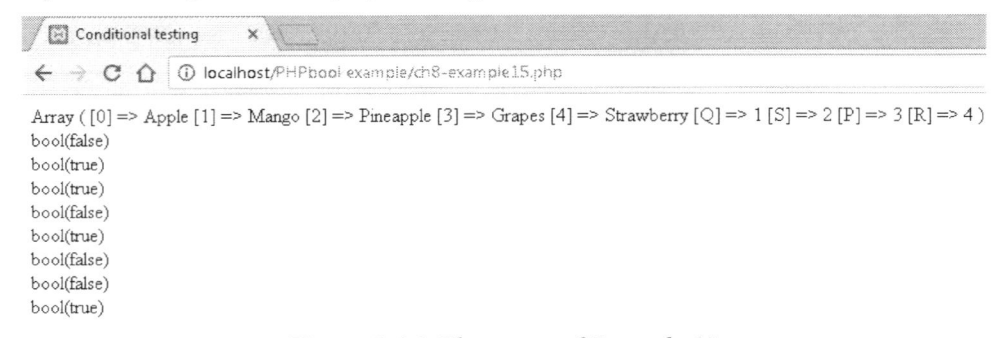

Figure 8-16 The output of Example 15

Self-Evaluation Test

Answer the following questions and then compare them to those given at the end of this chapter:

1. An _____ is a data type that can hold multiple data in a single variable.

Arrays 8-41

2. The _____ array consists of numeric keys.

3. The _____ array consists of named keys also known as named index.

4. The array of arrays is known as _____ array.

5. The _____ loop is used to make iteration over a collection of objects such as arrays.

6. The **asort()** function is an array function used to sort the array elements in descending order. (T/F)

7. The **count()** function is an array function used to count the total number of array elements in an array. (T/F)

8. The **explode()** function is an array function used to create an array from variables. (T/F)

Review Questions

Answer the following questions:

1. Which of the following data types can hold multiple data in a single variable?

   (a) Object   (b) String
   (c) Array   (d) Integer

2. Which of the following is the correct syntax of an indexed array?

   (a) `$array_name = array(list of array elements);`
   (b) `$array_name = array[list of array elements];`
   (c) `$array_name = "list of array elements";`
   (d) None of the above

3. Which of the following is the correct syntax of an associative array?

   (a) `$array_name = array(list of array elements);`
   (b) `$array_name = ["index_name"] "element";`
   (c) `$array_name = "list of array elements";`
   (d) `$array_name["index_name"]= "element";`

4. Which of the following functions will print the value of a variable declared inside the parentheses of the function in human readable format?

   (a) **count()**   (b) **print_r()**
   (c) **arsort()**   (d) **ksort()**

5. Which of the following functions is used to create an array from variables?

   (a) **explode()** (b) **asort()**
   (c) **compact()** (d) **count()**

EXERCISES

Exercise 1

Using the multidimensional associative array, write a program to display a list of fruits using named index.

Exercise 2

Write a program to arrange the elements of an array in descending order by using the **arsort()** array function.

Answers to Self-Evaluation Test

1. array, **2.** indexed, **3.** associative, **4.** multidimensional, **5. foreach**, **6.** F, **7.** T, **8.** F

Chapter 9

Form Implementation and Validation

Learning Objectives

After completing this chapter, you will be able to:
- *Understand the HTML form elements*
- *Understand form methods and action*
- *Understand the concept of JavaScript*
- *Understand the $_GET and $_POST superglobal variables*
- *Understand regular expressions*

INTRODUCTION

HTML forms are very important part of any dynamic website. An HTML form plays a key role to make any website interactive and user friendly. The forms are generally used to get the user details. You can create a form for your website using HTML 5. The PHP language is used along with HTML 5 to create dynamic forms in the website and to validate these forms, JavaScript is used. In this chapter, you will learn about HTML 5 form elements, form methods and action, JavaScript, and so on in detail.

HTML FORM ELEMENTS

HTML form elements are used to create a form in a website. The HTML form elements are form tags used to create different elements of form such as labels, buttons, drop-down list, input controls, and so on. The syntax to create HTML form is as follow:

```
<form>
 <!-- Form elements -->
</form>
```

In the given syntax, **<form>** is the start tag of HTML form body and **</form>** is the end tag of HTML form body. The form elements such as input text-box, labels, textarea, and so on are placed in between **<form>** and **</form>** tags.

Note
Every content from the start tag to the end tag of HTML is known as HTML element.

Attributes

An attribute in HTML provides additional information to the HTML elements. It is always written inside HTML start tag (HTML element) and contains a value. The syntax of attribute is as follow:

```
<tagname attribute="value">
```

In the given syntax, **<tagname>** represents any start tag (element) of HTML. Here, **attribute** represents any element attribute which provides additional information to the element and **value** represents any value related to the attribute also known as attribute description.

It is not necessary that every attribute will have a value. In that case, the syntax for attribute will be as follow:

```
<tagname attribute>
```

Form Input Element

An HTML form can contain various input controls such as text-box, check-box, radio-buttons, and so on. Therefore, form input elements are required to create these form input controls.

Form Implementation and Validation

The syntax of form input element is as follow:

```
<input type="value">
```

In the given syntax, **<input>** is the start tag (element) of the input control. The input element does not have end tag. Here, **type** is an input element attribute which provides additional information to the input element and **value** represents any value related to the **type** attribute.

There are various values available for the **type** attribute of the input element. Table 9-1 lists some of the possible values of the **type** attribute with their descriptions.

*Table 9-1 Values and descriptions of the **type** attribute*

Value	Description
text	It provides one-line input text box.
checkbox	It provides a single check box.
radio	It provides a single radio button.
submit	It provides a submit button for HTML form submission.
date	It provides the date calender for date selection.
email	It provides a input box with email validation in the form.
file	It provides the choose file button to browse a file to upload.
password	It provides the input box following the password pattern.
search	It provides the search box.
url	It provides the input box with URL validation in form.
button	It provides a button.

Example 1

The following program illustrates the use of HTML input elements. The program will create a static form containing various form controls by using the input element and display the output in the browser.

```
<!Doctype html>                                      1
<html>                                               2
<head>                                               3
<title>Form</title>                                  4
</head>                                              5
<body>                                               6
<h1>Form</h1>                                        7
    <form>                                           8
        <p><b>Name:</b>                              9
            <input type="text">                      10
        </p>                                         11
        <p><b>Gender:</b><br>                        12
            <input type="radio" name="gender" >Male  13
```

```
                    <input type="radio" name="gender" >Female      14
        </p>                                                        15
        <p><b>Languages:</b><br>                                    16
                    <input type="checkbox"> PHP                     17
                    <input type="checkbox"> HTML                    18
                    <input type="checkbox"> java                    19
                    <input type="checkbox"> c++                     20
        </p>                                                        21
        <p><b>Email:</b>                                            22
                    <input type="email" required>                   23
        </p>                                                        24
        <p><b>Password:</b>                                         25
                    <input type="password" required>                26
        </p>                                                        27
        <p><b>URL:</b>                                              28
                    <input type="url" required>                     29
        </p>                                                        30
        <p><b>Date:</b>                                             31
                    <input type="date">                             32
        </p>                                                        33
        <p>                                                         34
                    <input type="submit">                           35
        </p>                                                        36
        <p><b>File:</b>                                             37
                    <input type="file">                             38
                    <input type="button" value="upload">            39
        </p>                                                        40
    </form>                                                         41
</body>                                                             42
</html>                                                             43
```

Explanation
Line 8
<form>
In this line, **<form>** is the start tag of HTML form body.

Line 9 to Line 11
<p>Name:
    <input type="text">
</p>

In these lines, **<p>** and **</p>** are the paragraph elements of HTML. **Name** is the normal HTML content written in between the paragraph elements and **<input type="text">** is the input element of HTML where **type** is the attribute that has value **text**. It will create a one-line input text box inside the form.

Line 12 to Line 15
**<p>Gender:
**
    <input type= "radio" name="gender" >Male

Form Implementation and Validation   9-5

                <input type= "radio" name="gender" >Female
</p>

In these lines, **Gender:**, **Male**, and **Female** are the normal HTML content written in between the paragraph elements and **<input type="radio" name="gender">** is the input element of HTML where **type** is the attribute that has value **radio** and **name** is the attribute which can contain any name as its value. These lines will create two radio buttons in a paragraph inside the form.

> **Note**
> *Keep the values of attribute **name** same for the radio buttons of same category and keep the different value of attribute **name** for different category because if a user clicks on a radio button, it becomes checked and all other radio buttons with same name becomes unchecked.*

Line 16 to Line 21
**<p>Languages:
**
        <input type="checkbox"> PHP
        <input type="checkbox"> HTML
        <input type="checkbox"> java
        <input type="checkbox"> c++
</p>

In these lines, **<input type="checkbox">** is the input element of HTML where **type** is the attribute that has value **checkbox**. These lines will create 4 check boxes in a paragraph inside the form.

Line 23
<input type="email" required>
In this line, **<input type="email" required>** is the input element of HTML where **type** is the attribute that has value **email** and **required** is the attribute of input element which makes the particular that has field mandatory to be filled. This lines will create a single field text box with email validations in a paragraph inside the form.

Line 26
<input type="password" required>
In this line, **<input type="password" required>** is the input element of HTML where **type** is the attribute that has value **password** and **required** is the attribute of input element which makes this particular input field mandatory to be filled. This lines will create a single field text box which will follow the password pattern inside the form.

Line 29
<input type="url" required>
In this line, **<input type="url" required>** is the input element of HTML where **type** is the attribute that has value **url** and **required** is the attribute of input element which makes this particular input field mandatory to be filled. This lines will create a single field text box with the URL validations in a paragraph inside the form.

Line 32
<input type="date">
In this line, **<input type="date">** is the input element of HTML where **type** is the attribute

that has value **date**. This lines will create a text box which will display the date calender for date selection in the drop-down menu inside the text box.

Line 35
<input type="submit">
In this line, **<input type="submit">** is the input element of HTML where **type** is the attribute that has value **submit**. This lines will create a submit button of the form.

Line 38
<input type="file">
In this line, **<input type="file">** is the input element of HTML where **type** is the attribute that has value **file**. This lines will create the **choose file** button to browse a file in the system.

Line 39
<input type="button" value="upload">
In this line, **<input type="button" value="upload">** is the input element of HTML where **type** is the attribute that has value **button** and **value** is the attribute of input element which provide label to the button. This line will create the button with the label **upload**.

Line 41
</form>
In this line, **</form>** is the end tag of HTML form body.

The output of Example 1 is displayed in Figure 9-1.

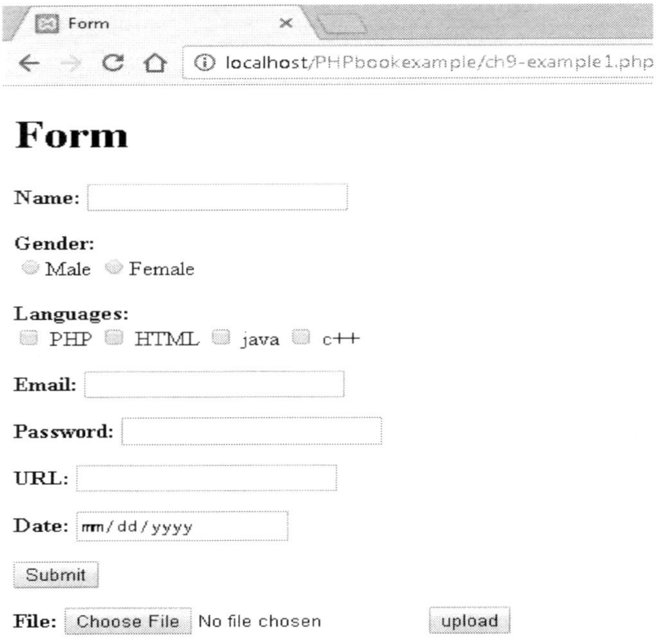

Figure 9-1 *The output of Example 1*

Form select Element

The form select element in HTML is used to create and define a drop-down list. The syntax of form select element is as follow:

```
<select name="val">
  <option value="item">Item</option>
  <option value="item2">Item2</option>
  ----
  ----
  <option value="itemN">ItemN</option>
</select>
```

In the given syntax, **<select>** and **</select>** are the select elements of HTML used to create drop-down list. Here, **name** is a select element attribute which provides additional information to the select element and **val** represents any name given to the select element through **name** attribute. To define the drop-down list, option element is used which is declared in between the select elements. Here, in the syntax, **<option>** and **</option>** are the option elements containing the attribute **value** which provides label or value to the option element and **Item** defined in between the option elements represents any name which is to be displayed in drop-down list. Therefore, to define N numbers of items in the drop-down list you need to define N numbers of option elements in between the select elements. By default the first item entered in the option elements is displayed in the drop-down text box.

Form datalist Element

The form datalist element in HTML is used to create a drop-down list which will display list of options when the user will start providing input data. The syntax of form datalist element is as follow:

```
<input list= "browsers">
  <datalist id="browsers">
    <option value="item1">
    <option value="item2">
    -----
    -----
    <option value="itemN">
  </datalist>
```

In the given syntax, **<datalist>** and **</datalist>** are the datalist elements of HTML used to create drop-down list which will display list of options when the user will start providing input data. Therefore, to get input from the user its important to have an input element to create the drop-down list using datalist elements. Here, **<input list="browsers">** is the input element that has an attribute **list** containing a value **browsers** which is fixed and cant not be changed. Now, the **<datalist>** element contains an attribute **id** having a value **browsers** which is also fixed and can not be changed. The attribute **id** provides identity to an element in an HTML. To define the drop-down list, option element is used which is declared in between the datalist elements. Here, in the syntax, **<option>** is the option element containing the attribute **value** which provides label or value to the option element which is to be displayed in drop-down list.

Therefore, to define N numbers of items in the drop-down list you need to define N numbers of option elements in between the datalist elements.

> **Note**
> *The datalist element is not supported by Safari, IE9, and earlier versions of IE.*

Form textarea Element

The form textarea element in HTML is used to create the multiple line input text box. The syntax of form textarea element is as follow:

```
<textarea>Content</textarea>
```

In the given syntax, **<textarea>** and **</textarea>** are the textarea elements of HTML used to create a multiple line input text box. Here, **Content** represents any content you want to write inside the text box which will get displayed in the browser. You can even skip writing content if you want user to provide the input.

Form button Element

The form button element in HTML is used to create the button. The syntax of form button element is as follow:

```
<button>button label</button>
```

In the given syntax, **<button>** and **</button>** are the button elements of HTML used to create the button. Here, **button label** represents any name or label of the button.

Form fieldset Element

The form fieldset element in HTML is used to create the form field (border) within which the form elements will exist. The syntax of form fieldset element is as follow:

```
<fieldset>
<!-- different form elements -->
</fieldset>
```

In the given syntax, **<fieldset>** and **</fieldset>** are the fieldset elements of HTML used to create the form field (border) within which the form elements will exist. You can place different form elements such as input, textarea, button, and so on elements in between fieldset elements.

Example 2

The following program will create a static form containing various form elements and display the output in the browser.

```
<!Doctype html>                                                 1
<html>                                                          2
<head>                                                          3
```

Form Implementation and Validation

```
<title>Form</title>                                         4
</head>                                                     5
<body>                                                      6
<h1>Form elements</h1>                                      7
    <form>                                                  8
         <fieldset style="width:300px">                     9
         <p><b>Name:</b>                                   10
             <input type="text">                           11
         </p>                                              12
         <p><b>Age group:</b>                              13
             <input list="browsers">                       14
             <datalist id="browsers">                      15
                  <option value="10-19">                   16
                  <option value="20-29">                   17
                  <option value="30-39">                   18
                  <option value="40-49">                   19
                  <option value="50">                      20
             </datalist>                                   21
         </p>                                              22
         <p><b>Language:</b>                               23
             <select>                                      24
                  <option value="English">English</option> 25
                  <option value="Hindi">Hindi</option>     26
                  <option value="Spanish">Spanish</option> 27
                  <option value="French">French</option>   28
             </select>                                     29
         </p>                                              30
         <p><b>Comment:</b>                                31
             <textarea></textarea>                         32
         </p>                                              33
         <button type="submit">Send</button>               34
         </fieldset>                                       35
    </form>                                                36
</body>                                                    37
</html>                                                    38
```

Explanation
Line 9
<fieldset style="width:300px">
In this line, **<fieldset>** is the start tag of HTML used to create the form field (border) within which the form elements will exist. Here, **style** is the attribute used to provide inline CSS to the fieldset element where **width** is CSS property followed by **:** (colon) and **300px** is its description. This will set the width of the fieldset to 300 pixels.

Line 14 to Line 21
<input list="browsers">
<datalist id="browsers">
    <option value="10-19">

```
            <option value= "20-29">
            <option value="30-39">
            <option value="40-49">
            <option value="50">
</datalist>
```

In these lines, **<input list="browsers">** is the input element having an attribute **list** that contains a value **browsers** which is fixed and cannot be changed. The **<datalist>** and **</datalist>** are the datalist elements of HTML used to create drop-down list which will display list of options when the user will start providing input data. Here, the **<datalist>** element contains an attribute **id** having a value **browsers** which is also fixed and can not be changed. Next, **<option>** is the option element containing the attribute **value** which provides label or value to the option element which is to be displayed in drop-down list.

Line 24 to Line 29
```
<select>
        <option value="English">English</option>
        <option value="Hindi">Hindi</option>
        <option value="Spanish">Spanish</option>
        <option value="French">French</option>
</select>
```

In these lines, **<select>** and **</select>** are the select elements of HTML used to create drop-down list. Next, **<option>** and **</option>** are the option elements that contain the attribute **value** which provides label or value to the option element and **English**, **Hindi**, **Spanish**, and **French** defined in between the option elements are the items which is to be displayed in drop-down list.

Line 32
<textarea></textarea>
In this line, **<textarea>** and **</textarea>** are the textarea elements of HTML used to create a multiple line input text box.

Line 34
<button type="submit">Send</button>
In this line, **<button>** and **</button>** are the button elements of HTML used to create the button where **type** is an attribute of button element having value **submit**. Here, **Send** is the label given to the button.

Line 35
</fieldset>
In this line, **</fieldset>** is the end tag of HTML used to end the form field (border) within which the form elements will exist.

The output of Example 2 is displayed in Figure 9-2.

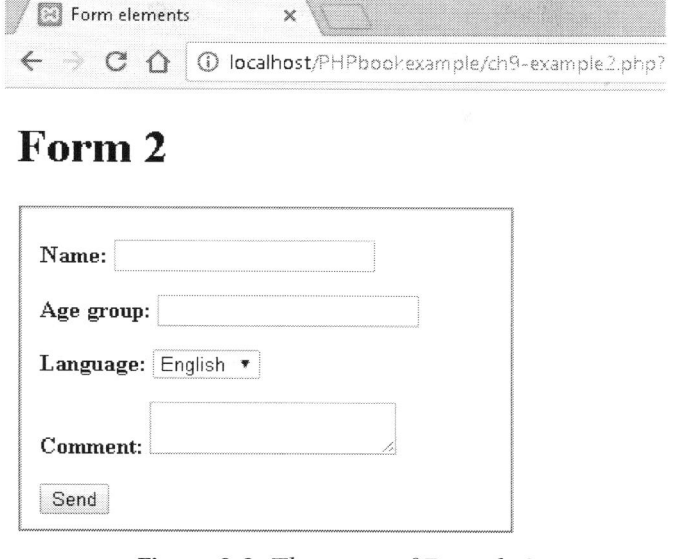

Figure 9-2 The output of Example 2

FORM METHODS AND ACTION

The form method specifies the method by which the form data will be sent. The form data is sent to the page which is specified by the form action. To specify the form method an attribute **method** is used inside the **<form>** tag and to specify the page where the data will be sent, the attribute **action** is used inside the **<form>** tag.

The attribute method can have two possible values that are as follow:

1. **get**
2. **post**

These form methods are discussed next.

The get Method

The **get** method is used when the user wants to send or append the form result into URL to bookmark the result. These results are appended into URL in the form of name/value pair. The **get** method is not secure as the input data of the form sent through the **get** method is visible to everyone in the URL. Therefore, never use the **get** method to send sensitive data such as password. The data that can be appended to URL through the **get** method is limited because the length of an URL is limited to 3000 characters approximately. You can use the **get** method to send data such as query strings similar to Google search.

The syntax of the **get** method is as follow:

```
<form method= "get">
```

In the given syntax, **<form>** is the start tag of HTML form where **method** is an attribute of form element and **get** is the method through which form data will be sent to the page.

The post Method

The **post** method is used to transfer data using HTTP header. This is the secure method to send the input data to another page, for example, to send sensitive data such as password you must use the **post** method instead of the **get** method. There is no data limit in post method, you can send multiple data to another page at a time. The data send by the **post** method can not be bookmarked and is not visible to everyone that is why it is more secure than the **get** method.

The syntax of the **post** method is as follow:

```
<form method= "post">
```

In the given syntax, **<form>** is the start tag of HTML form where **method** is an attribute of form element and **post** is the method through which form data will be sent to the page.

Form Action

The **action** is a form attribute used to specify the page where the form data will be sent by using the **get** or **post** method. The syntax of form action is as follow:

```
<form action="page.extension">
```

In the given syntax, **<form>** is the start tag of HTML form where **action** is an attribute of form element and **page.extension** represents the page where the form data will be sent.

RECEIVING FORM DATA IN PHP

The PHP file is used to receive or display the form data sent through the HTML file by using the two major form attributes: **method** and **action**. To receive the form data, you need to use some pre-defined PHP variables known as superglobals. You have already learned about superglobals in Chapter 4. In this section, you will learn and use some of them in PHP script to receive the data in PHP file as discussed next.

The $_GET Superglobial Variable

The **$_GET** superglobal variable is used in the PHP script when the form through which the PHP file is receiving the data is using the **get** method to send the data.

The syntax of using the **$_GET** superglobal variable to receive the form data in a PHP script is as follow:

```
$_GET["name"]
```

In the given syntax, **$_GET[]** is an array variable used to receive the data of form sent through the **get** method. Here, **name** represents the name of the form field through which the **$_GET[]** is receiving the data.

Example 3

In this example, you will create two programs, *ch9-example3-form.php* and *ch9-example3-formdata.php*, where the *ch9-example3-form.php* program will create a dynamic form containing various

Form Implementation and Validation

form elements and send the form data to *ch9-example3-formdata.php* program file using the **get** method and the **action** attribute. The *ch9-example3-formdata.php* program file will receive the form data from *ch9-example3-form.php* program file using the **$_GET** superglobal variable to display the output in the browser.

The *ch9-example3-form.php* program file.

```
<!Doctype html>                                                 1
<html>                                                          2
<head>                                                          3
<title>PHP Form</title>                                         4
</head>                                                         5
<body>                                                          6
<h1>PHP Form</h1>                                               7
    <form method="get" action="ch9-example3-formdata.php">      8
        <p><b>Name:</b>                                         9
            <input type="text" name="person" required>         10
        </p>                                                   11
        <p><b>Gender:</b>                                      12
            <br>                                               13
            <input type="radio" name="gender">Male             14
            <input type="radio" name="gender">Female           15
        </p>                                                   16
        <p><b>Email:</b>                                       17
            <input type="email" name="email" required>         18
        </p>                                                   19
        <p><b>Password:</b>                                    20
            <input type="password" name="pass" required>       21
        </p>                                                   22
        <input type="submit">                                  23
    </form>                                                    24
</body>                                                        25
</html>                                                        26
```

The *ch9-example3-formdata.php* program file.

```
<!Doctype html>                                                 1
<html>                                                          2
<head>                                                          3
<title>PHP Form Data</title>                                    4
</head>                                                         5
<body>                                                          6
<b>HELLO</b>                                                    7
    <?php                                                       8
echo $_GET["person"];                                           9
echo "<br>";                                                   10
echo "<b>Your email address is: </b>";                         11
echo $_GET["email"];                                           12
echo "<br>";                                                   13
```

9-13

```
        echo "<b>your password is: </b>". $_GET["pass"];        14
        ?>                                                      15
              <h3> Thank you for visiting :)</ h3>              16
    </body>                                                     17
    </html>                                                     18
```

Explanation (ch9-example3-form.php)
Line 8
<form method="get" action="ch9-example3-formdata.php">
In this line, **<form>** is the start tag of HTML form body where **method** and **action** are the two attributes that has **get** and **ch9-example3-formdata.php** values, respectively.

Line 10
<input type="text" name="person" required>
In this line, **name** is the attribute that has value **person** which is the name given to the input text field.

Explanation (ch9-example3-formdata.php)
Line 9
echo $_GET["person"];
In this line, **$_GET** [] is the superglobal variable used to receive the data of form sent through **get** method and **person** is the input text field name whose data is to be displayed.

The working of Line 12 and Line 14 is similar to Line 9

The output of Example 3 is displayed in Figure 9-3.

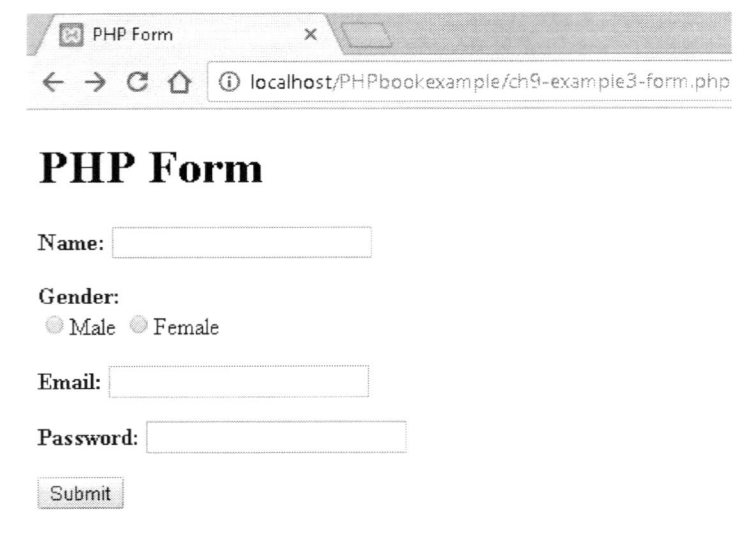

Figure 9-3 The output of Example 3

In Figure 9-3, the form is blank. Now, the user will enter the data to send it to another page as shown in Figure 9-4.

Form Implementation and Validation

Figure 9-4 The output of Example 3 with data in form

In *ch9-example3-formdata.php* data is filled as shown in Figure 9-4. Now the user will submit this data and the data will be sent to *ch9-example3-formdata.php* program. This program will receive the data and display the data in the URL because **get** method is used to send the data and the output will also be displayed, as shown in Figure 9-5.

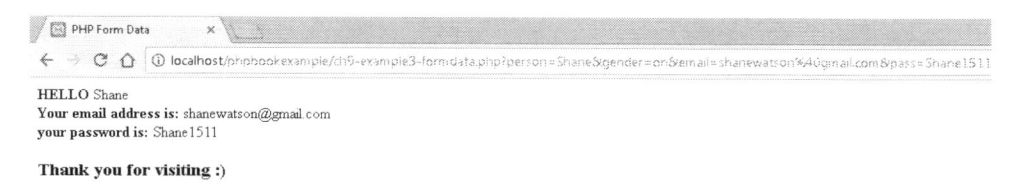

Figure 9-5 The output of Example 3 displaying form data

The $_POST Superglobal Variable

The **$_POST** superglobal variable is used in the PHP script when the form through which the PHP file is receiving the data is using the **post** method to send the data.

The syntax of using **$_POST** superglobal to receive the form data in a PHP script is as follow:

```
$_POST["name"]
```

In the given syntax, **$_POST[]** is an array variable used to receive the data of form sent through **post** method. Here, **name** represents the name of the form field through which the **$_POST[]** is receiving the data.

Example 4

In this example, you will create two programs, *ch9-example4-form.php* and *ch9-example4-formdata.php*, where the *ch9-example4-form.php* program will create a dynamic form containing various form elements and send the form data to *ch9-example4-formdata.php* program file using the **post** method and the **action** attribute. The *ch9-example4-formdata.php* program file will receive the form data from *ch9-example4-form.php* program file using the **$_POST** superglobal variable to display the output in the browser.

The *ch9-example4-form.php* program file.

```
<!Doctype html>                                                          1
<html>                                                                   2
<head>                                                                   3
<title>PHP post Form</title>                                             4
</head>                                                                  5
<body>                                                                   6
<h1>PHP Form 2</h1>                                                      7
    <form method="post" action="ch9-example4-formdata.php">              8
        <p><b>Name:</b>                                                  9
            <input type="text" name="person" required>                  10
        </p>                                                            11
        <p><b>Gender:</b>                                               12
            <br>                                                        13
            <input type="radio" name="gender">Male                      14
            <input type="radio" name="gender">Female                    15
        </p>                                                            16
        <p><b>Email:</b>                                                17
            <input type="email" name="email" required>                  18
        </p>                                                            19
        <p><b>Password:</b>                                             20
            <input type="password" name="pass" required>                21
        </p>                                                            22
        <input type="submit">                                           23
    </form>                                                             24
</body>                                                                 25
</html>                                                                 26
```

The *ch9-example4-formdata.php* program file.

```
<!Doctype html>                                                          1
<html>                                                                   2
<head>                                                                   3
<title>PHP POST Form Data</title>                                        4
</head>                                                                  5
<body>                                                                   6
<b>Hello</b>                                                             7
    <?php                                                                8
echo $_POST["person"];                                                   9
echo "<br>";                                                            10
echo "<b>Your email address is: </b>";                                  11
echo $_POST["email"];                                                   12
```

```
        echo "<br>";                                          13
        echo "<b>your password is: </b>". $_POST["pass"];     14
        ?>                                                    15
            <h3> Thank you for visiting :)</ h3>              16
    </body>                                                   17
    </html>                                                   18
```

Explanation (ch9-example4-form.php)
Line 8
<form method="post" action="ch9-example3-formdata.php">
In this line, <form> contain **method** and **action** attributes that has **post** and **ch9-example4-form-data.php** values, respectively.

Explanation (ch9-example4-formdata.php)
Line 9
echo $_POST["person"];
In this line, **$_POST []** is the superglobal variable used to receive the data of form sent through **post** method and **person** is the input text field name whose data is to be displayed.

The working of Line 12 and Line 14 is similar to Line 9

The output of Example 4 is displayed in Figure 9-6.

Figure 9-6 The output of Example 4

In Figure 9-6, the form is blank. Next, the user will enter the data to send it to another page, as shown in Figure 9-7.

Figure 9-7 The output of Example 4 with data in form

In Figure 9-7 the data is filled. Now the user will submit this data and then the data will be sent to *ch9-example4-formdata.php* program. This program will receive the data and the output will be displayed as shown in Figure 9-8.

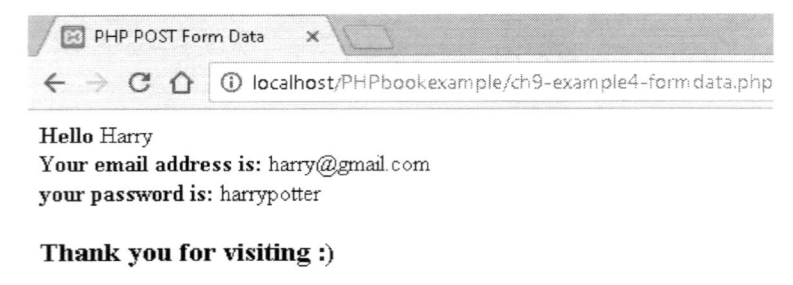

Figure 9-8 The output of Example 4 displaying form data

isset()

The **isset()** is the function used to check whether the variable is holding a value or not. If a variable is empty or have a **NULL** value then the **isset()** returns **false** otherwise **true**. The syntax of function **isset()** is as follow:

```
isset($var)
```

In the given syntax, **isset()** is the function and **$var** represents the variable. The **isset()** function will check whether the **$var** variable is holding a value or not.

trim()

The **trim()** function is used to remove the whitespace and other characters that are passed as parameter to the function, from the start and end point of a string. The syntax of function **trim()** is as follow:

```
trim($string,characters)
```

In the given syntax, **trim()** is the function containing two parameters where **$string** represents the variable holding string type value and **characters** represents any alphabet that is to be removed. The **$string** is the required parameter and **characters** is an optional parameter.

For example:

```
<?php
$str = "Hello User!";
echo trim($str,"Her!");
?>
//Output: llo Us
```

In the given example, **trim()** function will remove the **H,e,r**, and **!** characters from the **Hello User!** string assigned to **$str** variable and display the output **llo Us**.

stripslashes()

The **stripslashes()** function is used to remove the backslash(\) from the string. The syntax of function **stripslashes()** is as follow:

```
stripslashes($string)
```

In the given syntax, **stripslashes()** is the function containing a parameters **$string**. Here, **$string** represents the variable holding string type value.

For example:

```
<?php
$str = "Hello Ma\'am!!";
echo stripslashes($str);
?>
//Output: Hello Ma'am!!
```

In the given example, **stripslashes()** function will remove the backslash (\) from the **Hello Ma\'am!!** string assigned to **$str** variable and display the output **Hello Ma'am!!**.

htmlspecialchars()

The **htmlspecialchars()** function is used to convert the HTML special characters such as **<, >, &, ', ** and **"** into HTML entities. This means that the HTML special characters such as HTML tags will be treated as normal characters. The syntax of function **htmlspecialchars()** is as follow:

```
htmlsecialchars($string)
```

In the given syntax, **htmlspecialchars()** is the function containing a parameter **$string**. Here, **$string** represents the variable holding string type value which may contain HTML special characters.

For example:

```
<?php
$txt = "<h1> and </h1> are the start and end tags of HTML heading
    element.";
echo htmlspecialchars($txt);
?>
//Output: <h1> and </h1> are the start and end tags of HTML heading
    element.
```

In the given example, **htmlspecialchars()** function will convert the **<h1>** and **</h1>** tags into normal characters. Next, it will display the **<h1>** and **</h1>** tags in the browser by using the **echo** statement instead of performing the HTML heading element operation.

THE $_SERVER Superglobal Variable

The **$_SERVER** superglobal variable is used in the PHP script to get the entries in the array from the web server. The syntax of using **$_SERVER** superglobal is as follow:

```
$_SERVER['ELEMENT']
```

In the given syntax, **$_SERVER[]** is an array variable. Here, **ELEMENT** represents the predefined server elements, for example, **PHP_SELF**, **REQUEST_METHOD**, **SERVER_NAME** and so on.

Example 5

In this example, you will create two programs, *ch9-example5.php* and *ch9-example5-formdata.php*, where the *ch9-example5.php* program will create a dynamic form and send the form data to *ch9-example5-formdata.php* program file using the **post** method. The *ch9-example5-formdata.php* program file will receive the form data from *ch9-example5.php* program file by using the **$_POST** and **$_SERVER** superglobal variables and will check that data by using the **trim()**, **stripslashes()**, and **htmlspecialchars()** functions to display the output in the browser.

The *ch9-example5.php* program file.

```
<!Doctype html>                                           1
<html>                                                    2
<head>                                                    3
```

Form Implementation and Validation

```
<title>PHP Form 3</title>                                              4
<style>                                                                5
    .err {                                                             6
        color: red;                                                    7
        }                                                              8
    div {                                                              9
        border: double 5px black;                                     10
        padding: 25px;                                                11
        }                                                             12
    </style>                                                          13
</head>                                                               14
<body>                                                                15
<div>                                                                 16
    <h2>PHP Form 3</h2>                                               17
    <p><span class="err">* represents required field.</span></p>      18
    <form method="post" action="ch9-example5-Formdata.php">           19
    Name: <input type="text" name="name" required>                    21
    <span class="err">*</span>                                        22
    <br><br> Email:                                                   23
    <input type="email" name="email" required>                        24
    <span class="err">*</span>                                        25
    <br><br> Comment:                                                 26
    <textarea name="comment" rows="5" cols="40"></textarea>           27
    <br><br> Gender:                                                  28
<input type="radio" name="gender" value="Female" required>            29
Female
<input type="radio" name="gender" value="Male" required>              30
Male
<span class="err">*</span><br><br>                                    31
<input type="submit" name="submit" value="Submit">                    32
        </form>                                                       33
    </div>                                                            34
</body>                                                               35
</html>                                                               36
```

The *ch9-example5-formdata.php* program file.

```
<!Doctype html>                                                        1
<html>                                                                 2
<head>                                                                 3
<title>PHP Form 3 Data</title>                                         4
</head>                                                                5
<body>                                                                 6
<?php                                                                  7
$name = $email = $gender = $comment = "";                              8
    if ($_SERVER['REQUEST_METHOD'] == "POST") {                        9
    $name = check_data($_POST["name"]);                               10
    $email = check_data($_POST["email"]);                             11
```

```
    $comment = check_data($_POST["comment"]);                   12
    $gender = check_data($_POST["gender"]);                     13
}                                                               14
function check_data($fdata) {                                   15
    $fdata = trim($fdata);                                      16
    $fdata = stripslashes($fdata);                              17
    $fdata = htmlspecialchars($fdata);                          18
    return $fdata;                                              19
}                                                               20
echo "<h2>Your Details:</h2>";                                  21
echo $name;                                                     22
echo "<br>";                                                    23
echo $email;                                                    24
echo "<br>";                                                    25
echo $comment;                                                  26
echo "<br>";                                                    27
echo $gender;                                                   28
?>                                                              29
</body>                                                         30
</html>                                                         31
```

Explanation (ch9-example5.php)
Line 5
<style>
In this line, **<style>** is the start tag of HTML used to start the internal CSS of the web page.

Line 6 to Line 8
.err {
    color: red;
}

In these lines, **.err** is the class name (selector) which is to be styled. Here, inside the block of selector starting with the { and ending with }, **color** is the property used to color the HTML text, and **red** is the value of the property.

Line 9 to Line 12
div {
    border: double 5px black;
    padding: 25px;
}

In these lines, **div** is the tag name (selector) which is to be styled. Here, inside the block of selector, **border** is the property used to give the border to an element, it has different border values where **double** is the border style, **5px** is border width, and **black** is border color. Next, **padding** is another property given to the **div** element to create **25px** space from all sides between the **border** and elements of **div**.

Line 13
</style>
In this line, </style> is the end tag of HTML used to end the internal CSS of the web page.

Line 18
<p><span class="err">* represents required field.</span></p>
In this line, <span> is the start tag of HTML used to add some properties to the HTML content. Here, **class** is an attribute used to name an element through which users can add style to that element, as done in Line 6 to Line 8 and **err** is a class name given to the <span> element.

Line 27
<textarea name="comment" rows="5" cols="40"></textarea>
In this line, **name**, **rows**, and **cols** are three attributes given to the <textarea> element that has different values. Here, **rows** and **cols** defines the area of the textarea input box where **rows** is for number of rows and **cols** is for number of columns.

Explanation (ch9-example5-formdata.php)
Line 8
$name = $email = $gender = $comment = "";
In this line, **$name**, **$email**, **$gender**, and **$comment** variables are declared and no value is assigned to them.

Line 9
if ($_SERVER['REQUEST_METHOD'] == "POST") {
In this line, if condition is **$_SERVER['REQUEST_METHOD'] == "POST"**. Here **$_SERVER** superglobal variable has **REQUEST_METHOD** which is used to fetch the request method used to access the form data. Next, the condition is checked whether the request method is **POST** method or not. Here, the condition will get satisfied and the control will be transferred inside the **if** block and all statements (from Line 10 to Line 13) associated with the **if** block will be executed.

Line 10
$name = check_data($_POST["name"]);
In this line, **$name** is the variable which holds the **check_data()** function defined in Line 15 to Line 20. The **check_data()** function has **$_POST[]** superglobal variable which is used to fetch the data of **name** field from the form.

The working of Line 11 to Line 13 is similar to Line 10

Line 16
$fdata = trim($fdata);
In this line, **trim()** is the inbuilt function declared inside the user-defined function **check_data()**. This line will receive the data in **$fdata** variable from the **If** control structure and perform the **trim()** functionality on the received data.

Line 17
$fdata = stripslashes($fdata);
In this line, **stripslashes()** is the inbuilt function declared inside the user-defined function **check_data()**. This line will receive the data in **$fdata** variable from the **If** control structure and perform the **stripslashes()** functionality on the received data.

Line 18
$fdata = htmlspecialchars($fdata);
In this line, **htmlspecialchars()** is the inbuilt function declared inside the user-defined function **check_data()**. This line will receive the data in **$fdata** variable from the **If** control structure and perform the **htmlspecialchars()** functionality on the received data.

Line 19
return $fdata;
In this line, **return** will return the data of **$fdata** after performing all the functionality on the received data.

The output of Example 5 is displayed in Figure 9-9.

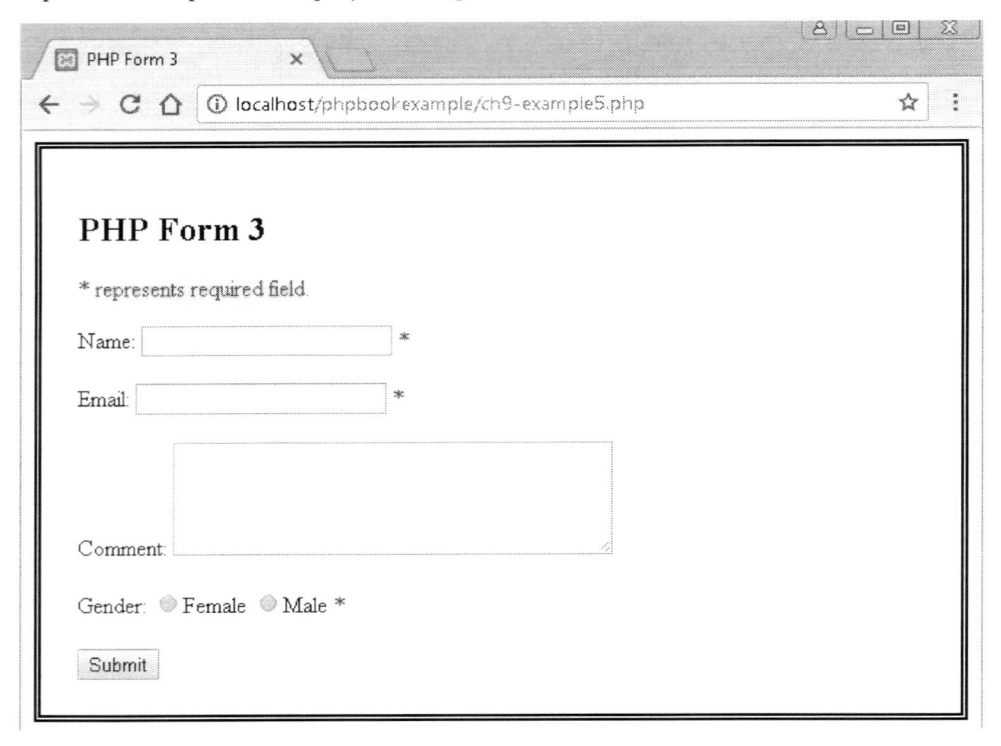

Figure 9-9 The output of Example 5

In Figure 9-9, the form is blank. Now, the user will enter the data to send it to another page as shown in Figure 9-10.

Form Implementation and Validation

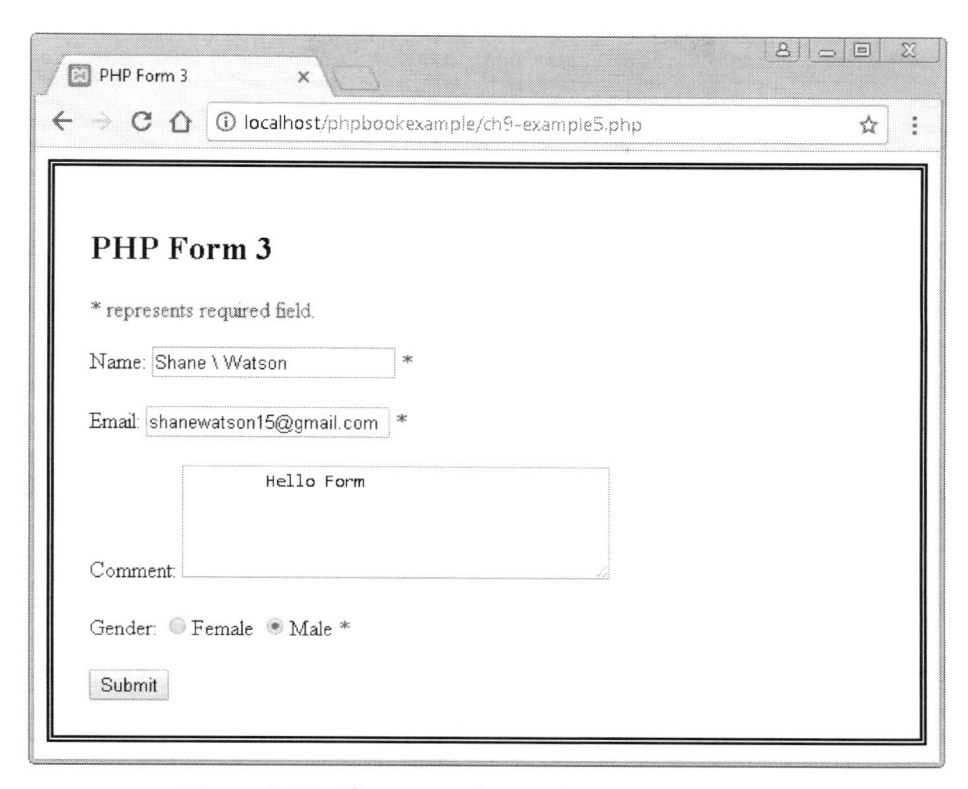

Figure 9-10 *The output of Example 5 with data in form*

In Figure 9-10 the data is filled. Now, the user will submit this data and the data will be sent to *ch9-example5-formdata.php* program. This program will receive the data and the output will be displayed as shown in Figure 9-11.

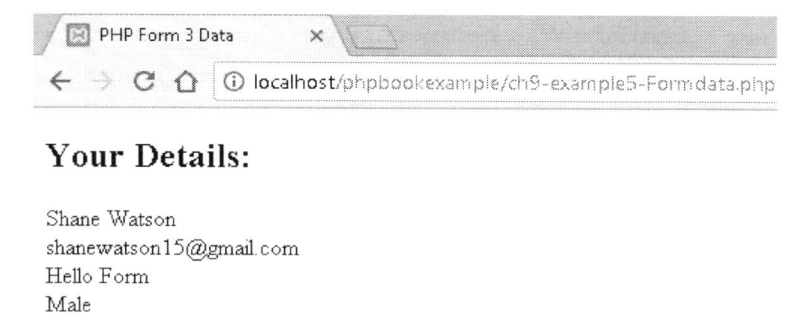

Figure 9-11 *The output of Example 5 displaying form data*

JavaScript(JS)
JavaScript is a lightweight object oriented scripting language which is used both for client-side scripting and server-side scripting. When JS is used to control the browser, to create dynamically updating content, validating form, and to control the Document Object Model, for example,

generating response to the user events when user provides any input to the form or clicks on button then the JS is working as client-side scripting language. When JS is used to communicate with a database or to manipulate files on server then the JS is working as server-side scripting language. JS is a case-sensitive language.

JS with HTML
The client-side scripting is done for the web browser by using JavaScript(JS) with HTML tags. The syntax of placing JS in HTML code is as follow:

```
<script>
         //JS code
</script>
```

In the given syntax, **<script>** is the start tag of HTML which is used to start the JavaScript code and **</script>** is the end tag of HTML which is used to end the Javascript code. The JavaScript code is placed between these tags.

You can place this syntax in the head section or in the body section of the HTML document. You can also create an external JS file and call it in the HTML document by following the syntax given next.

```
<script src="filename.js"></script>
```

In the given syntax, **src** is the attribute used to define the source path of the JS file inside the **<script>** tag and **filename.js** represents the complete path of JS file including the filename with its extension.

JS OUTPUT
You have already learned in the earlier chapters that to display the result or output of PHP script in the browser, PHP provides **echo** and **print** statements. Similarly, in JS there are four different way to display the output in the browser which are as follows:

1. **innerHTML**
2. **document.write()**
3. **window.alert()**
4. **console.log()**

innerHTML
The keyword **innerHTML** is used to access the HTML element to display the data declared inside the JS code. The syntax to use **innerHTML** is as follow:

```
document.getElementById('id').innerHTML = data;
```

In the given syntax, **document.getElementById('id')** is the method used to get the HTML element from the HTML document based on the element id. Here, **id** is the parameter passed inside the method which represents the value of the **id** attribute of an element that is to be accessed. Next, **innerHTML** is used with the method to access the element and display the **data** assigned to it where **data** represents a data of any type.

Form Implementation and Validation

Example 6

The following program illustrates the use of **innerHTML** of JS. The program will do the sum of two numbers and display the output in the browser.

```
<!Doctype html>                                                 1
<html>                                                          2
<head>                                                          3
<title>JavaScript innerHTML</title>                             4
</head>                                                         5
<body>                                                          6
<h1>First JS program</h1>                                       7
    <p>The sum of two numbers- 11 and 21 is</p>                 8
    <p id="p1"></p>                                             9
    <p><b id="p2"></b></p>                                     10
    <script>                                                   11
        document.getElementById("p1").innerHTML = 11 + 21;     12
        document.getElementById("p2").innerHTML = "The         13
        output is displayed";
    </script>                                                  14
</body>                                                        15
</html>                                                        16
```

Explanation
Line 9
<p id="p1"></p>
In this line, **<P>** and **</p>** are the start and end tags of HTML paragraph that has attribute **id** whose value is **p1**.

Line 11
<script>
In this line, **<script>** is the start tag of HTML used to add the JavaScript in the program.

Line 12
document.getElementById("p1").innerHTML = 11 + 21;
In this line, **document.getElementById()** is the method where **p1** is the id of a paragraph declared in Line 9. Next, **innerHTML** is used to display the sum of 11 and 21 inside the HTML paragraph element in the browser.

Line 13
In this line, **document.getElementById()** is the method where **p2** is the id of a bold element declared in Line 10. Next, **innerHTML** is used to display the string inside the HTML element in the browser.

Line 14
</script>
In this line, **<script>** is the end tag of HTML used to end the JavaScript in the program.

The output of Example 6 is displayed in Figure 9-12.

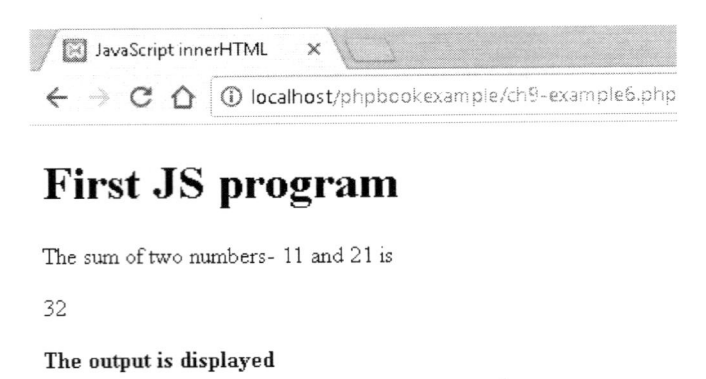

Figure 9-12 *The output of Example 6*

document.write()

The **documemt.write()** method of JS is used to write the content or HTML expressions for the document and display it on the web. It is mostly used to test the working of web page. The syntax to use **documemt.write()** of JS is as follow:

```
document.write(expression1, expexpression2,...)
```

In the given syntax, **documemt.write()** is the method used to write expressions in the document using JS where **expression1**, **expression2** represent multiple expressions that can be passed inside the method. These expressions will be displayed in the browser.

For example:

```
<script>
    document.write("Sum is <br>");
    document.write(11 + 21);
</script>
/*output: Sum is
         32 */
```

In the given example, **document.write()** will display the string **Sum is** and break the line in the browser because of the **
** tag. Next, **document.write()** will perform the addition operation and display the resultant value 32 in the browser.

window.alert()

The **window.alert()** method of JS is used to write the alert message for the document and display it in the alert box on the web which has the **ok** button. To proceed further, you will have to click on **ok** button of the alert box. The syntax to use **window.alert()** of JS is as follow:

```
window.alert("msg")
```

In the given syntax, **window.alert()** is the method used to write the alert message using JS where **msg** represents any message that is to be displayed in the alert box in the browser.

Form Implementation and Validation 9-29

Example 7

The following program illustrates the use of **window.alert()** method of JS. The program will display the message in the alert box as output in the browser.

```
<!Doctype html>                                      1
<html>                                               2
<head>                                               3
<title>window alert box</title>                      4
</head>                                              5
<body>                                               6
    <h2> You saw the alert box.</h2>                 7
    <script>                                         8
        window.alert("This is alert box msg");       9
    </script>                                        10
</body>                                              11
</html>                                              12
```

Explanation
Line 9
window.alert("This is alert box msg");
In this line, **window.alert()** method is used to display the message passed inside its parentheses in the alert box as output.

The output of Example 7 showing alert box is displayed in Figure 9-13.

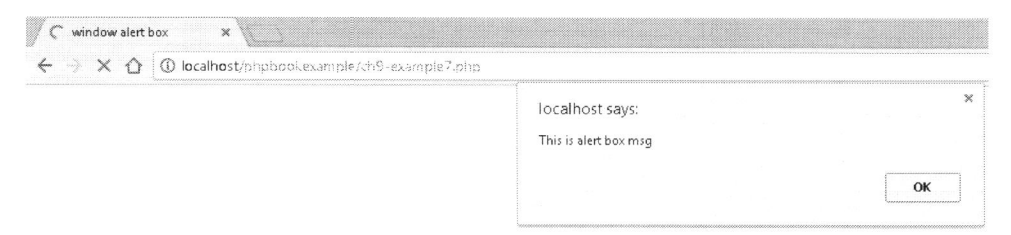

Figure 9-13 The output of Example 7 displaying alert box

Next, when the user will click the **ok** button of the alert box the other content of the web page defined in the program will be displayed as shown in figure 9-14.

Figure 9-14 The output of Example 7 displaying the content

console.log()

The **console.log()** method of JS is used to write and display any expression passed to it in the **Console** tab of the browser. It is used for debugging. Every browser has different path to reach the **Console** tab. The **Console** tab in the browser displays all the errors and other messages. The syntax to use **console.log()** of JS is as follow:

```
console.log(expression)
```

In the given syntax, **console.log()** is the method used to debug the code where **expression** represents any message or expression passed to it that is to be displayed in the **Console** tab in the browser.

The **Console** tab is not visible directly in the browser. It is displayed in different display box in the browser. For example, to open the **Console** tab in the Google Chrome browser, you can press **F12** button on the keyboard or you can right-click on the browser and then select **Inspect** option where you will find the **Console** tab in the separate display box in the browser.

Example 8

The following program illustrates the use of the **console.log()** method of JS. The program will display the message in the **Console** tab as output in the browser.

```
<!Doctype html>                                              1
<html>                                                       2
<head>                                                       3
<title>Console output</title>                                4
</head>                                                      5
<body>                                                       6
<p>To open console tab in Google chrome press <b>F12</b></p> 7
    <script>                                                 8
            console.log("No error found");                   9
    </script>                                                10
</body>                                                      11
</html>                                                      12
```

Explanation
Line 9
console.log("No error found");
In this line, the **console.log()** method is used to display the message or expression passed inside its parentheses in the **Console** tab in the browser.

The output of Example 8 is displayed in Figure 9-15.

Form Implementation and Validation

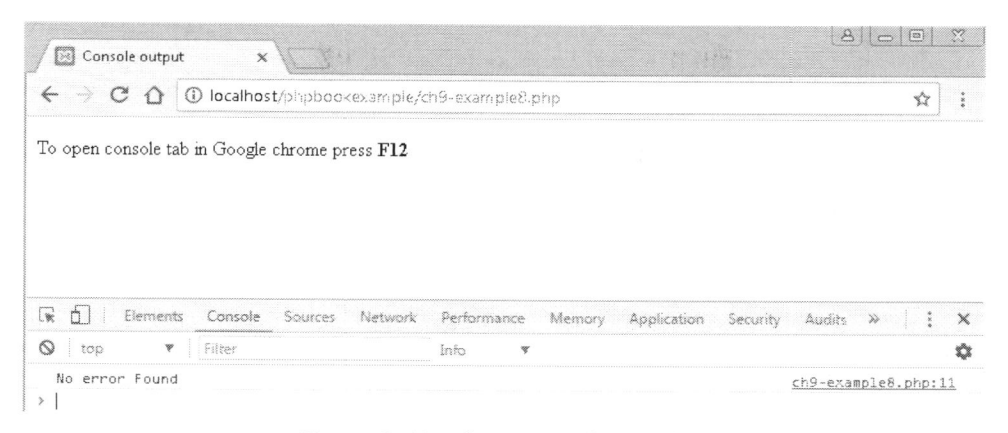

Figure 9-15 The output of Example 8

JavaScript Variables

The variables in JavaScript are declared by using the **var** keyword along with variable name. You can declare multiple variables at a time by separating them using comma.

For example:

```
<script> var a, b, c; </script>
```

In the given example, **var** is keyword used to declare the variable and **a,b**, and **c** are the variable names.

While naming a variable in JavaScript, you must follow certain rules. The rules are as follows:

1. Only alphabetic characters- both uppercase and lowercase, digits from 0 to 9, **$** symbol and underscore (_) can be used.
2. Variable name can start with an alphabet, **$**, or an underscore but not with a digit.
3. Variable name can not contain space. If variable name contain more than one word, it can be separated by using _ (underscore) character or can be written in camel case instead of using space.
4. Variable names are case sensitive. For example, **javascript** and **JavaScript** are two different variables, one in lowercase case and other in camel case.

> **Note**
> *If a value is assigned to the variable then it is optional to declare the variable with **var**. For example, **a = 5;** where **a** is a variable. But, to avoid errors declare all variables with **var**.*

Example 9

The following program illustrates the use of JavaScript variables. The program will use multiple JS variables to display the output in the browser.

```
<!Doctype html>                                                 1
<html>                                                          2
```

```
<head>                                                              3
<title>JS variables</title>                                         4
</head>                                                             5
<body>                                                              6
<h3>You can declare many variables in one statement.</h3>           7
<p><i>Hobby</i></p>                                                 8
<p id="par"></p>                                                    9
<h3>To open console tab in Google chrome press F12</h3>            10
    <script>                                                       11
        var v1;                                                    12
        var v2;                                                    13
        console.log(v1 = 5 * 10);                                  14
        v2 = v1 + 2;                                               15
        document.write("<i>The sum is : </i>" + v2);               16
        var name = "James Bond", age = 53, hobby = "Acting";       17
        document.getElementById("par").innerHTML = hobby;          18
    </script>                                                      19
</body>                                                            20
</html>                                                            21
```

Explanation
Line 13 and Line 14
var v1;
var v2;
In these lines, **v1** and **v2** are the JS variable names declared by using keyword **var.**

Line 14
console.log(v1 = 5 * 10);
In this line, **v1** variable is holding an expression where multiplication of 5 and 10 is done with the help of the * operator. The output of this line will be displayed in **Console** tab in the browser.

Line 16
document.write("<i>The sum is : </i>" + v2);
In this line, concatenation between the string and the variable passed inside the **document.write()** method is done with the + operator. This line will display the following in the browser.

The sum is : 52

Line 17
var name = "James Bond", age = 53, hobby = "Acting";
In this line, multiple variables are declared in one line by using the **var** keyword and each variable is holding a value.

The output of Example 9 is displayed in Figure 9-16.

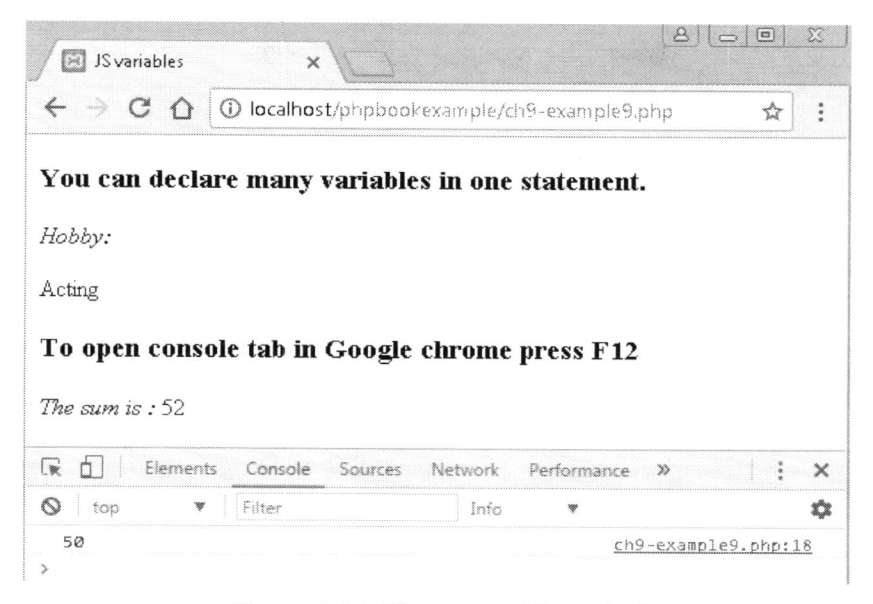

Figure 9-16 The output of Example 9

FORM VALIDATION USING JS

JavaScript is used for form validation to validate the user input to get the correct data instead of junk values. To validate any form, it is important to match every character that the user enters in a form field with the set of regular expression supported by both JS and PHP.

Regular Expression

Regular expressions are used to match the specified pattern or characters with the user input data. With the help of regular expressions, you can validate any form. It is helpful in construction of a pattern matching algorithms in a single expression. Every regular expression are enclosed in pair of forward slashes.

For example:

```
/Hello *User/
```

In the given example, **/Hello *User/** is a regular expression where **Hello *User** is a pattern to be matched which is enclosed in pair of forward slashes.

> **Note**
> *Regular expressions are case-sensitive.*

There are different groups of character matching used in regular expression which are as follow:

1. Metacharacters
2. Character classes

Metacharacters

Metacharacters are characters which have special meanings when used as regular expression. Table 9-1 shows a list of some of the metacharacters with their description and example.

Table 9-1 Metacharacters with their description

Metacharacter	Description	Example
*	Asterisk (*) matches any number of preceding characters including no character.	To match **HelloUser** or **Hello User**, the regular expression /**Hello *User**/ can be used.
+	It matches any number of preceding characters except empty case or no character.	To match **Hello User**, the regular expression /**hello +User**/ can be used but you cannot match **HelloUser** with the same expression.
.	It matches any single character. If written with * or + metacharacter it will match every character.	To match **bye**, **bee**, or **b2e**, the regular expression /**<b.e>**/ can be used.
\.	It matches the dot(.) symbol instead of reading it as metacharacter.	To match dot (.) symbol in string **gmail.com**, the regular expression /\./ is used.
\+	It matches the + symbol instead of reading it as metacharacter.	To match + symbol in the string **5 + 7**, the regular expression /\+/ is used.
*	It matches the asterisk(*) symbol instead of reading it as metacharacter.	To match * symbol in the string **5 * 7**, the regular expression /*/ is used.
\s	It matches a whitespace character.	To match the whitespace in the string **How are you?**, the regular expression /\s/g will be used where **g** is a modifier.
\S	It matches a nonwhitespace character.	To match every character other then space in the string **How are you?**, the regular expression /\S/g will be used where **g** is a modifier.
\w	It matches a word character (a-z,A-Z,0-9, and _).	To match the word character in any string /\w/ is used.
\W	It matches anything other than word character (a-z,A-Z,0-9, and _).	To match the word character in any string /\W/ is used.
\d	It matches a single digit.	To match only numbers such as 1, 2, 3 and so on, the regular expression /\d/ is used.
\D	It matches a single non-digit.	To match characters other then numbers, the regular expression /\D/ is used.
{n}	It matches anything **n** number of times.	To match 4 digit numbers such as 0000, 2000, and so on, the regular expression /\d{4}/ is used.

Character Classes

Character classes are used in regular expression to match one or more characters defined inside the character class. If any of the character defined inside the character class appears, the data matches. The character class starts with [and ends with] in a regular expression. You can place a list of characters inside the pair of square brackets [ ]. But, it matches exactly one character out of the list of characters. For example, if you want to match both **sun** and **son** then you can specify the regular expression as follow:

```
/s[ou]n/
```

In the given example, the regular expression can match **son** as well **sun** but not **soun** or **suon**. Because it matches exactly only one character out of the character list of character class. In this case, it can match either **o** or **u** but not **ou** or **uo** from the character class.

Character classes can also be used to define a range of characters from which a single data can appear in the data to be matched. To define a range, you can use the hyphen (-) inside the character class between two characters. For example, to match a single digit, you can use the regular expression **/[0-9]/**. This expression can match a single digit from the range 0 to 9.

If you do not want to match the characters given in the character class then you will have to use ^ symbol before that character inside the character class. For example, **/[^a-z]/** regular expression will match every character other than **a** to **z** characters.

Regular Expression Modifiers

Regular expression modifiers are used with regular expressions to modify them. These modifiers provides additional functionality to the regular expression. There are 3 regular expression modifiers listed in Table 9-2 with their description.

Table 9-2 Modifiers with their description

Modifiers	Description	Example
g	Globally search and matches the characters. This will search all matches.	**/girls/g** will match all the occurrence of word **girls** in the string.
i	Enables case-insensitive matching.	**/girls/i** will match **girls** as well as **Girls** in the string.
m	Search and matches the characters in multiple lines. If ^ (caret) is placed with the string inside the regular expression that has **m** modifier then it will match only at start of the each line. Similarly, if **$** is placed then it will match at the end of the each line.	**/^Hello/m** will match Hello in string **\nHello user\n Hello friends**. Here, **\n** is used for next line.

Example 10

In this example, you will create two programs, *ch9-example10.php* and *display.php*, where the *ch9-example10.php* program will create a dynamic form and validate the form by using JavaScript and send the form data to *display.php* program file using the **post** method. The *display.php* program file will receive the form data from *ch9-example10.php* program file to display the output in the browser.

The *ch9-example10.php* program file.

```
<!Doctype html>                                                   1
<html>                                                            2
<head>                                                            3
<title>JS validate</title>                                        4
<style>                                                           5
        .err {color: red;}                                        6
        div {                                                     7
              border: double 5px black;                           8
              padding: 25px;                                      9
              margin-right: 1000px;                              10
        }                                                        11
</style>                                                         12
<script>                                                         13
        function validateform(form) {                            14
           invalid = validateFname(form.firstname.value);        15
           invalid += validateLname(form.lastname.value);        16
           invalid += validateUsername(form.username.value);     17
           invalid += validatePassword(form.password.value);     18
           invalid += validateAge(form.age.value);               19
           invalid += validateEmail(form.email.value);           20
              if (invalid == "") return true;                    21
              else {                                             22
                   alert(invalid);                               23
                   return false;}}                               24
function validateFname(field) {                                  25
     return (field == "") ? "First Name Required.\n" : "";}      26
function validateLname(field) {                                  27
     return (field == "") ? "Last name Required.\n" : "";}       28
function validateUsername(field) {                               29
     if (field == "") return "Username Required.\n";             30
           else if (field.length < 5)                            31
     return "Username must be at least 5 characters.\n";         32
           else if (/[^a-zA-Z0-9_-]/.test(field))                33
return "Only a-z,A-Z,0-9,-,and _ allowed in Username.\n";        34
return "";}                                                      35
function validatePassword(field) {                               36
     if (field == "") return "Password Required.\n";             37
           else if (field.length < 6)                            38
```

```
            return "Password must be at least 6 characters.\n";       39
                else if (!/[a-z]/.test(field) ||                      40
                    !/[A-Z]/.test(field) ||
                    !/[0-9]/.test(field))
    return "Password require one each of a-z, A-Z, and 0-9.\n";       41
    return "";}                                                       42
    function validateAge(field){                                      43
        if (isNaN(field)) return "Age Required.\n";                   44
            else if (field < 18 || field > 110)                       45
        return "Age must be between 18 and 110.\n";                   46
        return "";}                                                   47
    function validateEmail(field){                                    48
        if (field == "") return "Email Required.\n";                  49
            else if (!((field.indexOf(".") > 0) &&                    50
                    (field.indexOf("@") > 0)) ||
                /[^a-zA-Z0-9.@_-]/.test(field))
        return "The Email address is invalid.\n";                     51
        return "";}                                                   52
    </script>                                                         53
</head>                                                               54
<body>                                                                55
<div>                                                                 56
    <h2>JS validate PHP Form</h2>                                     57
    <p><span class="err">* represents required field.</span></p>      58
    <form method="post" action="display.php"                          59
        onsubmit="return validateform(this)">
<p>First Name<input type="text" maxlength="32" name="firstname">      60
        <span class="err">*</span></p>                                61
<p>Last Name<input type="text" maxlength="32" name="lastname">        62
        <span class="err">*</span></p>                                63
<p>Username<input type="text" maxlength="16" name="username">         64
        <span class="err">*</span></p>                                65
    <p>Password<input type="password" maxlength="12"                  66
            name="password">                                          67
        <span class="err">*</span></p>                                68
    <p>Email<input type="email" maxlength="64" name="email">          69
        <span class="err">*</span></p>                                70
    <p>Age<input type="text" maxlength="3" name="age">                71
        <span class="err">*</span></p>                                72
    <input type="submit" value="Signup">                              73
    </form>                                                           74
</div>                                                                75
</body>                                                               76
</html>                                                               77
```

The *display.php* program file.

```
    <!Doctype html>                                                    1
    <html>                                                             2
```

```
<head>                                                              3
<title>JS validate Data</title>                                     4
</head>                                                             5
<body>                                                              6
<?php                                                               7
$fname = $lname = $uname = $email = $password = $age                8
= $gender = "";
    if ($_SERVER['REQUEST_METHOD'] == "POST") {                     9
  $fname = check_data($_POST["firstname"]);                         10
  $lname = check_data($_POST["lastname"]);                          11
  $uname = check_data($_POST["username"]);                          12
  $email = check_data($_POST["email"]);                             13
  $password = check_data($_POST["password"]);                       14
   $age = check_data($_POST["age"]);               }                15
function check_data($fdata) {                                       16
  $fdata = trim($fdata);                                            17
  $fdata = stripslashes($fdata);                                    18
  $fdata = htmlspecialchars($fdata);                                19
   return $fdata;                                                   20
                  }                                                 21
echo "<h2>Your Details:</h2>";                                      22
echo "Your first name is <b>$fname</b>";                            23
echo "<br>";                                                        24
echo "Your last name is <b>$lname</b>";                             25
echo "<br>";                                                        26
echo "Your username is <b>$uname</b>";                              27
echo "<br>";                                                        28
echo "Your email id is <b>$email</b>";                              29
echo "<br>";                                                        30
echo "Your password is <b>$password</b>";                           31
echo "<br>";                                                        32
echo "Your age is <b>$age</b>";                                     33
?>                                                                  34
</body>                                                             35
</html>                                                             36
```

Explanation (ch9-example10.php)
Line 13
<script>
In this line, **<script>** is the start tag used to start the JavaScript code.

Line 15
invalid = validateFname(form.firstname.value);
In this line, the **validateFname() function** is called to validate the form input field where **invalid** is a variable name, the **validateFname()** function is an user-defined function, and **form.firstname.value** is the parameter passed to the function. This parameter follows the Document Object Model (DOM) which breaks down the parts of an HTML into discrete objects. Here, **form** is used to call the HTML form tag **<form>**, **firstname** is the value of **name** attribute in the form input field, and **value** is for the user input value.

The working of Line 16 to Line 20 is similar to Line 15.

Line 21 to Line 24
if (invalid == " ") return true;
else {
      alert(invalid);
      return false;}}

In these lines, the **if** statement will check the condition that the **invalid** variable is empty or not. If it is empty, then it will return **true** otherwise an alert box will pop up that displays the string which contains the error message as specified in the functions.

Line 25 to Line 26
function validateFname(field) {
      return (field == "") ? " First Name Required.\n" : "";}

In these lines, the **validateFname()** function is testing whether the value in the **field** parameter is blank or not. The **field** parameter is receiving the value from **firstname** passed to the **validateFname()** function (Line 15). If the value of the **field** parameter is empty then the string **First Name Required.** is returned to the **validateform()** function and the string get displayed in the alert box. Otherwise, it returns an empty string to the **validateform()** function which signifies that no error is found in the received value.

The working of Line 27 to Line 28 is similar to the Lines 25 to 26.

Line 29 to Line 30
function validateUsername(field) {
  if (field == "") return "Username Required.\n";

In these lines, the **validateUsername()** function is testing whether the value in the **field** parameter is blank or not. The **field** parameter is receiving the value from **username** passed to the **validateUsername()** function (Line 17). If the value of the **field** parameter is empty then the string **Username Required.** is returned to the **validateform()** function and the string gets displayed in the alert box. Otherwise, the control will be transferred to Line 31.

Line 31 to Line 32
else if (field.length < 5)
return "Username must be at least 5 characters.\n";

In these lines, the **else if** condition is evaluated. If the length of the value received from the **validateUsername()** function (Line 17) is less than 5, then the next line (Line 32) will return the string **Username must be at least 5 characters.** to the **validateform()** function. Otherwise, the control will be transferred to Line 33.

Line 33 to Line35
else if (/[^ a-zA-Z0-9_-]/.test(field))
      return "Only a-z, A-Z, 0-9, -, and _ allowed in Username.\n";
return "";

In these lines, the **else if** condition is evaluated where /[^a-zA-Z0-9_-]/ is the regular expression and **test()** method is the JS inbuilt method which will test the **field**. The **else if** condition will check the value received from the **validateUsername()** function (Line 17). Here, if any character other than **a** to **z**, **A** to **Z**, **0** to **9**, **_**, and **-** exist then the control will be transferred to the next line (Line 34) where the string **Only a-z, A-Z, 0-9, - and _ allowed in Username.** is returned to the **validateform()** function. Otherwise, the control will be transferred to Line 35 which returns the empty string to the **validateform()** function which signifies that no error is found in the received value.

Line 40 to Line 41
else if (!/[a-z]/.test(field) ||!/[A-Z]/.test(field) ||!/[0-9]/.test(field))
return "Passwords require one each of a-z, A-Z, and 0-9.\n";

In these lines, the **else if** condition is evaluated. If the value received from the **validatePassword()** function (Line 18) does not contain at least one character each from **a** to **z**, **A** to **Z**, and **0** to **9** then the control will be transferred to the next line (Line 41) and the string **Password require one each of a-z, A-Z, and 0-9.** is returned to the **validateform()** function. Otherwise, the control will be transferred to Line 42.

Line 44
if (isNaN(field)) return "Age Required.\n";
In this line, **isNaN()** is the JS inbuilt method used to check whether a value is a number or not. If the value of the **field** parameter is other than a number or is empty then the string **Age Required.** is returned to the **validateform()** function and the string get displayed in the alert box. Otherwise, the control will be transferred to Line 45.

Line 45 to Line 46
else if (field < 18 || field > 110)
    return "Age must be between 18 and 110.\n";

In these lines, the **else if** condition is evaluated. If the value received from the **validateAge()** function (Line 19) is less than 18 or greater than 110 then the control is transferred to the next line (Line 46) and the string **Age must be between 18 and 110.** is returned to **validateform()** function. Otherwise, the control will be transferred to Line 47.

Line 50 to Line 51
else if (!((field.indexOf(".") > 0) &&(field.indexOf("@") > 0))
    ||/[^a-zA-Z0-9.@]/.test(field))
return "The Email address is invalid.\n";

In these lines, the condition will check the value received from the **validateEmail()** function (Line 20). If the index position of **.** and **@** are not greater than **0** or the value contain any character other than **a** to **z**, **A** to **Z**, **0** to **9**, **.**, and **@** then the condition will be true and the next statement (Line 51) is executed where the string **The Email address is invalid.** is returned to **validateform()** function. Otherwise, the control will be transferred to Line 52.

Form Implementation and Validation 9-41

Line 59
<form method="post" action="display.php" onsubmit="return validateform(this)">
In this line, **onsubmit** is an event attribute which executes the JavaScript function when the form is submitted by the user. Here, the **onsubmit** attribute will execute the **validateform()** function of Javascript.

Explanation (display.php)

The working of *display.php* program is similar to the *ch9-example5-formdata.php* program.

The output of Example 10 is displayed in Figure 9-17.

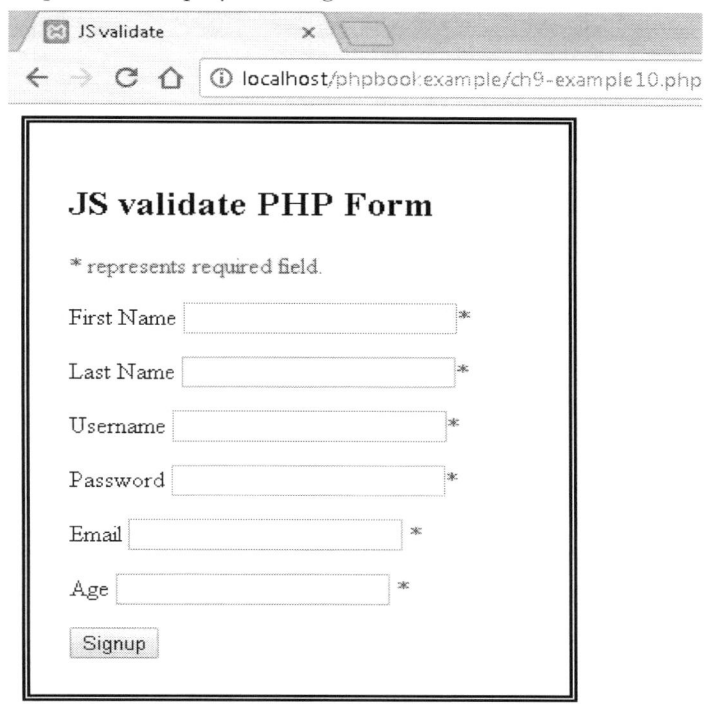

Figure 9-17 The output of Example 10

In Figure 9-17, the form is blank. Next, the user will enter the data and submit the data by clicking on **Signup** button in the form to send data to another page as shown in Figure 9-18.

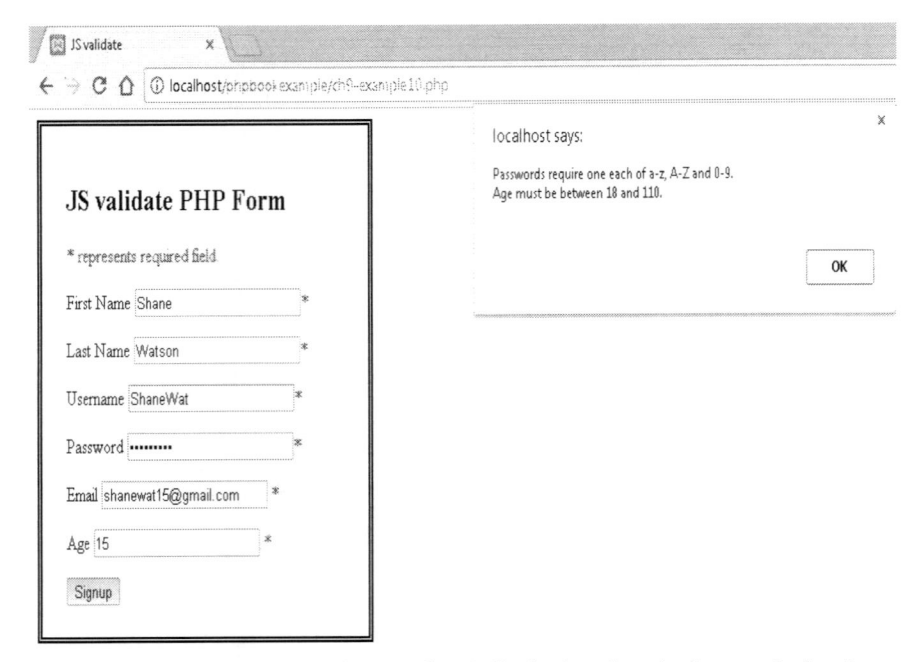

Figure 9-18 *The output of Example 10 displaying data in form and alert box*

In figure 9-18, the alert box is displayed because of JavaScript validation. The alert box in the Figure 9-18 displays the message to inform the user that the data entered is invalid. Now, the user will fill the data according to the validation rules set as shown in Figure 9-19.

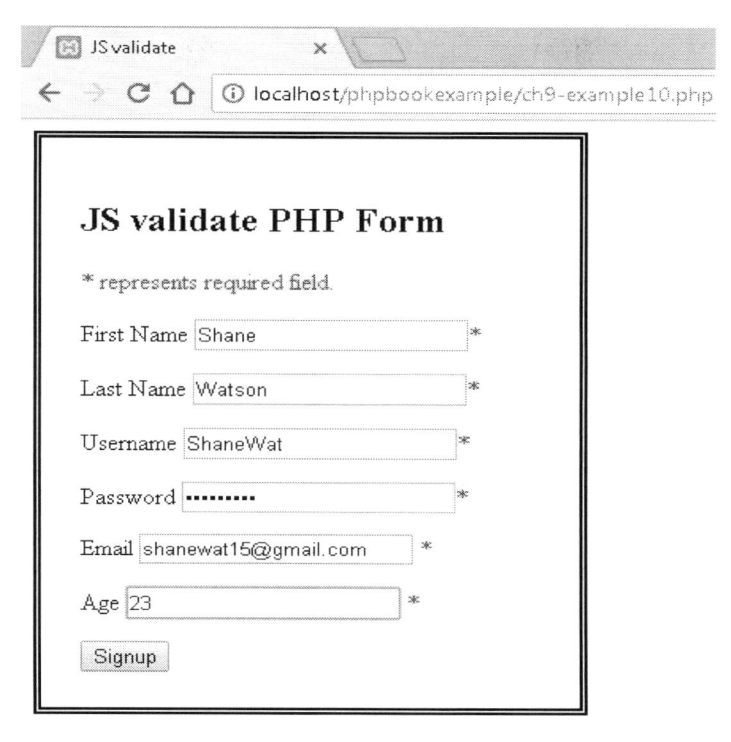

Figure 9-19 *The output of Example 10 displaying the valid form data*

In Figure 9-19 the data is filled. Now the user will again submit the form data by clicking on the **Signup** button. If the data is valid, the data will be sent to *display.php* program. This program will receive the data and the output will be displayed, as shown in Figure 9-20.

Figure 9-20 *The output of Example 10 displaying form data*

Regular Expression Functions in PHP

To use regular expression in PHP, you need to pass them as parameter to the regular expression function. The two most common regular expression functions are as follows:

1. preg_match()
2. preg_replace()

preg_match()

The **preg_match()** function is used to match a string with the help of regular expression. The syntax of **preg_match()** is as follows:

```
preg_match("/regularExp/","string",$match);
```

In the give syntax, **preg_match()** is the regular expression function and three parameters are passed to the **preg_match()** function. Here, **/regularExp/** represents regular expression which is to be matched with the text, **string** represents the text in which match is performed, and the third parameter passed to the function is **$match** which is optional, this represents the text that is matched.

For example:

```
<?php
preg_match("/php/i","Latest version of PHP is PHP 7",$result);
echo "$result[0]";
?>
//output: PHP
```

In the given example, the **preg_match()** function will match the first occurrence of the word **PHP** in the string **Latest version of PHP is PHP 7** and display **PHP** as output.

preg_replace()

The **preg_replace()** function is used to match and replace string with the help of regular expression. The syntax of **preg_replace()** is as follows:

```
preg_replace("/regularExp/","replacement","string");
```

In the given syntax, **preg_replace()** is the regular expression function and three parameters are passed to the **preg_replace()** function. Here, **/regularExp/** represents regular expression which is to be searched and replaced, **replacement** represents the replacement text, and **string** represents the string in which the replacement of text is done.

For example:

```
<?php
echo preg_replace("/php/i","HTML","PHP is a scripting language");
?>
//output: HTML is a scripting language
```

In the given example, the **preg_replace()** function will replace **PHP** with **HTML** in the string **PHP is a scripting language** and display **HTML is a scripting language** as output.

Form Implementation and Validation

Self-Evaluation Test

Answer the following questions and then compare them to those given at the end of this chapter:

1. An _____ in HTML provides additional information to the HTML elements.

2. The form _____ elements are required to create the form input controls.

3. The _____ value provides one-line input text box.

4. The form datalist element in HTML is used to create _____ list.

5. The _____ method is the secure method to send the input data to another page.

6. The **isset()** function is used to check whether the variable is holding a value or not. (T/F)

7. The keyword **innerHTML** is used to access the HTML element to display the data declared inside the PHP code. (T/F)

8. The **g** modifier enables case-insensitive matching. (T/F)

Review Questions

Answer the following questions:

1. Which of the following is the correct syntax of form input element?

    (a) `<input field="value">` (b) `<input element="value">`
    (c) `<input attr="value">` (d) `<input type="value">`

2. Which of the following form **method** is used to transfer data using HTTP header?

    (a) **get** (b) **post**
    (c) **header** (d) **URL**

3. Which of the following form attributes is used to specify the page where the form data will be sent by using **get** or **post** method.?

    (a) **action** (b) **enctype**
    (c) **title** (d) **method**

4. Which of the following functions is used to check whether the variable is holding a value or not?

    (a) **trim()** (b) **isset()**
    (c) **htmlspecialchars()** (d) **stripslashes()**

5. Which of the following regular expression modifiers is used for case-insensitive matching?

   (a) **g**   (b) **i**
   (c) **c**   (d) **m**

6. Which of the following JS methods is used to write and display any expression passed to it in the **Console** tab of the browser.

   (a) **window.alert()**   (b) **Console.error()**
   (c) **console.log()**   (d) **document.write()**

7. Which of the following functions is used to match and replace string with the help of regular expression?

   (a) **preg_replace()**   (b) **match_replace()**
   (c) **isset()**   (d) **preg_match()**

EXERCISES

Exercise 1

Create a form containing 5 types of input fields and a datalist drop-down.

Exercise 2

Create a form having 5 input elements and validate the form using JavaScript to display the form data in the browser.

Answers to Self-Evaluation Test

1. attribute, **2.** input, **3. text**, **4.** drop-down, **5. post**, **6.** T, **7.** F, **8.** F

Chapter 10

File Handling, Sessions, and Cookies

Learning Objectives

After completing this chapter, you will be able to:
- *Understand the concept of file handling*
- *Use file handling modes*
- *Use file functions*
- *Upload files*
- *Understand session and cookies*

INTRODUCTION

In this chapter, you will learn various aspects of file handling such as opening a file, opening modes of file, creating a file, and so on. In addition, you will learn about session and cookies.

FILE HANDLING

Files are created to store data in the system. You can manipulate these files by performing file operations such as read, write, delete, and so on. These file operations performed on the file is known as file handling.

File handling is classified into the following categories:

1. Opening a file
2. Creating a file
3. Writing in a file
4. Reading a file
5. Closing a file

Opening a File

To perform any file handling operation on a file, it is important to open the file. There are various file opening modes to open a file such as read only mode, write only mode, and so on. Once the file is open, you will get a file pointer according to the mode specified. This pointer points to the part of the file where file handling operation will be performed. While opening a file, you need to specify the file opening mode as required. File opening modes are discussed next.

File Opening Modes

To perform any file handling operation, it is important to specify the file opening mode. For example, you can open a file in read and write mode, read only mode, or in write only mode. Table 10-1 lists some file opening modes with their description.

Table 10-1 File opening modes with their description

Modes	Description
r	It opens the file in read only mode. In this mode, the file pointer will be at the beginning of the file.
r+	It opens the file in read and write mode. In this mode, the file pointer will be at the beginning of the file.
w	It opens the file in write only mode. In this mode, the file pointer will be at the beginning of the file. This mode will clear the content of file if any or will create a new file if no file exists.
w+	It opens the file in read and write mode. In this mode, the file pointer will be at the beginning of the file. This mode will clear the content of file if any or will create a new file if no file exists.
a	It opens the file in write only mode. In this mode, the file pointer will be at the end of the file. This mode will preserve the content of the file if exist, because the pointer is placed at the end of the file or will create a new file if no file exists.

File Handling, Sessions, and Cookies

a+	It opens the file in read and write only mode. In this mode, the file pointer will be at the end of the file. This mode preserves the content of the file if exist, because the pointer is placed at the end of the file. This mode will also create a new file if file does not exist.
x	It opens and create a new file in write only mode. This mode will return FALSE if the file already exists and will throw warning.
x+	It creates a new file and open it in a read and write mode. This mode will return FALSE if the file already exists and will throw warning.

fopen() Function

The **fopen()** function in used to open a file in PHP. The syntax to open a file is as follow:

```
$file = fopen('file_name.txt' , 'mode');
```

In the given syntax, **$file** is a variable and **fopen()** is the function used to open the file. This function has **file_name.txt** and **mode** as its two parameters where **file_name.txt** represents the file name or path of the file to be opened with its extension and **mode** represents the file opening mode.

For example:

```
<?php
    $newfile = fopen("new_file.txt","r");
?>
```

In the given example, **$newfile** is a variable and **fopen()** is the function used to open the file. This function has **new_file.txt** and **r** as its two parameters where **new_file.txt** is the file name to be opened with its extension to perform file handling operations and **r** is the file opening mode which will open file in read only mode. This example will throw an error if the **new_file.txt** file does not exist. So, its important to create a file to open it in read only mode.

> **Note**
> *If the file handling PHP file and the text file to be opened are not in the same folder then you need to mention the complete location of the text file along with its name and extension. For example, in the above example, you need to mention **location\new_file.txt** as the parameter of **fopen()** function instead of **new_file.txt**.*

CREATING A FILE

To create a file using PHP program, you need to open a file using **fopen()** function in the following modes according to the requirement:

1. **w**
2. **w+**
3. **a**
4. **a+**
5. **x**
6. **x+**

Refer to Table 10-1 for complete description of the given modes.

For example:

```
<?php
    $newfile = fopen("new_file.txt","w");
?>
```

In the given example, **$newfile** is a variable and **fopen()** is the function used to open the file. This function has **fnew_file.txt** and **w** as its two parameters where **new_file.txt** is the file name to be opened with its extension and **w** is the file opening mode which will open file in write only mode. This example will create a new file with the name **new_file.txt** if the file does not exist.

Checking the Existence of File

To check the existence of a file, the **file_exists()** function is used. This function will return either TRUE or FALSE. The syntax of **file_exists()** function is as follow:

```
file_exists("file_name.txt")
```

In the given syntax, **file_exists()** is the function used to check whether a file exists or not. This function has **file_name** as its parameter where **file_name.txt** represents the name of the file whose existence is to be checked.

For example:

```
<?php
    if (file_exists('old_file.txt'))
        {
            echo "The file exists";
        }
    else {
            echo "The file does not exist";
        }
?>
```

In the given example, **file_exists()** is the function used to check the existence of **old_file.txt** file. This example will display **The file exists** if the **old_file.txt** exists, otherwise, it will display **The file does not exist**.

exit() or die()

The **exit()** function is used to terminate the current running script and to display the specified message in the browser. The **die()** function is the alias of **exit()** function. This means the working of both the functions is same. You can use any of these functions to terminate the current running script.

The syntax of the **exit()** function is as follow:

```
exit("msg");
```

In the given syntax, **exit()** is the function and **msg** is optional parameter of this function. This parameter represents any message that will get displayed in the browser when script terminates. The working and syntax of **die()** function is same as **exit()** function. The syntax of **die()** function is as follow:

```
die("msg");
```

filesize()

The **filesize()** function is an inbuilt function used to get the size of the specified file. This function either returns FALSE on failure or returns the size of the file in bytes on success. The syntax of **filesize()** function is as follow:

```
filesize("file_name.txt");
```

In the given syntax, **filesize()** is the function and **file_name.txt** is the parameter of this function. This parameter represents the name of the text file with its extension. Here, the **filesize()** function will return the size of the **file_name.txt** text file.

> **Note**
> *The **filesize()** function may return unexpected output for the files having size greater than 2GB.*

WRITING IN THE FILE

To write in a file using PHP program, first you need to open a file using the **fopen()** function in write only mode or in read and write mode. Then, by using the **fwrite()** function, you can either write into the new file or append the text into existing file. The syntax of the **fwrite()** function is as follow:

```
fwrite($filename, "Text", "length" );
```

In the given syntax, three parameters are passed to the **fwrite()** function. First two parameters of the function, **$filename** and **Text**, are required. **$filename** represents the file pointer (the variable holding the **fopen()** function) and **Text** represents the text to be written or appended in the file. Third parameter, **length**, is optional and represents the maximum length of the data that can be written in the file.

> **Note**
> *The **fputs()** function is the alias of **fwrite()** function. You can use any of the functions to write in the file.*

Example 1

The following program will create a new file with the name *ch10-example1.txt* and write into the file using the **fopen()** and **fwrite()** functions.

```
<?php                                                          1
    $New_File = "ch10-example1.txt";                           2
    $newfile = fopen($New_File,"w");                           3
    if($newfile == false )                                     4
    {                                                          6
        echo ( "Error in opening file" );                      7
        exit();                                                8
    }                                                          9
    fwrite( $newfile, "This text file is created by using     10
           PHP program.." );
    echo ("<i>You successfully, wrote into file.</i> <br>     11
    <b>To see the text file you can navigate to the folder   12
        where you have saved the current program file.</b>")
?>                                                            13
```

Explanation
Line 2
$New_File = "ch10-example1.txt";
In this line, **ch10-example1.txt** is the string type data assigned to the **$New_File** variable. Here, **$New_File** will act as the file pointer throughout the program.

Line 3
$newfile = fopen($New_File, "w");
In this line, two parameters, **$New_file** and **w**, are passed to the **fopen()** function. Here, **$New_File** is the variable which is holding a value (see Line 2) and **w** is the file in write only mode. This line will create a new file with the name *ch10-example1.txt* if the file with the same name does not exist.

Line 8
exit();
In this line, the **exit()** function is used to terminate the current running script if any problem occurred in opening the file.

Line 10
fwrite($newfile, "This text file is created by using PHP program..");
In this line, two parameters are passed to the **fwrite()** function. Here, **$newfile** is the file pointer and **"This text file is created by using PHP program.."** is the text that will be written inside the file.

Note
To check the newly created file, navigate to the folder where you have saved the program and look for the file.

The output of Example 1 is displayed in Figure 10-1.

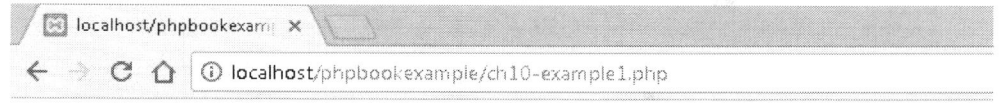

You successfully, wrote into file.
To see the text file you can navigate to the folder where you have saved the current program file.

Figure 10-1 The output of Example 1

READING A FILE

To read the text file using PHP program, you need to open the file using the **fopen()** function in read only mode or in read and write mode. After opening the file, you can read the file by using the **fread()** function. The syntax of the **fread()** function is as follow:

```
fread($filepointer, filesize("file_name.txt") );
```

In the given syntax, two parameters are passed to the **fread()** function where **$filepointer** represents the file pointer and **filesize()** function is an inbuilt function used to get the size of the given file. Here, **file_name.txt** represents the text file which is passed as parameter to the **filesize()** function. You can also pass the complete location of the file in place of **file_name.txt** text file, if required.

Example 2

The following program will read the *ch10-example1.txt* file using the **fread()** function and display the output in the browser.

```
<?php                                                    1
    $old_File = "ch10-example1.txt";                     2
    $oldFile = fopen($old_File, "r");                    3
    if($oldFile == false )                               4
    {                                                    5
        die("Unable to open and read the file!");        6
    }                                                    7
    echo fread($oldFile,filesize($old_File));            8
?>                                                       9
```

Explanation
Line 3
$oldFile = fopen($old_File, "r");
In this line, two parameters, **$old_File** and **r**, are passed to the **fopen()** function. Here, **$old_File** is the variable which is holding the file to be opened and **r** is the file in read only mode. This line will read the file with the name *ch10-example1.txt*.

Line 6
die("Unable to open and read the file!");
In this line, the **die()** function is used to terminate the current running script if any problem occurred in opening the file. This line will display the following in the browser:

Unable to open and read the file!

Line 8
echo fread($oldFile,filesize($old_File));
In this line, two parameters are passed to the **fread()** function where **$oldFile** is the file pointer and **filesize()** is an inbuilt function. The **$old_File** is the variable, passed as parameter to the **filesize()** function which is holding the text file (see Line 2). This line will display the following in the browser:

The output of Example 2 is displayed in Figure 10-2.

Figure 10-2 The output of Example 2

fgets()
The **fgets()** function is an inbuilt function used to read the single line of the specified file at a time. The pointer moves to the next line after reading the first line. The syntax of the **fgets()** function is as follow:

```
fgets($file_name, length);
```

In the given syntax, two parameters are passed to the **fgets()** function where **$file_name** represents the file pointer which is a required parameter and **length** represents the number of bytes to be read. Here, length parameter is optional.

Example 3
The following program will create, write and read the *ch10-example3.txt* file using **fopen()** and **fgets()** functions. This program will read one line of the file and display the output in the browser.

```
<?php                                                   1
    $Next_File = "ch10-example3.txt";                   2
    $writefile = fopen($Next_File,"w");                 3
    if($writefile == false )                            4
    {                                                   5
        echo ( "Error in opening file" );               6
        exit();                                         7
    }                                                   8
    fwrite($writefile, "This is Line 1.                 9
```

File Handling, Sessions, and Cookies

```
        This is Line 2.                                        10
        This is Line 3." );                                    11
    $read_File = "ch10-example3.txt";                          12
    $readFile = fopen($read_File, "r");                        13
    if($readFile == false )                                    14
        {                                                      15
            die("Unable to open and read the file!");          16
        }                                                      17
    echo fgets($readFile);                                     18
?>                                                             19
```

Explanation
Line 18
echo fgets($readFile);
In this line, **fgets()** is the function and **$readFile** is the parameter passed to this function. This function will read only one line of the *ch10-example3.txt* file. This line will display the following in the browser:

This is Line 1.

The output of Example 3 is displayed in Figure 10-3.

Figure 10-3 *The output of Example 3*

feof()
The **feof()** function is an inbuilt function used to check the End-Of-File (EOF). This function is mostly used as the looping condition when the file length or end of file data is unknown. The syntax of **feof()** function is as follow:

```
feof($file_name);
```

In the given syntax, **$file_name** is the parameter passed to the **feof()** function where **$file_name** represents the file pointer.

Example 4

The following program will read the *ch10-example3.txt* file by using the **fgets()** and **feof()** functions with **while** loop. This program will read the file line by line, until End-Of-File is reached and display the output in the browser.

```
<?php                                                          1
    $read_File = "ch10-example3.txt";                          2
    $readFile = fopen($read_File, "r");                        3
```

```
        if($readFile == false)                           4
        {                                                5
                die("Unable to open and read the file!");6
        }                                                7
        while(!feof($readFile))                          8
          {                                              9
                echo fgets($readFile) . "<br>";         10
          }                                             11
    ?>                                                  12
```

Explanation
Line 8
while(!feof($readFile))
This line contains the **while** loop statement. In this line, the conditional expression, **!feof($readFile)** will be evaluated. This condition states that **feof()** function will read the file until it reaches the end of file where **$readFile** is the file pointer. This file pointer is pointing the *ch10-example3.txt* file (Line 2). So, if the **while** condition evaluates to true, the block of **while** loop will be executed (from Line 9 to Line 11). Otherwise, the loop will get terminate.

The output of Example 4 is displayed in Figure 10-4.

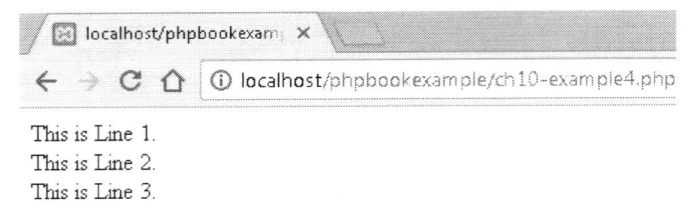

Figure 10-4 The output of Example 4

CLOSING A FILE
After opening the file with the **fopen()** function, if you are done with all the file handling operations such as read and write then it is important to close the opened file. The **fclose()** function is used to close the file. The syntax of the **fclose()** function is as follow:

```
    fclose($file_name);
```

In the given syntax, **$file_name** is the required parameter passed to the **fclose()** function where **$file_name** represents the file pointer.

> **Note**
> *In PHP, files get automatically closed after the entire execution of PHP script. But, it is good practice to close all the files by using **fclose()** functions to free the server resources earlier instead of waiting for the execution of entire PHP script.*

File Handling, Sessions, and Cookies

Example 5

The following program will create, open, write, read, and close the *ch10-example5.txt* file by using file handling functions and display the output in the browser.

```
<?php                                                          1
   $file_name = "ch10-example5.txt";                            2
   $file_pointer = fopen( $file_name, "w" );                    3
   if( $file_pointer == false ) {                               4
      echo ( "Error in opening new file" );                     5
      exit();                                                   6
   }                                                            7
   fwrite( $file_pointer, "Hello User. How are you?" );         8
   fclose( $file_pointer );                                     9
?>                                                              10
<html>                                                          11
<head>                                                          12
    <title>fclose() function</title>                            13
</head>                                                         14
<body>                                                          15
  <?php                                                         16
      $file_name = "ch10-example5.txt";                         17
      $file_pointer = fopen( $file_name, "r" );                 18
      if( $file_pointer == false ) {                            19
         echo ( "Error in opening file" );                      20
         exit();                                                21
      }                                                         22
      $file_size = filesize( $file_name );                      23
      $file_text = fread( $file_pointer, $file_size );          24
      fclose( $file_pointer );                                  25
      echo ( "File size :<b> $file_size </b> bytes <br>" );     26
      echo ( "<b>$file_text</b> <br>" );                        27
      echo("File name: <b> $file_name </b>");                   28
  ?>                                                            29
</body>                                                         30
</html>                                                         31
```

Explanation
Line 9
fclose($file_pointer);
In this line, **fclose()** function will close the *ch10-example5.txt* file.

The output of Example 5 is displayed in Figure 10-5.

Figure 10-5 The output of Example 5

COPYING A FILE

The **copy()** function is used to create a copy of some existing file. The file which is copied is known as source file and the copy of the file is known as destination file. If the destination file already exists then the **copy()** function will replace the existing file. The syntax of the **copy()** function is as follow:

```
copy('old_file.txt','copy_file.txt');
```

In the given syntax, two parameters are passed to **copy()** function where **old_file.txt** represents the file name which is to be copied and **copy_file.txt** represents the name of the file by which the copy of **old_file.txt** file will be saved.

Example 6

The following program will create the copy of *ch10-example5.txt* file by using the **copy()** function and display the output in the browser.

```
<?php                                                                  1
    $file_name = 'ch10-example5.txt';                                  2
    $copyfile_name = 'ch10-example6.txt';                              3
        copy($file_name, $copyfile_name)                               4
        or die("failed to copy $file");                                5
    echo "File successfully copied <br> Check the folder where         6
    you have saved the current program, to see the copy of file";
?>                                                                     7
```

Explanation
Line 4
copy($file_name, $copyfile_name)
In this line, two parameters are passed to the **copy()** function where, **$file_name** is the variable holding the *ch10-example5.tx*t file (Line 2) and **$copyfile_name** is the variable holding the name of the file by which the copy of the source file will be saved (Line 3). Here, the **copy()** function will create the copy of *ch10-example5.txt* file with the name *ch10-example6.txt*.

The output of Example 6 is displayed in Figure 10-6.

File Handling, Sessions, and Cookies   10-13

> ![Browser screenshot showing localhost/phpbookexample/ch10-example6.php]
>
> File successfully copied
> Check the folder where you have saved the current program, to see the copy of file

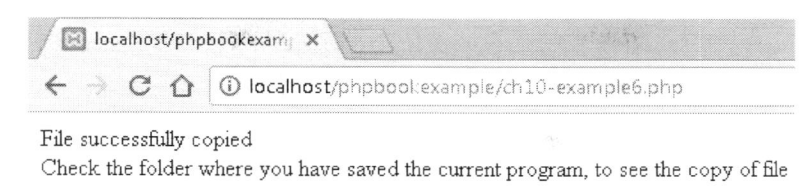

Figure 10-6 The output of Example 6

RENAMING A FILE

The **rename()** function is used to rename some existing file. The syntax of the **rename()** function is as follows:

```
rename('name.txt','rename.txt');
```

In the given syntax, two parameters are passed to the **rename()** function where **name.txt** represents the file name which is to be renamed and **rename.txt** represents the new name of that file.

> **Note**
> *The **rename()** function is also be used to rename directories.*

Example 7

The following program will rename the *ch10-example6.txt* file by using the **rename()** function and display the output in the browser.

```
<?php                                                              1
    $old_name = 'ch10-example6.txt';                               2
    $new_name = 'ch10-example7.txt';                               3
        rename($old_name, $new_name)                               4
        or die("failed to rename the $old_name");                  5
    echo "File successfully renamed <br> Check the folder where    6
    you have saved the current program, to see the changes";
?>                                                                 7
```

Explanation
Line 4
rename($old_name, $new_name)
In this line, two parameters are passed to **rename()** function where **$old_name** is the variable holding the *ch10-example6.tx*t file (Line 2) and **$new_name** is the variable holding the new name of *ch10-example6.tx*t file (Line 3). Here, the **rename()** function will rename the *ch10-example6.txt* file name to *ch10-example7.txt*.

The output of Example 7 is displayed in Figure 10-7.

DELETING A FILE

To delete an existing file, the **unlike()** function is used. The syntax of **unlike()** function is as follow:

```
unlike('name.txt');
```

In the given syntax, **unlike()** function is the inbuilt function. Here, the parameter passed to the **unlike()** function is **name.txt** which represents the file name or path of the file which is to be deleted.

Example 8

The following program will delete the *ch10-example7.txt* file by using the **unlike()** function and display the output in the browser.

```
<?php                                                           1
    $del_file = 'ch10-example7.txt';                            2
    unlink($del_file)                                           3
    or die("failed to delete a $del_file file");                4
    echo "File successfully deleted <br> Check the folder       5
    where you have saved the current program, to see if the
    file is deleted or not";
?>                                                              6
```

Explanation
Line 3
unlink($del_file)
In this line, one parameter is passed to the **unlike()** function where **$del_file** is the variable holding the *ch10-example7.tx*t file (Line 2). Here, the **unlike()** function will delete the *ch10-example7.txt* file.

The output of Example 8 is displayed in Figure 10-8.

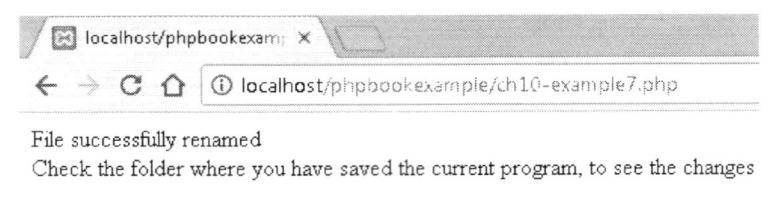

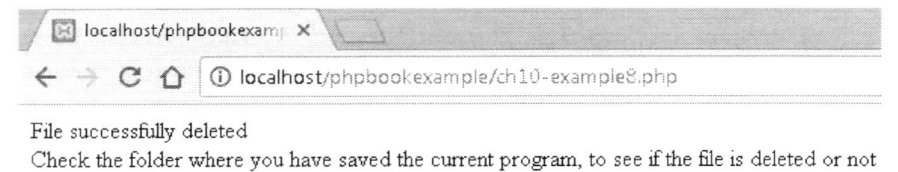

Figure 10-8 The output of Example 8

HANDLING FILE UPLOAD

File upload is part of HTML form. You have already learned about form with its different form input elements and attributes in the previous chapter. To upload the files in the web server, various attributes and inbuilt functions are used that are discussed next.

enctype Attribute

The **enctype** form attribute should be used to encode the form data while submitting the data to the server. The **enctype** form attribute can only be used with **post** method. The syntax of **enctype** form attribute is as follow:

```
<form method="post" enctype="value">
```

In the given syntax, **<form>** is the start tag of HTML form where **post** method is used to send the form data to the server page. Here, **enctype** is a form attribute and **value** represents any value related to the **enctype** form attribute.

There are various values available for the **enctype** form attribute. Table 10-2 lists all the possible values of the **enctype** form attribute with their descriptions.

Table 10-2 Values and descriptions of enctype attribute

Value	Description
application/x-www-form-urlencoded	It encodes all the special characters into ASCII HEX values and all the spaces into + symbol before sending them to server.
multipart/form-data	It does not encode any character. It is required when the file upload control is used in the HTML form.
text/plain	It only converts spaces into + symbols.

Note
*To upload the files to the web server, it is important to use **enctype= "multipart/form-data"** in the form.*

The $_FILES Superglobal Variable

The **$_FILES** superglobal variable contains an array of items uploaded to the current script through the **post** method. There are five type of **$_FILES** array element. Table 10-3 lists all the possible array elements of the **$_FILES** superglobal variable with their descriptions.

Table 10-3 $_FILES array elements

$_FILES array element	Description
$_FILES['fieldname']['name']	The **fieldname** represents the name of the input field in an HTML form. For example, in an input element of HTML form **name="file"** is an attribute where **file** is the name of the input field. The **name** in **['name']** represents the name of the uploaded file. For example, flower.jpeg (image file).
$_FILES['fieldname']['type']	The **fieldname** represents the name of the input field in an HTML form and **type** represents the content type of the file. There are various media content type. For example, **image/jpeg**, **image/gif**, **video/mp4**, and so on.
$_FILES['fieldname']['size']	The **fieldname** represents the name of the input field in an HTML form and **size** represents the size of files in bytes
$_FILES['fieldname']['tmp_name']	The **fieldname** represents the name of the input field in an HTML form and **tmp_name** represents the name of the temporary file. This temporary file is stored on the server.
$_FILES['fieldname']['error']	The **fieldname** represents the name of the input field in the form and the **error** represents the error code.

move_uploaded_file() Function

The **move_uploaded_file()** function is an inbuilt function which is used to move an uploaded file to a new location. The syntax of **move_uploaded_file()** function is as follow:

```
move_uploaded_file(file_name, new_location)
```

In the given syntax, two parameters are passed to the **move_uploaded_file()** function where **file_name** represents the name of the file and **new_location** represents the new location of the file where you have to move the file.

> **Note**
> *The **move_uploaded_file()** function works only on the files uploaded by using the **post** method. If a file with same name already exist at the new location then this function overwrites the existing file.*

Example 9

The following program will use **$_FILES** superglobal variable and **move_uploaded_file()** function to upload the image file and display the output in the browser.

File Handling, Sessions, and Cookies

```php
<!DOCTYPE html>                                                      1
<html>                                                               2
<head>                                                               3
   <title>PHP Image Upload</title>                                   4
</head>                                                              5
<body>                                                               6
   <h1>PHP Image Upload</h1>                                         7
   <form action="ch10-example9.php" method="post"                    8
     enctype="multipart/form-data">
   <p><b>Upload a JPG, GIF, PNG or TIF File:</b></p>                 9
   <input type="file" name="upload_img">                            10
   <input type="submit" value= "Upload image">                      11
   <br><br>                                                         12
   </form>                                                          13
</body>                                                             14
</html>                                                             15
<?php                                                               16
if ($_FILES)                                                        17
{                                                                   18
   $name = $_FILES['upload_img']['name'];                           19
   switch($_FILES['upload_img']['type']){                           20
        case 'image/jpeg': $extension = 'jpg'; break;               21
        case 'image/gif': $extension = 'gif'; break;                22
        case 'image/png': $extension = 'png'; break;                23
        case 'image/tiff': $extension = 'tif'; break;               24
        default: $extension = '';                                   25
   }                                                                26
   if($extension){                                                  27
        $new_name ="image.$extension";                              28
move_uploaded_file($_FILES['upload_img']['tmp_name'],$new_name);    29
echo "<b>The '$name' image is uploaded as '$new_name':             30
</b><br><br>";
echo "<img src='$new_name' height='300px' width='500px' >";        31
   }                                                                32
   else echo "<p><b>'$name' is not an accepted image file.<b></p>"; 33
}                                                                   34
else echo "<b>No image uploaded</b>";                               35
?>                                                                  36
```

Explanation
Line 8
<form action="ch10-example9.php" method="post" enctype="multipart/form-data">
In this line, **<form>** is the start tag of HTML form body and enctype is the attribute having **multipart/form-data** as its value. This value is required when the file upload control is used in the HTML form to upload the file.

Line 19
$name = $_FILES['upload_img']['name'];
In this line, **$_FILES** is the superglobal variable having two array elements, **upload_img** and **name**, where **upload_img** is the name of the input field (Line 10) and **name** represents the name of the uploaded file.

Line 20
switch($_FILES['upload_img']['type']){
In these lines, **$_FILES['upload_img']['type']** is passed as the parameter to the **switch** statement. Here, the **type** array element represents the type of file. The values of **type** array element is compared with all the **case** literal values.

Line 21
case 'image/jpeg': $extension = 'jpg'; break;
In this line, if the **case 'image/jpeg'** matches with the type of file uploaded, it will assign **jpg** to the **$extension** variable. Otherwise, the control will be transferred to the next line. Here, **image/jpeg** is the type of file.

The working of Lines 21 to 24 is similar to Line 21.

Line 25
default: $extension = '';
This line contain the **default** case. This case will be executed only when no match is found in all other cases.

Line 29
move_uploaded_file($_FILES['upload_img']['tmp_name'],$new_name);
In this line, two parameters are passed to the **move_uploaded_file()** function where **$_FILES['upload_img']['tmp_name']** is the first parameter which represents the name of the file. Here, **upload_img** is the name of the input field and **tmp_name** represents the temporary name of file. **$new_name** is the second parameter of **move_uploaded_file()** function which is holding the new name of uploaded file (Line 28).

The output of Example 9 is displayed in Figure 10-9.

PHP Image Upload

Upload a JPG, GIF, PNG or TIF File:

Choose File   No file chosen   Upload image

No image uploaded

Figure 10-9 *The output of Example 9 when no file is chosen*

File Handling, Sessions, and Cookies 10-19

In Figure 10-9, No file is chosen to upload. Now, the user will browse for the file by clicking on **Choose File** button. The file name of the chosen file will be displayed in the browser as shown in Figure 10-10.

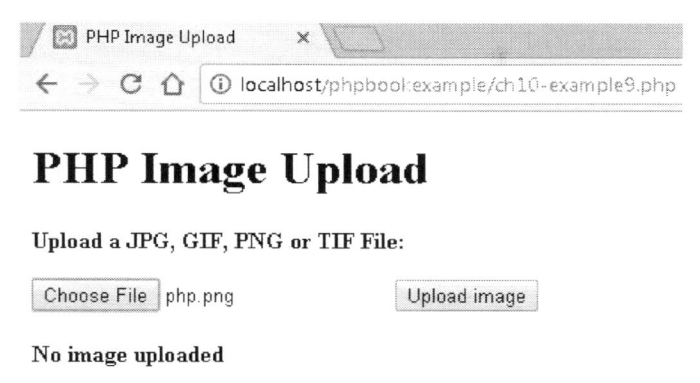

Figure 10-10 The output of Example 9 after the file is chosen

After choosing the file to be uploaded, refer Figure 10-10, user will click on the **Upload image** button which will display the chosen image in the browser as shown in Figure 10-11.

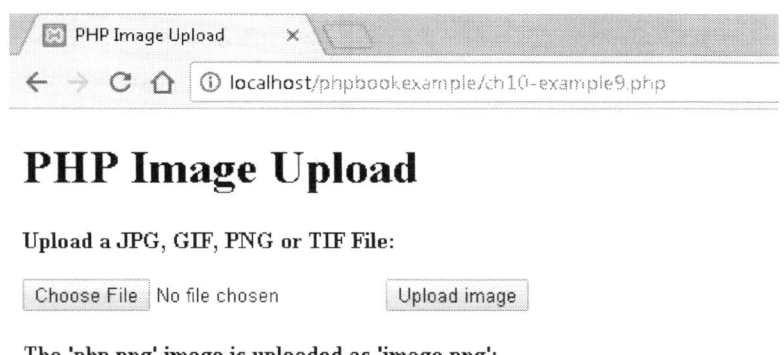

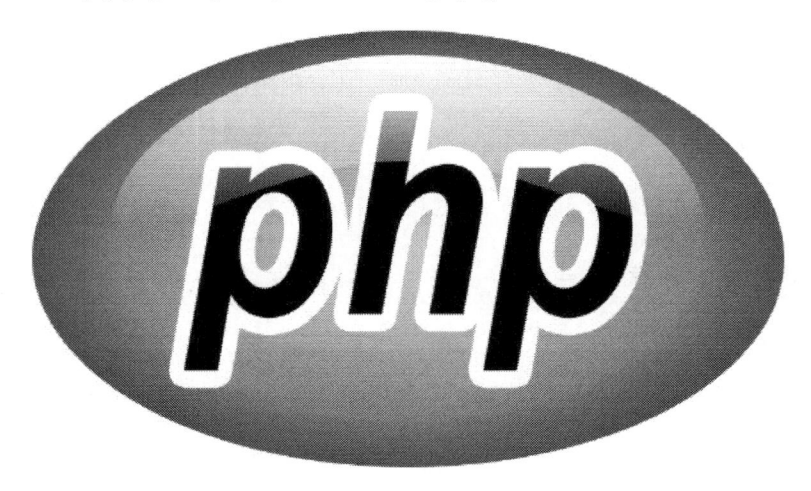

Figure 10-11 The output of Example 9 displaying the chosen image

SESSIONS

Sessions are group of variables that store data for every individual by providing the user with unique session ID. This data is stored on the server but not on the user computer or system. The session of a particular user starts when the user opens the browser application or logs into a particular website and is maintained until that browser application is closed completely or the user logs out from that website.

PHP creates a new session and generates a new ID for the session if a session is not passed in the program otherwise it uses existing session ID. Session easily stores user information and makes that information available across multiple pages of that particular website in the browser.

Starting a Session

The **session_start()** function is used to start a new session or to resume any session. A session can be resumed with the help of session identifier passed through **GET** or **POST** request. In PHP 7, new options parameter was introduced for the **session_start()** function. The syntax for using the **session_start()** function is as follow:

```
session_start([options]);
```

In the given syntax, **session_start()** function is an inbuilt function for resuming or creating a session. An array that has various options is passed as parameter to the **session_start()** function, and this parameter is an optional parameter.

The array options can override the session configuration directives of PHP. Various array options of **session_start()** functions are **session.lazy_write**, **read_and_close**, **session.sid_length**, and so on. The **session.lazy_write** option is set **on** by default and it overwrites the session file if any data has been changed in the session. The **read_and_close** option reads the session data and closes it immediately without making any changes. To specify the length of session ID **session.sid_length** is used. By default, the length value of session ID is set to 32 but it can vary from 22 to 256.

For example:

```php
<?php
    session_start([
        'cache_limiter' => 'private',
        'read_and_close' => true,
    ]);
?>
```

In the given example, **session_start()** function is used to start the session. Here, **cache_limiter** and **read_and_close** are the array options passed as a parameter to the **session_start()** function. The **cache_limiter** option is set to **private** where cache limiter defines which cache control HTTP headers are sent to the client and **private** allows client to cache the content and disallows caching by proxies. The **read_and_close** option is set **true** and will therefore read and then close the session data immediately.

File Handling, Sessions, and Cookies

> **Note**
> The **session_start()** function must be placed at the top of the PHP document before starting any HTML or any other PHP code.

The $_SESSION Superglobal Variable

The **$_SESSION** superglobal variable is used to set the session variables. Once the session starts, you can set various session variables by using **$_SESSION** superglobal variable.

Example 10

The following program will create a new session by using **session_start()** function. This program will also set the session variables with **$_SESSION** superglobal variable and display the output in the browser.

```
<?php                                                            1
    session_start();                                             2
?>                                                               3
<!DOCTYPE html>                                                  4
<html>                                                           5
<head>                                                           6
        <title>Session variables</title>                         7
</head>                                                          8
<body>                                                           9
    <?php                                                       10
        $_SESSION["username"] = "Shane";                        11
        $_SESSION["password"] = "Kathe";                        12
        echo "Session variables are set. To check its working   13
        run ch10-example11.php file in the same browser.";
    ?>                                                          14
</body>                                                         15
</html>                                                         16
```

Explanation
Line 2
session_start();
In this line, **session_start()** function will start a new session.

Line 11
$_SESSION["username"] = "Shane";
In this line, **$_SESSION** is a superglobal array variable having **username** as an array element and the value assigned to this session variable is **Shane**.

The working of Line 12 is same as Line 11.

The output of Example 10 is displayed in Figure 10-12.

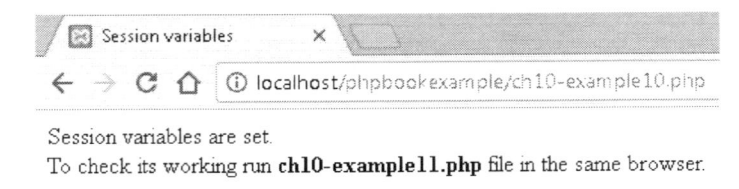

Figure 10-12 The output of Example 10

Note
To check the working of session, you can run Example 11 in the new tab of same browser given in the next section.

Get the Session Values
To get the values of session variables which is already set, you can **echo** the session variables in the new or same file by using **$_SESSION** supergloabal array variable.

Example 11

The following program will get the session values which are already set in the previous program with **$_SESSION** superglobal variable and display the output in the browser.

```
<?php                                                               1
    session_start();                                                2
?>                                                                  3
<!DOCTYPE html>                                                     4
<html>                                                              5
<head>                                                              6
        <title>Get session values</title>                           7
</head>                                                             8
<body>                                                              9
<?php                                                              10
echo "The Username is <b>" . $_SESSION["username"]."</b>.<br>";    11
echo "The password is <b>" . $_SESSION["password"]."</b>.";        12
?>                                                                 13
</body>                                                            14
</html>                                                            15
```

Explanation
Line 2
session_start();
In this line, **session_start()** function will resume the old session as the session was already created in previous example.

Line 11
**echo "The Username is " . $_SESSION["username"]. ".
";**
In this line, the **$_SESSION["username"]** session variable is used to get the value of **username** which was set in the previous example. This line will display the following in the browser:

File Handling, Sessions, and Cookies

The Username is Shane.

The working of Line 12 is same as Line 11.

The output of Example 11 is displayed in Figure 10-13.

Figure 10-13 The output of Example 11

Modifying the Session Variables
To change or modify the value of existing session variables, you can replace the old value with new value in the new or old file.

Example 12

The following program will modify the session values which were already set with **$_SESSION** superglobal variable and display the output in the browser.

```
<?php                                                                    1
    session_start();                                                     2
?>                                                                       3
<!DOCTYPE html>                                                          4
<html>                                                                   5
<head>                                                                   6
        <title>Modifying session values</title>                          7
</head>                                                                  8
<body>                                                                   9
<?php                                                                   10
$_SESSION["username"] = "Harry";                                        11
echo "The new username is <b>" . $_SESSION["username"] .                12
"</b>.<br>";
echo "The old password is  <b>" . $_SESSION["password"] .               13
"</b>.";
?>                                                                      14
</body>                                                                 15
</html>                                                                 16
```

Explanation
Line 11
$_SESSION["username"] = "Harry";
In this line, the old value **Shane** (see Example 10) is replaced by **Harry**.

The output of Example 12 is displayed in Figure 10-14.

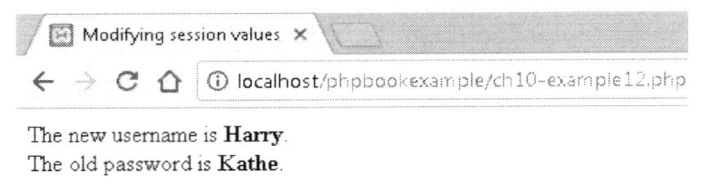

Figure 10-14 The output of Example 12

Destroying a Session

A session is destroyed when the user closes an application or logs out from the website in the browser. You can destroy or end the session by using **session_destroy()** function in the PHP file. You can also unset the already set session variables by using **session_unset()** function which will only unset the session variables instead of destroying or ending the session.

Example 13

The following program will unset the session values by using **session_unset()** function. This program will also destroy the session by using **session_destroy()** function and display the output in the browser.

```
<?php                                                             1
    session_start();                                              2
?>                                                                3
<!DOCTYPE html>                                                   4
<html>                                                            5
<head>                                                            6
        <title> Destroying Session </title>                       7
</head>                                                           8
<body>                                                            9
<?php                                                            10
    session_unset();                                             11
        echo "Variables are unset. <br>";                        12
    session_destroy();                                           13
        echo "Session is destroyed. <br>";                       14
echo "To check whether the session is expired or not, <br>       15
run <b>ch10-example11.php</b> file again in the browser."
?>                                                               16
</body>                                                          17
</html>                                                          18
```

Explanation
Line 11
session_unset();
In this line, **session_unset()** function will unset all the session values which were already set in the current session.

File Handling, Sessions, and Cookies 10-25

Line 13
session_destroy();
In this line, **session_destroy()** function will destroy or end the current session.

The output of Example 13 is displayed in Figure 10-15.

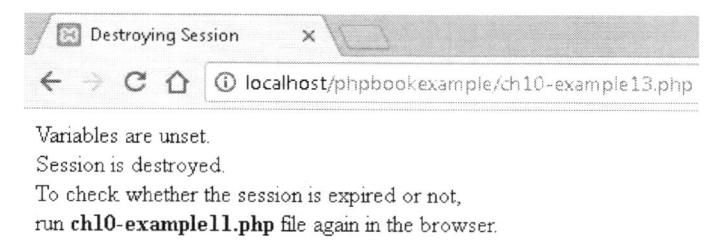

Figure 10-15 *The output of Example 13*

> **Note**
> *To check whether a particular session is destroyed or not, you can run Example 11 (ch10-example11.php file) in the new tab of same browser. You will notice that the values of session variables are undefined as session is destroyed.*

COOKIES

The web server stores the browsing data in the hard disk of your computer which is known as cookies. These cookies maintain the data and stores the login details of the user that helps in tracking or identifying the users. The cookies can be easily retrieved from the hard disk of same computer in which it was stored. Whenever user will browse for visited pages in the browser of same computer, the browser will send the cookies back to the web server to get the requesting page faster.

Every website with a unique domain can issue its own cookies which can be retrieved by the website only. This maintains the privacy of the user and the domain company.

Creating a Cookie

You can create or set a cookie in PHP by using **setcookie()** function. Cookies are set in an HTTP header and are exchanged when the header is transfered. It is important to set a cookie before sending any HTML code because cookies cannot be transfered once HTML code is sent. The syntax of **setcookie()** function is as follow:

```
setcookie(name, value, expire, path, domain, secure, httponly);
```

In the given syntax, the **setcookie()** function is used to set the cookie. It has multiple parameters where **name** and **value** are required parameters and remaining are optional parameters. Table 10-4 lists all the parameters of the **setcookie()** function with their descriptions.

Table 10-4 setcookie() function parameters and their description

Parameter	Description
name	It represents the name of the cookie. Your server uses this name to access the cookie.
value	It represents the value of the cookie.
expire	It represents the expiry date or expiry time of a cookie. **time()** function is used to set the time including number of seconds. For example, in **time() + 86400**, 86400 is time in seconds. By default cookie expires when the browser is closed if time is not set.
path	It represents the path of the directory for which you want to set the cookie. For example if you use only forward slash(/) then the cookie is valid for the entire domain or directory else will be available only for the subdirectory mentioned. By default it is available for the current directory where the cookie is set.
domain	It represents the domain or subdomain for which the cookie is set. For example, *.cadcim.com* (domain).
secure	It represents secure transportation of cookie. If this value is set to **TRUE** (1), the cookie is transferred only in secured connection through *https://*. By default it is set to **FALSE** (0) which means cookie is sent through *http://*.
httponly	It represents the medium through which the cookie will be transferred across the web. If this value is set to **TRUE**, the cookie will be sent through HTTP only and the JavaScript will not be able to access that cookie. By default it is set to **FALSE** as all the browsers do not support **httponly**.

Get the Cookie Values

To get already set values of cookie variables, you can display the cookie value by using **$_COOKIE** supergloabal array variable.

Example 14

The following program will set the cookie by using **setcookie()** function. This program will also get the value of cookie by using **$_COOKIE** superglobal variable and display the output in the browser.

```
<?php                                                        1
   $name = "username";                                       2
   $value = "Shane Kathe";                                   3
   setcookie($name, $value, time() + (86400 * 30), "/");     4
?>                                                           5
```

File Handling, Sessions, and Cookies

```
<!DOCTYPE html>                                                      6
<html>                                                               7
<head>                                                               8
      <title> Set and Display Cookie </title>                        9
</head>                                                             10
<body>                                                              11
<?php                                                               12
  if(!isset($_COOKIE[$name])) {                                     13
     echo "Cookie named ' <b>" . $name . "</b>' is not set!";       14
        } else {                                                    15
     echo "Cookie name'<b>" . $name . "</b>' is set!<br>";          16
     echo "Cookie value is: <b>" . $_COOKIE[$name] ."</b>";         17
  }                                                                 18
?>                                                                  19
<p><b>Note:</b>Please <b>reload</b> the web page if it is           20
   displaying the message that cookie is not set.</p>
</body>                                                             21
</html>                                                             22
```

Explanation
Line 4
setcookie($name, $value, time() + (86400 * 30), "/");
In this line, **setcookie()** function has multiple parameters where **$name** is a variable holding cookie name (Line 2), **$value** is holding the cookie value (Line 3) and **time()** function is used to set the expiry time of the cookie which is set to **+ (86400 * 30)**. This means, cookie will get expired after 30 days, because 86400 seconds is equal to 1 day which is multiplied by 30 and positive sign (**+**) is used for future time. Forward slash(/) states that cookie is available for the entire directory.

Line 17
echo "Cookie value is: " . $_COOKIE[$name] ."";
In this line, the **$_COOKIE[$name]** superglobal variable is used to get the value of cookie which was set by using **setcookie()** function (Line 4). This line will display the following in the browser:

Cookie value is: Shane Kathe

> **Note**
> *To see the correct output, reload the web page once again after running every program in which cookie is set on the browser.*

The output of Example 14 is displayed in Figure 10-16.

Figure 10-16 The output of Example 14

Deleting a Cookie

You can delete a cookie in PHP by using **setcookie()** function again by setting the past time in the function parameter instead of the future time. To do so, follow the same syntax of **setcookie()** function as already discussed in the last section with all the parameters same except the **time()** function. To delete the cookie you will have to pass negative time in seconds instead of positive time.

Example 15

The following program will delete the cookie which was already set by using **setcookie()** function and display the output in the browser.

```
<?php                                                              1
   $name = "username";                                             2
   $value = "Shane Kathe";                                         3
   setcookie($name, $value, time() - 86400, "/");                  4
?>                                                                 5
<!DOCTYPE html>                                                    6
<html>                                                             7
<head>                                                             8
        <title> Delete a Cookie </title>                           9
</head>                                                            10
<body>                                                             11
<?php                                                              12
   if(!isset($_COOKIE[$name])) {                                   13
      echo "Cookie named ' <b>" . $name . "</b>' is not set!";     14
         } else {                                                  15
      echo "Cookie name'<b>" . $name . "</b>' is set!<br>";        16
      echo "Cookie value is: <b>" . $_COOKIE[$name] . "</b>";      17
   }                                                               18
?>                                                                 19
<p><b>Note:</b>Please <b>reload</b> the web page once again        20
   to see the correct output</p>
</body>                                                            21
</html>                                                            22
```

File Handling, Sessions, and Cookies

Explanation

Line 4

setcookie($name, $value, time() - 86400, "/");

In this line, **setcookie()** function is used to delete a cookie. Here **time()** function is used to set the expiry time of the cookie which is set to **- 86400**. Here a negative value of 86400 indicates past time which means the cookies has already expired.

The output of Example 15 is displayed in Figure 10-17.

Figure 10-17   The output of Example 15

Self-Evaluation Test

Answer the following questions and then compare them to those given at the end of this chapter:

1. File Handling is used to perform _____ related operations.

2. The _____ function in used to open a file in PHP.

3. The _____ function is an inbuilt function used to read single line of a particular file at a time.

4. The _____ function is used to delete an existing file.

5. The _____ function is used to start a session.

6. The **move_upload_file()** function is used to move an uploaded file to a new location. (T/F)

7. The **session_destroy()** function is used to destroy a session. (T/F)

8. You can create or set a cookie in PHP by using the **setcookie()** function. (T/F)

Review Questions

Answer the following questions:

1. Which of the following file opening modes is used to open a file in read only mode?

   (a) **r+** (b) **w**
   (c) **w+** (d) **r**

2. Which of the following functions is used to read a single line of a file at a time?

   (a) **fread()** (b) **fgets()**
   (c) **feof()** (d) None of them

3. Which of the following functions is used to delete a file?

   (a) **destroy()** (b) **unlike()**
   (c) **remove()** (d) **del()**

4. Which of the following superglobal variables is used to upload a file?

   (a) **$_UPLOAD** (b) **$_SERVER**
   (c) **$_GET** (d) **$_FILES**

5. Which of the following functions is used to start a new session?

   (a) **session_start()** (b) **start_session()**
   (c) **session()** (d) **new_session()**

6. Which of the following functions is used to set a cookie?

   (a) **get_cookie()** (b) **start_cookie()**
   (c) **setcookie()** (d) **set_cookie()**

EXERCISES

Exercise 1

Write a program to upload only jpeg and png files in the browser.

Exercise 2

Write a program to create, write, and read a file and also to display the output in the browser.

Exercise 3

Write a program to create cookie. Set its expiry time to 5 days after its creation and also display the output in the browser.

Answers to Self-Evaluation Test

1. file, 2. fopen(), 3. fgets(), 4. unlike(), 5. session_start(), 6. F, 7. T, 8. T

Chapter 11

Introduction to MySQL

Learning Objectives

After completing this chapter, you will be able to:
- *Understand the RDBMS terminologies*
- *Interact with MySQL*
- *Create database and table*
- *Understand Data types*
- *Understand and use constraints*
- *Use the SELECT statement*
- *Alter the table*
- *Manage transaction with COMMIT and ROLLBACK*

INTRODUCTION

MySQL is an open source Relational Database Management System (RDBMS). It is all about working with database by using various MySQL platforms and SQL commands. The name MySQL is the combination of two words: My (the name of co-founder Michael Widenius's daughter) and SQL (Structured Query Language). SQL is a specialized non-procedural language used to perform various tasks such as inserting, updating or retrieving data to communicate with a database. According to ANSI (American National Standards Institute), SQL is a standard language for the relational database management system which must support the same major keywords such as **SELECT**, **INSERT**, **UPDATE**, **DELETE**, **WHERE**, and so on in every database products.

In this chapter, you will learn about the basics of each SQL commands and also to execute these commands on various MySQL platforms. You will also learn about basic RDBMS terminologies such as database, row, column which are used in MySQL.

RDBMS TERMINOLOGIES

RDBMS terminologies create the base of relational database. So, it is important to understand basic RDBMS terminologies which are discussed next.

Database

A database is a collection of data that is used to store and retrieve related information. MySQL manage a large amount of data and provides multi-user environment and these multiple users can concurrently access the same data in a database.

Table

Tables are the basic unit of data storage in the MySQL database which holds data in form of rows and columns. For example, a table **EMPLOYEES**, holds the details of employees such as **EMPLOYEE_ID**, **FIRST_NAME**, and **SALARY**, as shown in Figure 11-1. A table can contain a number of records. Once a table has been created with columns and rows, you can retrieve, delete, update, or insert data in it.

EMPLOYEES

EMPLOYEE_ID	FIRST_NAME	SALARY
1	Shane	1500000
2	Harry	1300000
3	Liza	1100000
4	Lucy	1000000

Figure 11-1 Table of employees

Record

A record in a database is equivalent to a row, but is not usually referred to as a row. A record is composed of various cells and each cell contains data such as all the data about one particular person, company, or item in a database. For example, in the **EMPLOYEES** table, refer Figure 11-1, there are details of four employees. So, the detail of one employee is a single record (row) of a **EMPLOYEES** table, such as **1**, **Shane**, and **1500000**, as shown in Figure 11-2.

*Figure 11-2 Record of the **EMPLOYEES** table*

Field
A field in a database is part of a record. It contains single unit for the subject of the record and appear as columns in a database table. For example, in the **EMPLOYEES** table, refer Figure 11-1, there are three fields, **EMPLOYEE_ID**, **FIRST_NAME**, and **SALARY** in the **EMPLOYEES** table.

Column
A column is also comprises of various cells. Each cell represents data of a particular type, one for each row of the table. A column is a set of row corresponding to the multiple record. For example, in the **EMPLOYEES** table (refer to Figure 11-1), a set of cells that contains different data for different employee in a particular field will represent a column in the **EMPLOYEES** table, as shown in Figure 11-3.

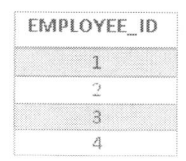

*Figure 11-3 Column of the **EMPLOYEES** table*

INTERACTING WITH MYSQL
MySQL is embedded within the XAMPP, so there is no need to perform any database setup externally to use MySQL. There are three interface to interact with MySQL that are as follow:

1. Using Command-Line on Windows **Command Prompt**
2. Using MySQL commands in **phpMyAdmin**
3. Using PHP programming Language

Using Command-Line on Windows Command Prompt
You can run MySQL commands on command-line interface. Click on the **START** menu and choose **Command Prompt**. Check the drive or directory where XAMPP is installed. By default XAMPP is installed in **C** drive. Enter the following command in the command prompt to run **mysql.exe** file:

```
C:\xampp\mysql\bin\mysql -u root
```

Here, **C** is the drive, **xampp\mysql\bin\mysql** is the path followed to run the **mysql.exe** file and **-u root** will log you into MySQL as shown in Figure 11-4. By default, the MySQL user is set as **root** which does not have password.

Figure 11-4 Command-line to run MySQL executable file

Note
*Before executing this command on command prompt, make sure that **Apache** and **MySQL** are in running state in XAMPP control panel.*

To check the working of MySQL, you can enter the following command in the **Command Prompt**:

SHOW DATABASES;

Here, this command will display the name of the databases that is on your server, as shown in Figure 11-5.

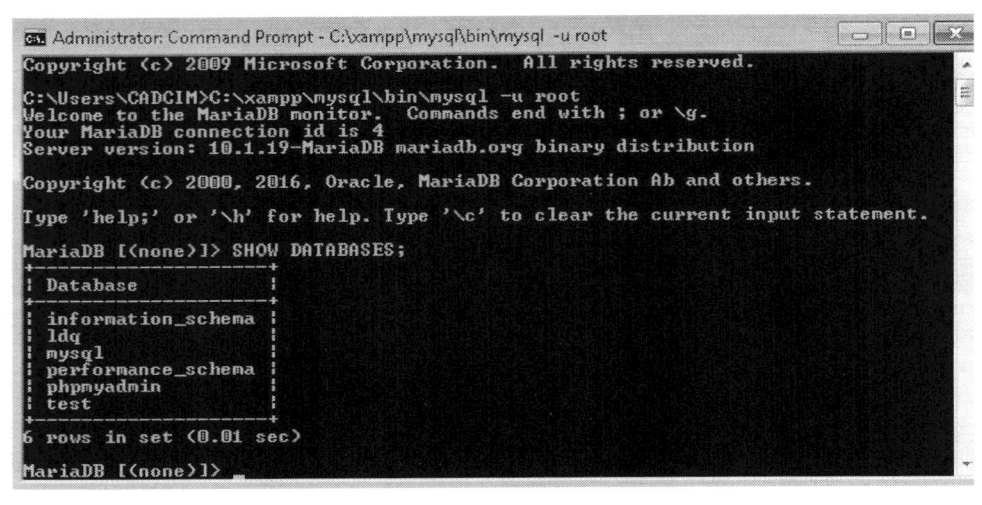

Figure 11-5 SHOW DATABASES command

Introduction to MySQL

> **Note**
> MySQL commands are case-insensitive. You will learn various MySQL commands later in this chapter.

Using Command-Line in phpMyAdmin

You can also run MySQL commands in **phpMyAdmin**. To open **phpMyAdmin**, first open the **XAMPP Control Panel** and start **Apache** by choosing the **Start** button if the application is not already running. Once **Apache** gets started, open your web browser and enter the URL - *http://localhost/phpmyadmin/*. This will open **phpMyAdmin** in your browser, as shown in Figure 11-6.

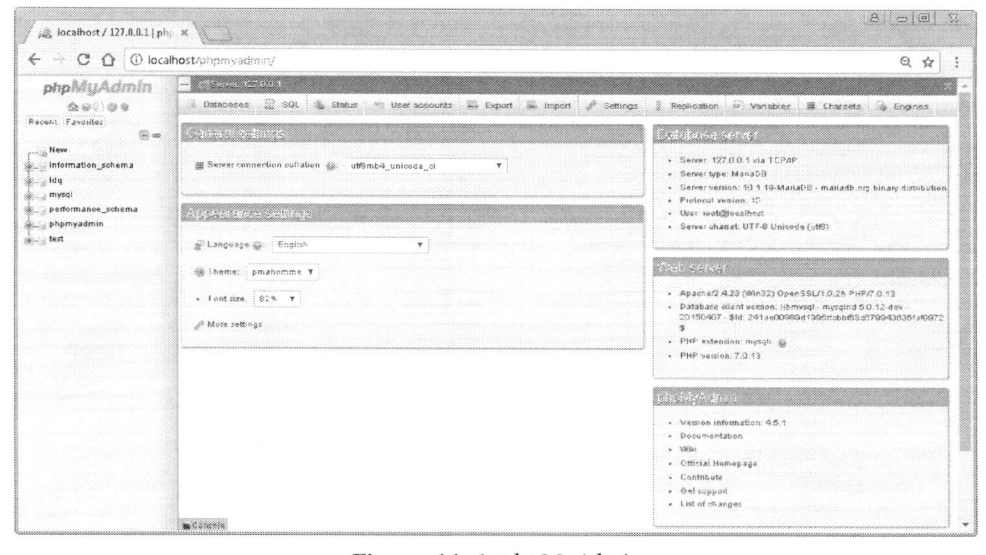

Figure 11-6 phpMyAdmin

To write the MySQL commands in **phpMyAdmin**, choose the **SQL** tab from the navigation bar. This will open the **SQL** tab area, as shown in Figure 11-7 where you can write the commands and to execute the commands, choose the **Go** button.

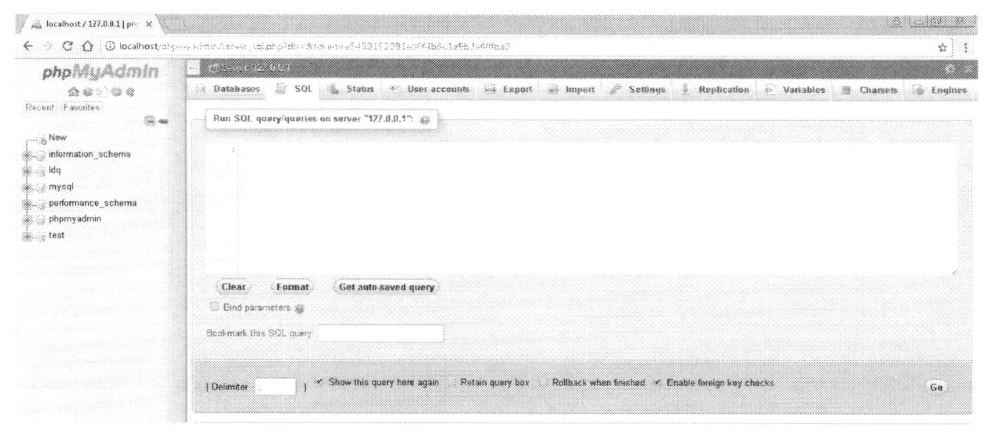

Figure 11-7 SQL tab area

To check the database in **phpMyAdmin**, you can enter the following command in the **SQL** tab area of **phpMyAdmin**:

```
SHOW DATABASES;
```

Here, this command will display the name of the databases that is on your server, as shown in Figure 11-8.

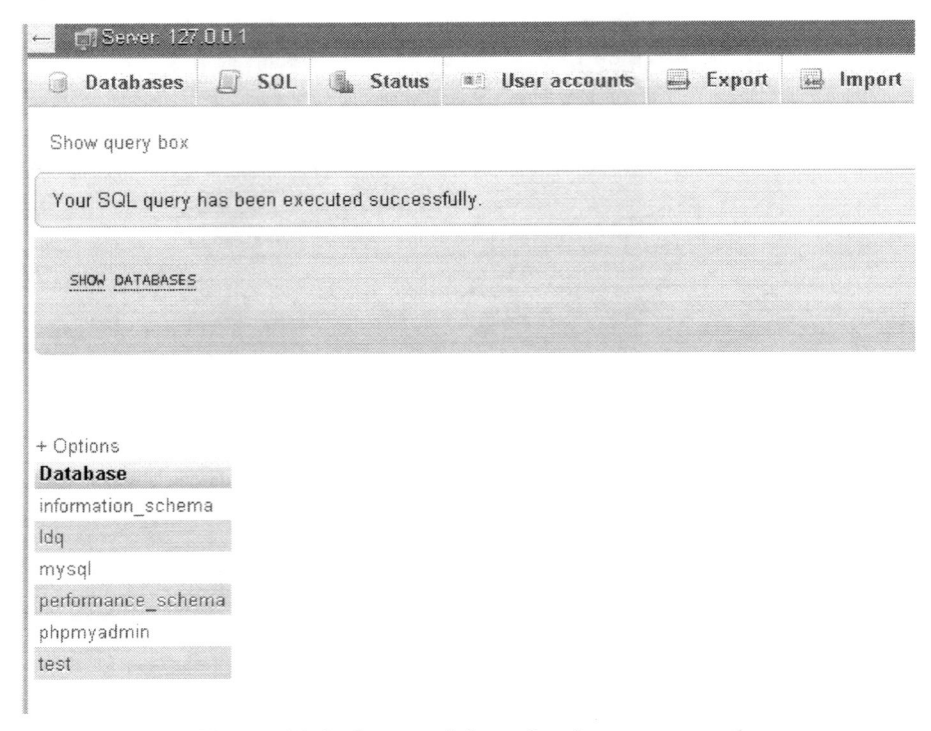

*Figure 11-8 Output of **show databases** command*

> **Note**
> *In this book, **phpMyAdmin** interface is used to interact with database in MySQL. As MySQL commands are same for all the three MySQL interfaces, you can also use PHP language or **Command Prompt** to access and work with the databases on your server. You will learn to access database by using PHP in the next chapter.*

CREATING DATABASE

You can create database on your server by using MySQL command according to the requirements of your website. The syntax of creating database using MySQL command is as follow:

```
CREATE DATABASE database_name;
```

In the given syntax, **CREATE** and **DATABASE** are the SQL keywords used to create the database on server. **CREATE** keyword is also used to create table, index, and so on. **database_name** represents the name of the new database that will be created.

Introduction to MySQL

For example:

To create a new database with the name **cadcim**, you can enter the following command in the **SQL** tab area of **phpMyAdmin**:

    CREATE DATABASE cadcim;

You will find the list of databases in the left panel of the **phpMyAdmin** including **cadcim** database. The output of this command is shown in Figure 11-9.

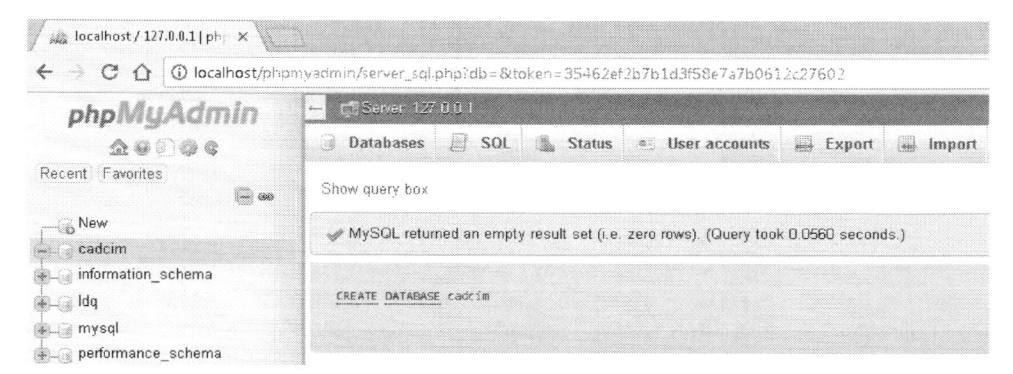

*Figure 11-9 Creating **cadcim** database*

You can create multiple databases by running same command but with different database name on your server. To work with a particular database, **USE** keyword is used. The syntax to work with a database using MySQL command is as follow:

    USE database_name;

In the given syntax, **USE** is a SQL keyword for using the specified database on server and **database_name** represents name of the database to be used.

For example:

To work with **cadcim** database that was already created in the last example, enter the following command in the **SQL** tab area of **phpMyAdmin**:

    USE cadcim;

The output of this command is shown in Figure 11-10.

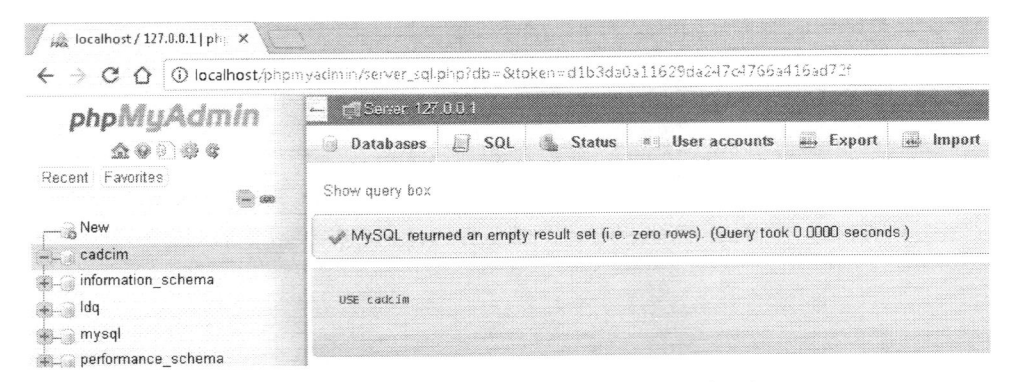

*Figure 11-10 The output of using **cadcim** database*

After the execution of **USE** command, you can start working with the specified database by using different SQL commands and queries.

Creating Users for Accessing Database

Now a days, security is a major concern for everyone. If a website or a web page is not secured, it can get hacked very easily. So, for the security purpose it is important to create users for all the databases.

To create user for a particular database or for all the databases, **GRANT** command is used. **GRANT** command sets the privileges for the users so that only the specified user can access the specified database with user-name and password. The syntax to grant privileges to user using MySQL command is as follow:

```
GRANT PRIVILEGES ON database_name.object TO 'username'@'hostname'
    IDENTIFIED BY 'password';
```

In the given syntax, **database_name** represents name of the particular database and **object** represents various database objects on which privileges will be granted to user. Here, **username** represents the name of the user to whom the privileges will be granted and **hostname** represents the host where the database is hosted and **password** represents the password that is assigned to the user to access the database. Rest all the words written in capital letters are keywords that will remain same.

In the **GRANT** command syntax, **database_name.object** parameter can be replaced. Table 11-1 lists all the possible parameters of **GRANT** command with their descriptions. You can replace **database_name.object** with any one of them.

*Table 11-1 **GRANT** parameters and their description*

Parameter	Description
.	* represent all, So this parameter represents all the database with all their objects.
database_name.*	It represents name of a particular database with all its objects.

Introduction to MySQL

For example:

To **GRANT** privileges to **cadcim** database, you can enter the following command:

```
GRANT ALL ON cadcim.* TO 'cad'@'localhost' IDENTIFIED BY 'cimPASS';
```

Note
*You can execute this command in **phpMyAdmin**, but you would not be able to see the result. To see the result, execute this command on command-prompt.*

To execute the given example, run the **mysql.exe** file in the Command Prompt as you have learned in the previous section. Then, execute the **GRANT** command given in the example as shown in Figure 11-11.

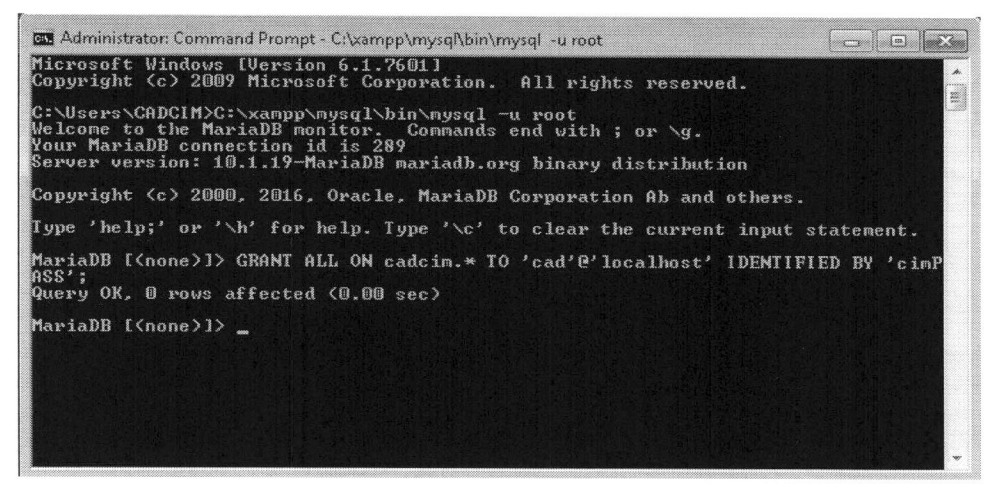

*Figure 11-11 Execution of **GRANT** command in Command Prompt*

Now, enter **quit** command to quit the MySQL and re-run the **mysql.exe** file by replacing **-u root** with **-u cad -p**. It will prompt you to enter password (In this example, it is **cimPASS**). Enter the password to work with **cadcim** database as shown in Figure 11-12.

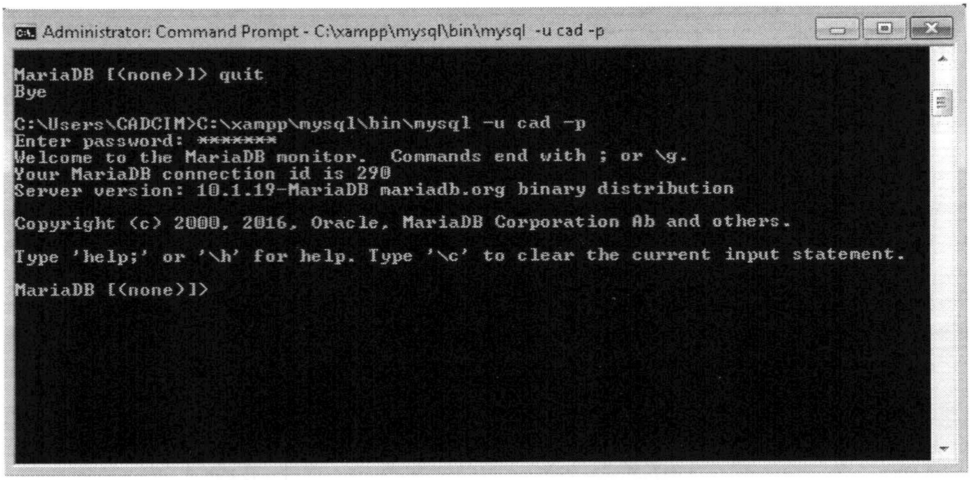

Figure 11-12 Result of GRANT command

Now, after logging into MySQL you can start making tables and run various SQL queries. But before creating tables in database, you must be aware of data types used in the table which is discussed next.

DATA TYPES IN MySQL

All the data that is stored or manipulated by MySQL database has a certain data type. Data type is the type of value a column or an argument can store. The data type of a column associates a fixed set of properties with the values stored in the column. These properties cause MySQL to treat the values of one data type differently from the values of another data type. When you create or alter a table, you need to specify the data type for each of its columns and arguments respectively.

MySQL database provides many data types. The data types of MySQL can be broadly classified into the categories, as listed in Table 11-2.

Table 11-2 Data types of MySQL

Category	Data Type
Character	**CHAR** and **VARCHAR**
Binary	**BINARY** and **VARBINARY**
BLOB	**TINYBLOB, BLOB, MEDIUMBLOB,** and **LONGBLOB**
TEXT	**TINYTEXT, TEXT, MEDIUMTEXT,** and **LONGTEXT**
Numeric	**BIT, TINYINT, SMALLINT, MEDIUMINT, INT/INTEGER, BIGINT, DECIMAL, FLOAT,** and **DOUBLE**
Date and Time	**DATETIME, DATE, TIMESTAMP, TIME,** and **YEAR**
ENUM	**ENUM**

Character Data Type

The MySQL database provides character data types to store character values. The character values include alphanumeric data which comprises letters, numbers, spaces, symbols, and punctuations. These character data types are discussed next.

CHAR

The **CHAR** data type is used to store the fixed length character data. The maximum length of data that it can store is 255 bytes or characters. The syntax for declaring column with the **CHAR** data type is as follows:

```
column_name CHAR(length)
```

In the given syntax, **column_name** is the name of the column that has the **CHAR** data type. And **length** is required parameter which represents any integer value ranging from 1 to 255. If you do not specify the value of **length**, MySQL will return an error.

Also if you enter a value exceeding the specified column length of **CHAR** data type, the MySQL database will return an error. If the inserted value is shorter than the specified column length, MySQL will insert blank spaces in that value to match the column length of **CHAR** data type.

VARCHAR

The **VARCHAR** data type is used to store a variable-length character string. The maximum length of the **VARCHAR** data type is 65535 bytes or characters. The syntax for declaring column with the **VARCHAR** data type is as follows:

```
column_name VARCHAR(length)
```

In the given syntax, **column_name** is the name of the column that has the **VARCHAR** data type and **length** is required parameter which represents an integer value ranging from 1 to 65535. If you do not specify the value of **length**, MySQL will return an error.

The MySQL database will also return an error, if you will try to enter value exceeding the specified column length of **VARCHAR** data type.

Binary Data Type

The MySQL database provides binary data types to store binary values which are always in HEX form. Binary data types are discussed next.

BINARY

BINARY data type is similar to **CHAR** but instead of character set, it contains binary string. The maximum length of data that it can store is 255 bytes. The syntax for declaring column with the **BINARY** data type is as follows:

```
column_name BINARY(length)
```

In the given syntax, **column_name** is the name of the column that has the **BINARY** data type and **length** is required parameter which represents any integer value ranging from 1 to 255. If you do not specify the value of **length**, MySQL will return an error.

VARBINARY

The **VARBINARY** data type is similar to **VARCHAR** but instead of character set, it contains binary string. The maximum length of data that it can store is 65535 bytes. The syntax for declaring column with the **VARBINARY** data type is as follows:

    column_name VARBINARY(length)

In the given syntax, **column_name** is the name of the column that has the **VARBINARY** data type and **length** is required parameter which represents any integer value ranging from 1 to 65535. If you do not specify the value of **length**, MySQL will return an error.

BLOB Data Type

The **BLOB** stands for Binary Large OBject which is to store binary data in excess size. You can store images such as GIF images or JPEG images in this data type. These **BLOB** data types are discussed next.

TINYBLOB

The **TINYBLOB** data type can store the maximum length of 255 bytes. The syntax for declaring column with the **TINYBLOB** data type is as follows:

    column_name TINYBLOB

In the given syntax, **column_name** is the name of the column that has the **TINYBLOB** data type. There is no default length set for **TINYBLOB** data type. If you do not specify the length, MySQL will not return any error.

BLOB

The **BLOB** data type can store the maximum length of 65536 bytes. The syntax for declaring column with the **BLOB** data type is as follows:

    column_name BLOB

In the given syntax, **column_name** is the name of the column that has the **BLOB** data type. There is no default length set for **BLOB** data type. If you do not specify the length, MySQL will not return any error.

MEDIUMBLOB

The **MEDIUMBLOB** data type can store the maximum length of 1.67e+7 bytes. The syntax for declaring column with the **MEDIUMBLOB** data type is as follows:

    column_name MEDIUMBLOB

In the given syntax, **column_name** is the name of the column having the **MEDIUMBLOB** data type. There is no default length set for **MEDIUMBLOB** data type. If you do not specify the length, MySQL will not return any error.

LONGBLOB

The **LONGBLOB** data type can store the maximum length of 4.29e+9 bytes. The syntax for declaring column with the **LONGBLOB** data type is as follows:

    column_name LONGBLOB

In the given syntax, **column_name** is the name of the column that has the **LONGBLOB** data type. There is no default length set for **LONGBLOB** data type. If you do not specify the length, MySQL will not return any error.

Text Data Type

The MySQL database provides text data types to store string type data with character set in excess size. There is no default length set for these data types. If you do not specify the length, MySQL will not return any error. These text data types are discussed next.

TINYTEXT

The **TINYTEXT** data type can store the maximum length of 255 bytes. The syntax for declaring column with the **TINYTEXT** data type is as follows:

    column_name TINYTEXT

In the given syntax, **column_name** is the name of the column that has the **TINYTEXT** data type.

TEXT

The **TEXT** data type can store the maximum length of 65536 bytes. The syntax for declaring column with the **TEXT** data type is as follows:

    column_name TEXT

In the given syntax, **column_name** is the name of the column that has the **TEXT** data type.

MEDIUMTEXT

The **MEDIUMTEXT** data type can store the maximum length of 1.67e+7 bytes. The syntax for declaring column with the **MEDIUMTEXT** data type is as follows:

    column_name MEDIUMTEXT

In the given syntax, **column_name** is the name of the column that has the **MEDIUMTEXT** data type.

LONGTEXT

The **LONGTEXT** data type can store the maximum length of 4.29e+9 bytes. The syntax for declaring column with the **LONGTEXT** data type is as follows:

```
column_name LONGTEXT
```

In the given syntax, **column_name** is the name of the column that has the **LONGTEXT** data type.

Numeric Data Type

The numeric data types stores numeric data that can be either signed or unsigned where signed can be any number from negative to positive, including zero and unsigned can be any number from zero to positive. By default all the numeric data types are signed so there is no need to specify it. To specify unsigned value the UNSIGNED keyword is used.

The maximum length of data that numeric data type except BIT can store is 255 bytes. There are various types of numeric data type that are discussed next.

BIT

The **BIT** data type is used to store bit type data. The maximum length of data that it can store is 64 bit. The syntax for declaring column with the **BIT** data type is as follows:

```
column_name BIT(length)
```

In the given syntax, **column_name** is the name of the column that has the **BIT** data type and **length** is required parameter which represents any integer value ranging from 1 to 64. If you do not specify the value of **length**, MySQL will return an error.

TINYINT

In the **TINYINT** data type, you can insert any number from -128 to 127 if it is signed or insert any number from 0 to 255 if it is unsigned. The maximum length of data that it can store is 255 bytes. If the length is not specified, by default it sets to 4. The syntax for declaring column with the **TINYINT** data type is as follows:

```
column_name TINYINT(length)UNSIGNED
```

In the given syntax, **column_name** is the name of the column that has the **TINYINT** data type and **length** is optional parameter which represents any number from 1 to 255. Here, **UNSIGNED** is also optional which is used to set the unsigned number.

SMALLINT

In the **SMALLINT** data type, you can insert any number from -32768 to 32767 if it is signed or insert any number from 0 to 65535 if it is unsigned. If the length is not specified, by default it sets to 6. The syntax for declaring column with the **SMALLINT** data type is as follows:

```
column_name SMALLINT(length)UNSIGNED
```

In the given syntax, **column_name** is the name of the column that has the **SMALLINT** data type and **length** is optional parameter which represents any number from 1 to 255. Here, **UNSIGNED** is also optional which is used to set the unsigned number.

Introduction to MySQL

MEDIUMINT

In the **MEDIUMINT** data type, you can insert any number from -8388608 to 8388607 if it is signed or insert any number from 0 to 16777215 if it is unsigned. If the length is not specified, by default it sets to 9. The syntax for declaring column with the **MEDIUMINT** data type is as follows:

```
column_name MEDIUMINT(length)UNSIGNED
```

In the given syntax, **column_name** is the name of the column that has the **MEDIUMINT** data type and **length** is optional parameter which represents any number from 1 to 255. Here, **UNSIGNED** is also optional which is used to set the unsigned number.

INT/INTEGER

In the **INT** or **INTEGER** data type, you can insert any number from -2147483648 to 2147483647 if it is signed or insert any number from 0 to 4294967295 if it is unsigned. If the length is not specified, by default it sets to 11. The syntax for declaring column with the **INT/INTEGER** data type is as follows:

```
column_name INT(length)UNSIGNED
            or
column_name INTEGER(length)UNSIGNED
```

In the given syntax, **column_name** is the name of the column that has the **INT** data type and **length** is optional parameter which represents any number from 1 to 255. Here, **UNSIGNED** is also optional which is used to set the unsigned number. You can also replace **INT** with **INTEGER** as given in the other syntax of **INT** data type.

BIGINT

In the **BIGINT** data type, you can insert any number from -9223372036854775808 to 9223372036854775807 if it is signed or insert any number from 0 to 18446744073709551615 if it is unsigned. If the length is not specified, by default it sets to 20. The syntax for declaring column with the **BIGINT** data type is as follows:

```
column_name BIGINT(length)UNSIGNED
```

In the given syntax, **column_name** is the name of the column that has the **BIGINT** data type and **length** is optional parameter which represents any number from 1 to 255. Here, **UNSIGNED** is also optional which is used to set the unsigned number.

Table 11-3 lists all the numeric data type having signed and unsigned range with their default value.

Table 11-3 Numeric data type and their range with default value

Numeric data type	Signed Range	Unsigned Range	Default value
TINYINT	-128 to 127	0 to 255	4
SMALLINT	-32768 to 32767	0 to 65535	6
MEDIUMINT	-8388608 to 8388607	0 to 16777215	9
INT/INTEGER	-2147483648 to 2147483647	0 to 4294967295	11
BIGINT	-9223372036854775808 to 9223372036854775807	0 to 18446744073709551615	20

DECIMAL

The **DECIMAL** data type is used to store fixed-point numeric type data. To define the DECIMAL data type, you have to specify the values of both precision and scale. The syntax for declaring column with the **DECIMAL** data type is as follows:

```
column_name DECIMAL(P,S)
```

In the given syntax, **column_name** is the name of the column that has the **DECIMAL** data type. **P** represents the precision or the total number of digits including decimal place with precision up to 65 digits and **S** represents the scale or the number of digits on the right of the decimal point. The maximum digits of **S** can be 30. If you do not specify the value of **P** by default it will be 10 and for **S** it will be 0.

The precision value denotes all digits on the left of the decimal point, whereas the scale value denotes all digits to right of the decimal point.

FLOAT

The **FLOAT** data type is used to store floating-point numeric type data. It can have a decimal point anywhere between the first and the last digits, or it can be a number without any decimal point as there is no restriction for the decimal point. The syntax for declaring column with the **FLOAT** data type is as follows:

```
column_name FLOAT(P,S)
```

In the given syntax, **column_name** is the name of the column that has the **FLOAT** data type. **P** represents the precision or the total number of digits including decimal place with precision up to 24 places and **S** represents the scale or the number of digits on the right of the decimal point. If you do not specify the value of **P** and **S**, MySQL will not return any error. The precision value denotes all digits on the left of the decimal point, whereas the scale value denotes all digits on right of the decimal point.

DOUBLE

The **DOUBLE** data type is also used to store floating-point numeric type data. It can have a decimal point anywhere between the first and the last digits. The syntax for declaring column with the **DOUBLE** data type is as follows:

Introduction to MySQL

```
column_name DOUBLE(P,S)
```

In the given syntax, **column_name** is the name of the column that has the **DOUBLE** data type. **P** represents the precision or the total number of digits including decimal place with precision up to 53 places and **S** represents the scale or the number of digits on the right of the decimal point. If you do not specify the value of **P** and **S**, MySQL will not return any error. But, if you will specify the **P** then it is mandatory to specify **S**, otherwise it will return an error. The precision value denotes all digits on the left of the decimal point, whereas the scale value denotes all digits to right of the decimal point.

Date and Time Data Type

The date and time data types store date and time values. The date and time data types are discussed next.

DATE

The **DATE** data type is used to store date. MySQL stores the following information for each date value: year, month, date. The default date format is YYYY-MM-DD. The valid date range is from 1000-01-01 to 9999-12-31. The syntax for declaring a column with the **DATE** data type is as follows:

```
Column_Name DATE
```

In the given syntax, **Column_Name** specifies the name of the column that has the **DATE** data type.

DATETIME

The **DATETIME** data type is used to store date and time. MySQL stores the following information for each date value: year, month, date, hour, minute, and second. The default date and time format is YYYY-MM-DD HH:MM:SS using the 24-hours clock. The valid date and time range is from 1000-01-01 00:00:00 to 9999-12-31 23:59:59. The syntax for declaring a column with the **DATETIME** data type is as follows:

```
Column_Name DATETIME(Fractional_Seconds_Precision)
```

In the given syntax, **Column_Name** specifies the name of the column that has the **DATETIME** data type. If you specify a date value without the time component, the default time will be midnight (00:00:00 for 24-hour clock time). **Fractional_Seconds_Precision** is an optional value that indicates the number of digits that MySQL will store in the fractional part of the seconds, date, and time field. Its value can be vary from 0 to 6. If you do not specify this value, MySQL will take its default value, which is 0.

TIMESTAMP

The **TIMESTAMP** data type is exactly same as **DATETIME** data type with only difference that the valid date and time range of **TIMESTAMP** is very less as compare to **DATETIME** data type that is from 1970-01-01 00:00:01.000000 UTC to 2038-01-19 03:14:07.999999 UTC. The syntax for declaring a column with the **TIMESTAMP** data type is as follows:

```
Column_Name TIMESTAMP(Fractional_Seconds_Precision)
```

In the given syntax, **Column_Name** specifies the name of the column that has the **TIMESTAMP** data type. If you specify a date value without the time component, the default time will be midnight (00:00:00 for 24-hour clock time). **Fractional_Seconds_Precision** is an optional value. If you do not specify this value, MySQL will take its default value, which is 0.

> **Note**
> *TIMESTAMP is very useful in MySQL, because if you do not specify the value of TIMESTAMP while adding a row then MySQL automatically inserts the current time in that row.*

TIME
The **TIME** data type is used to store time. MySQL stores the following information for each date value: hour, minute, and second. The default time format is HH:MM:SS using the 24-hours clock. The syntax for declaring a column with the **TIME** data type is as follows:

```
Column_Name TIME(Fractional_Seconds_Precision)
```

In the given syntax, **Column_Name** specifies the name of the column that has the **TIME** data type. **Fractional_Seconds_Precision** is an optional value. If you do not specify this value, MySQL will take its default value, which is 0.

YEAR
The **YEAR** data type is used to store year. The default year format is YYYY. The valid year range is from 1901 to 2155. The syntax for declaring a column with the **YEAR** data type is as follows:

```
Column_Name YEAR
```

In the given syntax, **Column_Name** specifies the name of the column that has the **YEAR** data type.

ENUM Data Type
An **ENUM** data type is used to create your own list of options or elements among which only one (or none) can be selected and stored in MySQL. The syntax for declaring a column with the **ENUM** data type is as follows:

```
Column_Name ENUM('element1','element2', ....... , 'elementN')
```

In the given syntax, **Column_Name** specifies the name of the column that has the **ENUM** data type where **element1**, **element2**, and so on represents list of elements from which one can be selected. For example, If you define your **ENUM** as **ENUM ('CAR', 'BUS', 'TRAIN')** then only CAR or BUS or TRAIN values (or none) could ever populate your specified column.

CONSTRAINTS
Constraints are a set of predefined rules, which ensure that the valid data is stored in a table. These predefined rules are applied on one or more columns in a table. When the table undergoes

Introduction to MySQL

any data action (creation, modification, or deletion), these rules are validated and an exception is raised on any violation. Constraints are applied at the time of creation of a table or you can add them later using the **ALTER** statement. Constraints can be disabled when not needed. The constraints increase the accuracy and reliability of the data in a table. Following are the important constraint types: **PRIMARY KEY**, **UNIQUE**, and **FOREIGN KEY**.

The basic structure of a constraint used in MySQL is as follows:

The keyword **CONSTRAINT** is followed by a unique constraint name and then by a constraint definition. The constraint name is used to manipulate the constraint once a table has been created. The syntax for declaring a constraint is as follows:

```
CONSTRAINT [Constraint_Name] Constraint_Type
```

In the given syntax, **Constraint_Type** may be any of the above mentioned constraint type.

> **Note**
> *If you omit the name of the constraint, MySQL will assign an arbitrary name to it. This constraint name is used to drop the constraint by using the **ALTER** statement, which will be discussed later in this chapter.*

The constraints used in MySQL are discussed below.

PRIMARY KEY Constraint

The **PRIMARY KEY** constraints ensure that the Null values are not entered in a column and also the value entered is unique. Thus, this constraint avoid the duplication of records. A primary key constraint can be defined in the **CREATE TABLE** and **ALTER TABLE** commands.

The syntax for declaring a **PRIMARY KEY** constraint with the column declaration is as follows:

```
column_name column_Datatype(length) PRIMARY KEY
```

In the given syntax, **PRIMARY KEY** is the keyword and **Column_Name** specifies the name of the column. **column_Datatype** represents the data type having **length** depending on the data type used.

The syntax for declaring a **PRIMARY KEY** constraint at the end of the column declaration is as follows:

```
PRIMARY KEY (Column_Name)
```

In the given syntax, **PRIMARY KEY** is keyword and **Column_Name** represents the name of the column for which you want to declare the constraint.

You can also create a **PRIMARY KEY** constraint for more than one column. The syntax for declaring a **PRIMARY KEY** constraint at the end of the column declaration for more than one column is as follows:

```
PRIMARY KEY(Column_Name1,Column_Name2, Column_Name3, ...)
```

In the given syntax, **PRIMARY KEY** is keyword. **Column_Name1**, **Column_Name2**, **Column_Name3**, and so on represents the names of the columns for which you want to declare the **PRIMARY KEY** constraint.

The syntax for declaring a **PRIMARY KEY** constraint with Constraint name at the end of the column declaration is as follows:

```
CONSTRAINT Constraint_Name PRIMARY KEY (Column_Name)
```

In the given syntax, **CONSTRAINT** and **PRIMARY KEY** are keywords. **Constraint_Name** represents the name of the constraint and **Column_Name** represents the name of the column for which you want to declare the constraint.

UNIQUE Constraint

The **UNIQUE** constraint is used to prevent the duplication of data values within the rows of a specified column or a set of columns in a table. It allows a null value so, multiple null values in **UNIQUE** constraint are accepted and it does not returns any error. You can even pass multiple columns in **UNIQUE** constraint. But the combination of all the values in the **UNIQUE** constraint should be unique otherwise it returns error.

The syntax for declaring a **UNIQUE** constraint with Constraint name at the end of the column declaration is as follows:

```
CONSTRAINT Constraint_Name UNIQUE (Column_Name)
```

In the given syntax, **CONSTRAINT** and **UNIQUE** are keywords. **Constraint_Name** represents the name of the constraint and **Column_Name** represents the name of the column for which you want to declare the constraint.

FOREIGN KEY Constraint

The **FOREIGN KEY** constraint is the property that guarantees the dependency of data values of one column with column of another table. A **FOREIGN KEY** constraint, also known as referential integrity constraint, is declared for a column to ensure that the value in one column is found in the column of another table with the **PRIMARY KEY** constraint. The table containing the **FOREIGN KEY** constraint is referred to as the child table, whereas the table containing the referenced (**PRIMARY KEY**) is referred to as the parent table. The **FOREIGN KEY** reference will be created only when a table with the **PRIMARY KEY** column already exists. The **FOREIGN KEY** constraint can be declared in two ways: within the column declaration and at the end of the column declaration.

The syntax for declaring a **FOREIGN KEY** constraint at the end of the column declaration is as follows:

```
FOREIGN KEY (foreign_key_column_name)REFERENCES
Primary_Key_Table_Name(Primary_Key_Column_Name)
```

Introduction to MySQL

```
ON DELETE action
ON UPDATE action
```

In the given syntax, **FOREIGN KEY, REFERENCE, ON DELETE,** and **ON UPDATE** are keywords where **ON DELETE** and **ON UPDATE** operations are optional. These operations have different types of **action** such as **RESTRICT, CASCADE, SET NULL, NO ACTION,** or **SET DEFAULT.** You can choose any of these actions according to the requirement. **foreign_key_column_name** represents the name of column for which you want to declare the foreign key constraint. **Primary_Key_Table_Name** represents the name of the table that contains the referenced column. The referenced column **Primary_Key_Column_Name** represents the primary key of the table **Primary_Key_Table_Name**.

The syntax for using the **FOREIGN KEY** constraint with Constraint name at the end of the column declaration is as follows:

```
CONSTRAINT Constraint_Name FOREIGN KEY (foreign_key_column_name)
    REFERENCE Primary_Key_Table_Name(Primary_Key_Column_Name)
ON DELETE action
ON UPDATE action
```

In the given syntax, **CONSTRAINT, FOREIGN KEY, REFERENCE, ON DELETE,** and **ON UPDATE** are keywords. **Constraint_Name** represents the name of the constraint. **foreign_key_column_name** represents the name of column for which you want to declare the foreign key constraint. **Primary_Key_Table_Name** represents the name of the table that contains the referenced column. The referenced column **Primary_Key_Column_Name** represents the primary key of the table **Primary_Key_Table_Name**.

CREATING A TABLE

A database holds data in the tabular form, which is in rows and columns. A table such as **EMPLOYEES** can contain various columns such as **Employee_Id, First_Name, Last_Name,** and so on. Each column has a length and data types, such as **VARCHAR, DATE, INT,** and so on. The width can be pre-determined by the data type, as in case of the data type **VARCHAR**. But, if a column has a **FLOAT, DOUBLE,** or **DECIMAL** data type, you can define precision and scale instead of length.

A row is a set of columns corresponding to a single record. A table can contain number of such records. For each column, you can specify rules, called constraints. For example, the NOT NULL constraint ensures that each column of a row contains some data values. The constraints maintain the integrity of data in a database.

While creating a table, the naming convention for tables and columns should be properly followed. The naming conventions used while creating tables and columns are as follows:

1. Names cannot contain space.

2. The reserve words used in MySQL cannot be used as names of columns or tables.

3. Names can contain characters a to z, 0 to 9, _, $, and #. Using other symbols will not throw an error but will create problem while executing queries. So, avoid other symbols.

4. Names are not case-sensitive.

A table column can also have different characteristics that are as follows:

1. **NOT NULL**: The **NOT NULL** applied on a column ensures that the column does not accept any Null value. You cannot leave a value blank in this column.

2. **AUTO_INCREMENT**: The **AUTO_INCREMENT** applied to a column automatically generates a unique number for that column in each row.

The syntax for creating a table in MySQL is as follows:

```
CREATE TABLE Table_Name
(
Field_Name1 Field_Datatype (length),
Field_Name2 Field_Datatype (length),
Field_Name3 Field_Datatype (length),
Field_Name4 Field_Datatype (length),
.......
.......
.......
);
```

In the given syntax, **CREATE** and **TABLE** are keywords and **Table_Name** represents the name of the table to be created. **Field_Name1**, **Field_Name2**, **Field_Name3**, **Field_Name4**, and so on represents the names of columns. **Field_Datatype** represents the data type of the column and **length** represents the length of the column.

For example:

To create a table **student** containing student data such as roll number, name, and date of birth. Enter and execute the following command given below in **SQL** tab area of **phpMyAdmin**:

```
CREATE TABLE student
( roll_number INT AUTO_INCREMENT PRIMARY KEY,
  name VARCHAR(255) NOT NULL,
  date_of_birth DATE );
```

You will find the name of the created table under the database name in the left panel of the **phpMyAdmin**. The output of this command is shown in Figure 11-13.

Introduction to MySQL

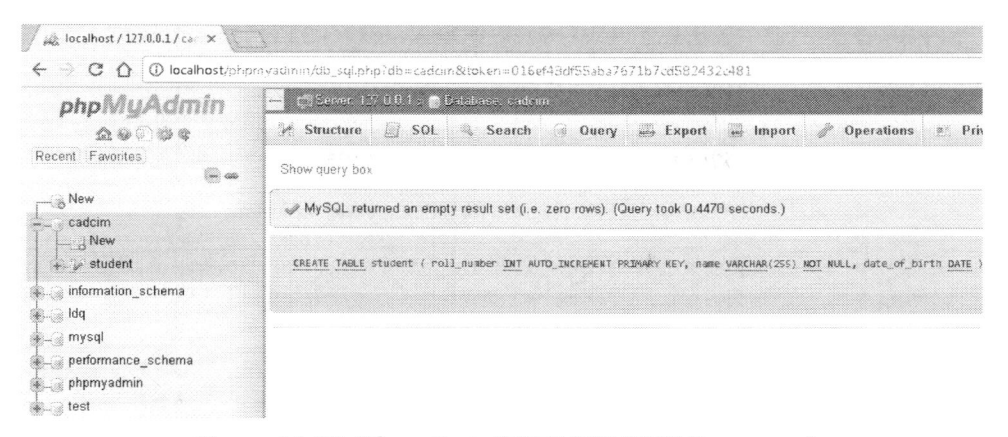

*Figure 11-13 The output of **CREATE TABLE** command*

Describing a Table

You can describe the table to see the complete details of a table such as all the columns, their data types, and other characteristics. The syntax for describing a table is as follows:

```
DESCRIBE Table_name;
```

In the given syntax, **DESCRIBE** is a keyword used to describe the details of a table where **Table_name** represents the name of the table.

For example:

To check the details of **student** table (created in previous example), enter and execute the following command given below in **SQL** tab area of **phpMyAdmin**:

```
DESCRIBE student;
```

You will find the descriptions of all the fields in the **student** table as the output of the given command, as shown in Figure 11-14.

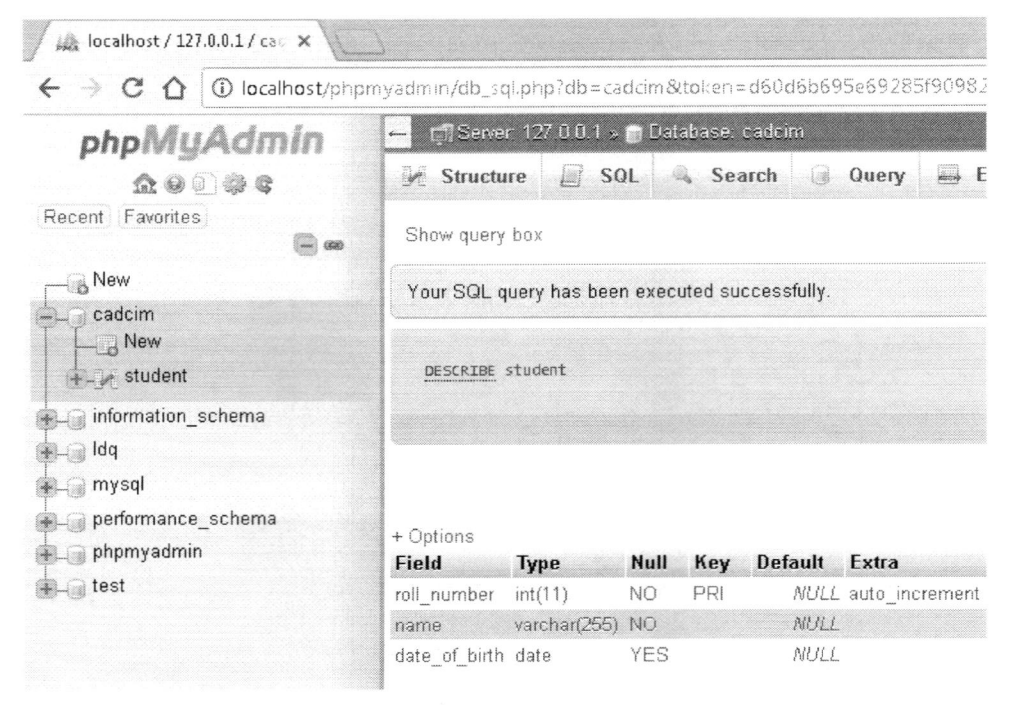

*Figure 11-14 The output of **DESCRIBE** table command*

ALTER TABLE

You can modify and make changes in the structure of existing table by using **ALTER TABLE** command. You can modify the existing table by adding or removing a column in the existing table. You can even rename the table or a column of the existing table by using **ALTER TABLE** command. This command also helps in changing the data type or length of the existing column. The various **ALTER TABLE** commands are discussed next.

Renaming a Table

You can also rename the existing table any time, if required. In such case, instead of old name the new name will be used in all the commands. The syntax to rename a table by using the **ALTER TABLE** command with the **RENAME** option is as follows:

```
ALTER TABLE table_name RENAME new_table_name
```

In the given syntax, **ALTER TABLE** and **RENAME** are the keywords. **table_name** represents the old table name of the existing table to be renamed and **new_table_name** represents the new name for the **old table name**.

Introduction to MySQL

For example:

To rename the existing **student** table, enter and execute the following command given below in the **SQL** tab area of **phpMyAdmin**:

```
ALTER TABLE student RENAME student_detail;
```

The output of this command is shown in Figure 11-15. You will find the new name **student_detail** of the existing table under the database name in the left panel of the **phpMyAdmin**.

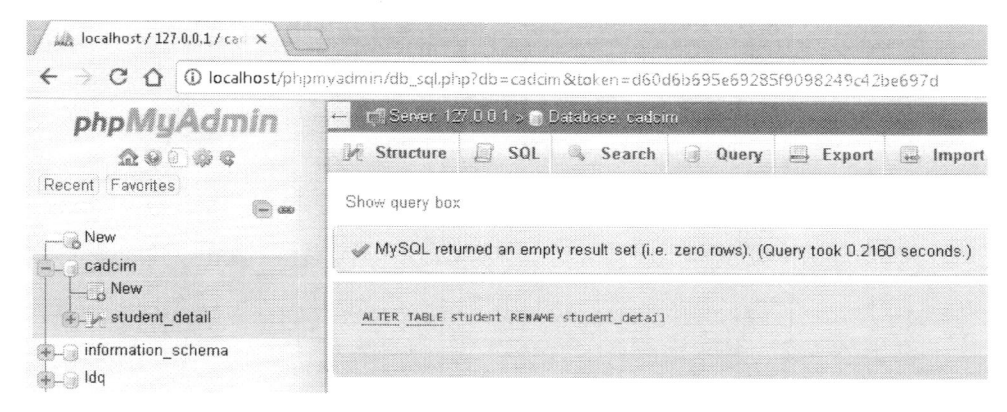

*Figure 11-15 The output of **RENAME** command*

Renaming a Column

You can rename the existing column of existing table by **ALTER TABLE** command with the **CHANGE** option. The syntax to rename a column by using the **ALTER TABLE** command with the **CHANGE** option is as follows:

```
ALTER TABLE table_name CHANGE old_col_name new_col_name DT(length);
```

In the given syntax, **ALTER TABLE** and **CHANGE** are the keywords. **table_name** represents the name of the existing table in which you want to rename a column. **old_col_name** represents the existing name of the column that you want to rename. **new_col_name** represents the new name of the **old_col_name** column and **DT** represents the data type of **old_col_name** column that may or may not have **length** depending on the data type.

For example:

To rename the **roll_number** column of the existing **student_detail** table (renamed the **student** table in last example), enter and execute the following command given below in the **SQL** tab area of **phpMyAdmin**:

```
ALTER TABLE student_detail CHANGE roll_number id int;
```

To see the changes in the table execute the following command in **SQL** tab area of **phpMyAdmin**:

```
DESCRIBE student_detail;
```

You will find that the **roll_number** column name is changed to **id** in the output of the given command, as shown in Figure 11-16.

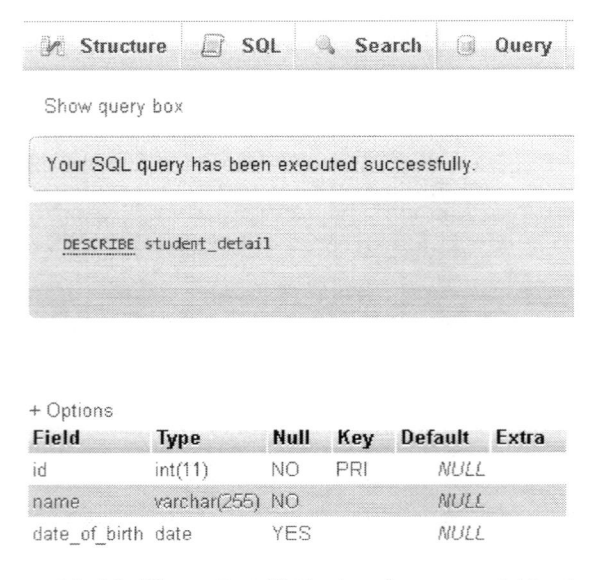

*Figure 11-16 The output displaying the renamed **id** column*

Modifying the Data Type

You can modify or change the data type of any existing column in a table by using the **ALTER TABLE** command with the **MODIFY** option. The syntax to modify the data type of a column in the table by using the **ALTER TABLE** command with the **MODIFY** option is as follows:

```
ALTER TABLE table_name MODIFY col_name New_Dt(length);
```

In the given syntax, **ALTER TABLE** and **MODIFY** are the keywords. **table_name** represents the table in which you want to modify the column data type. **col_name** represents the name of the existing column in **table_name** table that you want to modify. **New_Dt** represents the new data type of the **col_name** column that may or may not have **length** depending on the data type.

For example:

To modify the **VARCHAR(255)** data type to **VARCHAR(300)** of the **name** column in the existing **student_detail** table, enter and execute the following command given below in the **SQL** tab area of **phpMyAdmin**:

```
ALTER TABLE student_detail MODIFY name VARCHAR(300);
```

To see the changes in the table execute the following command in the **SQL** tab area of **phpMyAdmin**:

```
DESCRIBE student_detail;
```

Introduction to MySQL

You will find that the data type of **name** column is changed to **varchar(300)** in the output of the given command, as shown in Figure 11-17.

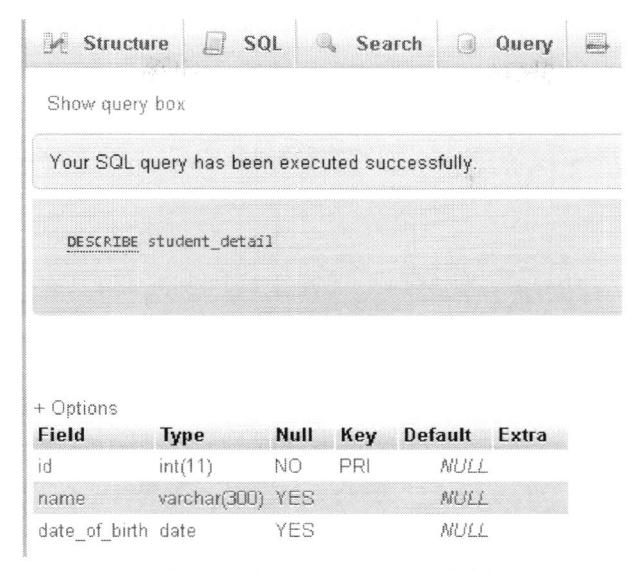

Figure 11-17 *The output of modified data type*

Adding a Column

You can add new columns to the existing table by using the **ALTER TABLE** command with the **ADD** option. The syntax to add a new column in the existing table is as follows:

    ALTER TABLE Table_Name ADD Column_Name Data_Type Constraints;

In the given syntax, **ALTER TABLE** and **ADD** are the keywords. **Table_Name** represents the name of an existing table to which you want to add the new column. **Column_Name** represents the name of the new column. **Data_Type** represents the data type of the new column **Column_Name** and **Constraints** represents any constraint that you want to set for the new column which is optional.

For example:

To add a new column **contact** to the existing **student_detail** table, enter and execute the following command given below in the **SQL** tab area of **phpMyAdmin**:

    ALTER TABLE student_detail ADD contact INT;

To see the changes in the table execute the following command in the **SQL** tab area of **phpMyAdmin**:

    DESCRIBE student_detail;

You will find a new **contact** column having **INT** data type in the output of the given command, as shown in Figure 11-18.

Figure 11-18 *The output displaying new* **contact** *column*

Deleting a Column

You can delete an existing column from the database table by using the **ALTER TABLE** command with the **DROP** option. The syntax for delete an existing column from table is as follows:

    ALTER TABLE Table_Name DROP Column_Name;

In the given syntax, **ALTER TABLE** and **DROP** are the keywords. **Table_Name** represents the name of the existing table from which you want to delete or remove a column and **Column_Name** specifies the name of the column that you want to delete or remove from the **Table_Name** table.

For example:

To delete the **contact** column from the **student_detail** table, enter and execute the following command given below in the **SQL** tab area of **phpMyAdmin**:

    ALTER TABLE student_detail DROP contact;

To see the changes in the table execute the following command in the **SQL** tab area of **phpMyAdmin**:

    DESCRIBE student_detail;

You will find that the **contact** column is deleted from the **student_detail** table in the output of the given command, as shown in Figure 11-19.

Introduction to MySQL

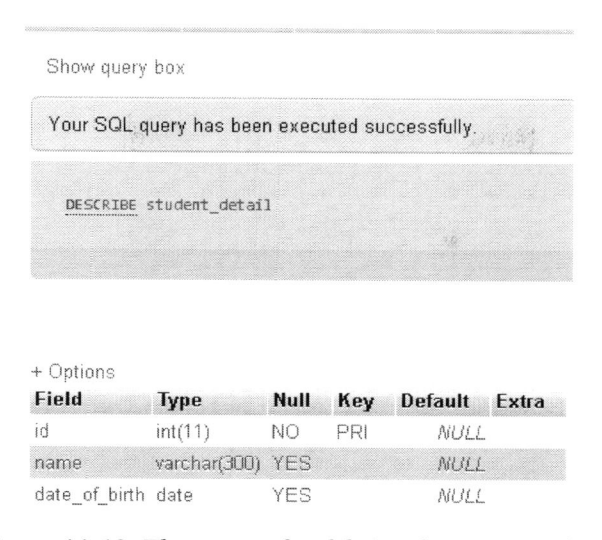

*Figure 11-19 The output after deleting the **contact** column*

Deleting a Constraint

You can also remove an existing constraint from a database table by using the **ALTER TABLE** command with the **DROP** option. The syntax for deleting an existing constraint from the table is as follows:

```
ALTER TABLE Table_Name DROP CONSTRAINT;
```

In the given syntax, **ALTER TABLE** and **DROP** are the keywords. **Table_Name** represents the name of an existing table from which you want to remove the constraint and **CONSTRAINT** represents the constraint that you want to remove.

For example:

To delete the **PRIMARY KEY** constraint from the **student_detail** table, enter and execute the following command given below in the **SQL** tab area of **phpMyAdmin**:

```
ALTER TABLE student_detail DROP PRIMARY KEY;
```

To see the changes in the table execute the following command in the **SQL** tab area of **phpMyAdmin**:

```
DESCRIBE student_detail;
```

You will find that the **KEY** column is blank which means **PRIMARY KEY** constraint is removed from the **id** column of the **student_detail** table in the output of the given command, as shown in Figure 11-20.

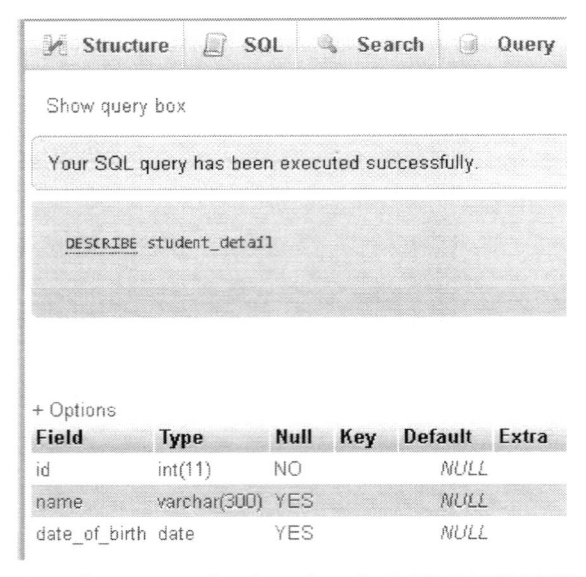

*Figure 11-20 The output after dropping the **PRIMARY KEY** constraint*

DELETING A TABLE

You can use the **DROP TABLE** command to delete or remove the database tables. It deletes the table completely. The syntax for using the **DROP TABLE** command is as follows:

```
DROP TABLE Table_Name;
```

In the given syntax, **DROP** and **TABLE** are keywords and **Table_Name** represents the name of the table to be deleted or removed from the database.

For example:

To delete the **student_detail** table from the **cadcim** database, enter and execute the following command given below in **SQL** tab area of **phpMyAdmin**:

```
DROP TABLE student_detail;
```

To check the tables in the database in **phpMyAdmin**, enter the following command in the **SQl** tab area of **phpMyAdmin**:

```
SHOW TABLES;
```

The given command displays the list of tables in the database. As **student_detail** table of the **cadcim** database is deleted, you will not find any list of tables in the output, as shown in Figure 11-21. You can also notice that there is no sub division of **cadcim** database that displays list of tables in the left panel of the **phpMyAdmin**.

Introduction to MySQL

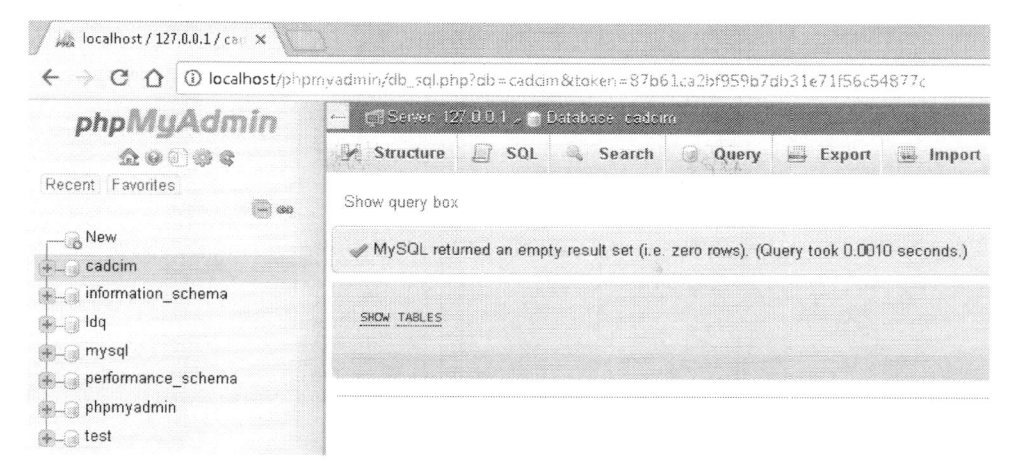

*Figure 11-21 The output of **SHOW TABLES** command after deleting a table*

Note
1. If any column of the table **Table_Name** has a reference in another table, the **DROP TABLE** command cannot delete or remove the table **Table_Name** from the database.

2. The best method to drop a table that has a reference in another table, is to delete or remove all tables that have foreign key references with other tables.

INSERTING DATA IN A TABLE

In this section, you will learn how to insert values into an existing table by using the **INSERT** command. You can insert a single row or multiple rows into a table by using the **INSERT** command.

The syntax for inserting a single row using the **INSERT** command is as follows:

```
INSERT INTO table_name
(column-1, column-2, ... column-n)VALUES
(value-1, value-2, ... value-n);
```

In the given syntax, **INSERT INTO** and **VALUES** are the keywords. **table_name** represents the name of the table in which you will insert a new row. **column-1**, **column-2**, and so on represents the names of columns of the **table_name** table, and **value-1**, **value-2**, and so on are the corresponding values to be inserted in specified columns. If the number of column values differs from the number of columns specified in the table, MySQL will throw an error.

For example:

Create a table **author** with 5 fields: **a_name**, **book_title**, **book_category**, **year**, and **ISBN_num** to insert a single row using **INSERT** statement.

To create the **author** table, enter and execute the following command given below in **SQL** tab area of **phpMyAdmin**:

```
CREATE TABLE author
( a_name VARCHAR(200),
book_title VARCHAR(300),
book_category VARCHAR(50),
year INT,
ISBN_num CHAR(13)PRIMARY KEY );
```

Note
*You can check the list of tables in the database by choosing **cadcim** database in the left panel of **phpMyAdmin**.*

To insert the data in **author** table, enter the following command in the **SQL** tab area of **phpMyAdmin**:

```
INSERT INTO author
(a_name, book_title, book_category, year, ISBN_num)VALUES
('William Shakespeare','Hamlet','Play', 1609, '9899308355971');
```

To view the table data, enter the following command in the **SQL** tab area of **phpMyAdmin**:

```
SELECT * FROM author;
```

The given command will display the **author** table data, as shown in Figure 11-22.

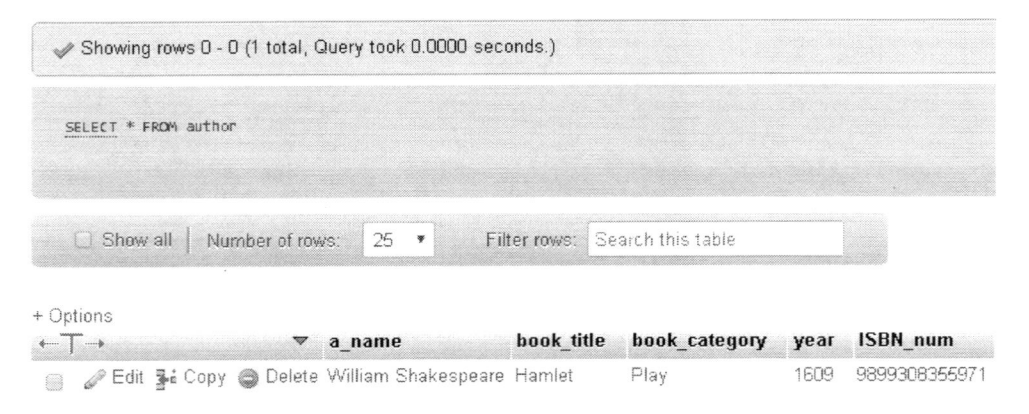

*Figure 11-22 The output displaying single row inserted with **INSERT** command*

Note
*You will learn about **SELECT** command in next section of this chapter.*

Alternatively, you can insert the above row by using the statement given below:

```
INSERT INTO author VALUES
('William Shakespeare','Hamlet','Play', 1609, '9899308355971');
```

Introduction to MySQL

The given MySQL statement will also insert the same row as inserted by the previous statement. The only difference between both the queries is that in the second statement, you do not need to specify the names of the columns if you know the sequence and number of columns in the table. If the values specified in the given query do not match with the number of columns in the **author** table, MySQL will throw an error.

You can also insert data into specific columns of a table. In such cases, you need to specify the names of the columns in the **INSERT** command.

The following command will insert a new row into the **author** table, and the data will get inserted in the **a_name**, **book_title**, **book_category**, and **ISBN_num** columns.

```
INSERT INTO author
(a_name, book_title, book_category,ISBN_num)VALUES
('Charles Darwin','The Voyage of the Beagle',
 'Biography','9711438741989');
```

To view the table data, enter the following command in the **SQL** tab area of **phpMyAdmin**:

```
SELECT * FROM author;
```

The given command will display the **author** table data, as shown in Figure 11-23.

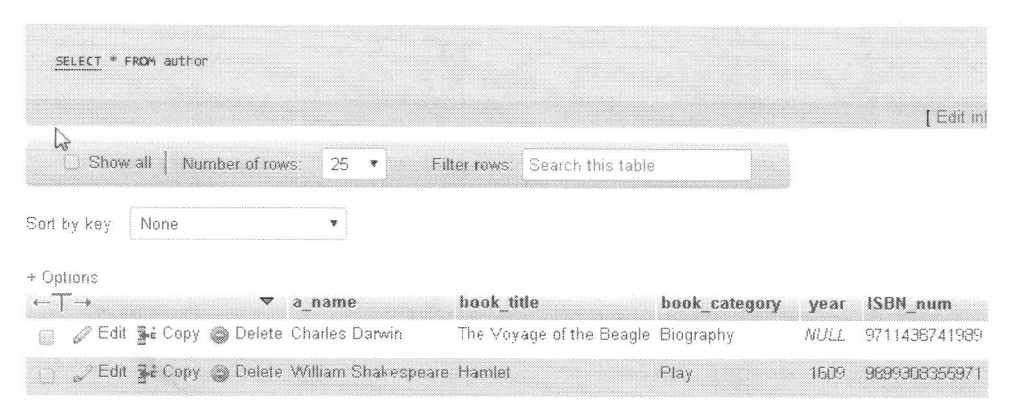

Figure 11-23 Data inserted in specific columns

The syntax for inserting multiple rows using the **INSERT** command is as follows:

```
INSERT INTO table_name
(column-1, column-2, ... column-n)VALUES
(value1-1, value1-2, ... value1-n),
(value2-1, value2-2, ... value2-n),
(value3-1, value3-2, ... value3-n),
.......
.......
.......
(valueN-1, valueN-2, ... valueN-n);
```

In the given syntax, **INSERT INTO** and **VALUES** are the keywords. **table_name** represents the name of the table in which you will insert a new row. **column-1**, **column-2**, and so on represents the names of columns of the **table_name** table, and **value1-1**, **value1-2**, and so on are the corresponding values to be inserted in the columns for the multiple rows. If the number of column values differs from the number of columns specified in the table, MySQL will throw an error.

For example:

To insert multiple rows together in **author** table, enter the following command in the **SQL** tab area of **phpMyAdmin**:

```
INSERT INTO author
(a_name, book_title, book_category, year, ISBN_num)VALUES
('Stephenie Meyer','Twilight','Fiction', 2005, '9899308355682'),
('Charles Dickens','Oliver Twist','Fiction', 1838, '9899308355783'),
('Malcolm Gladwell','Blink','Non-Fiction', 2005, '9711438741881'),
('George Martin','A Game of Thrones','Fiction', 1996, '9711438741874'),
('Kristin Hannah','The Nightingale','Fiction', 2015, '9899308355654');
```

The output of the given example is shown in Figure 11-24.

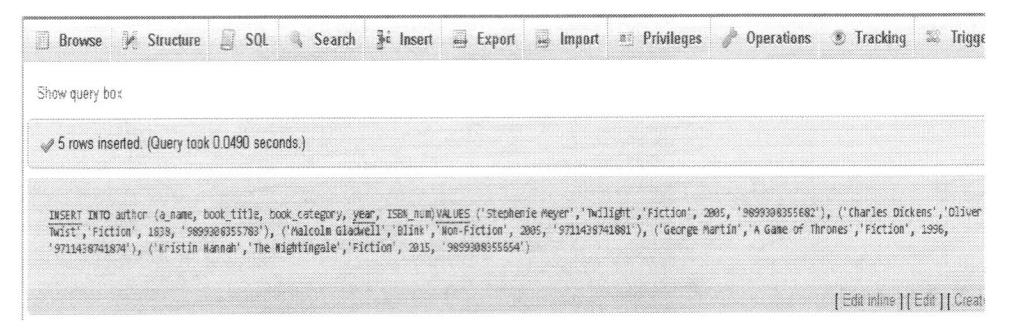

Figure 11-24 Multiple rows inserted

THE SELECT STATEMENT

The **SELECT** statement is the most popular SQL statement used for querying a table. This statement is used to retrieve or view the data of one or more tables. The syntax for using the **SELECT** statement is as follows:

```
SELECT * FROM Table_Name;
```

In the given syntax, **SELECT** and **FROM** are keywords and **Table_Name** represents the name of the table from which you want to retrieve data. * (asterisk) is also a keyword and is used to retrieve data from all columns or fields of a table.

For example:

To view the data of **author** table, enter the following command in the **SQL** tab area of **phpMyAdmin**:

Introduction to MySQL

```
SELECT * FROM author;
```

The given SQL query retrieves all information contained within the **author** table. Note that the asterisk is used as a wildcard in SQL. Literally, it means "Select all records from a table.". The given command will display all the data of **author** table, as shown in Figure 11-25.

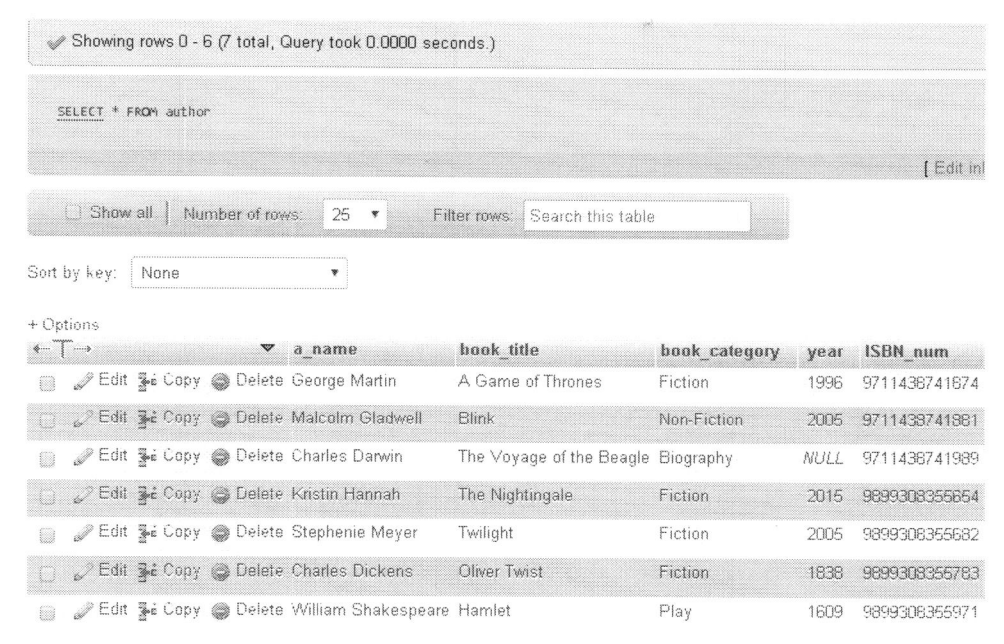

*Figure 11-25 The output of **SELECT** statement*

You can use the following syntax to limit the attributes retrieved from a table:

```
SELECT Column1, Column2, ..., ColumnN FROM Table_Name;
```

In the given syntax, **SELECT** and **FROM** are keywords and **Column1, Column2, ..., ColumnN** represents the names of the columns for which you want to retrieve data. **Table_Name** represents name of the table from which you want to retrieve data.

For example:

To view or retrieve the limited column data of **author** table, enter the following command in the **SQL** tab area of **phpMyAdmin**:

```
SELECT a_name, year, ISBN_num FROM author;
```

The given command will display only the data of columns **a_name**, **year**, and **ISBN_num** of **author** table, as shown in Figure 11-26.

*Figure 11-26 The output displaying limited columns using **SELECT** statement*

Selecting Distinct Rows

You can retrieve distinct rows from a table by using the **DISTINCT** clause with the **SELECT** statement. Retrieving distinct rows from the table prevents the selection of duplicate rows. Following is the syntax for using the **DISTINCT** clause with the **SELECT** statement:

    SELECT DISTINCT Column_Name FROM Table_Name;

In the given syntax, **SELECT**, **DISTINCT**, and **FROM** are keywords. **Column_Name** represents the name of the column for which you want to retrieve distinct values and **Table_Name** represents the name of the table which contains the column **Column_Name**.

For example:

To retrieve the distinct data of **book_category** column in **author** table, enter the following command in the **SQL** tab area of **phpMyAdmin**:

    SELECT DISTINCT book_category FROM Table_Name;

The given command will display only the distinct data of **book_category** column of **author** table, as shown in Figure 11-27. You will note that no data is repeated where as the **author** table has repeated data in **book_category** column, refer Figure 11-25.

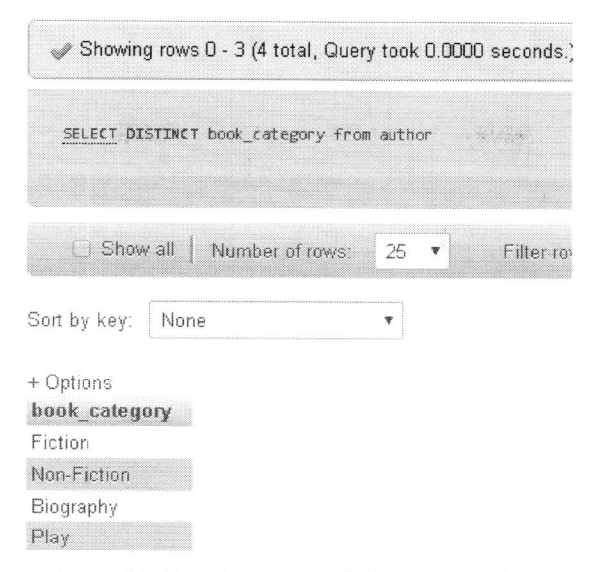

Figure 11-27 The output of DISTINCT clause

Selecting Rows with the WHERE Clause

The **WHERE** clause is used with the **SELECT**, **DELETE**, or **UPDATE** statement to select, delete, or update the data of a table on the basis of a condition. Also, this clause is used to filter the data from the database. The **WHERE** clause selects, deletes, or updates only those rows in which expressions evaluate to true.

The syntax for using the **WHERE** clause is as follows:

```
SELECT Column_Name FROM Table_Name
WHERE Column_Name/Expression Operator Value/Expression;
```

In the above syntax, **SELECT**, **FROM**, and **WHERE** are the keywords; **Column_Name** represents the name of the column that you want to select from the table; and **Table_Name** represents the name of the table. The **WHERE** clause used with both the **DELETE** and **UPDATE** statements will be discussed later in this chapter.

For example:

To retrieve all the data of **author** table where the **book_category** is equal to **Fiction**, enter the following command in the **SQL** tab area of **phpMyAdmin**:

```
SELECT * FROM author WHERE book_category= "Fiction";
```

The given command will display the output, as shown in Figure 11-28.

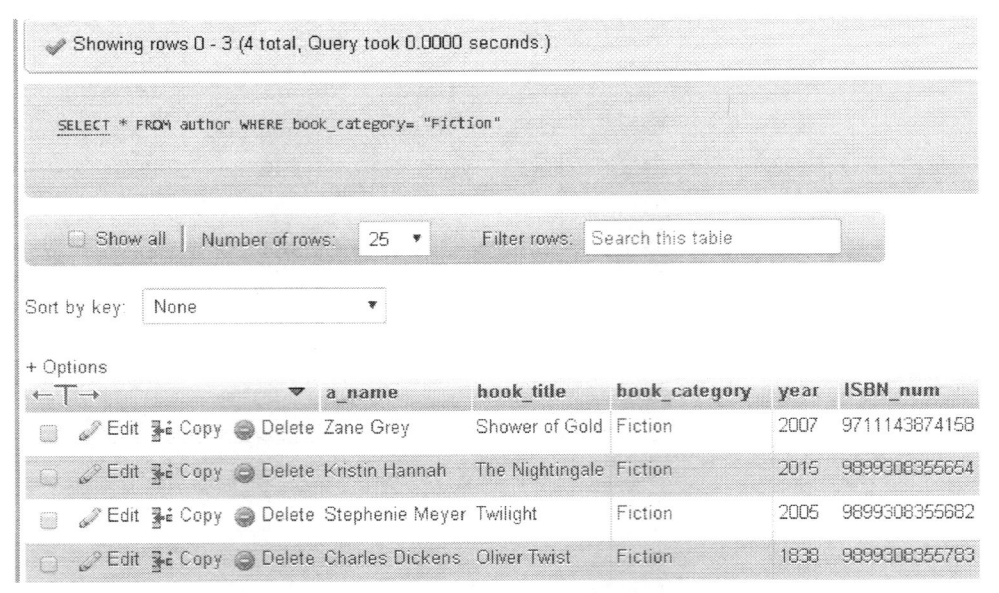

Figure 11-28 The output of SELECT statement with WHERE clause

COUNT Function

The **COUNT()** function counts the number of rows according to the column passed as parameter to it. This function is used with **SELECT** statement. The syntax of using **COUNT()** function is as follow:

```
SELECT COUNT(*) FROM Table_Name;
```

In the given syntax, **SELECT** and **FROM** are keywords and **Table_Name** represents the name of the table from which you want to retrieve data. **COUNT()** function is used to count the number of rows and * (asterisk) is a keyword used to retrieve all the columns or fields of a table.

For example:

To view the number of rows in **author** table, enter the following command in the **SQL** tab area of **phpMyAdmin**:

```
SELECT COUNT(*) FROM author;
```

The given SQL query counts all the rows contained within the **author** table. The given command will display the number of rows in **author** table, as shown in Figure 11-29.

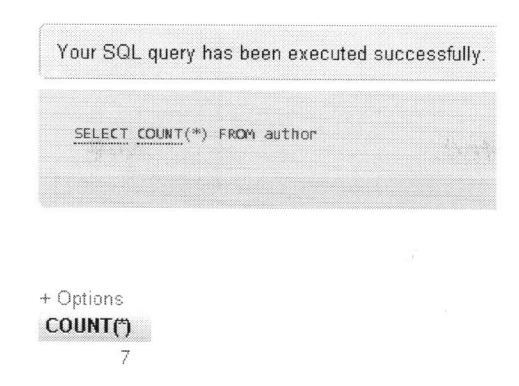

*Figure 11-29 The output of **COUNT()** function*

UPDATING AND DELETING EXISTING TABLE ROWS

In this section, you will learn how to update and delete the existing records from a table. You can update and delete the existing records from a table by using the **UPDATE** and **DELETE** statements.

Updating Table Rows

You can update table rows using the **UPDATE** statement. Using this statement, you can change the values of the specified columns in one or more rows in a table or View. It is recommended that you always execute the **UPDATE** statement with the **WHERE** clause; otherwise, all rows of the table will be affected.

The syntax for using the **UPDATE** statement is as follows:

```
UPDATE TableName
SET column_name = {sql_expression | (subquery)}
[WHERE {search_condition}];
```

Note
Anything written in between [ ] (square brackets) represents optional value.

The keywords, parameters, and clause in the above syntax are explained next.

TableName
It specifies the name of the table that you want to update.

column_name
column_name represents the name of the column to be updated. The column name cannot be repeated in the **column_name** list. Also, it is not necessary that the column names should appear in the **UPDATE** statement in the same order as in the table.

SET column_name = sql_expression
This clause assigns the value of the expression **sql_expression** to the **column_name** column.

SET column_name = (subquery)
This clause assigns the value retrieved by executing a subquery to the **column_name** column. The subquery must return a single value.

For example:

To update the **year** data of a book in **author** table, enter the following command in the **SQL** tab area of **phpMyAdmin**:

```
UPDATE author SET year=1839 WHERE book_category="Biography";
```

The given SQL query will update the **year** column data from **NULL** to **1839** where the **book_category** is **Biography** in the **author** table, to see the old value, refer Figure 11-26.

To view the updated data, enter the following command in the **SQL** tab area of **phpMyAdmin**:

```
SELECT year FROM author Where book_category="Biography" ;
```

The given command will display the output, as shown in Figure 11-30.

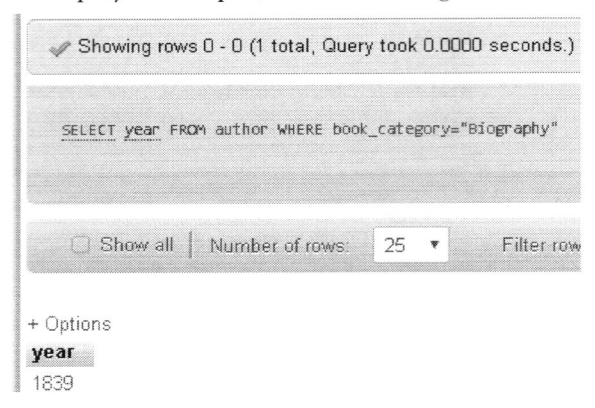

Figure 11-30 The output after updating a row

Deleting Table Rows

The **DELETE** statement is used to delete one or multiple rows from a table. If you do not specify the **WHERE** clause in the **DELETE** statement, all rows will be deleted from the table. The syntax for using the **DELETE** statement is as follows:

```
DELETE FROM Table_name WHERE search_condition;
```

In the given syntax, **Table_name** represents the name of the table from which you want to remove rows. The **DELETE** statement can delete rows from a single table only. You can specify the **WHERE** clause to restrict the number of rows being deleted in the table.

Introduction to MySQL

For example:

To delete a row from **author** table, enter the following command in the **SQL** tab area of **phpMyAdmin**:

```
DELETE FROM author WHERE year=1996;
```

The given SQL query will delete the row where the **year** is **1996** in the **author** table, to see the old table, refer Figure 11-25.

To view the table after deleting the row, enter the following command in the **SQL** tab area of **phpMyAdmin**:

```
SELECT * FROM author;
```

The given command will display the output, as shown in Figure 11-31.

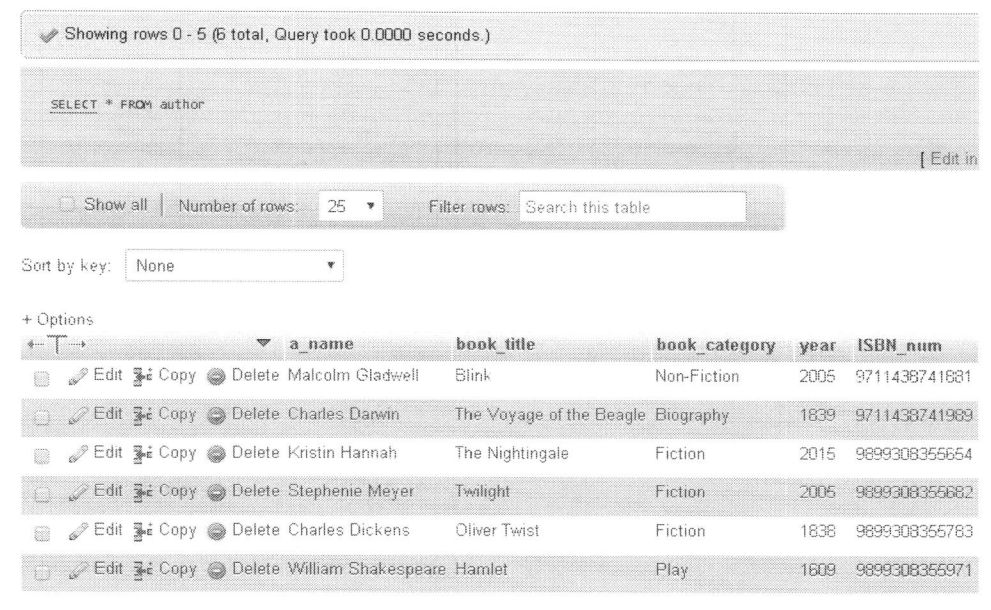

Figure 11-31 The output after deleting a row

ORDER BY CLAUSE

The **ORDER BY** clause allows you to arrange the data retrieved from a table in a sorted order. The rows retrieved are sorted either in the ascending or in the descending order.

The syntax for using the **ORDER BY** clause is as follows:

```
SELECT Column_name FROM Table_name
WHERE Condition
ORDER BY column_name ASC/DESC;
```

In the above syntax, **ORDER BY** is the keyword and **Column_name** represents the name of column of the **Table_name** table. The result will be sorted depending upon the column or columns specified in the **ORDER BY** clause. The keyword **ASC** indicates that the result set will be sorted in the ascending order and **DESC** indicates that the result set will be sorted in the descending order. If the **ASC** or **DESC** value is omitted, MySQL will assume the ascending order as the default value.

For example:

```
SELECT a_name, year FROM author ORDER BY year DESC;
```

In the given example, the query will return the data of **a_name** column and **year** column of the **author** table. Here, the records will be sorted by the **year** field in the descending order, as shown in Figure 11-32.

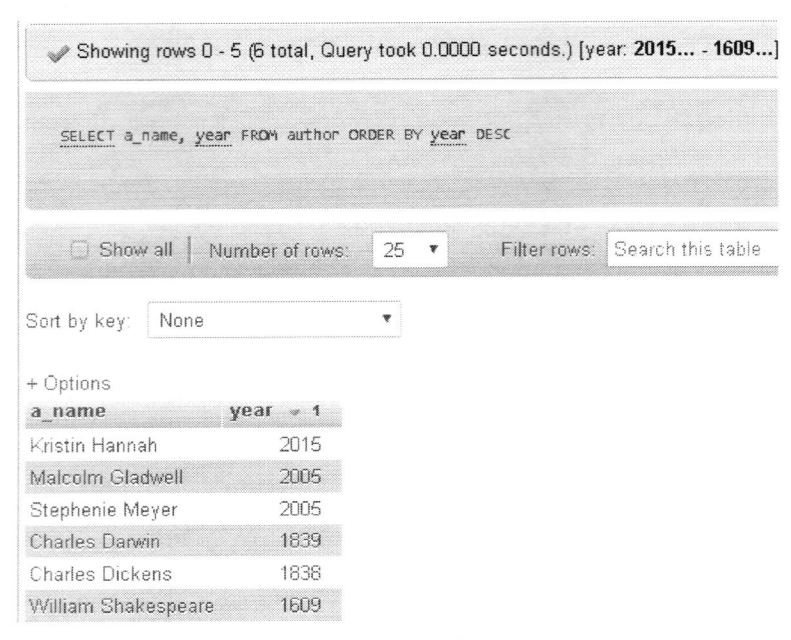

Figure 11-32 Sorting records by year (DESC)

GROUP BY CLAUSE

The **GROUP BY** clause is used in the **SELECT** statement to collect data from multiple records and group the results that have matching values for one or more columns. The syntax for using the **GROUP BY** clause is as follows:

```
SELECT Column1, Column2, ..., Column-n
FROM Table_name [WHERE Condition]
GROUP BY Column1, Column2, ..., Column-n;
```

Introduction to MySQL

In the given syntax, the **GROUP BY** is a keyword and **Column1**, **Column2**, and **Column-n** are the names of columns of the **Table_name** table. You can group the result set by one or more columns.

You can also use the aggregate function in the **SELECT** statement with the **GROUP BY** clause. The syntax for using the **GROUP BY** clause while using the aggregate function in the **SELECT** statement is as follows:

```
SELECT Column1, Column2, ..., Column-n,
aggregate_Function(Expression)
FROM Table_name WHERE Condition
GROUP BY Column1, Column2, ..., Column-n;
```

In the above syntax, the **aggregate_Function** can be any aggregate function such as **SUM**, **COUNT** and so on. The **SUM** function returns the total sum of a column in a given selection. You have already learned about **COUNT** function previously in this chapter.

For example:

```
SELECT book_category, COUNT(a_name) FROM author GROUP BY
book_category;
```

The given SQL query will return the book category (**book_category** columns data) with the total numbers of authors (**a_name** columns data) writing the book in each category. Figure 11-33 shows the output of the given query.

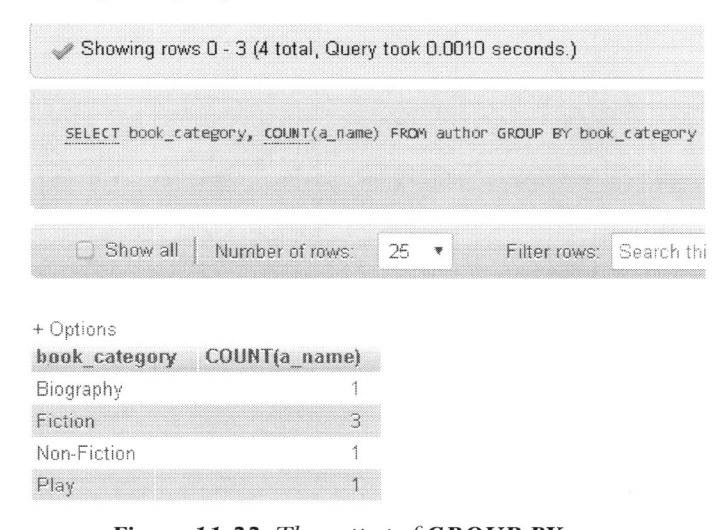

Figure 11-33 The output of GROUP BY query

TRANSACTION MANAGEMENT

In MySQL, a transaction is a logical unit of work done by a bunch of SQL statements. You can make changes in a database during the transaction only. A transaction must be committed or rolled back. The data changed in a transaction remains invisible to another user or session until it is committed. A transaction begins with the execution of the first SQL statement and ends when it is committed or rolled back. You can commit or rollback a transaction explicitly by executing the **COMMIT** or **ROLLBACK** statement

Transaction Storage Engine

MySQL require transaction storage engine to perform MySQL transaction. MySQL uses MySQL's InnoDB storage engine. For this you need to pass **ENGINE InnoDB** as a parameter while creating a table.

For example:

To create a transaction-ready **reader** table containing readers data such as id and name, enter and execute the following command given below in the **SQL** tab area of **phpMyAdmin**:

```
CREATE TABLE reader
( id INT AUTO_INCREMENT PRIMARY KEY,
  name VARCHAR(255) NOT NULL) ENGINE InnoDB;
```

To check the details of **reader** table, enter and execute the following command given below:

```
DESCRIBE reader;
```

You will find the descriptions of all the fields in the **reader** table as the output of the given command, as shown in Figure 11-34.

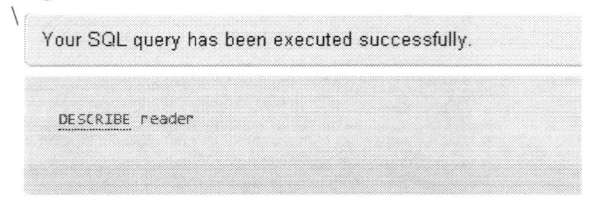

*Figure 11-34 The output describing **reader** table*

To insert the table data in **author** table, enter the following command:

```
INSERT INTO reader
(id, name)VALUES
(1, 'Shane Katson'),
(2, 'Rosy Hawkins'),
(3, 'Maria Haden');
```

Introduction to MySQL

To view the table data, enter the following command:

```
SELECT * FROM reader;
```

The given command will display the **reader** table data, as shown in Figure 11-35.

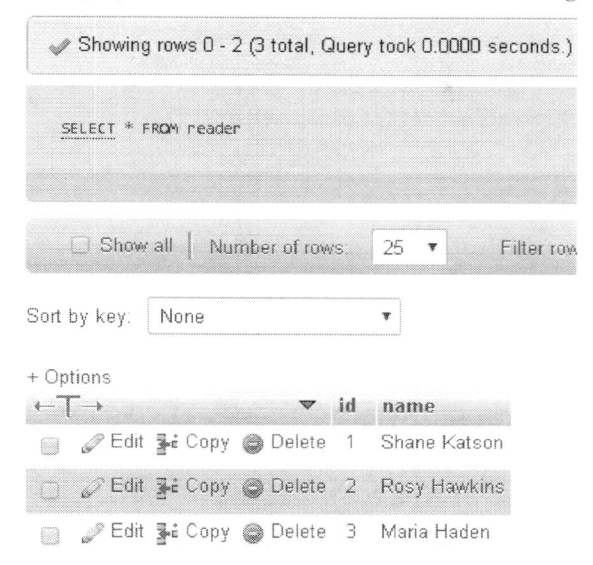

*Figure 11-35 The output displays **reader** table data*

MySQL provides the following statements for transaction management:

1. **BEGIN**
2. **COMMIT**
3. **ROLLBACK**

These statements are discussed next.

The BEGIN Statement

The transaction in MySQL starts with **BEGIN** statement. So, before executing any MySQL query you need to begin the transaction. The syntax for using the **BEGIN** statement is as follows:

```
BEGIN;
```

In the given syntax, **BEGIN** is the keyword used to begin the transaction in MySQL.

For example:

To update the data of **reader** table in transaction mode, enter the following command in the **SQL** tab area of **phpMyAdmin**:

```
BEGIN;
UPDATE reader SET name="Harry" WHERE id=3;
COMMIT;
```

The given SQL query will update the **name** column data from **Maria Haden** to **Harry** where the **id** is **3** in the **reader** table, to see the old value, refer Figure 11-36. Note that you will learn about **COMMIT** statement in next section of this chapter.

To view the updated data, enter the following command in the **SQL** tab area of **phpMyAdmin**:

```
SELECT * FROM reader;
```

The given command will display the output, as shown in Figure 11-36.

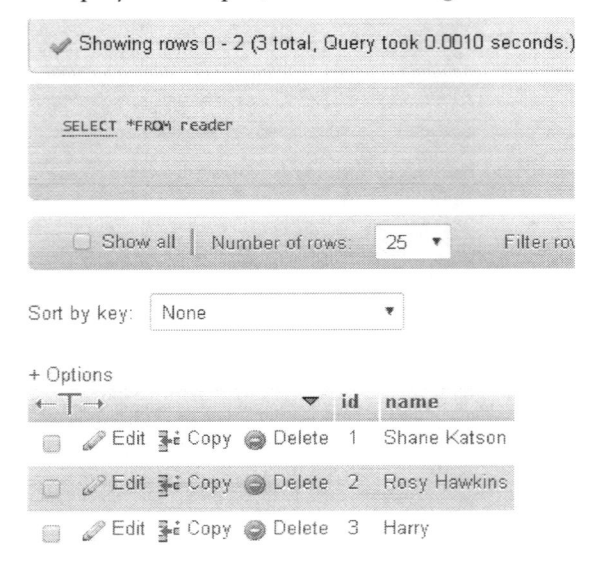

*Figure 11-36 The output of **reader** table in transaction mode*

The COMMIT Statement

The **COMMIT** statement is used to make the changes made by SQL statements permanent. Therefore, you can use this statement only after executing the SQL statements. All the changes made to the MySQL database are considered to be temporary until you do not commit the changes. So, commit the changes with **COMMIT** statement only if you are sure that all the changes done are correct. The syntax for using the **COMMIT** statement is as follows:

```
COMMIT;
```

In the given syntax, **COMMIT** is the keyword used to make the changes permanent on server.

The ROLLBACK Statement

The **ROLLBACK** statement is used to undo the changes made in the current session of the database by the current transaction. However, the **ROLLBACK** statement cannot undo the

Introduction to MySQL

changes that have been made permanent by issuing the **COMMIT** statement. The **ROLLBACK** statement gives you a chance to rectify mistakes.

The syntax for using the **ROLLBACK** statement is as follows:

```
ROLLBACK;
```

In the given syntax, **ROLLBACK** statement roll backs the changes made by the current transaction.

For example:

To roll back any changes made in the database, you need to first start the transaction and make some changes to the database. So, to update the data of **reader** table in transaction mode, enter the following command in the **SQL** tab area of **phpMyAdmin**:

```
BEGIN;
UPDATE reader SET name="Maria Savion" WHERE id=3;
SELECT * FROM reader
```

Note
Do not commit the changes, otherwise you would not be able to rollback the changes.

The given SQL query will update the **name** column data from **Harry** to **Maria Savion** where the **id** is **3** in the **reader** table, to see the old value, refer Figure 11-36 and the last **SELECT** statement will display the updated data in the output, as shown in Figure 11-37.

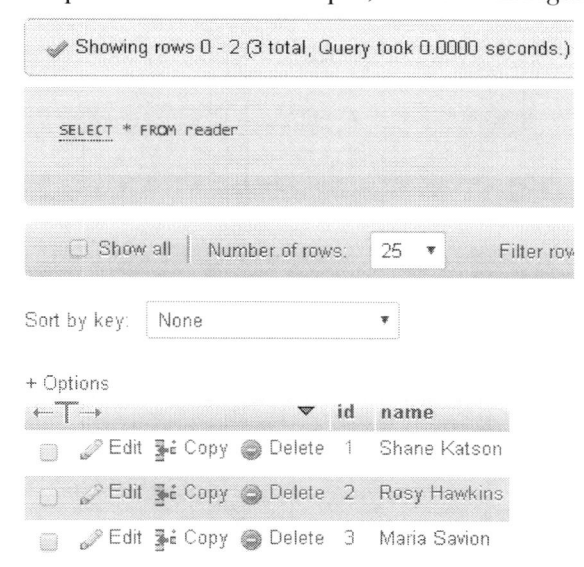

*Figure 11-37 The updated data of **reader** table in transaction mode*

Now, to rollback the updated data, enter the following command in the **SQL** tab area of **phpMyAdmin**:

```
ROLLBACK;
SELECT * FROM reader;
```

The **ROLLBACK** statement will undo the changes made previously (refer Figure 11-37) and the **SELECT** statement will display the output, as shown in Figure 11-38.

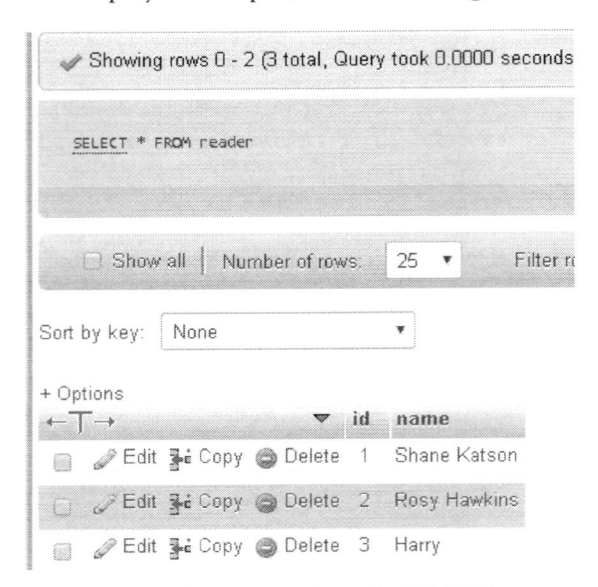

*Figure 11-38 The output after **ROLLBACK** statement*

Self-Evaluation Test

Answer the following questions and then compare them to those given at the end of this chapter:

1. A _____ is a collection of data that is used to store and retrieve related information.

2. The _____ data type is used to store the fixed length character data.

3. The _____ data type is used to store date and time.

4. **BLOB** stands for _____.

5. The _____ statement in SQL is used for querying a table.

6. You can retrieve distinct rows from a table by using the **DIFFERENT** clause with the **SELECT** statement. (T/F)

Introduction to MySQL

7. The **DELETE** statement is used to delete one or multiple rows from a table. (T/F)

8. The **COMMIT** statement is used to make the changes made by SQL statements permanent. (T/F)

Review Questions

Answer the following questions:

1. Which of the following **ALTER TABLE** options is used to delete a column from a database table?

   (a) **DROP** (b) **MODIFY**
   (c) **DELETE** (d) All the above

2. Which of the following clauses allows you to arrange the data retrieved from a table in a sorted order?

   (a) **ARRANGE** (b) **LIST**
   (c) **ORDER BY** (d) **UPDATE**

3. Which of the following clauses is used with the **SELECT**, **DELETE**, or **UPDATE** statement to select, delete, or update data from a table on the basis of a condition?

   (a) **CONDITION** (b) **MODIFY**
   (c) **SELECT BY** (d) **WHERE**

4. Which of the following **ALTER TABLE** options is used to add new columns to a existing database table?

   (a) **ADD** (b) **JOIN**
   (c) **MODIFY** (d) All the above

5. Which of the following statements is used to undo the changes made in the current session of the database by a current transaction?

   (a) **BEGIN** (b) **ROLLBACK**
   (c) **UNDO** (d) **COMMIT**

EXERCISE

Exercise 1

Create a table using SQL command with the name **Employee** having the following columns **Empid**, **Ename**, **Designation**, **Salary**, **Commission**, **Deptno**. Also, declare a primary key constraint for the **Empid** column.

Answers to Self-Evaluation Test
1. database, 2. **CHAR**, 3. **DATETIME**, 4. Binary Large OBject, 5. **SELECT**, 6. F, 7. T, 8. T

Chapter 12

PHP and MySQL Integration

Learning Objectives

After completing this chapter, you will be able to:
- *Connect to the database*
- *Change the default database*
- *Perform SQL query on table*
- *Fetch data from the table*
- *Send data to the database through form*

INTRODUCTION

There are three ways to interact with MySQL: by using Command-Line on Windows Command Prompt, by using MySQL commands in phpMyAdmin, and by using PHP programming Language. You have already learned about first two ways in previous chapter. In this chapter, you will learn to interact with MySQL through PHP programming Language.

You can link the MySQL database with any of your website form by integrating MySQL queries and commands with PHP. In this chapter, you will learn to connect with MySQL database, build SQL queries, fetch the result, store form data to the database, and display the form data in the browser by using PHP programming language along with MySQL.

CONNECTING TO THE DATABASE

You can connect your website or web page with the MySQL database server by using some in-built PHP functions. The PHP MySQLi functions are used to access MySQL database. MySQLi stands for MySQL Improved. The functions required to connect with MySQL database are discussed next.

mysqli_connect() Function

The **mysqli_connect()** function is used in PHP to open a new connection to the MySQL database server. The syntax of **mysqli_connect()** function is as follows:

```
mysqli_connect(Hostname,Username,Password,Database_name,Port,
Socket);
```

In the given syntax, the **mysqli_connect()** function is the in-built function. Six parameters are passed inside the parentheses of **mysqli_connect()** function. Here, **Hostname** represents the name of the host or an IP address, which by default is **localhost** for the local server. **Username** represents the MySQL username that is used to log in to the MySQL server. By default, it is **root** for the local MySQL server. **Password** represents the MySQL log in password associated with the **Username** and its default value is blank for local MySQL server. **Database_name**, **Port**, and **Socket** are the optional parameters and represent the name of the existing database to be used, the port number that attempts to connect the MySQL server, and the socket to be used, respectively.

To create connection as object, you can use the **mysqli()** method in place of **mysqli_connect()** function. The syntax of **mysqli()** method is as follows:

```
$connect = new mysqli(Hostname,Username,Password,
Database_name,Port,Socket);
```

In the given syntax, **mysqli()** is the method used to open a new connection to the MySQL database server. Six parameters are passed inside the parentheses of **mysqli()** method where all the parameters are same as the parameters of **mysqli_connect()** function. Here, **$connect** represents the object of **mysqli()** method which is created by assigning the **mysqli()** method, prefixed with the **new** keyword to the **$connect** variable.

PHP and MySQL Integration

Resource

You have already learned about resource in previous chapters. Resource is a special data type which is used to hold the reference of external resource. The variable that holds the function such as **mysqli_connect()** are of resource type, as it holds a reference to an external resource which is database in case of database connectivity.

For example:

```
$conn_var = mysqli_connect("localhost","root","pass","db");
```

In the given example, **$conn_var** is a resource type variable which is holding an **mysqli_connect()** function. This function is connecting to an external resource.

mysqli_connect_errno() Function

The **mysqli_connect_errno()** function is used in PHP to return error code, if there is any connection error. The procedural style syntax of **mysqli_connect_errno()** function is as follows:

```
mysqli_connect_errno();
```

In the given syntax, **mysqli_connect_errno()** function is the in-built PHP function. No parameter is passed inside this function. If any error occurs while connecting to the MySQL database server, it returns the error code otherwise, it returns zero.

The object oriented style syntax to return error code is as follows:

```
$connect->connect_errno;
```

In the given syntax, **$connect** represents the object of the **mysqli()** method (variable that holds the **mysqli()** method). The **->** operator indicates that the data on the right side of the operator is a property or a method of the object on the left side. The **connect_errno** is the method which returns the error code if any error occurs while connecting to the MySQL database server. Otherwise, it returns zero.

Example 1

The following program will connect to the **cadcim** database in local MySQL server by using **mysqli_connect()** function and display the output in the browser.

```
<!DOCTYPE html>                                                             1
<html>                                                                      2
<head>                                                                      3
        <title> Connecting to Database </title>                             4
</head>                                                                     5
<body>                                                                      6
<?php                                                                       7
$connection = mysqli_connect("localhost","root","","cadcim");               8
// Check connection                                                         9
```

```
  if (mysqli_connect_errno())                                    10
  {                                                              11
     echo "<b>Error occurred, Failed to connect with MySQL:"     12
     .mysqli_connect_error()."</b>";
  }                                                              13
  else                                                           14
  {                                                              15
     echo "Connection established with MySQL <b>cadcim</b>       16
     database";
  }                                                              17
  ?>
  </body>                                                        18
  </html>                                                        19
```

Explanation

Line 8
$connection = mysqli_connect("localhost","root"," ","cadcim");
In this line, **$connection** is the resource type variable holding **mysqli_connect()** function. Four parameters are passed to the **mysqli_connect()** function. Here, **localhost** is the host name, **root** is the MySQL username, third parameter is password which is blank in this case, and **cadcim** is the database name.

Line 10 to Line 17
if (mysqli_connect_errno())
 {
  echo "**Error occurred, Failed to connect with MySQL:**". mysqli_connect_error()."****";
 }
else
{
  echo "Connection established with MySQL **cadcim** database";
}

In these lines, **mysqli_connect_errno()** is the function passed as condition to the **if** statement. If there is any error in connection then the **if** block statement will be executed, otherwise, the else block statement will be executed.

The output of Example 1 is displayed in Figure 12-1.

Note
*In Example 1, **cadcim** is the name of the database that you have already created in previous examples of Chapter 11. This **cadcim** database is used in every example of this chapter.*

Figure 12-1 The output of Example 1

PHP and MySQL Integration

Example 2

The following program will return an error while connecting to the **cadcim** database in local MySQL server by using **mysqli_connect_errno()** and display the output in the browser.

```
<!DOCTYPE html>                                                            1
<html>                                                                     2
<head>                                                                     3
        <title> Connection Error </title>                                  4
</head>                                                                    5
<body>                                                                     6
<?php                                                                      7
$connection = mysqli_connect("localhost","wrong_username","",              8
"cadcim");
// Check connection                                                        9
if (mysqli_connect_errno())                                               10
 {                                                                        11
    echo "<b>Error occurred, Failed to connect with MySQL:"               12
    .mysqli_connect_error()."</b>";
 }                                                                        13
else                                                                      14
{                                                                         15
    echo "Connection established with MySQL <b>cadcim</b>                 16
    database";
}                                                                         17
?>
</body>                                                                   18
</html>                                                                   19
```

Explanation
Line 8
$connection = mysqli_connect("localhost","wrong_username", " ", "cadcim");
In this line, four parameters are passed to the **mysqli_connect()** function. Here, **localhost** is the host name, **wrong_username** is the MySQL username (which does not exist), third parameter is password which is blank in this case, and **cadcim** is the database name.

Line 10 to Line 17
if (mysqli_connect_errno())
 {
 echo "****Error occurred, Failed to connect with MySQL:". mysqli_connect_error()."****";
 }
else
{
   echo "Connection established with MySQL ****cadcim**** database";
}

In these lines, **mysqli_connect_errno()** is the function passed as condition to the **if** statement. If there is any error in connection then it will execute the **if** block statement. Inside the **if** block, the **echo** statement contain the **mysqli_connect_errno()** function which will display the error code in the browser. Otherwise, it will execute the **else** block statement

The output of Example 2 is displayed in Figure 12-2.

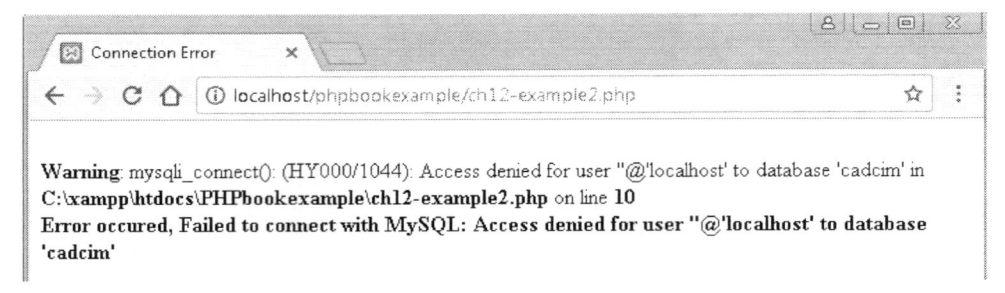

Figure 12-2 The output of Example 2

Example 3

The following program will return an error while connecting to the **cadcim** database in local MySQL server by using **connect_errno** method and display the output in the browser.

```
<!DOCTYPE html>                                                  1
<html>                                                           2
<head>                                                           3
        <title>Object Oriented Connection error </title>         4
</head>                                                          5
<body>                                                           6
<?php                                                            7
$connection = new mysqli("localhost","wrong_username","",        8
"cadcim");
// Check connection                                              9
if ($connection->connect_errno)                                  10
 {                                                               11
    echo "<b>Error occurred, Failed to connect with MySQL:"      12
    .$connection->connect_errno."</b>";
 }                                                               13
else                                                             14
 {                                                               15
    echo "Connection established with MySQL <b>cadcim</b>        16
    database using <b>mysqli()</b> function";
 }                                                               17
?>
</body>                                                          18
</html>                                                          19
```

Explanation
Line 8
$connection = new mysqli("localhost","wrong_username", " ", "cadcim");
In this line, the **$connection** variable is the object of the **mysqli()** method which is created by

PHP and MySQL Integration

assigning the **mysqli()** method, prefixed with the **new** keyword to the **$connection** variable. Here, four parameters are passed to the **mysqli()** function where **localhost** is the host name, **wrong_username** is the MySQL username (which does not exist), third parameter is password which is blank in this case, and **cadcim** is the database name.

Line 10 to Line 17
if ($connection->connect_errno)
 {
    echo "\<b\>Error occurred, Failed to connect with MySQL:"
    .$connection->connect_errno."\</b\>";
 }
else
{
    echo "Connection established with MySQL \<b\>cadcim\</b\>
    database using \<b\>mysqli()\</b\> function";
}

In these lines, **$connection->connect_errno** is passed as condition to the **if** statement. If there is any error in connection then it will execute the **if** block statement. Inside the **if** block, **echo** statement contains **$connection->connect_errno** which will display the error code in the browser. If there is no error, then the **else** block statement will be executed.

The output of Example 3 is displayed in Figure 12-3.

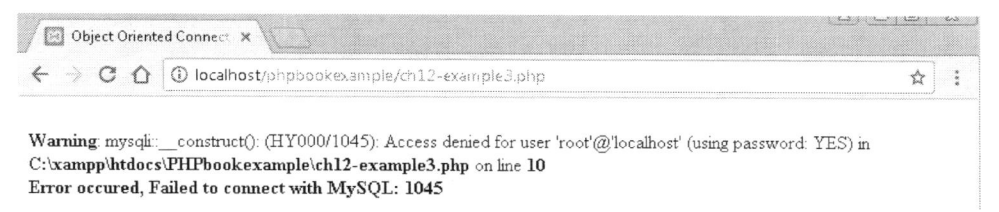

Figure 12-3 The output of Example 3

mysqli_select_db() Function
The **mysqli_select_db()** function is used in PHP to change the default database or to select the desired database for the particular connection. The procedural style syntax of **mysqli_select_db()** function is as follows:

```
mysqli_select_db(Connection_var, Database_name);
```

In the given syntax, **mysqli_select_db()** function is the in-built PHP function. Two parameters are passed inside this function which are required. **Connection_var** represents the variable that is holding the **mysqli_connect()** function used for connection and **Database_name** represents the name of the database that is to be selected.

The object oriented style syntax to change the default database is as follows:

```
$conn_db->select_db(Database_name);
```

In the given syntax, **$conn_db** represents the object of the **mysqli** method (variable that holds the **mysqli()** method). The **->** operator indicates that the data on the right side of the operator is a property or a method of the object on the left side. The **select_db()** is the method which is used to change the default database and **Database_name** represents the name of the database that is to be selected for particular connection.

Example 4

The following program will change the default database to **cadcim** database by using **mysqli_select_db()** for the connection and display the output in the browser.

```
<!DOCTYPE html>                                                    1
<html>                                                             2
<head>                                                             3
        <title>Selecting Database</title>                          4
</head>                                                            5
<body>                                                             6
<?php                                                              7
$connect = mysqli_connect("localhost","root","", "test");          8
if (mysqli_connect_errno())                                        9
  {                                                                10
   echo "<b>Error occurred, Failed to connect with MySQL:"         11
     .mysqli_connect_error()."</b>";
  }                                                                12
elseif (mysqli_select_db($connect,"cadcim"))                       13
  {                                                                14
     echo "<b>cadcim</b> database selected for this connection";   15
  }                                                                16
else                                                               17
  {                                                                18
    echo "No database Selected";                                   19
  }                                                                20
?>                                                                 21
</body>                                                            22
</html>                                                            23
```

Explanation
Line 8
$connect = mysqli_connect("localhost","wrong_username", " ", "test");
In this line, **$connect** is the resource type variable holding **mysqli_connect()** function. Inside the parentheses of **mysqli_connect()** function, **localhost** is the host name, **root** is the MySQL username, third parameter is password which is blank in this case, and **test** is the database name. In this case, **test** is the default database.

Line 13
elseif (mysqli_select_db($connect,"cadcim"))
In this line, **mysqli_select_db()** is the function passed as condition to the **elseif** statement. Two required parameters are passed inside this function where **$connect** is the variable that is holding the **mysqli_connect()** function used for the connection in Line 8. **cadcim** is name

PHP and MySQL Integration

of the database that is to be selected in place of the **test** database. If this condition is true, the **elseif** block statement will be executed. Otherwise, the **else** block statement will be executed.

The output of Example 4 is displayed in Figure 12-4.

Figure 12-4 The output of Example 4

BUILDING SQL QUERY

SQL query in PHP program is similar to queries such as **SELECT, INSERT**, and **UPDATE** queries that you have learned in previous chapter. The only difference between them is that they use different platform. In previous chapter, you executed the queries in Command Prompt and phpMyAdmin but, here you will write those queries in the PHP program to send them from PHP to MySQL. To perform these queries, PHP has an in-built function which is discussed next.

mysqli_query() Function

The **mysqli_query()** function is used to perform a single query at a time on the database. The procedural style syntax of the **mysqli_query()** function is as follows:

```
mysqli_query(Connection_var, Query, Result_mode);
```

In the given syntax, **mysqli_query()** is the in-built PHP function. Three parameters are passed inside this function. **Connection_var** is the required parameter which represents the variable that is holding the **mysqli_connect()** function used for connection. **Query** is also a required parameter which represents any SQL query that is to be performed on database and **Result_mode** is the optional parameter that can be either **MYSQLI_USE_RESULT** or **MYSQLI_STORE_RESULT**. If you do not pass **Result_mode** in the function, by default it is set to be **MYSQLI_STORE_RESULT**. To retrieve large amount of data **MYSQLI_USE_RESULT** is passed as parameter to the **mysqli_query()** function.

The **mysqli_query()** function returns **mysqli_result** object for successful **SELECT, SHOW**, or **DESCRIBE** queries. This function returns **TRUE** for other successful queries and returns **FALSE** on failure.

The object oriented style syntax to perform a single query is as follows:

```
$conn->query(Query, Result_mode);
```

In the given syntax, **$conn** represents the object of the **mysqli** method (variable that holds the **mysqli()** method). The **->** operator indicates that the **query()** on the right side of the operator is a method of the **$conn** object on the left side. Here, **query()** is the method which is used to perform single query on the database table. Two parameters are passed to the **query()** method where **Query** and **Result_mode** are same as the parameter of the **mysqli_query()** function.

Example 5

The following program will insert the data into the **author** table of **cadcim** database by using the **mysqli_query()** function and then display the output in the browser.

```
<!DOCTYPE html>                                                      1
<html>                                                               2
<head>                                                               3
        <title>INSERT query</title>                                  4
</head>                                                              5
<body>                                                               6
<?php                                                                7
$connect = mysqli_connect("localhost","root","","cadcim");           8
if (mysqli_connect_errno())                                          9
   {                                                                 10
     echo "<b>Error occurred, Failed to connect with MySQL:"         11
    .mysqli_connect_error()."</b>";}
    //Executing queries                                              12
else                                                                 13
{                                                                    14
    $query = "INSERT INTO author(a_name,book_title,                  15
      book_category,year,ISBN_num)VALUES('Zane Grey',
      'Shower of Gold','Fiction','2007','9711143874158')";
mysqli_query($connect, $query);                                      16
echo "Data Inserted successfully ..";                                17
echo "<br>";                                                         18
echo "Check the <b>author</b> table of <b>cadcim</b> database        19
      in <b>phpMyAdmin</b>, by running <b>SELECT * FROM author
      </b> in <i><b>SQL</b></i> tab area of <i><b>phpMyAdmin</b>
      </i>, to see if the data is inserted or not.";
   }                                                                 20
?>                                                                   21
</body>                                                              22
</html>                                                              23
```

Explanation
Line 15
$query = "INSERT INTO author(a_name,book_title,book_category,year,ISBN_num) VALUES('Zane Grey','Shower of Gold','Fiction','2007','9711143874158')";
In this line, **INSERT** query is assigned to **$query** variable. This **INSERT** query will insert data into **author** table in a single row.

Line 16
mysqli_query($connect, $query);
In this line, **$connect** and **$query** variables are two parameters passed to the **mysqli_query()** function to perform a query. Here, **$connect** variable is holding the **mysqli_connect()** function (Line 8) and **$query** variable is holding the **INSERT** query (Line 15).

PHP and MySQL Integration

The output of Example 4 is displayed in Figure 12-5.

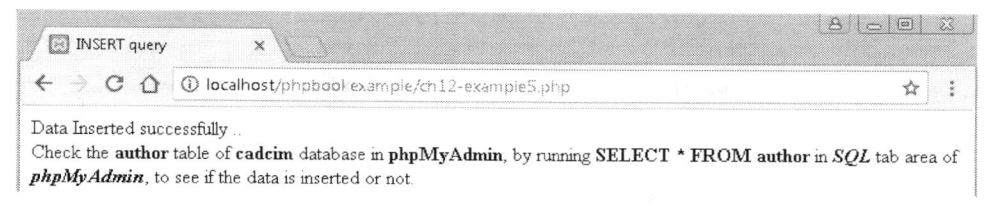

Figure 12-5 The output of Example 5

To view the **author** table data of **cadcim** database in **phpMyAdmin**, enter the following command in the **SQL** tab area of **phpMyAdmin**:

```
SELECT * FROM author;
```

The given command will display the **author** table data, as shown in Figure 12-5.

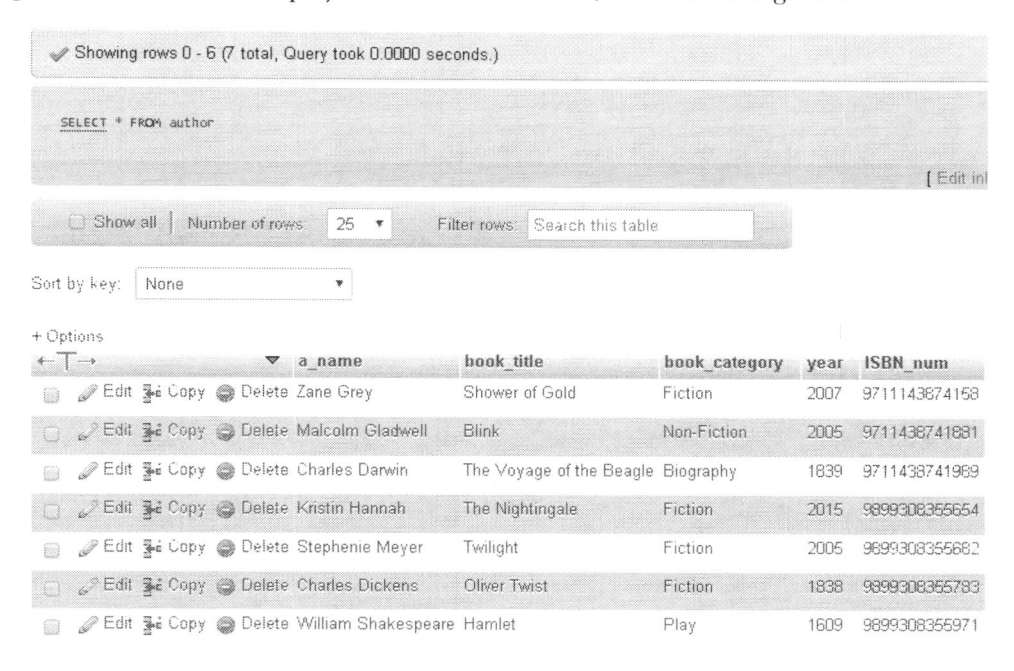

*Figure 12-6 Single row inserted in **author** table by using **mysqli_query()** function*

You can notice in the output of **SELECT** statement, refer to Figure 12-6, that the **mysqli_query()** function of Example 5 has inserted data in the **author** table of **cadcim** database.

FETCHING THE SQL QUERY RESULT

To fetch the result of SQL queries such as **SELECT**, **SHOW**, or **DESCRIBE** queries, you need to store the **mysqli_query()** function result in a variable. You can easily fetch that result and display it on the browser with the help of some PHP in-built functions that are discussed next.

mysqli_num_rows() Function

The **mysqli_num_rows()** function returns the total number of rows in the table that is stored in the result set of the **mysqli_query()** function. The procedural style syntax of **mysqli_num_rows()** function is as follows:

    mysqli_num_rows(Result);

In the given syntax, **mysqli_num_rows()** is the in-built PHP function. **Result** is the required parameter passed to the function. Here, **Result** represents the result set returned by the **mysqli_query()** function (the variable that holds the **mysqli_query()** function).

The object oriented style syntax to return the total number of rows is as follows:

    $result->num_rows;

In the given syntax, **$result** represents the result set of **query()** method (variable that holds the **$conn->query()** method). The **->** operator indicates that the **num_rows** on the right side of the operator is a method of the result set **$result** on the left side. **num_rows** is the method which returns the total number of rows in the table that is stored in the result set **$result**.

mysqli_fetch_assoc() Function

The **mysqli_fetch_assoc() function** is used to fetch the result row as an associative array. This function fetches the data of the tables in the database. You can fetch that data easily by passing the field name of that table in an associated array. The procedural style syntax of **mysqli_fetch_assoc()** function is as follows:

    mysqli_fetch_assoc(Result);

In the given syntax, **mysqli_fetch_assoc()** is the in-built PHP function. **Result** is the required parameter passed to the function. Here, **Result** represents the result set returned by the **mysqli_query()** function (the variable that holds the **mysqli_query()** function).

The object oriented style syntax to fetch the result row as an associative array is as follows:

    $result->fetch_assoc();

In the given syntax, **$result** represents the result set of **query()** method (variable that holds the **$conn->query()** method). The **->** operator indicates that the **fetch_assoc()** on the right side of the operator is a method of the result set **$result** on the left side. **fetch_assoc()** is the method which fetches the result row as an associative array of the table that is stored in the result set **$result**.

Note
*The field names returned from the **mysqli_fetch_assoc()** function are case-sensitive.*

Example 6

The following program will select the data from the **author** table of **cadcim** database by using **mysqli_query()** function. The program will also fetch the data by using **mysqli_num_rows()** and **mysqli_fetch_assoc()**, and display the output in the browser.

```
<!DOCTYPE html>                                                                 1
<html>                                                                          2
<head>                                                                          3
        <title>SELECT query</title>                                             4
</head>                                                                         5
<body>                                                                          6
<?php                                                                           7
$connect = mysqli_connect("localhost","root","","cadcim");                      8
if (mysqli_connect_errno())                                                     9
   {                                                                           10
     echo "<b>Error occurred, Failed to connect with MySQL:"                   11
   .mysqli_connect_error()."</b>";
   }                                                                           12
   //Executing queries                                                         13
else                                                                           14
{                                                                              15
   $query = "SELECT * FROM author";                                            16
   if ($result = mysqli_query($connect, $query))                               17
   {                                                                           18
      /* fetch associative array */                                            19
         if (mysqli_num_rows($result) > 0)                                     20
             {                                                                 21
                while($row = mysqli_fetch_assoc($result))                      22
           {                                                                   23
     echo "<b>Author Name:</b> " .$row["a_name"]. "<br>";                      24
     echo "<b>Book Title:</b> " .$row["book_title"]. "<br>";                   25
     echo "<b>Book Category:</b> " .$row["book_category"]."<br>";26
     echo "<b>Year:</b> " .$row["year"]. "<br>";                               27
     echo "<b>ISBN Number: </b> " .$row["ISBN_num"]. "<br>";                   28
     echo "<br><hr>";                                                          29
           }                                                                   30
         }                                                                     31
   else {                                                                      32
          echo "No results";                                                   33
       }                                                                       34
     }                                                                         35
}                                                                              36
mysqli_close($connect);                                                        37
?>                                                                             38
</body>                                                                        39
</html>                                                                        40
```

Explanation
Line 16
$query = SELECT * FROM author
In this line, **SELECT** query is assigned to **$query** variable. This **SELECT** query will select all the data from the **author** table.

Line 17
if ($result = mysqli_query($connect, $query))
In this line, **$result = mysqli_query($connect, $query)** is passed as condition to the **if** statement. Here, **$connect** and **$query** variables are two parameters passed to the **mysqli_query()** function to perform a query. The **$connect** variable is holding the **mysqli_connect()** function (Line 8) and the **$query** variable is holding the **SELECT** query (Line 16). **$result** is the variable that is holding the **mysqli_query()** function. So, **$result** will store the result returned by the **mysqli_query()** function. If this function works correctly, then the given condition will become true and the block of **if** statement (Line 18 to Line 35) will be executed.

Line 20
if (mysqli_num_rows($result) > 0)
In this line, **mysqli_num_rows($result) > 0** is passed as condition to the **if** statement. Here, **$result** is the parameter passed to the **mysqli_num_rows()** function where **$result** is the result set returned by **mysqli_query()** function (the variable that holds the **mysqli_query()** function). Here, the **mysqli_num_rows()** function will return the total number of **rows** in the **author** table of **cadcim** database. If this function works correctly and the result is greater than 0, then the given condition will become true and the block of **if** statement (Line 21 to Line 31) will be executed.

Line 22
while($row = mysqli_fetch_assoc($result))
In this line, **$row = mysqli_fetch_assoc($result)** is passed as condition to the **while** statement. Here, **$result** is the parameter passed to the **mysqli_fetch_assoc()** function where **$result** is the result set returned by **mysqli_query()** function (the variable that holds the **mysqli_query()** function). Here, the **mysqli_fetch_assoc()** function will fetch the data from the **author** table of **cadcim** database and return the total number of rows as an associated array to the **$row** variable. So, if this function works correctly then the given condition will become true and the block of **while** loop (Line 23 to Line 30) will get executed until the given condition becomes false.

Line 24
echo "Author Name: " .$row["a_name"]. "<br>";
In this line, **$row["a_name"]** is an associated array where **$row** is the associated array name that is holding the data returned by **mysqli_fetch_assoc()** function. Here, **a_name** is the field name of **author** table. So, this line will display the data stored in **a_name** field of author table.

The working of Lines 25 to 28 are similar to Line 24.

Line 29
**echo "
<hr>";**
In this line, **<hr>** is the HTML tag which is used to separate the content from each other. So, the **<hr>** tag will add line for the content separation.

PHP and MySQL Integration

Line 37
mysqli_close($connect);
In this line, the **mysqli_close()** function is used to close the connection stored in the **$connect** variable.

The output of Example 6 is displayed in Figure 12-7.

> **Note**
> *You will learn about the **mysqli_close()** function in next section of this chapter.*

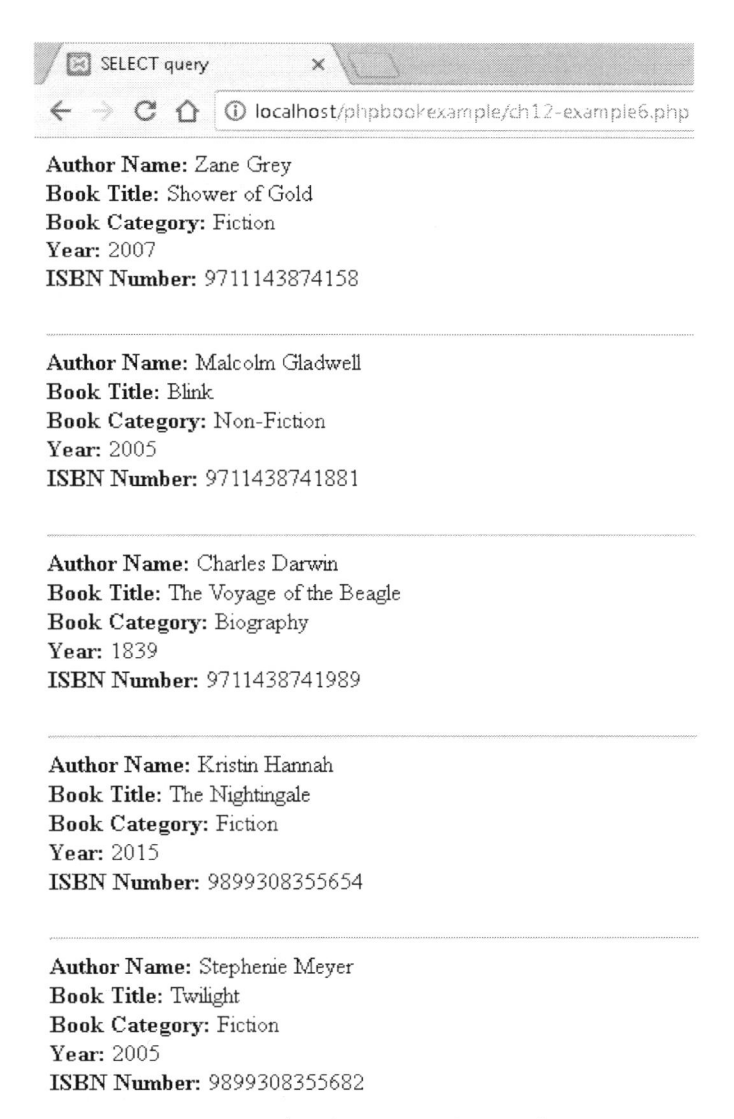

Author Name: Zane Grey
Book Title: Shower of Gold
Book Category: Fiction
Year: 2007
ISBN Number: 9711143874158

Author Name: Malcolm Gladwell
Book Title: Blink
Book Category: Non-Fiction
Year: 2005
ISBN Number: 9711438741881

Author Name: Charles Darwin
Book Title: The Voyage of the Beagle
Book Category: Biography
Year: 1839
ISBN Number: 9711438741989

Author Name: Kristin Hannah
Book Title: The Nightingale
Book Category: Fiction
Year: 2015
ISBN Number: 9899308355654

Author Name: Stephenie Meyer
Book Title: Twilight
Book Category: Fiction
Year: 2005
ISBN Number: 9899308355682

Figure 12-7 *The output of Example 6*

CLOSING MySQL DATABASE CONNECTION

The **mysqli_close()** function is used to close the previously opened MySQL database connection. It is not compulsory to close the MySQL connection as it gets closed automatically after the complete execution of script. But, you can explicitly close the database connection in between the script when the requirement of database connection is finished. This will free up resources and reduce the overheads which will improve the overall performance.

The procedural style syntax of the **mysqli_close()** function is as follows:

```
mysqli_close(Connection);
```

In the given syntax, the **mysqli_close()** function is the in-built PHP function. **Connection** is a required parameter which represents the variable that is holding the **mysqli_connect()** function used for connection.

The object oriented style syntax to close the MySQL connection is as follows:

```
$connection->close();
```

In the given syntax, **$connection** represents the object of the **mysqli** method (variable that holds the **mysqli()** method). The **->** operator indicates that the **close()** on the right side of the operator is a method of the **$connection** object on the left side. Here, the **close()** method is used to close the connection.

PRACTICAL IMPLEMENTATION

You have learned many PHP functions and methods to connect and work with MySQL database in previous sections. In this section, you will learn to implement these functions on your website form to dynamically send the data from your HTML form to the MySQL database.

Creating Table for Form Data

To insert the user data in the database through form, you need to create a table for that form in the existing database or in new database. In this section, you will create a table for the input fields of the form with the help of MySQL query using PHP program.

Example 7

The following program will create a **userdata** table containing various form fields in the existing **cadcim** database and display the output in the browser.

```
<!DOCTYPE html>                             1
<html>                                      2
<head>                                      3
    <title>Create Table</title>             4
</head>                                     5
<body>                                      6
<?                                          7
```

PHP and MySQL Integration   12-17

```
    $connect = mysqli_connect("localhost", "root", "", "cadcim");      8
    if (!$connect) {                                                    9
        die("Connection failed: " . mysqli_connect_error());           10
    }                                                                  11
    // sql to create table                                             12
    $sql = "CREATE TABLE userdata (                                    13
    id INT(6) UNSIGNED AUTO_INCREMENT PRIMARY KEY,                     14
    name VARCHAR(30) NOT NULL,                                         15
    email VARCHAR(50) NOT NULL,                                        16
    password VARCHAR(50) NOT NULL,                                     17
    contact VARCHAR(50) NOT NULL,                                      18
    gender TINYTEXT NOT NULL,                                          19
    education VARCHAR(30),                                             20
    country VARCHAR(30)                                                21
    )";                                                                22
    if (mysqli_query($connect, $sql))                                  23
    { echo "<b>userdata</b> table created successfully";               24
    } else {                                                           25
        echo "Error";                                                  26
    }                                                                  27
    mysqli_close($connect);                                            28
    ?>                                                                 29
    </body>                                                            30
    </html>                                                            31
```

Explanation

Line 13 to Line 22
$sql = "CREATE TABLE userdata (
id INT(6) UNSIGNED AUTO_INCREMENT PRIMARY KEY,
name VARCHAR(30) NOT NULL,
email VARCHAR(50) NOT NULL,
password VARCHAR(50) NOT NULL,
contact VARCHAR(50) NOT NULL,
gender TINYTEXT NOT NULL,
education VARCHAR(30),
country VARCHAR(30)
)";
In these lines, **CREATE TABLE** query is assigned to the **$sql** variable. This query will create the **userdata** table with specified fields and data types in the existing **cadcim** database.

Line 23
if (mysqli_query($connect, $sql))
In this line, **mysqli_query($connect, $sql)** is passed as condition to the **if** statement. Here, the **$connect** and **$sql** variables are two parameters passed to the **mysqli_query()** function to perform a query. **$connect** variable holds the **mysqli_connect()** function (Line 8) and **$sql** variable holds the **CREATE TABLE** query (Line 13 to Line 22). If this function works correctly, then the given condition will become true and the block of **if** statement will be executed.

The output of Example 6 is displayed in Figure 12-8.

Figure 12-8 The output of Example 7

To check the **userdata** table in **cadcim** database, enter the following command in the **SQL** tab area of **phpMyAdmin** after selecting the **cadcim** database:

```
DESCRIBE userdata;
```

The given command will describe the **userdata** table, as shown in Figure 12-8.

Figure 12-9 The output of DESCRIBE userdata query

Creating HTML Form and Sending Data in Database

You need to create an HTML form to send the user data directly from form to the database. You have already learned to create an HTML form in previous chapters. In this section, you will create a form and connect it with another PHP file which will connect to the database and store the data in the database table.

Example 8

The following program will create a dynamic form containing various form elements and send the form data to another web page using the **post** method and the **action** attribute. This example will also create a *ch12-example8-conn.php* file to connect and send data to the **userdata** table of the **cadcim** database.

PHP and MySQL Integration

The *ch12-example8-form.php* program file to create the form and send the form data using **post** method.

```
<!DOCTYPE html>                                                      1
<html>                                                               2
<head>                                                               3
   <title>User Registration form</title>                             4
   <style>                                                           5
   body {                                                            6
         background: -webkit-linear-gradient(left,lightgreen,        7
         yellow);
         }                                                           8
         form {                                                      9
               border: solid;                                       10
               background: lightyellow;                             11
               width: 400px;                                        12
               padding: 20px;                                       13
         }                                                          14
         h1 {                                                       15
               color: green;                                        16
         }                                                          17
   </style>                                                         18
</head>                                                             19
<body>                                                              20
   <h1>USER REGISTRATION FORM</h1>                                  21
   <form action="ch12-example8-conn.php" method="post"              22
         enctype="multipart/form-data">
   <p> Name                                                         23
   <input name="name" type="text" placeholder="name" required       24
   autofocus></p>
   <p> Email                                                        25
   <input type="email" placeholder="email" name="email"             26
   required> </p>
   <p> Password                                                     27
   <input type="password" placeholder="password"                    28
   name="password" required></p>
   <p> Contact                                                      29
   <input type="text" placeholder="contact" name="contact"></p>     30
   <p> Gender: Male                                                 31
   <input name="gender" type="radio" value="Male" required>         32
   Female <input value="Female" name="gender" type="radio"          33
   required></p>
   <p> Education                                                    34
         <select name="education" required>                         35
               <option>Undergraduate</option>                       36
               <option>Graduate</option>                            37
               <option>Post Graduate</option>                       38
         </select></p>                                              39
```

```
            <p>Country                                                      40
            <input list="country" required name="country"                   41
placeholder="Country">
                        <datalist id="country">                             42
                                <option>Australia </option>                 43
                                <option> India </option>                    44
                                <option> Pakistan </option>                 45
                                <option> England </option>                  46
                                <option> Bangladesh </option>               47
                                <option> Others</option>                    48
                        </datalist></p>                                     49
    <p><input name="submit" type="submit"></p>                              50
    </form>                                                                 51
</body>                                                                     52
</html>                                                                     53
```

The *ch12-example8-conn.php* program file to setup the connection with **cadcim** database and to insert the form data to the **userdata** table using **INSERT** query.

```
<!DOCTYPE html>                                                             1
<html>                                                                      2
<head>                                                                      3
    <title>Database Connection</title>                                      4
    <style>                                                                 5
    body {                                                                  6
            background: -webkit-linear-gradient(left,lightgreen,            7
            yellow);
            }                                                               8
            h1 {                                                            9
                    text-align: center;                                     10
                    color: green;                                           11
            }                                                               12
    </style>                                                                13
</head>                                                                     14
<body>                                                                      15
<?php  $con=mysqli_connect('localhost', 'root', '');                        16
if(!$con)                                                                   17
{                                                                           18
    echo 'not connected';                                                   19
}                                                                           20
if(!mysqli_select_db($con, 'cadcim'))                                       21
{                                                                           22
    echo 'database not selected';                                           23
}                                                                           24
$name =$_POST['name'];                                                      25
$email = $_POST['email'];                                                   26
$password=$_POST['password'];                                               27
$gender=$_POST['gender'];                                                   28
```

PHP and MySQL Integration

```
$contact=$_POST['contact'];                                        29
$education=$_POST['education'];                                    30
$country=$_POST['country'];                                        31
$sql = "INSERT INTO userdata (name,email,password,gender,          32
contact,education,country)VALUES('$name','$email',
'$password','$gender','$contact','$education','$country')";
if(!mysqli_query ($con,$sql))                                      33
{                                                                  34
    echo 'not inserted';                                           35
}                                                                  36
else                                                               37
{                                                                  38
    echo "<h1>Thanks For your Registration</h1>";                  39
}                                                                  40
header ("refresh:3; url=ch12-example8-form.php");     ?>           41
</body>                                                            42
</html>                                                            43
```

Explanation (ch12-example8-form.php)
Line 5
<style>
In this line, **<style>** is the start tag of HTML used to start the internal CSS of the web page.

Line 6 to Line 8
body {
background: -webkit-linear-gradient(left, lightgreen, yellow);
}
In these lines, **body** is the tag name (selector) which is to be styled. Inside the block of the **body** selector, **background** is the short hand property used to give the background color to the specified selector. **-webkit-linear-gradient(left, lightgreen, yellow)** is the value of the property. So, here the HTML **body** will have **linear-gradient** background color having two shades, **lightgreen** and **yellow**, starting from **left** side of the browser. **-webkit-** is used to run the code properly on Safari and Google chrome web browsers if the browser do not support some specific values or property such as **linear-gradient**.

Line 9 to Line 14
form {
    border: solid;
    background: lightyellow;
    width: 400px;
    padding: 20px;
}
In these lines, **form** is the tag name (selector) which is to be styled. Inside the block of the **form** selector, **border** is the short hand property which is used to provide all side border. **solid** is the value of border property. **background** is the second property which will give the **lightyellow** background color to the **form**. **width** is third property which will set **form** width to **400px** and **padding** is the last property which will give **20px** padding from all side inside the **form**.

Line 15 to Line 17
h1 {
    color: green;
}
In these lines, **h1** is the tag name (selector) which is to be styled. Inside the block of **h1** selector, **color** is the property which will give **green** color to the **h1** text.

Line 18
</style>
In this line, **</style>** is the end tag of HTML used to end the internal CSS of the web page.

Line 22
<form method="post" action="ch12-example8-conn.php" enctype="multipart/form-data">
In this line, **<form>** tag contain **method** and **action** attributes having **post** and **ch12-example8-conn.php** values, respectively. **enctype** is the attribute having value **multipart/form-data**. This value is required when the file upload control is used in the HTML form to upload the file.

Line 24
<input type="text" name="name" placeholder="name" required autofocus></p>
In this lines, **placeholder** is the attribute having text value **name** that is hold by an input box temporarily. **autofocus** is an attribute that creates automatic focus on the input box by placing cursor in that input box.

The working of Line 25 to Line 51 is similar to the form tags.

Explanation (ch12-example8-conn.php)
Line 25
$name =$_POST['name'];
In this line, **$_POST [ ]** is the **superglobal** variable used to receive the data of form sent through the **post** method and **name** is the input text field name whose data is to be stored in the **$name** variable.

The working of Line 26 to Line 31 is similar to Line 25.

Line 32
$sql = "INSERT INTO userdata (name,email,password,gender,contact,education,country) VALUES ('$name','$email','$password','$gender','$contact','$education','$country')";
In this line, **INSERT** query is assigned to the **$sql** variable. This **INSERT** query will insert data into **username** table in a single row dynamically with the help of variables specified in **VALUES**.

Line 41
header ("refresh:3; url=ch12-example8-form.php");
In this line, the **header()** function is in-built function of PHP. Here, **refresh** will refresh the existing page in **3** seconds and redirect it to the **ch12-example8-form.php** URL.

PHP and MySQL Integration

The output of example 8 is displayed in Figure 12-10.

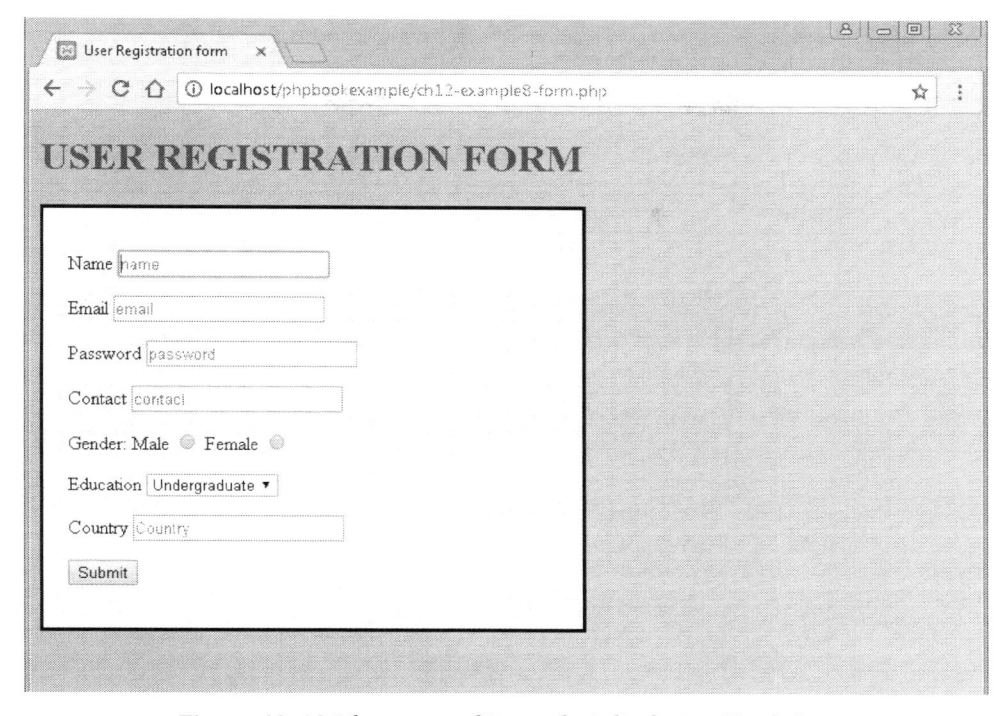

Figure 12-10 *The output of Example 8 displaying blank form*

In Figure 12-10, the form is blank. Next, the user will enter the data to send it to the database as shown in Figure 12-11.

Figure 12-11 The output of Example 8 having data in the form

In Figure 12-11 the data is filled. Now the user will submit this data and the data will be sent to *ch12-example8-conn.php* program. This program will receive the data and insert the data in the **userdata** table of the **cadcim** database. The output will be displayed as shown in Figure 12-12 and will be redirected to URL *ch12-example8-form.php* in 3 seconds.

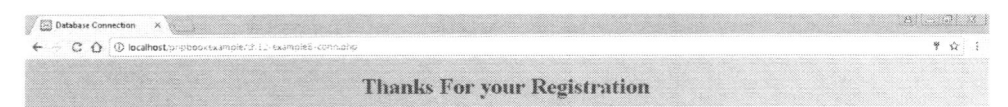

Figure 12-12 The output of Example 8 after submitting the data

To check if the data is inserted in the **userdata** table of the **cadcim** database, enter the following command in the **phpMyAdmin SQl** tab area after selecting the **cadcim** database:

```
SELECT * FROM userdata;
```

The given command will display the data of **userdata** table, as shown in Figure 12-13.

PHP and MySQL Integration

12-25

Figure 12-13 The data of **userdata** table inserted with a PHP form

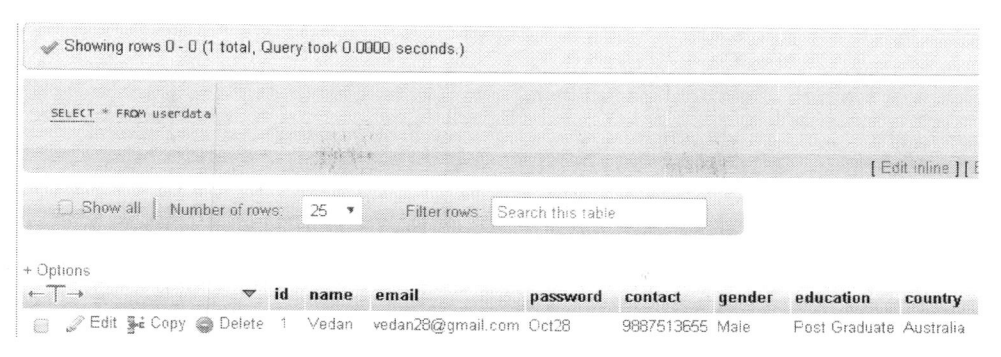

Self-Evaluation Test

Answer the following questions and then compare them to those given at the end of this chapter:

1. In PHP, _____ function is used to open a new connection to the MySQL database server.

2. In PHP, _____ function is used to return error code.

3. In PHP, _____ function is used to perform a single query at a time on the database.

4. The _____ function is used to fetch the result row as an associative array in PHP.

5. The _____ function is used to close the previously opened MySQL database connection.

6. The **mysqli_change_db()** function is used in PHP to change the default database. (T/F)

7. Resource is a special type of data type which is used to hold the reference of external resource. (T/F)

Review Questions

Answer the following questions:

1. Which of the following functions is used to perform a single query on the database at a time?

    (a) **mysqli_single()** (b) **mysqli_query()**
    (c) **mysqli_one_query()** (d) All the above

2. Which of the followings function is used in PHP, to return the total number of rows of the MySQL database table?

   (a) **mysqli_return_row()**
   (c) **mysqli_num_rows()**
   (b) **mysqli_total_rows()**
   (d) None of them

3. Which of the following functions is used in PHP to change the default database?

   (a) **mysqli_db()**
   (c) **mysqli_correct_db()**
   (b) **mysqli_change_db()**
   (d) **mysqli_select_db()**

4. Which of the following is the full form of MySQLi?

   (a) MySQL Important
   (c) MySQL Improved.
   (b) MySQL Integration
   (d) None of them

5. Which of the following functions is used to refresh the existing page and redirect it to the new URL in given time.

   (a) **redirect()**
   (c) **destroy()**
   (b) **refresh()**
   (d) **header()**

EXERCISES

Exercise 1

Create a table using PHP program with the name **Details** having the following columns **Roll_no**, **name**, **class**, and **fees**. Also, declare a primary key constraint for the **Roll_no** column.

Exercise 2

Create a form having 4 input fields for students **Roll number**, **Name**, **Class**, and **Fees** where every field will be required. Also, create a PHP program to send students data to the **Details** table on click of submit button of form.

Answers to Self-Evaluation Test
1. mysqli_connect(), 2. mysqli_connect_errno(), 3. mysqli_query(), 4. mysqli_fetch_assoc(), 5. mysqli_close(), 6. F, 7. T

Index

Symbols

$_FILES Superglobal Variable 10-15
$_GET Supergloblal Variable 9-12
$_POST Superglobal Variable 9-15
$_SERVER Supergloblal Variable 9-20
$_SESSION Superglobal Variable 10-21

A

ALTER TABLE commands 11-24
Anonymous class 7-43
application/x-www-form-urlencoded 10-15
Arithmetic Operator 5-2
Array Functions 8-27
Array Operators 5-24
Arrays 8-2
arsort() 8-28
asort() 8-28
Associative Array 8-7
Attributes 9-2
AUTO_INCREMENT 11-22

B

Basic Assignment Operator 5-5
BEGIN Statement 11-45
BIGINT 11-15
bin2hex() 7-10
Binary Data Type 11-11
BIT 11-14
Bitwise AND (&) Operator 5-9
Bitwise Compliment (~) Operator 5-10
Bitwise Exclusive OR (^) Operator 5-10
Bitwise Operator 5-9
Bitwise OR (|) Operator 5-10
BLOB 11-12
Boolean 3-16
break Statement 6-27

C

cache_limiter 10-20
Case Sensitivity 3-10
CHAR 11-11
Character Classes 9-35
Character Data Type 11-11
Class constant 7-24
Classes 7-14
Coercive Mode 3-20
Column 11-3
Combined Assignment Operators 5-5
Command-Line 11-3
COMMIT Statement 11-46
compact() 8-34
Comparison Operators 5-14
Compound Data Types 3-16
Concatenation 4-20
Concatenation Assignment Operator 5-23
Conditional Control Structure 6-3
Conditional(? :) Operator 5-25
Condition Expression 6-18
console.log() 9-30
constant() 4-16
Constant Name 4-13
Constants 4-13
const keyword 7-24
Constraints 11-18
Constructor 7-22
continue Statement 6-32
Control Structures 6-3
Cookies 10-25
copy() function 10-12
count() 8-33
COUNT() function 11-38
CREATE keyword 11-6
CSPRNG Functions 7-9

D

Database 11-2
Data Types 3-11

date() 7-7
Date and Time Data Type 11-17
DATETIME 11-17
DECIMAL 11-16
define() 4-13
Destructor 7-22
die() 10-4
Distinct Rows 11-36
Document root 2-13
document.write() 9-28
DOUBLE 11-16
Double-Quoted String 4-18
do-while Loop 6-21
DROP TABLE command 11-30
Dynamic Function Call 7-7
Dynamic Website 1-6

E

Echo 3-4
elseif Control Structure 6-10
enctype Attribute 10-15
ENUM Data Type 11-18
Equality(==) Operator 5-24
Equal(==) Operator 5-15
exit() 10-4
explode() 8-36
extends keyword 7-40

F

fclose() function 10-10
feof() 10-9
fgets() 10-8
Field 11-3
file_exists() function 10-4
FILE INCLUSION statements 7-12
filesize() 10-5
final Keyword 7-35
Float 3-15
FLOAT 11-16
Flowchart 6-2
fopen() Function 10-3
foreach Loop 8-20
Foreign Key Constraint 11-20
for Loop 6-24
Form Action 9-12

Form button Element 9-8
Form datalist Element 9-7
Form Elements 9-2
Form fieldset Element 9-8
Form select Element 9-7
FORM Validation 9-33
fputs() function 10-5
fread() function 10-7
Function Arguments 7-4
Function Name 7-3
Function Return Value 7-6
Functions 7-2
fwrite() function 10-5

G

get Method 9-11
Global Variables 4-7
goto Statement 6-34
GRANT privileges 11-9
GROUP BY Clause 11-42

H

htmlspecialchars() 9-20
httponly 10-26

I

Identical(===) Operator 5-15
Identity(===) Operator 5-24
if Control Structure 6-3
if-else Control Structure 6-6
In-built Functions 7-7
include Statement 7-12
Increment or Decrement Expression 6-18
Increment(++) or Decrement(--) Operators 5-20
Indexed Array 8-2
Inequality(!= / <>) Operator 5-24
Inheritance 7-30
Initialization Expression 6-18
innerHTML 9-26
Input Element 9-2
Insert command 11-31
instanceof Operator 7-37
Integer 3-14
Interface 7-38

Index

Int/Integer 11-15
isset() 9-18

J

JavaScript Variables 9-31
Jump Statements 6-27

K

krsort() 8-30
ksort() 8-29

L

LAMP 2-3
Left Shift (<<) Operator 5-11
Left to Right Associativity 5-27
Local Variables 4-4
Logical AND(and / &&) Operators 5-18
Logical NOT(!) Operator 5-19
Logical Operators 5-17
Logical OR(or / ||) Operator 5-18
Logical XOR(xor) Operator 5-19
LONGBLOB 11-13
LONGTEXT 11-13
Loop Control Structure 6-17

M

Magic Constants 4-16
MAMP 2-3
MEDIUMBLOB 11-12
MEDIUMINT 11-15
MEDIUMTEXT 11-13
Metacharacters 9-34
Methods and Action 9-11
Method Scope 7-15
move_uploaded_file() Function 10-16
Multidimensional Array 8-9
multipart/form-data 10-15
Multiple Line Comment 3-3
mysqli_close() function 12-16
mysqli_connect_errno() Function 12-3
mysqli_connect() Function 12-2
mysqli_fetch_assoc() Function 12-12
mysqli_num_rows() Function 12-12
mysqli_query() Function 12-9
mysqli_select_db() Function 12-7

N

Non-identical(!==) Operator 5-16
Non-identity(!==) Operator 5-25
Not equal(!= and <>) Operators 5-16
NOT NULL 11-22
NULL 3-18
Null Coalescing(??) Operator 5-25
Numeric Data Type 11-14

O

Object 3-17
Object Cloning 7-20
Object-Oriented Programming 7-2
Objects 7-16
One-Line Comment 3-3
Operator Associativity 5-27
Operator Precedence 5-26
ORDER BY Clause 11-41

P

Parallelogram 6-2
parent Keyword 7-33
PHP Frameworks 1-9
phpMyAdmin 11-5
Postfix Notation 5-20
post Method 9-12
Prefix Notation 5-21
preg_match() 9-44
preg_replace() 9-44
PRIMARY KEY Constraint 11-19
Print 3-7
print_r() Function 8-24
private 7-16
protected 7-16
public 7-15

R

random_bytes() 7-9
random_int() 7-11
RDBMS Terminologies 11-2
Record 11-2
Regular Expression 9-33
Regular Expression Functions 9-43
Regular Expression Modifiers 9-35
rename() function 10-13
require Statement 7-12
return Statement 6-36
Return Type Declaration 3-21
Right Shift (>>) Operator 5-12
Right to Left Associativity 5-27
ROLLBACK Statement 11-46

S

Scalar Data Types 3-12
Scalar Type Declaration 3-19
SELECT Statement 11-34
session_destroy() function 10-24
Sessions 10-20
session_start() function 10-20
session_unset() function 10-24
setcookie() function 10-25
Single-Quoted String 4-18
sort() 8-27
Spaceship(<=>) Operator 5-17
Special Data Types 3-18
Static Methods and Properties 7-25
Static Variables 4-9
Static Website 1-6
Strict Mode 3-21
String 3-12
String Operators 5-23
stripslashes() 9-19
strlen() 4-25
str_replace() 4-26
strrev() 4-26
strtolower() 4-24
strtoupper() 4-24
str_word_count() 4-25
substr_compare() 4-27
Superglobal variables 4-12
switch Control Structure 6-13

T

textarea Element 9-8
Text Data Type 11-13
time() function 10-28
TIMESTAMP 11-17
TINYBLOB 11-12
TINYINT 11-14
TINYTEXT 11-13
Transaction Management 11-43
Transaction Storage Engine 11-44
trim() 9-19
Type declaration 3-19

U

Union(+) Operator 5-24
UNIQUE Constraint 11-20
unlike() function 10-14
USE keyword 11-7
User Defined Functions 7-2

V

VARBINARY 11-12
VARCHAR 11-11
var_dump() 7-8
Variables 4-2
Variable scope 4-4

W

WAMP 2-3
Web Server 1-7
WHERE Clause 11-37
while Loop 6-18
window.alert() 9-28
Windows Command Prompt 11-3

X

XAMPP 2-3
XAMPP Control Panel 2-12
XOR 5-19

Z

Zend Engine 1-8

Other Publications by CADCIM Technologies

The following is the list of some of the publications by CADCIM Technologies. Please visit *www.cadcim.com* for the complete listing.

Computer Programming Textbooks
- Introduction to C++ programming, 2nd Edition
- Learning Oracle 12c - A PL/SQL Approach
- Learning ASP.NET AJAX
- Introduction to Java Programming, 2nd Edition
- Learning Visual Basic.NET 2008

CINEMA 4D Textbooks
- MAXON CINEMA 4D Studio R19: A Tutorial Approach, 6th Edition
- MAXON CINEMA 4D Studio R18: A Tutorial Approach, 5th Edition
- MAXON CINEMA 4D Studio R17: A Tutorial Approach, 4th Edition
- MAXON CINEMA 4D Studio R16: A Tutorial Approach, 3rd Edition

Autodesk 3ds Max Design Textbooks
- Autodesk 3ds Max Design 2015: A Tutorial Approach, 15th Edition
- Autodesk 3ds Max Design 2014: A Tutorial Approach
- Autodesk 3ds Max Design 2013: A Tutorial Approach
- Autodesk 3ds Max Design 2012: A Tutorial Approach
- Autodesk 3ds Max Design 2011: A Tutorial Approach

Autodesk 3ds Max Textbooks
- Autodesk 3ds Max 2018 for Beginners: A Tutorial Approach, 18th Edition
- Autodesk 3ds Max 2017 for Beginners: A Tutorial Approach, 17th Edition
- Autodesk 3ds Max 2016 for Beginners: A Tutorial Approach, 16th Edition
- Autodesk 3ds Max 2018: A Comprehensive Guide, 18th Edition
- Autodesk 3ds Max 2017: A Comprehensive Guide, 17th Edition
- Autodesk 3ds Max 2016: A Comprehensive Guide, 16th Edition
- Autodesk 3ds Max 2015: A Comprehensive Guide, 15th Edition
- Autodesk 3ds Max 2014: A Comprehensive Guide
- Autodesk 3ds Max 2013: A Comprehensive Guide

Autodesk Maya Textbooks
- Autodesk Maya 2018: A Comprehensive Guide, 10th Edition
- Autodesk Maya 2017: A Comprehensive Guide, 9th Edition
- Autodesk Maya 2016: A Comprehensive Guide, 8th Edition
- Autodesk Maya 2015: A Comprehensive Guide, 7th Edition

- Autodesk Maya 2014: A Comprehensive Guide
- Autodesk Maya 2013: A Comprehensive Guide

Digital Modeling Textbook
- Exploring Digital Modeling using 3ds Max and Maya 2015

Fusion Textbooks
- Blackmagic Design Fusion 7 Studio: A Tutorial Approach, 3rd Edition
- The eyeon Fusion 6.3: A Tutorial Approach

Flash Textbooks
- Adobe Flash Professional CC 2015: A Tutorial Approach, 3rd Edition
- Adobe Flash Professional CC: A Tutorial Approach
- Adobe Flash Professional CS6: A Tutorial Approach

ZBrush Textbooks
- Pixologic ZBrush 4R8: A Comprehensive Guide, 3rd Edition
- Pixologic ZBrush 4R7: A Comprehensive Guide, 3rd Edition

Premiere Textbooks
- Adobe Premiere Pro CC: A Tutorial Approach
- Adobe Premiere Pro CS6: A Tutorial Approach
- Adobe Premiere Pro CS5.5: A Tutorial Approach

Nuke Textbook
- The Foundry NukeX 7 for Compositors

Coming Soon from CADCIM Technologies
- SolidCAM 2016: A Tutorial Approach
- Autodesk Fusion 360: A Tutorial Approach
- Project Management Using Microsoft Project 2016 for Project Managers

Online Training Program Offered by CADCIM Technologies

CADCIM Technologies provides effective and affordable virtual online training on various software packages including computer programming languages, Computer Aided Design and , Manufacturing, and Engineering (CAD/CAM/CAE), animation, architecture, and GIS. The training will be delivered 'live' via Internet at any time, any place, and at any pace to individuals as well as the students of colleges, universities, and CAD/CAM/CAE training centers. For more information, please visit the following link: *www.cadcim.com*

Printed in Great Britain
by Amazon